Tomcat 6 Developer's Guide

Build better web applications by learning how a servlet
container actually works

Damodar Chetty

[PACKT]
PUBLISHING

BIRMINGHAM - MUMBAI

Tomcat 6 Developer's Guide

First published: December 2009

Production Reference: 1091209

Published by Packt Publishing Ltd.
32 Lincoln Road
Olton
Birmingham, B27 6PA, UK.

ISBN 978-1-847197-28-3

www.packtpub.com

Cover Image by Vinayak Chittar (vinayak.chittar@gmail.com)

Credits

Author
Damodar Chetty

Reviewers
David O'Meara

Michael Besosa

Karl Espe

Alok Gupta

Arun Lakkakula

Giridhar Reddy

David Gordhamer

Chad LaVigne

Vladan Pulec

Raghu Ramakrishnan

Dan Syrstad

Acquisition Editor
Sarah Cullington

Development Editor
Swapna Verlekar

Technical Editor
Akash Johari

Copy Editor
Leonard D'Silva

Editorial Team Leader
Akshara Aware

Project Team Leader
Manjiri Nadkarni

Project Coordinator
Leena Purkait

Indexer
Hemangini Bari

Monica Ajmera

Proofreader
Jeff Orloff

Graphics
Nilesh R. Mohite

Production Coordinator
Shantanu Zagade

Cover Work
Shantanu Zagade

About the author

Damodar Chetty is a lifelong programmer with almost two decades in the computer software industry. During that period he's worked in a variety of languages, tools, and technologies, journeying from programming in assembly language, all the way through to Java and Ruby, making some interesting side trips along the way.

He has also been fortunate to have worked in a number of Fortune 500 organizations, and to have engaged with a number of world class software engineers, all of which have helped him perfect his craft.

He is also the recipient of the US Department of Interior Information Technology award for 2001.

Damodar has an undergraduate degree in Electronics & Telecommunications Engineering from the University of Bombay and graduate degrees in Management Sciences from the University of Goa and in Computer Engineering from the University of Minnesota.

He is the owner of Software Engineering Solutions, Inc., a provider of Java EE web development consulting services. He is an avid blogger on his web site at `www.swengsol.com`.

He currently lives in Woodbury, Minnesota with his wife Devi, his children Ashwin and Anita, and a passion for photography.

Acknowledgement

No book is the product of just the author. He just happens to be the one with his name on the cover.

A number of people contributed to the success of this book, and it would take more space than I have to thank each one individually.

A special shout out goes to Sarah Cullington, my editor, who is the reason that this book exists. Thank you Sarah for believing in me and for being a wonderful guide through this process. Thank you also to the entire Packt Publishing team for working so diligently to help bring out a high quality product.

No words can express my gratitude to my amazing development cohort, with whom it is my privilege to work. In particular, thanks are due to Michael Besosa, Karl Espe, David Gordhamer, Alok Gupta, Arun Lakkakula, Chad LaVigne, Vladan Pulec, Raghu Ramakrishnan, Giridhar Reddy, and Dan Syrstad. Your encouragement and support were invaluable to me. You guys are the best!

I must also thank the talented team of developers who have contributed to the Apache Tomcat project. This product is truly an engineering marvel, and it was an instructive experience to rummage through its source. It is a credit to this team that the Tomcat mailing lists are not just civil places, but are also full of interesting tips and tricks, and well worth a visit.

Finally, I'd like to acknowledge Joginder Nahil, who provided me with an early taste for the written word.

About the reviewers

David O'Meara is an experienced developer, architect, and technical manager with over 10 years based in Australia and the USA. Primarily focusing on the Java language and related technologies, his experience is mainly based on web, distributed, and integration projects.

He has previously worked on many business domains, but currently devotes the bulk of his time in the maintenance and programming of highly adaptive, semi-autonomous, self-aware bipedal hominids, also known as child raising. The rest of his spare time is often spent answering questions on the JavaRanch, moderating on DZone, or working on open source projects.

Michael Besosa is a Principal Architect at Pearson VUE, Inc.

Karl Espe and **Alok Gupta** are Web Engineering Leads at Pearson VUE, Inc.

Arun Lakkakula and **Giridhar Reddy** are Senior Web Software Developers at Pearson VUE, Inc.

David Gordhamer is a Web Software Developer at Pearson VUE, Inc.

Chad LaVigne, **Vladan Pulec**, **Raghu Ramakrishnan**, and **Dan Syrstad** are web development consultants based in Minnesota.

This book is dedicated to:

- *My wife Devi, every day with you is a joy and a blessing*
- *My children, Ashwin and Anita, you are the lights of my world*
- *My parents, Nagarathnam and Shanmugam, who taught me all that is important*

This book would not have been possible without your love and understanding.

Thank you from the bottom of my heart.

Table of Contents

Preface

Current books on Tomcat are primarily focused on the application deployer or administrator. As a result, they invariably focus on the issues related to managing a Tomcat installation, configuring the runtime environment, and on deploying web applications.

On the other hand, while books on servlet programming are targeted at Java web developers, they often provide a container-agnostic view of the servlet specification. Tomcat is often a bit player in these books and has very few speaking lines.

This book fills the void between these two approaches.

It will take you on a guided tour of a living implementation of an industrial-strength servlet container.

Along the way, you will learn how various elements of the Servlet 2.5 specification as well as how the HTTP RFCs are implemented.

By the end of your journey, you will have acquired specialist grade skills in a range of technologies that contribute to the arena of Java server-side development.

This book intended to provide Tomcat administrators, deployers, and developers an introduction into the internal workings of the Tomcat servlet container.

At the same time, it provides Java web programmers with a deep appreciation of the Servlet API by exploring its reference implementation—the Tomcat container.

While this book provides you with the conceptual background of all that is necessary to take your skills to the next level, it assumes that the reader has a general understanding of the Java programming language and Java web programming.

What this book covers

Chapter 1 – Introduction to Tomcat introduces you to the Tomcat container and provides you with the tools necessary to begin to take it apart. The key objective of this chapter is to allow you to make a current source distribution of Tomcat active in a development environment (Eclipse Galileo) so that you can trace the path that a request takes through the container's code.

Chapter 2 – Servlet API Overview provides the prerequisite information necessary to navigate the remainder of the book. It describes the Java Enterprise Edition Platform, the HTTP protocol, and the Servlet API, and serves as a refresher for those who are already familiar with Java EE web development.

Chapter 3 – Servlet Container Overview introduces the reader to the Tomcat container. This is the 10,000 foot overview of the container that provides a backdrop to the chapters that follow. All the components of Tomcat are described with just enough detail, so as not to overwhelm the reader with too much information, too early in the process.

Chapter 4 – Starting up Tomcat takes a closer look at the startup process for Tomcat. This is also where you will be first introduced to the Apache Digester project – a key component that we will revisit in later chapters. The chapter ends with an example that demonstrates how a web application can be deployed to a dissected Tomcat container living within an Integrated Development Environment.

Chapter 5 – The Server and Service Components discusses the `Server` component and investigates one of its key services – an implementation of the **Java Naming and Directory Interface (JNDI)** API. We are also introduced to the `Lifecycle` interface that almost every component within Tomcat implements in order to participate in a standardized event based listener mechanism. To show JNDI in action, our example considers connecting to a MySQL database to retrieve data.

Chapter 6 – The Connector Component introduces our first Tomcat luminary, the Coyote Connector. We take a closer look at the standard Java I/O implementation of an HTTP connector. In this chapter, we get a closer look at socket programming, advanced elements of the HTTP protocol, and the internals of the request processing mechanism.

Chapter 7 – The Engine Component describes the first request processing 'Container' within Tomcat and gives us an inkling of things to come. We are also introduced to the `Pipeline` and its `Valves`, which are the standard request processing mechanism for Tomcat components.

Chapter 8 – The Host Component discusses the Tomcat implementation of a Virtual Host. This is the key component responsible for the deployment of web application contexts, as well as for the error page mechanism.

Chapter 9 – The Context Component is at the central core of this book. You get an up-close-and-personal look at how a `Context` is configured, how it accesses its resources, and how it implements its class loading magic.

Chapter 10 – The Wrapper Component takes us to the workhorse of the Tomcat component hierarchy. This component wraps an actual servlet, and as a result is close to a web developer's heart. In addition to reviewing the mapping rules dictated by the Servlet API, we also look at the implementation of servlet filters and the request dispatcher mechanism.

Chapter 11 – The Session Component discusses how sessions are implemented in Tomcat to enable stateful behavior over the stateless HTTP protocol. In addition to looking at some core concepts, such as Java serialization and entropy gathering for random number generation, we look at the standard memory based session implementation, as well as an implementation that uses files to persist sessions.

What you need for this book
You should have knowledge of the Java programming language and web development on the Java platform.

Who this book is for
This book is written for the following classes of readers:

1. Web developers who want to take their programming skills to the next level.
2. Server administrators who want to get a better understanding of the software they manage.
3. Hobbyists who want to contribute to the Tomcat project.
4. Academics and students who want to look at a production grade web server and servlet container from the inside out.
5. Open source auditors who want to understand whether a particular open source project passes audit for usage in highly secure environments or not.
6. Developers who want to understand how to architect high availability, high performance software.

Conventions

In this book, you will find a number of styles of text that distinguish between different kinds of information. Here are some examples of these styles, and an explanation of their meaning.

Code words in text are shown as follows: "You will end up with a file named jdk-6u14-windows-i586.exe on your workstation."

A block of code will be set as follows:

```
[request-method] [/path/to/resource] [HTTP protocol version]
[request-header=value]+
[blank-line to indicate the end of the request headers]
[POST:request-payload]
```

When we wish to draw your attention to a particular part of a code block, the relevant lines or items will be shown in bold:

```
<?xml version="1.0" encoding="UTF-8"?>
<Context antiResourceLocking = "false" reloadable = "true"
         privileged = "false">
  <ResourceLink name = "contactsTableCaption"
                global = "contactsCaption"
                type = "java.lang.String"/>
  <ResourceLink name = "jdbc/swengsolDB" global = "jdbc/swengsolDB"
                type = "javax.sql.DataSource"/>
</Context>
```

Any command-line input or output is written as follows:

```
mysql> help contents;
```

New terms and important words are shown in bold. Words that you see on the screen, in menus or dialog boxes for example, appear in our text like this: "Once the installation has completed, run the MySQL Server Instance Configuration Wizard".

Warnings or important notes appear in a box like this.

Tips and tricks appear like this.

Reader feedback

Feedback from our readers is always welcome. Let us know what you think about this book—what you liked or may have disliked. Reader feedback is important for us to develop titles that you really get the most out of.

To send us general feedback, simply drop an email to feedback@packtpub.com, and mention the book title in the subject of your message.

If there is a book that you need and would like to see us publish, please send us a note in the **SUGGEST A TITLE** form on www.packtpub.com or email suggest@packtpub.com.

If there is a topic that you have expertise in and you are interested in either writing or contributing to a book, see our author guide on www.packtpub.com/authors.

Customer support

Now that you are the proud owner of a Packt book, we have a number of things to help you to get the most from your purchase.

> **Downloading the example code for the book**
>
> Visit http://www.packtpub.com/files/code/7283_Code.zip to directly download the example code.
>
> The downloadable files contain instructions on how to use them.

Errata

Although we have taken every care to ensure the accuracy of our contents, mistakes do happen. If you find a mistake in one of our books—maybe a mistake in text or code—we would be grateful if you would report this to us. By doing so, you can save other readers from frustration, and help us to improve subsequent versions of this book. If you find any errata, please report them by visiting http://www.packtpub.com/support, selecting your book, clicking on the **let us know** link, and entering the details of your errata. Once your errata are verified, your submission will be accepted and the errata added to any list of existing errata. Any existing errata can be viewed by selecting your title from http://www.packtpub.com/support.

Piracy

Piracy of copyright material on the Internet is an ongoing problem across all media. At Packt, we take the protection of our copyright and licenses very seriously. If you come across any illegal copies of our works in any form on the Internet, please provide us with the location address or website name immediately so that we can pursue a remedy.

Please contact us at `copyright@packtpub.com` with a link to the suspected pirated material.

We appreciate your help in protecting our authors, and our ability to bring you valuable content.

Questions

You can contact us at `questions@packtpub.com` if you are having a problem with any aspect of the book, and we will do our best to address it.

Introduction to Tomcat

1

It is hard to overemphasize the importance of Apache Tomcat in the realm of Java Enterprise Edition web development. Tomcat began its life as source code that was donated by Sun Microsystems to the **Apache Software Foundation (ASF)**. Since then, it has played a central role in the development and validation of the Java Servlet and JavaServer Pages specifications and has been the official reference implementation for these specifications.

Its early popularity stemmed from the fact that it was easily integrated with two of the world's most popular web server software, Apache httpd and Microsoft's **Internet Information Services (IIS)** server.

However, since then, it has evolved into a production-grade product used by multiple large corporations (see a partial list at `http://wiki.apache.org/tomcat/PoweredBy`).

Tomcat is also found embedded, in part or whole, in various open source application server offerings. Even when using competing commercial application server offerings such as IBM's WebSphere and BEA's WebLogic, developers often use Tomcat to validate the vendor-independence of their applications.

It is also priced just right. It is open source and distributed under the Apache license, meaning it is free for use and modification (see `www.apache.org/licenses` for details). This also has the side effect of having the source code readily available for examination.

This availability of source code, strict adherence to specifications, and proven track record, combine to make Tomcat a unique learning opportunity for us. This book will assist you in taking the covers off this unique project, so that you get to see exactly how a production-grade servlet container is implemented.

What's the story behind Tomcat?

As I write this, the most current version of Tomcat is 6.0.20, where 6 is the major version, 0 is the minor version, and 20 is the bug fix release number. This version implements, and is completely compliant with, version 2.5 of the Java Servlet specification, and version 2.1 of the JavaServer Pages (JSP) specification.

That's a pretty hefty mouthful, so let's start at the beginning.

Every superhero has an origins story, and Tomcat is no exception. The Tomcat web site lists the available versions at `http://tomcat.apache.org/whichversion.html`, which shows the first stable release listed as Tomcat 3.x. So what happened to versions 1 and 2?

Tomcat was conceived in November 1998 by James Duncan Davidson at Sun Microsystems, who wrote it to form the core of the **JavaServer Web Development Kit (JSWDK)** for the Servlet 2.1 specification.

The name 'Tomcat' came to him when he was trying to decide a package name for the code he was working on. He ended up using `com.sun.tomcat`.

At the time, Apache JServ, a free servlet container, was in the process of being updated to support the Servlet 2.1 specification.

However, this effort was abandoned due to the donation of Tomcat by Sun Microsystems to the Apache Software Foundation, at JavaOne in 1999. It soon came to life as Tomcat version 3.0, the successor to JSWDK 2.1.

This was a major milestone for the open source community as it meant that a commercial package owned and developed by Sun Microsystems, and which implemented the latest Servlet 2.2 and JSP 1.1 specifications, was now being offered to the general public for free.

All of this made the decision to abandon Apache JServ rather uncontroversial.

The focus soon shifted from updating JServ to support the new specification, to getting Tomcat to implement features that were missing. The most important one being the ability to cooperate with the Apache web server. This was critical to the popularity of Tomcat, as it meant that developers could leverage the static file handling capabilities of the Apache web server together with the dynamic capabilities of Tomcat to achieve a well rounded solution. Subsequent Tomcat releases have actually strengthened this connection component.

In addition, Tomcat can now directly serve static content and so is often deployed in standalone mode without a separate web server.

It is interesting to note that Tomcat began life not as its own top level project. Instead, it started humbly as a subproject within the Jakarta project (an umbrella project that covers many subprojects such as Apache Commons, Cactus, and JMeter). It was only in 2005 that it was upgraded to the status of a top level project at Apache.

What exactly is Tomcat?

For most users, the typical web interaction can be represented as follows: Joe User enters a **Uniform Resource Locator** (**URL**) in the browser's location box to request the resource that is identified by that URL. A URL is composed of a host name, an optional port (which defaults to 80), and the resource being requested.

When a web server receives that request, it first determines whether the resource being requested is static or dynamic in nature.

A static resource is one that is identical no matter how many times, or in what order, that resource is requested. Some examples of these would be a company's logo on a web page, a CSS style sheet, or a typical HTML page.

The web server handles the request for a static resource by simply fetching the identified resource from the appropriate path in which its static content resides (for example, htdocs for Apache), and returning those bytes in the response to the user.

For static resources, a depiction of this request flow is as shown below.

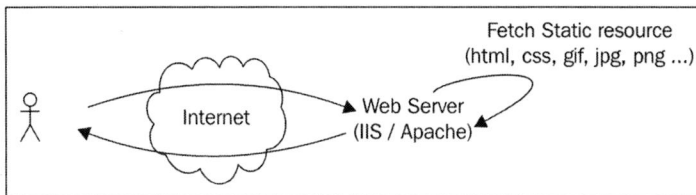

A dynamic resource, on the other hand, indicates a resource that varies its content based on various factors that may include the specific user making the request, the time of day when the request is made, or the presence of additional information in the request that affects how the request is interpreted. Some examples of these would include the current inventory for a specific product in an online store, or the availability of a seat on an airplane.

Most web servers are tuned to deliver blazing fast request handling for static resources. However, they require additional help when dealing with dynamic resources. This help is typically provided by an additional software component that is registered with the web server, called a **servlet container** on the Java EE platform.

In the IIS world, access to this servlet container is offered by implementing an **Internet Server Application Programming Interface (ISAPI)** extension, which is a Dynamic Link Library (DLL) that allows you to extend the functionality of IIS. In the Apache world, you access the container using code written in C or C++.

When a request comes in that is directed at a dynamic resource, the web server simply hands off that request to its associated servlet container.

The container then springs into action, invokes the appropriate servlet that represents the requested dynamic resource. This servlet is responsible for generating the response. The generated response is returned by the servlet container to the web server which, in turn, returns it to the requesting user. This interaction is depicted in the following diagram.

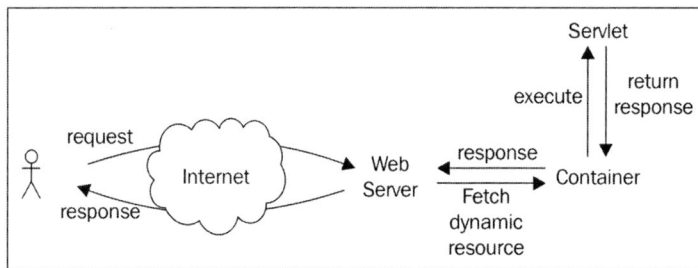

A **servlet** in its most basic form is a Java class that acts as a dynamic web resource. In other words, it can be the target of a client browser's request.

Being a Java class, it can tailor its response according to the payload of the incoming request, the conversation that this request is a part of, as well as other environmental criteria (such as the time of the day or the inventory status from a database).

> It is important to note that there is nothing special about this delegation mechanism that restricts it only to dynamic resources. You could configure a web server to also delegate requests for a certain subset of static resources (for example, those within a given URL path) to the servlet container.

JSPs

The problem with using Java code to generate HTML content is that you end up with a lot of string generation and concatenation to generate the actual HTML content, interspersed with actual program logic written in Java. This is an unholy combination as it tends to make the program logic impervious to the person tasked with maintaining your code. In addition, changes to static content now require you to compile the servlet class.

Applying the 80-20 rule very loosely to dynamic content, you might find that 80% of the content of a page is in reality static content. The JavaServer Pages specification was evolved as the solution to this situation. A **JSP (JavaServer Page)** is a template made up primarily of static content with very specific (and hopefully, few) invocations of Java code to retrieve the dynamic aspects of the page.

The problem of requiring a compilation step was resolved by making a JSP an artificial construct. The container is responsible for transparently parsing a JSP and converting it into a bona fide servlet, compiling it, and then invoking it in the same manner as the other servlets in the application.

As long as the ratio of static to dynamic content is high, that is, as long as there are more static elements than dynamic elements on a page, even non programmers, such as graphic artists, can find their way around a JSP file with some comfort.

This is about as much as we will cover on JavaServer Pages technology in this book.

Servlet container

With all that behind us, we are now ready to answer the question posed by this section's title – what exactly is Tomcat?

Tomcat is classified as a servlet container, that is, an environment within which servlets can live and prosper. As a container, it provides a lot of administrative support to servlets, allowing programmers to focus on the core application logic that is to be implemented, without having to bother about low level specifics such as session management and class loading.

The servlet and JSP specifications describe the service contract that the container promises to provide to the servlets and JSP files that we write. Together, the specifications describe all the services that a container should provide, and specify how the servlet may make use of those services. As with all other **Application Programming Interfaces (APIs)**, the specifications describe the 'what' and leave the 'how' to the implementer of the specific container.

Tomcat serves as the 'reference implementation' of these specifications, and as a result, serves as a guinea pig or canary in the mine shaft for them. In other words, it provides a sample implementation to prove that the specification can indeed be implemented, and serves as a guide for other implementers.

The following diagram provides an early bird's eye view of the responsibilities of a servlet container.

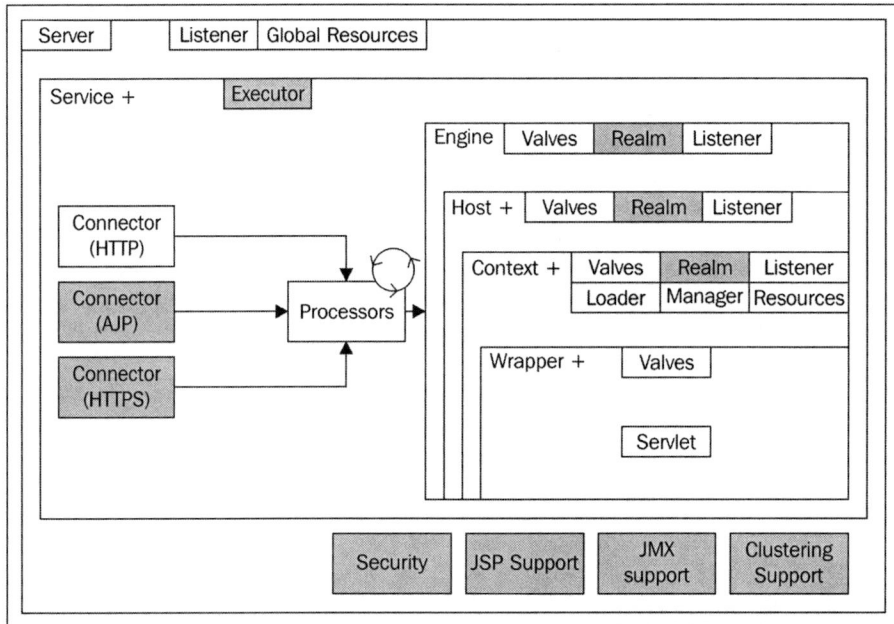

The primary responsibility of a container is to process an incoming request and to generate a corresponding response that is then returned to the client.

A **Connector** component provides the external interface that allows clients to connect to the container. This component not only accepts incoming connections, but is also responsible for delegating the processing of the request to an available request processor thread. The 'Processors' block in the image denotes multiple threads in a pool that may be used to process the incoming request.

The request processing framework is implemented using a multiple level hierarchy of sub containers (the servlet **Engine**, virtual hosts, web application contexts, and servlet **Wrappers**) and nested components (**Valves, Listeners, Loaders, Resources,** and **Security Realms**). Note that the '+' sign in the above image indicates that there can be more than one instance of that component. For instance, more than one Host, Context, and servlet Wrapper component may be contained within its parent container.

The result of processing a request is represented by a response, which is then returned through the same **Connector**.

In addition to the core request processing components, the container also provides support for other aspects of operation, such as logging, security, and JMX monitoring.

In this book, our primary focus will be on the request processing responsibilities of a servlet container. These components form the unshaded boxes in the previous image. Additional topics will be considered only when they are crucial to understanding a request processing component's actions.

It is important to note that a servlet container is a completely different beast from an application server.

In the simplest sense, an application server contains a servlet container, along with other containers, such as an EJB container, an applet container, and an application client container. In addition, an application server provides implementations for a number of Service APIs that are required for heavy duty applications. We will take a closer look at the Java EE platform in Chapter 2.

Examples of application servers include the JBoss Application Server, GlassFish, IBM's WebSphere, and BEA's WebLogic.

Whether or not you should use a full fledged application server, with its support for Enterprise JavaBeans and other Java EE heavy artillery, depends on your application needs.

Why this book?

Tomcat is one of the few technology areas that is particularly blessed with a plethora of very well written books, and the Tomcat mailing lists are rather friendly places for new developers. So really, why another book on Tomcat?

The answer is simple. Most of these books and material focus primarily on the set up, administration, and management, of a Tomcat server.

This is no accident. Most web developers rarely have to concern themselves with anything more challenging than setting up a context fragment or changing the default port for Tomcat from 8080 to 80.

As long as a developer understands the basic terminology of web applications (such as the context, the context root) and the structure of a WAR file, most modern **Integrated Development Environments (IDEs)**, such as Eclipse and IntelliJ IDEA, do all the heavy lifting for you.

It seems only appropriate then, for authors to target their books at the typical administrator or deployer.

For its part, Tomcat exposes a myriad of configuration files that enable even an obsessive administrator to fine tune the installation and the Java Virtual Machine as much as desired.

The net result is that your average book contains the customary chapter on installing Tomcat, chapters on configuring it, on deploying servlets into it, on integration with either the Apache httpd web server or Microsoft's IIS, and on securing the installation.

The downside with this approach is that it provides a one-sided view of the software engineering marvel that is Tomcat. You tend to see it as a black box with lots of control switches that you can throw, but you never ever really get a chance to peer into the open vents on the sides of that box.

In this book, I hope to correct that imbalance. I'm going to pry open the service door on the side of that black box, and take you in on an interesting journey through some of the sights that most people rarely get to see. A connector shimmering in the moonlight, the rays of the early morning sun catching an application class loader in its native state, a lumbering valve caught in motion capture frames as it springs into action with surprising agility. There are a lot of fantastical beings that populate this world, if you only dare to venture into it.

In the course of the next few chapters, we will look at Tomcat from the perspective of someone attempting to understand what makes it tick. Our goal will be to understand Tomcat as few others do. We'll not only see the control switches on the outside, but we'll also learn about how these switches affect the machinery within.

Gathering our tools

In this section, I'm going to get together all the pieces that you will need for the remainder of this book. If you would like to follow along with the rest of this book, then this section is crucial.

The software that we will download and install includes the following:

- The **Java SE Development Kit (JDK)** version 6.0
- A download verifier
- Apache Ant 1.7.1
- Subversion 1.6.3
- Eclipse 3.5 Galileo

The workstation that I use throughout this book runs a Microsoft Windows operating system (XP Professional or Vista).

The version numbers that are specified were current at the time of writing this text. However, with the speed of product cycles in the open source arena, it is likely that newer versions will be available by the time you read this.

Java Development Kit (JDK) 6.0

JDK 6 can be found at `http://java.sun.com/javase/downloads/index.jsp`.

As with every download page on the Sun web site, there are enough choices to make your head spin. For our needs, we need the plain vanilla JDK 6.0 that at the time of writing is **JDK 6 Update 14**.

Once you've picked the **Platform: (Windows)** and **Language: (Multi-language)**, you will end up with a file named `jdk-6u14-windows-i586.exe` on your workstation.

Execute this file to install it. Once you have accepted the terms and conditions, and have picked an install directory, the installation process will begin.

Once the JDK has been installed, the installer will prompt you to install the JRE. You may do so if you wish.

The JDK for 64-bit platforms
There are 64-bit versions of the JDK that are available for Windows, Linux, and Solaris. The file for 64-bit Windows is named `jdk-6u14-windows-x64.exe`.

Verifying downloaded files

Most open source software is hosted on multiple mirror sites, and you are expected to pick your nearest mirror from which to download it. A key question here is how do you ensure that the file that you just downloaded is an exact copy of the version that the open source team intended for download, and there isn't a malicious hacker chuckling with glee to see you install a Trojan on your workstation?

There are a couple of answers to this question—using PGP keys or using a message digest.

The former is more secure as it uses public key cryptography, but as a result is also more complex.

The latter, while simpler to use, is not quite as secure, as the most common digest algorithm (MD5) has some well documented flaws, allowing different files to generate the same digest. In addition, the MD5 digest value itself may have been modified by the hacker so that it matches the compromised file.

Using the principle that any security is better than none, you would compute the MD5 message digest for the downloaded file, and compare that computed value against the published digest for the file.

You can download a digest generator from either `www.formilab.ch/md5/` or `www.nullriver.com/index/products/winmd5sum`.

For example, the MD5 digest for the ZIP file distribution of Tomcat 6.0.18 is:

```
f7d0c15df19fedf52476767f7ce0b6f8
 *apache-tomcat-6.0.18.zip
```

Apache Ant

Apache Ant or Another Neat Tool is a build automation utility that owes its existence to James Duncan Davidson and Tomcat. It originated as a tool used to build Tomcat itself. But its widespread popularity ensured that it was promoted into its own project, independent of Tomcat, in January 2000.

As Ant is written in Java, it inherits its Write Once Run Anywhere aspect, making it platform independent. Its build directives (by default, in a file named `build.xml`) are written using XML - another cross platform advantage.

Ant build directives take the form of targets that describe the actions or tasks that must be performed, whether creating, deleting, or copying files and directories, setting classpaths, compiling Java classes, or even packaging your applications.

The ability to define dependencies on targets adds to its flexibility. You can indicate that a compile target depends on other targets that clear out the output directories, fetch the latest changes from your source code repository, and set the classpath.

Finally, throw in the ability to define your own targets, and the sky's the limit!

Download the latest version from `http://ant.apache.org/bindownload.cgi` and extract the Ant distribution. The version that was current when I wrote this, was Ant 1.7.1.

You need to add Ant to your **PATH**. On Windows, this is accomplished by opening the System Properties box – by right clicking your **My Computer** icon and clicking **Properties.** Pick **System** from the Control Panel's classic view or press the keyboard shortcut *Windows + Pause/Break.*

On the **Advanced system settings** tab, click on **Environment Variables** tab and edit the **Path** variable. Add [ANT_HOME]\bin to the end of the path variable, replacing [ANT_HOME] with the absolute path to the location where you extracted the downloaded file.

Note that path variables in Windows are delimited by a semicolon.

Subversion

Next, we need a way to retrieve the latest version of the Tomcat source code, which is currently housed in a Subversion repository.

Subversion was conceived in 2000, when CollabNet, Inc. decided that it was time to write a brand new version control system, and brought on Karl Fogel to head this effort. The stated goal of the original team was to write a better version of CVS, while retaining the familiar elements of CVS, to make it easier for developers to switch without much effort.

Subversion has since dethroned CVS as the system of choice. In particular, it has been adopted as the standard version control mechanism by the Apache Software Foundation.

Subversion, like CVS, uses a copy-modify-merge model. In the copy phase, each developer makes a private copy of the project's source code on to their individual workstations. This copy acts as a sandbox within which each developer may work.

In the modify phase, each developer makes changes in his or her own working copy. The changes made by one developer are not visible to the others. If you need visibility into another developer's changes, you would need to update your working copy from the repository.

In the merge phase, a developer commits his changes back into the source code. If a file was modified by another developer since you checked out your copy, you would then need to merge your changes back into the repository resolving any conflicts as necessary.

Get the latest version of the **Subversion Command-Line Client for Windows** from http://www.collab.net/downloads/subversion/, which is currently 1.6.3. Execute the downloaded file, CollabNetSubversion-client-1.6.3-3.win32.exe.

The installation is fairly straightforward and only requires that you specify a path name for your installation.

To verify that the software was successfully installed, run the `svn --version` command from the command prompt. This command should output the version of Subversion that is installed on your workstation.

Obtaining the Tomcat source code

You have two options when trying to download the Tomcat source. You could either use the Subversion version control software, which was described in the last section, or you could simply download the compressed source distribution of Tomcat as a ZIP file. The former option is preferred if you expect to be developing in Tomcat, whereas the latter is simply a snapshot of the code at a given version.

Using Subversion

To obtain the latest source code for Tomcat from the Subversion repository at the ASF, change your working directory to where you want to download your working copy (for example, `c:\tomcat`), and execute the following at the command line (all on one line):

```
svn checkout http://svn.apache.org/repos/asf/tomcat/tc6.0.x/trunk/
```

When this completes, you will notice that your current directory now contains a `trunk` subfolder with the source directories for Tomcat.

> The above command downloads the most up-to-date version of the source `trunk` and may result in code that may differ from the descriptions in this text.
>
> If you would like to ensure that you are working with the exact codebase covered in this book, then you should use the following command instead:
>
> ```
> svn checkout http://svn.apache.org/repos/asf/tomcat/
> tc6.0.x/tags/TOMCAT_6_0_20/
> ```

This is the 'copy' phase of your interaction with the Subversion version control system. The result of this operation is to make a local copy of Tomcat's latest development code line from the Subversion repository. This lets you play in your own little sandbox, making changes and experimenting for as long as you need.

Tomcat source distribution

If you'd rather not install Subversion, a less invasive option would be to simply download the Tomcat source from the **Source Code Distributions** section at `http://tomcat.apache.org/download-60.cgi`.The source for a previous version can be downloaded from `http://archive.apache.org/dist/tomcat/tomcat-6/`. The only downside with this approach is that the source distribution does not contain a project file for use with the Eclipse IDE. To get these files, point your browser at `http://svn.apache.org/repos/asf/tomcat/tc6.0.x/trunk` (or to `http://svn.apache.org/repos/asf/tomcat/tc6.0.x/tags/TOMCAT_6_0_20` for the version used in this book) and download the `.classpath` and `.project` files. Ensure that the downloaded files are named exactly the same as their originals.

Getting ready to build Tomcat

Now, we're ready to get started with building the source that we just downloaded. This is a two step process that utilizes the power of Ant and the `build.xml` file that exists in the `trunk` directory. First change directory to the directory to which your source code has been downloaded (or unzipped.).

Downloading dependencies

Now, run the `download` target:

```
ant download
```

The `download` target downloads a number of binaries that are needed for this build. These artifacts are downloaded to the folder that is identified by the `base.path` property in the Ant `build.properties.default` file. By default, this will be `/usr/share/java`. However, you can change this to a different absolute path such as `c:/tomcat/downloads/trunk`.

The files that are downloaded include:

- The native Tomcat connectors (currently at version 1.1.15).
- The Commons daemon library (version 1.0.1), which is used with `jsvc`—a Java Service Wrapper that is used to run Tomcat as a non-root user listening on the privileged port 80 on non Windows operating systems.

- The Eclipse JDT JAR, which is used by Tomcat to compile JSPs.

- The **Nullsoft Scriptable Install System (NSIS)**—an open source system to create Windows installers.

- The Commons Collections library.

- The Commons Database Connection Pool (version 1.2.2) and Commons Pool (version 1.4). The `build-tomcat-dbcp` Ant target renames the packages for these Commons projects, for example, by replacing `org.apache.commons` with `org.apache.tomcat.dbcp`. The stated goal here is to ensure that the DBCP and Pool classes, used by Tomcat internally, do not conflict with any versions of DBCP or Pool classes that are packaged with individual web applications.

> **Download errors**
>
> I have noticed that the `download` target sometimes fails when trying to unzip the NSIS with the following error: `java.io.IOException: Negative seek offset`
>
> In such cases, a manual workaround is to simply download the target ZIP file (in this case `http://downloads.sourceforge.net/nsis/nsis-2.37.zip`) and unzip it to the folder into which the build script is downloading files. Then, ensure that the test file is present, which in this case is `c:/tomcat/downloads/trunk/nsis-2.37/makensis.exe`.

Building Tomcat

We're finally ready to build Tomcat using Ant, so run the `deploy` target.

```
ant deploy
```

This target compiles the Java code and builds the binary distribution of Tomcat. Note that you can omit the target name because `deploy` is defined as the default target in the `build.xml` file. So the following would be equivalent:

```
ant
```

The `deploy` target builds the Tomcat binaries and copies files out to `output\build`.

> **The "clean" target**
>
> If you need to start with a clean build, then the `clean` target is your friend. It clears out all the output folders for a fresh distribution to be laid into it.

Starting up your shiny new Tomcat

From the `output\build\bin` directory within your Tomcat `trunk` folder, execute the `startup.bat` batch file.

startup

This starts up your Tomcat server in a separate command window. Reassuring log messages should be output to your console as shown.

```
Aug 1, 2009 9:46:28 AM org.apache.catalina.core.AprLifecycleListener init
INFO: The APR based Apache Tomcat Native library which allows optimal performance in produ
ction environments was not found on the java.library.path: C:\java\jdk1.5.0_19\bin;.;C:\Wi
ndows\system32;C:\Windows;C:\Windows\system32;C:\Windows;C:\Windows\System32\Wbem;C:\Progr
am Files (x86)\CyberLink\Power2Go\;C:\Program Files (x86)\CollabNet Subversion;C:\java\jdk
1.5.0_19\bin;c:\java\apache-ant-1.7.1\bin;C:\usr\share\java\tomcat-native-1.1.15
Aug 1, 2009 9:46:29 AM org.apache.coyote.http11.Http11Protocol init
INFO: Initializing Coyote HTTP/1.1 on http-8080
Aug 1, 2009 9:46:29 AM org.apache.catalina.startup.Catalina load
INFO: Initialization processed in 2767 ms
Aug 1, 2009 9:46:29 AM org.apache.catalina.core.StandardService start
INFO: Starting service Catalina
Aug 1, 2009 9:46:29 AM org.apache.catalina.core.StandardEngine start
INFO: Starting Servlet Engine: Apache Tomcat/6.0-snapshot
Aug 1, 2009 9:46:29 AM org.apache.catalina.startup.HostConfig deployDescriptor
INFO: Deploying configuration descriptor host-manager.xml
Aug 1, 2009 9:46:31 AM org.apache.catalina.startup.HostConfig deployDescriptor
INFO: Deploying configuration descriptor manager.xml
Aug 1, 2009 9:46:31 AM org.apache.catalina.startup.HostConfig deployDirectory
INFO: Deploying web application directory docs
Aug 1, 2009 9:46:31 AM org.apache.catalina.startup.HostConfig deployDirectory
INFO: Deploying web application directory examples
Aug 1, 2009 9:46:32 AM org.apache.catalina.startup.HostConfig deployDirectory
INFO: Deploying web application directory ROOT
Aug 1, 2009 9:46:32 AM org.apache.coyote.http11.Http11Protocol start
INFO: Starting Coyote HTTP/1.1 on http-8080
Aug 1, 2009 9:46:32 AM org.apache.jk.common.ChannelSocket init
INFO: JK: ajp13 listening on /0.0.0.0:8009
Aug 1, 2009 9:46:32 AM org.apache.jk.server.JkMain start
INFO: Jk running ID=0 time=0/132  config=null
Aug 1, 2009 9:46:32 AM org.apache.catalina.startup.Catalina start
INFO: Server startup in 3831 ms
```

Now, using your favorite browser, type in the URL `http://localhost:8080`, and marvel at what you have wrought.

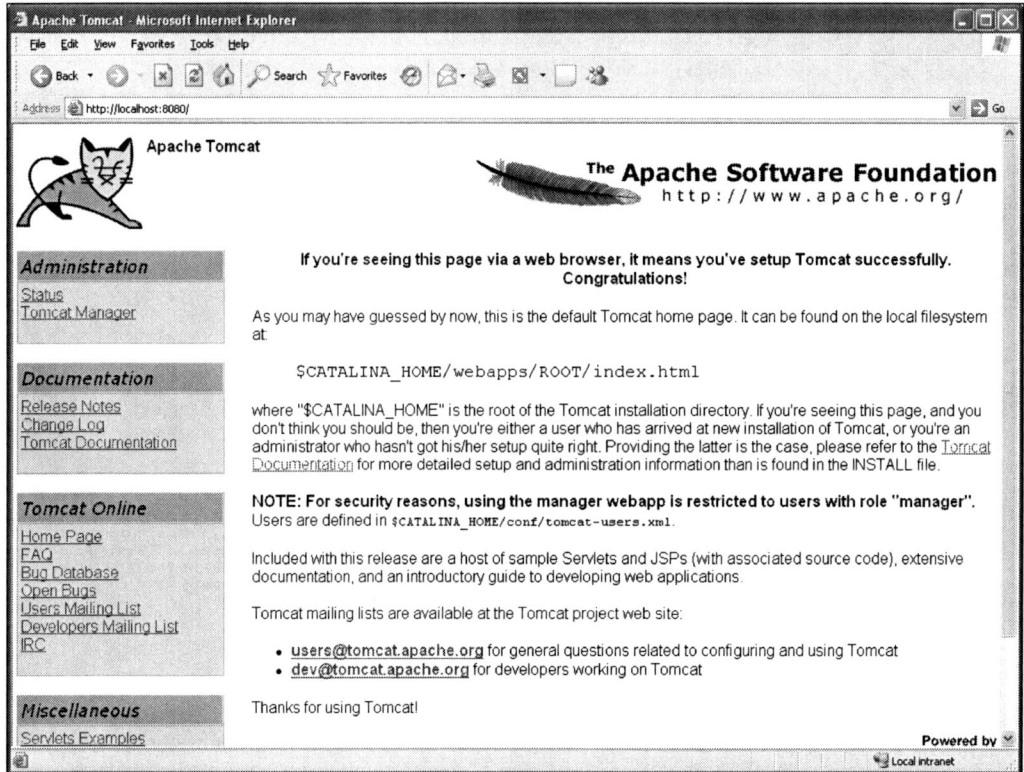

Finally, to shut down your server, execute the `shutdown.bat` batch file.

shutdown

This command closes down the Tomcat server gracefully, and you're done.

Eclipse

We're now on to the home stretch. The ultimate prize for us is to be able to use an **IDE** to run the Tomcat server. What would be more appropriate for investigating Tomcat, than the free and full featured open source IDE—Eclipse!

> While you can simply use your favorite IDE, the Tomcat source distributions include project metadata files only for the Eclipse IDE.

In particular, let's pick Eclipse Galileo, which is the most recent in an annual series of releases that package multiple major projects. Previous releases have been code named Callisto, Europa, and Ganymede.

Galileo was released in June 2009, and includes the core Eclipse project along with almost three dozen other major projects, including the Web Tools Platform project, the Rich Ajax Platform project, and the SOA Tools Platform project.

Eclipse downloads are available at `http://www.eclipse.org/downloads/`. Make sure that you pick the **Eclipse IDE for Java EE Developers** version. For Windows, this results in the file `eclipse-jee-galileo-win32.zip` being copied down to your workstation.

> **Eclipse for 64-bit Windows**
>
> The above link works fine for downloading Eclipse for the most common platforms, including 64-bit Linux. However, you have to work a bit harder to get the 64-bit version for Windows. The downloads for the Eclipse project are available at `http://download.eclipse.org/eclipse/downloads/`. For safety, click the link associated with the **Latest Release** version, which is currently at 3.5. These downloads are named `eclipse-SDK-[versionNumber]-[platform].zip`. For Vista 64, this download is `eclipse-SDK-3.5-win32-x86_64.zip`.

Unzip the Eclipse distribution to a folder of your choice, and execute `eclipse.exe` to verify that your IDE starts up.

At startup, you are prompted for a workspace location. A workspace folder is used to house your projects as well as to store metadata about your plugins and your IDE preferences.

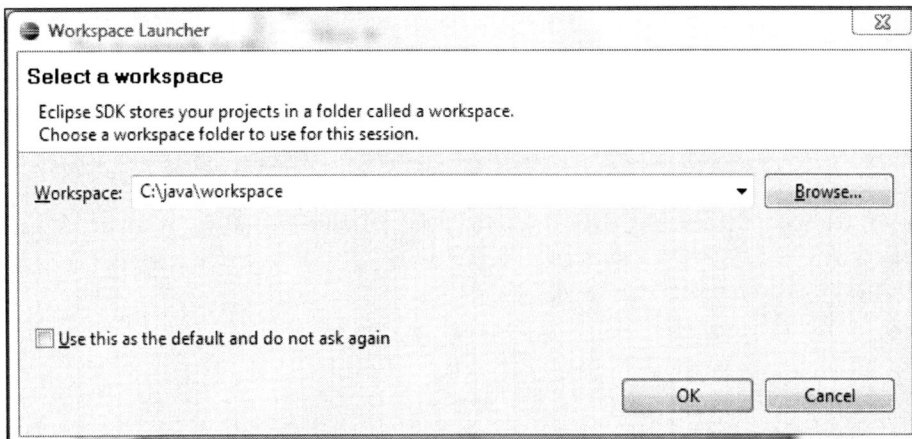

In this dialog, you can either point to an existing workspace folder if you have one, or to a new folder location. It is recommended that you pick a folder that lies outside of your Eclipse installation directory so that when you upgrade your Eclipse version, you can simply delete the old installation folder without losing your workspace.

Once Eclipse starts up, dismiss the Welcome screen to proceed to the Workbench, and then select the **Window | Preferences** menu option to display the Preferences dialog.

In the left pane of this dialog, drill down to **Java | Installed JREs**, and verify that your previously installed version of JDK 6 shows up. If it doesn't, then click on the **Add** button to add a reference to your JDK.

We will also set up two classpath variables as shown next—ANT_HOME to point at the base directory for your Ant installation and TOMCAT_LIBS_BASE to point to the directory that holds the files downloaded by the download ant target that you executed while building Tomcat.

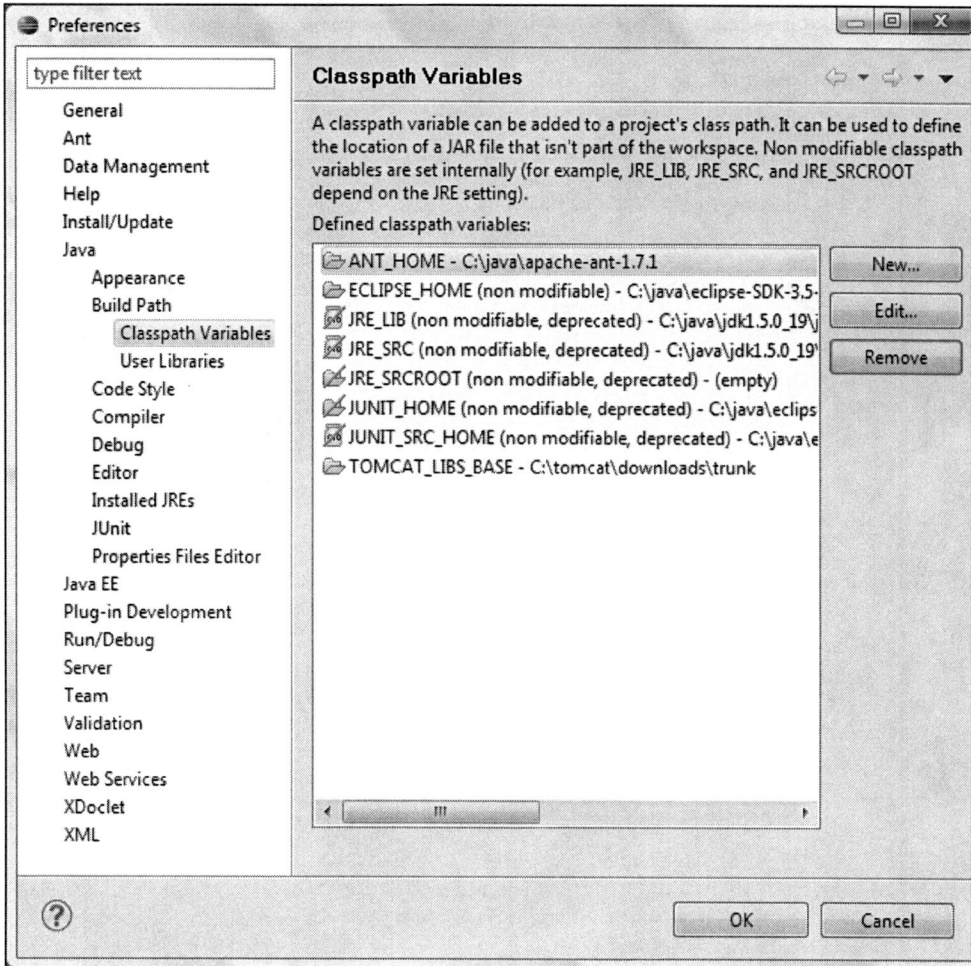

> If you are building a non-trunk version of Tomcat, then ensure that your TOMCAT_LIBS_BASE classpath variable points to the path to where the ant download target downloads its dependencies.

Next, import the project file that is present in the working copy of the Tomcat trunk. Choose **File | Import** to open the **Import** dialog. From this dialog, choose **General | Existing Projects into Workspace** to import the Eclipse project present in the Tomcat trunk into your new workspace.

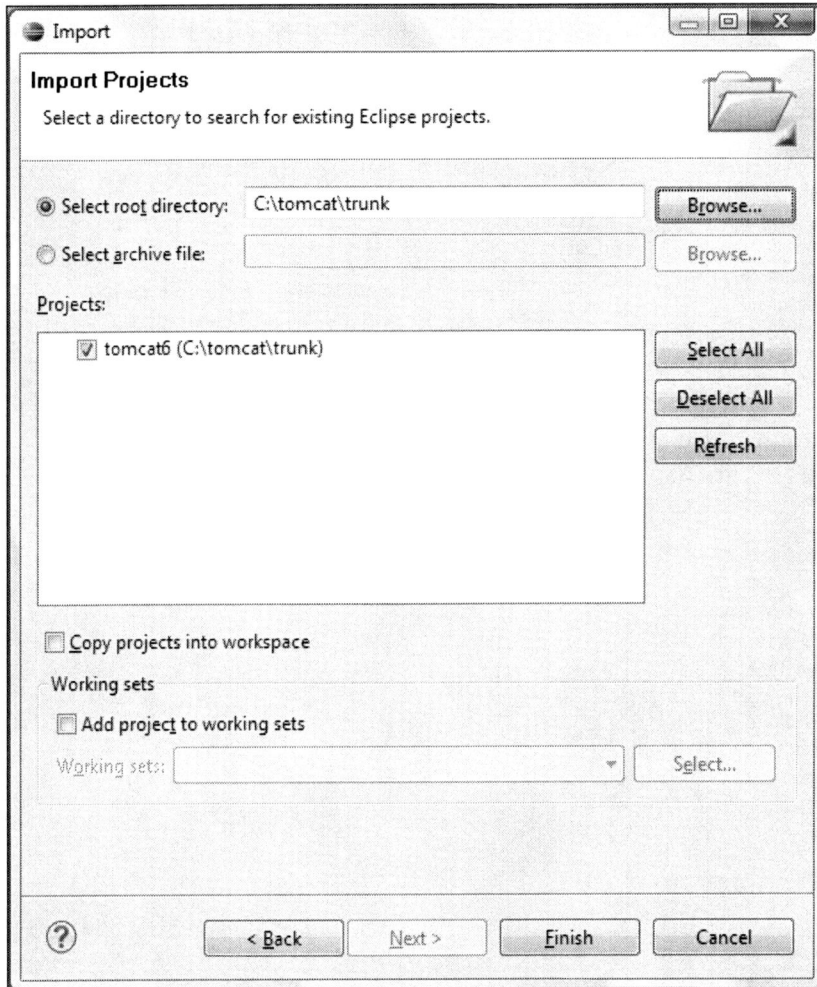

Click on **Finish** to import the project.

A project build begins automatically, and you will get the following screen.

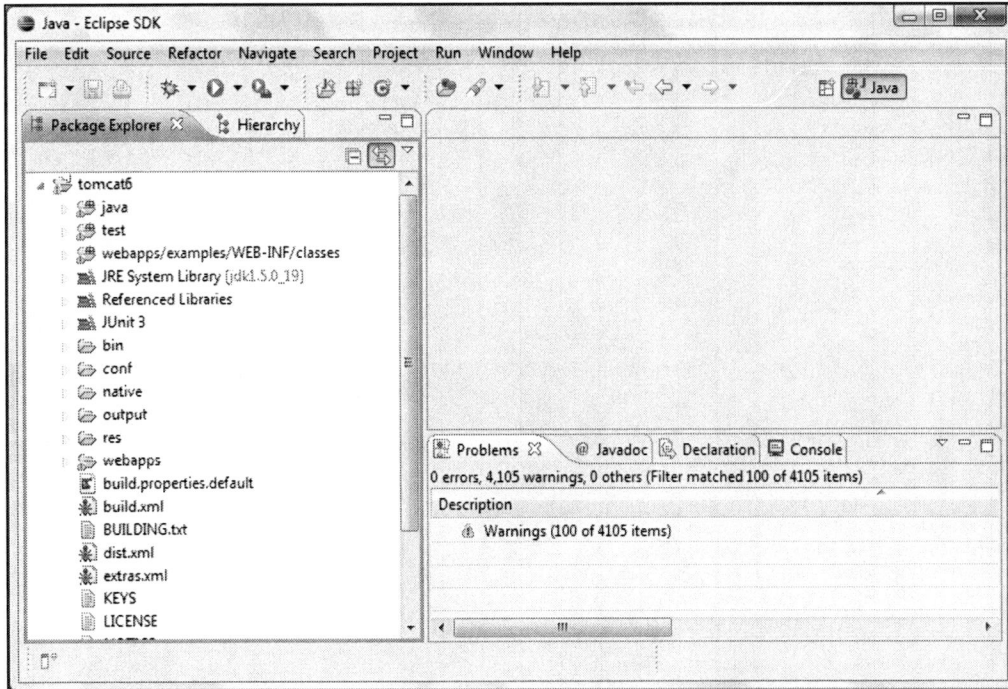

To start up your Tomcat server from within Eclipse, create a Run configuration by choosing the **Run | Run Configurations...** menu option, and select `org.apache.catalina.startup.Bootstrap` as the Main class.

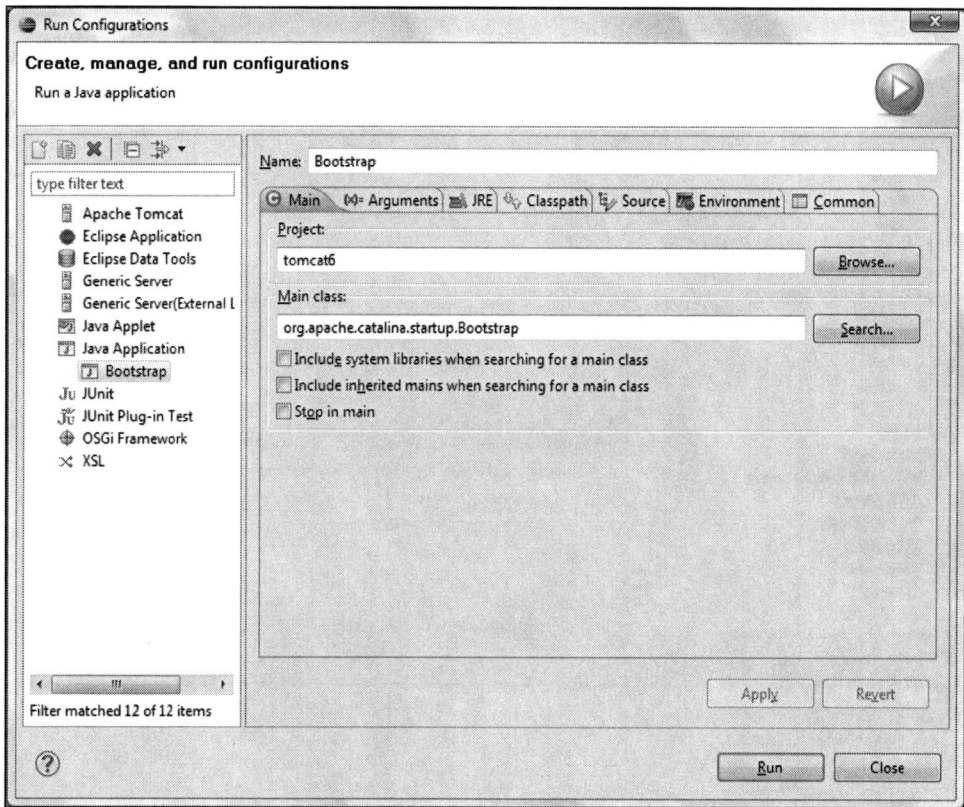

Click on **Run,** and watch the Console pane for output indicating that Tomcat was successfully started.

Now browse on over to `http://localhost:8080` to view the Tomcat welcome page.

Congratulations! You're done.

For now, play with this code by placing breakpoints and stepping through interesting code sections. We'll explore these sections in far greater detail in the chapters to come.

In the next couple of chapters, we'll regroup and visit concepts that are necessary for the exploring that we'll be doing in later chapters.

Summary

We covered a lot of ground in this chapter. We began by looking at the principles behind a servlet container. We looked at the origins of Tomcat, and we built ourselves our very own server by cobbling together a number of software helpers.

We looked at the JDK, the Ant build tool, the Subversion version control tool, and the Eclipse IDE. We retrieved the latest source from the Tomcat Subversion repository, and we compiled the Java sources to result in a binary distribution of the container.

In the next chapter, we'll explore some of the ideas embodied in the servlet specification.

2
Servlet API Overview

In the preceding chapter, Apache Tomcat was described as a reference implementation of the Servlet and JSP specifications.

There are two concepts here that go together like peanut butter and jelly—a specification and its implementation.

While the bulk of this book is focused on the implementation aspect, this chapter takes a bit of a detour to review the actual specification that is under discussion. Think of it as a walk through the actual requirements that the Tomcat development teams were given to implement.

We will begin by taking a look at how specifications are born and nurtured in the world of Java. We will then look at the Java Enterprise Edition specification, the uber-specification of which the Servlet and JSP specifications are but a part. We will end our tour by examining the Servlet and JSP specifications themselves.

There is a lot of ground to cover, and concepts will be coming at you from every direction. But at the end of this chapter, you will be able to appreciate exactly how servlets fit into the grand scheme of things, and you will be very well positioned to appreciate the huge effort undertaken by the Apache Tomcat project teams.

Readers who are familiar with the Servlet API and the **Hypertext Transfer Protocol (HTTP)** may safely skip this chapter.

Java Community Process

The **Java Community Process (JCP)** was introduced by Sun Microsystems in 1998. Its primary goal was to engage the greater Java community in the process of developing and revising Java Application Programming Interfaces (APIs). The process is currently at version 2.6 (http://jcp.org/en/procedures/jcp2).

The JCP works by bringing together a group of experts in the subject area, under the guidance of a *technical specification lead* to not only develop or revise a specification, but also to build a reference implementation as well as a technology compatibility kit.

The process starts with the submission of a **Java Specification Request (JSR)**, which either proposes a brand new specification or a significant revision to an existing specification.

An API is the contract that is made by a software package in terms of the functionality that it makes available to the developer. There is an implicit guarantee that APIs can be relied upon to exist for a very long time. You can see this at work in many Java APIs, where even questionable API decisions live on in perpetuity, as deprecated methods.

A *specification* has, at its core, the API for some aspect of the technology. For example, the Servlet 2.5 specification of August 2007 devotes almost half its pages to the API embodied in its `javax.servlet` and `javax.servlet.http` packages. The rest of its pages are split between the description of concepts that are introduced by the specification (servlets, the servlet context, sessions, filters, and so on) and a description of the functional requirements of a Java Enterprise Edition 5 servlet container.

A *platform edition specification* is a more involved animal and defines a baseline set of APIs that provide a foundation upon which applications can be built. For example, the Java Enterprise Edition platform describes a set of APIs (such as the JDBC, JNDI, and Servlet APIs) that are guaranteed to be available to any application that runs within a Java EE compliant server.

A *reference implementation* is the proof of concept implementation for a given specification, and is intended to prove that the specification can actually be implemented. Apache Tomcat serves as the reference implementation for the Servlet and JSP APIs; whereas the Sun Java System Application Server (GlassFish) is the reference implementation for the entire Java EE 5 stack.

A *technology compatibility kit* is used to verify that a given implementation is compliant with its specification. It consists of a set of tests, a mechanism to automate these tests, useful tools, and documentation. The reference implementation also serves as a useful platform against which to validate the tests in the TCK.

The current version for the Servlet API is the Java™ Servlet Specification version 2.5 Maintenance Release 6 specification. This specification was developed using the JCP as Java Specification Request 154.

This document can be downloaded from `http://jcp.org/en/jsr/detail?id=154`.

A more recent maintenance release specification of the API can be obtained from
`http://jcp.org/aboutJava/communityprocess/mrel/jsr154/index.html`.

Java Enterprise Edition platform

The Java Enterprise Edition platform is nothing more than a set of API specifications that act as building blocks that you can use to build enterprise applications.

> With its most recent release, the name of the Java Enterprise Edition platform has been simplified.
>
> Instead of being called the **Java 2 Platform, Enterprise Edition (J2EE) v1.5**, the version up from J2EE v1.4 is now labeled Java Enterprise Edition 5 or Java EE 5. It is incorrect to abbreviate this name as 'JEE'.
>
> The main drivers for this change are a desire to do away with the '2', which really was beginning to lose its meaning anyway; and to provide center stage to the word 'Java', which is the core technology underlying the different platform editions.
>
> While this may seem like just a rebranding decision, there are some real issues associated with it. Firstly, you need to be aware that you might come across JARs named `j2ee.jar` and `javaee.jar` and will need to know which one to pick. Secondly, you need to remember that this is more like deprecation, rather than a replacement, that is, most people will continue to use the term J2EE long into the future—on resumes, job requisitions, design documents, and on blogs.

An 'enterprise application', just by the sound of it, seems more forbidding than plain old 'application'. It is therefore interesting to look at what exactly makes an application, an 'enterprise application'.

What is an enterprise application?

To help us see the difference here, let us consider prototypical examples of both types of applications. A representative 'application' might be the standard personal finance management applications, such as Microsoft's Money™ or Intuit's Quicken™. A prototypical 'enterprise application', on the other hand, would be an online banking system.

Both applications are fairly similar in that you can view the transactions for one or more accounts, transfer money either into or out of an account, schedule bills that come due, and you can reconcile your checkbook based on statements. In addition, you may also have the ability to run reports on amortization tables, spending patterns, or transaction histories.

So what makes one an enterprise application and the other not? The essence of an enterprise application can be boiled down into four concepts—simultaneous users, highly performant systems, heterogeneous environments, and a distributed nature.

Simultaneous users

An enterprise application is expected to be used simultaneously by more than one user. In fact, such applications are often expected to be accessed simultaneously by hundreds or even thousands of users.

This adds complexity as you now need to apportion system resources across these users. In addition, you must also ensure that one user does not interfere with the operations of another, even if they happen to be working on the same data.

Highly available, reliable, and scalable

An enterprise application is one where there is usually significant potential for loss if its users are unable to access and use it in a predictable manner. This encompasses the concepts of availability, reliability, and scalability.

An online banking application has to be available when the customer needs it, irrespective of the time of day. It has to function reliably when used by that customer and should be able to handle higher peak loads over certain periods such as major holidays like Christmas or the periods when paychecks are deposited by employers.

A failure on any one of these criteria results in a loss of customers, a loss of revenue, or both.

While these characteristics are equally important to non-enterprise applications, the impacts of failure are often much less dramatic as such applications are generally designed to be used either by a single user, or by a very small set of users.

Heterogeneous environment

A typical enterprise application has very little control over its destiny. Most often it is cobbled together from various collaborating systems, many of which have been in operation for a number of years (or decades).

An enterprise typically already has a significant investment in terms of software, hardware, staffing, and infrastructure in its existing legacy systems. By necessity, any new development needs to play nice with these. This may include software systems (such as Enterprise Resource Planning systems, Custom Relationship Management products, and mainframe systems), operating systems, data sources (such as IMS, Oracle, and SQL Server), application servers (such as WebSphere, WebLogic, and JBoss), communication protocols, and data formats. An ability to integrate nicely with these disparate technologies is the hallmark of an enterprise application.

A point of note is that one of the most significant investments that an enterprise makes is in its data. Most of the time this investment is locked within silos throughout the enterprise, making the task of turning it into useful information a very daunting one. Most enterprise applications have, as their central focus, the ability to access this shared data, freeing it from the grips of traditional systems.

On the other hand, non-enterprise applications are fairly standalone entities. For instance, installations of Microsoft Money never need to deal with the issues of application or system integration, or with the issues of integrating data from multiple data stores.

The only real complexity often arises from data transfer format requirements. For example, personal finance software will typically download transaction data from financial institutions using either the **Open Financial Exchange (OFX)** or the **Web Connect (QFX)** formats.

Distributed nature

An enterprise application rarely runs on a single computer host. This is almost always necessitated because of performance and scalability, as there is a practical limit on how much work can be assigned to a particular computer; as well as of heterogeneity, since the collaborating systems may run on their own dedicated hardware.

As a result, when describing your enterprise application, you tend to speak in terms of server farms, clusters, load balancers, DMZs, firewalls, and so on.

A corollary of this fact is that portions of the enterprise application itself may be distributed across multiple hosts. For instance, the logic that determines what is rendered to the user can be separated into its own tier from that of the logic that defines the business rules for the application, and there can be yet another tier that houses the persistent data store used by the application.

It is important to note that these tiers can either be logical (when all these tiers run on the same physical machine, possibly within the same Java Virtual Machine) or physical (when each of these tiers runs on a dedicated physical machine.)

On the other hand, the typical vanilla application runs on a single workstation and is designed to serve a single user. You will be hard pressed to find a distributed implementation of either Money or Quicken.

To summarize, there are very valid reasons as to why enterprise application development is crucial to a corporation's survival - it serves as the best way to leverage your existing technology investments.

Java EE architecture

In its most basic form, the Java Enterprise Edition platform describes a set of APIs that must be implemented by any Java EE compliant application server platform. These APIs are guaranteed to be available to any application that runs on a Java EE compliant server.

The API implementations that are provided by a Java EE application server provider make it easy for a developer to focus on the business requirements, instead of having to implement infrastructural aspects of a complex enterprise application, such as having to figure out how to implement 2-phase commits to ensure that transactions work across disparate data sources.

A **transaction** is defined as a grouping of tasks that must be either executed completely or must not be executed at all. The typical example is that of a transfer of funds between two accounts, which is comprised of two tasks—a withdrawal from the first account and a deposit into the second. If a system failure occurs between these two tasks, then data corruption is likely as the withdrawal has taken place but no corresponding deposit has occurred. The complexity of transactions in an enterprise application is compounded by the fact that the individual tasks may involve completely different database servers or other legacy data stores.

An additional benefit of writing applications based on the standard Java EE APIs is that your application is now implementation independent. In other words, your application can be deployed on any vendor's Java EE compliant application server.

In fact, a popular recommendation is to deploy applications on the reference implementation, as well as on the target application server. This ensures that you have not inadvertently locked yourself into a particular vendor's platform implementation.

However, you need to take this advice with a pinch of common sense. Vendor lock-in is not always bad, especially if you are getting something material in return (such as improved reliability, stability, or functionality). The choice of a vendor is often based on numerous factors, such as licensing costs, administrative/deployment staff expertise, and proven performance on existing production applications. As a result, changing vendors rarely happens as often as one might fear.

There are a few key features about the Java EE architecture that merit mention.

Java based

The Java EE platform is a superset of the Java SE platform. As a result, it inherits its basic advantages, such as the ability to run Java applications on diverse operating systems, its mature and flexible object-oriented programming model, its ability to work well across a network (including over the Internet), its automatic garbage collection mechanism, and its inherent multithreaded nature, all of which make for a very compelling package.

Generic APIs

A key aspect of enterprise application development is the need to work and integrate with a variety of disparate systems. Learning the individual APIs of each of these diverse systems can be an insurmountable task. Java EE provides a solution for this problem—by separating the vendor-agnostic aspect of an interaction, the API, from the vendor-implementation aspect, termed the Service Provider Interface (SPI).

This design provides for an astonishing decrease in the level of complexity that developers need to contend with during enterprise development.

As an example, consider the Java Naming and Directory Interface API. The published API is generic enough to be used against any particular vendor implementation, whether LDAP, the RMI Registry, or even just the file system.

As a developer, all you need is to be aware of the vendor-agnostic API. You will also supply some configuration information that is appropriate for your choice of vendor such as the URL at which to access the service, authentication credentials, and the factory class for the initial context.

A service provider implements not only the SPI that defines the core service implementation, but also any abstract classes and interfaces that are left undefined in the API itself. Service providers may be linked into the Java EE platform server either statically (through configuration files or deployment descriptors) or dynamically at runtime. When multiple providers implement the same functionality, an application may choose, at runtime, which particular provider's implementation to use.

As an application programmer, you will typically use a factory method to interact with the service provider, which will return to you the appropriate instance, which implements an interface within the Java EE API. Your application interacts with this generic interface using the functions defined by the API and is completely oblivious to the specific implementation class.

This basic theme is repeated over and over again within the Java EE.

Java EE containers and container services

The Java EE platform is designed around a containment hierarchy, where an application server hosts containers, each of which in turn hosts components.

A container is responsible for configuring its components based on the deployment descriptor, allowing component behavior to be controlled using configuration rather than code. For example, a deployment descriptor may specify that a particular Enterprise JavaBeans method may not be invoked unless the user belongs to a given security role.

It is also responsible for managing the life cycle of its components. For instance, a servlet container will load the servlet class, instantiate it, call its initialization method, will repeatedly call its service method as requests come in, and will finally call its destruction method when it is being taken out of service.

The container is also the gateway through which its components may access their runtime environment. It is also the intercessor when one component needs to communicate with another Java EE component. This intercession allows the container to add value by transparently propagating transactions, implementing security checks, and so on.

This container-based architecture provides an effective way of providing a separation of concerns. The deployed components can now focus on the business problem being solved, whereas the container can provide the plumbing and infrastructure required to make everything work.

Each platform vendor must implement these containers so as to maintain the contract with its components as specified in the appropriate API specification. While this does not stop the vendor from providing additional services through the container, it does ensure that each component can be guaranteed to find a baseline set of services, irrespective of the particular vendor implementation that it is deployed into.

The Java EE specification defines four types of containers.

An **application client** container provides the runtime environment for Java programs (either graphical user interface based or command line) that execute on a client workstation. Application clients are the same as standard Java SE applications, so no special life cycle calls are made by this container.

An **applet container** contains applets that typically execute natively within a browser or through the Java Plug-in product.

A **servlet container** hosts Servlet API and JavaServer Pages API components, which are used to service HTTP requests from web clients.

Finally, an **Enterprise JavaBeans (EJB)** container hosts EJB components, which houses the business logic that is usually found in the middle tier of a Java EE application.

A typical servlet container (such as Apache Tomcat) will, among other things, allow a developer to package a web application as per the Servlet specification. It will load the appropriate servlets as necessary, will invoke a servlet's lifecycle and service methods, and will provide the servlet instance with access to information about its operating context.

Similarly, an EJB container will provide its contained components (Enterprise JavaBeans) with services for security, transactions, instance pooling, and so on.

A container is usually controlled through configuration files, such as Tomcat's `server.xml` file.

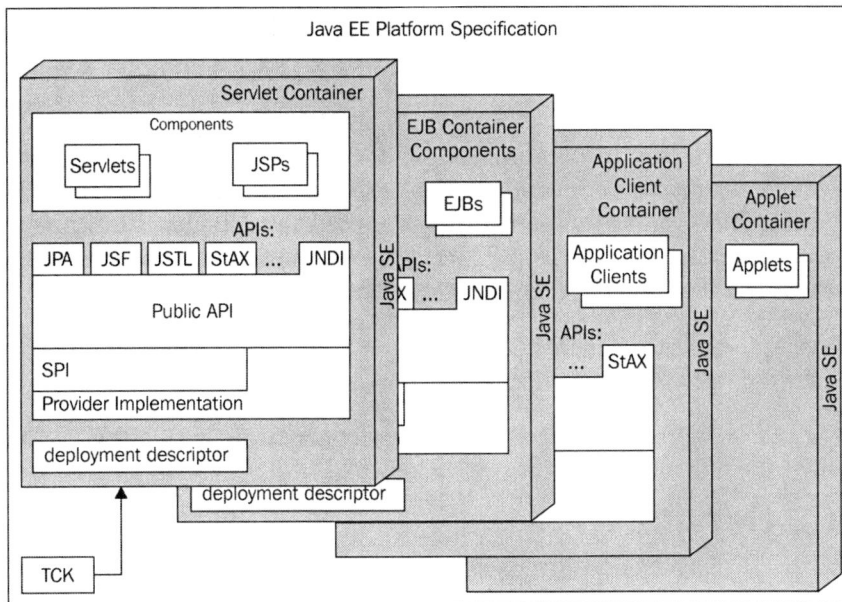

This figure summarizes the concepts that we've introduced so far—the distinction between the API and the SPI, the Java EE containers, and the component model. The specification of the platform is comprised of the specifications for multiple containers. Each container is responsible for hosting its own component model. The components for each container expect certain services to be provided by their container.

The face that services expose to components is defined by the service's API. The vendor implements each service by providing code that implements the SPI, the abstract classes, and interfaces that are defined by the API.

Finally, a deployment descriptor may be used to configure the container's services and runtime environment, as well as to define how the components are deployed into that service.

The **Technology Compatibility Kit (TCK)** is a set of tests that allow you to validate the compliance of a container implementation with its specification.

Java EE components and their APIs

The Java EE platform uses a component-based development model. This is different from a class-based model as a component typically consists of more than one class cooperating to achieve some reusable unit of functionality.

A Java EE application is built by assembling multiple such standalone components and deploying them with their configurations into their associated containers.

The power of Java EE comes from the fact that components can be independently developed, tested, assembled, and deployed into any Java EE compliant vendor's server implementation.

Each container can deploy its own unique set of components. The application client container can contain application client components, which are standard Java programs. The applet container contains applet components. The web container contains web components, such as JSP, Servlet, Filter, and event listener components, whereas the EJB container contains enterprise bean components.

Application logic typically resides in the components, and business logic usually resides in the enterprise bean components.

In this book, we will primarily focus on the servlet container and web components.

Java EE Service APIs

The Service APIs serve to simplify your programming tasks by providing standard APIs to access diverse systems or alternative implementations.

The key APIs that are defined by the Java EE platform include:

- **Java Database Connectivity (JDBC) API**: The JDBC API provides a database-independent mechanism to access a relational database server. Note that even application client components may access a database directly via the JDBC API. However, the preferred mechanism in Java EE 5 is to use the Java Persistence API whenever possible.

- **Java Naming and Directory Interface (JNDI)**: A naming service allows applications to bind an object to a logical name and to use that logical name at a later time to retrieve that object. Examples of a naming service include the file system, where a file name maps to a file object, or the Domain Naming Service, where a URL is used to lookup an IP address.

  A Java EE container implements a naming service. A component within that container can access this naming service to look up various system- or user-defined objects, such as a `DataSource`, an environment variable, or an Enterprise JavaBean.

  A directory service lets you manage a hierarchical tree of objects and their attributes. Examples of directory services include **Lightweight Directory Access Protocol (LDAP)** directories that can be used to store user information such as user names, passwords, and contact details.

- **Java EE Connector Architecture (JCA)**: This API lets you access data that is contained in existing corporate assets such as non-relational databases and mainframe applications, from within the Java EE platform.

- **Java API for XML Processing (JAXP)**: JAXP allows a Java EE application to process XML documents, using DOM, SAX, or StAX APIs that are independent of the underlying XML processor implementation.

- **Java Message Service (JMS) API**: A messaging service allows distributed applications to communicate using messages. This communication is usually asynchronous. The JMS API provides a generic API that can be used to access enterprise messaging implementations from different vendors such as TIBCO or IBM MQ Series.

- **JavaMail API**: This API provides an interface that an application can use to interact with different email systems. It uses the **JavaBeans Activation Framework (JAF)** API to handle MIME data that are included in email messages.

- **Java Transaction (JTA) API**: This is a generic API for transaction management that even supports the complexity of transactions involving distributed databases. The **Java Transaction Service (JTS)** provides an implementation of this API.

- **Remote Method Invocation (RMI) over Internet Inter-ORB protocol (RMI/IIOP)**: This API allows distributed EJB components to communicate with each other and with distributed CORBA services.

- **Java Persistence API (JPA)**: This API provides an object/relational mapping facility for developers. Applications should use this technology in preference to either CMP entity beans or JDBC access.

- **Web Service APIs**: The **Java API for XML Web Services (JAX-WS)** and **Java API for XML-based RPC (JAX-RPC)** support the invocation of web services using the SOAP/HTTP protocol. The **Java Architecture for XML Binding (JAXB)** defines the mapping between Java classes and XML. In addition, the **Java API for XML Registries (JAXR)** provides client access to XML registry servers.

- **Java IDL**: It allows Java EE application components to invoke external CORBA objects.

- **JavaServer Faces (JSF)**: This API provides a standard way to build component-oriented web applications that run within a web container.

- **JavaServer Pages Standard Tag Library (JSTL)**: This library defines tags that provide core functionality required by web applications.

- **Streaming API for XML (StAX)**: The StAX API provides for a simple pull parsing programming model for XML. Rather than waiting for program callback, as with the push-parsing that is used by the **Simple API for XML (SAX)** parser model, StAX lets the programmer retain control of the parsing operation.

- **Java Management Extensions (JMX)**: This API supports the web-based management and monitoring of applications and services.

What is a typical Java EE application architecture?

In the typical multitier model, the enterprise application's functionality is divided into three tiers.

- The Presentation tier, which is comprised of the web container, and which houses web components like servlets and JSP pages.

- The Middle tier, which is comprised of the EJB container, and which houses enterprise bean components.

- The Persistence or Enterprise Information Systems tier, which houses the persistent data store.

The presentation tier reacts to client requests by invoking business logic that resides in the middle tier and is responsible for generating the view that is rendered at the client. The business logic for the application is housed in enterprise beans that live in the middle tier. This tier is responsible for updating the data stores in the persistence tier, based on the client's actions.

The creation of multiple tiers gives us the opportunity for scalability, but at the cost of performance.

However, most applications don't require this level of complexity, and so the Java EE specification does not require that all three tiers should actually be present.

In particular, the presence of an EJB container in the middle tier often adds unnecessary complexity. In such cases, you do not need a full blown Java EE application server, such as JBoss or GlassFish. Instead, you can make do with just a servlet container such as Tomcat.

In this scenario, the client is a browser, which communicates with the servlet container using HTML over HTTP. Web components receive these incoming requests, process them, access the data store as necessary, and return a HTML over HTTP response to the client browser. In this case, the business domain classes, the business rules, and the presentation logic are typically interwoven into the web components.

This is the application architecture that we will consider for the remainder of this book.

Hypertext Transfer Protocol (HTTP)

Any communication between two parties requires a clear understanding of how the communication will be conducted. For example, a telephone conversation is initiated by the caller lifting the handset from the cradle, checking for a dial tone, and if the dial tone is present, beginning to dial the desired number. This is usually comprised of a country code prefix, followed by the country code, an area code, and the phone number. If the call is made to another phone within the same country, or within the same area code, the caller might skip these elements.

At the receiving end, the protocol is much simpler. The called party waits until the phone begins to ring, at which point, she picks up the phone and indicates that she is ready to receive the communication by saying 'Hello'.

This telephony protocol has been in place for so many years that it has now become second nature to us, and seems quite unremarkable. Until of course, you move to a different country, and suddenly realize that your international dialing prefix is not 011, but is 00 instead, or that the area code prefix is now a 0 rather than a 1.

HTTP is just another communication protocol, except that it defines how one computer may connect to another to request a particular resource. This particular protocol has been wildly successful since its introduction in 1990 as HTTP/0.9 and is today the lingua franca of the Internet.

There are some characteristics that are common to the two communication models.

First, there is a connection that needs to be established between the two parties. This connection has to be held open until the interaction has been completed and the information has been completely exchanged. In the HTTP/1.1 protocol, this is called **a persistent connection**.

Second, there are two aspects to the communication, the protocol and the actual payload. In the case of HTTP, the payload is usually text marked up using tags that are defined by the HyperText Markup Language (HTML). However, HTTP may be used to transfer other data, including audio and video content. The protocol aspects are carried in communication headers that indicate various capabilities of the client (such as the client's preferred character encoding), metadata about the resource being retrieved (such as the length of the payload data), the server's success at retrieving this resource, and so on.

Third, there is the question of conversational state. In the typical interaction, a client (usually a web browser) makes a request for a resource, such as a text file or an image, and a server responds with that resource.

In reality, a single interaction may consist of multiple such request/response pairs. This usually happens when a browser requests a page that contains one or more images. In this case, the connection is held open while a request/response pair occurs for each of the images on that page. However, once the interaction has been completed, the connection between the two computers is terminated.

This is why HTTP is considered a stateless protocol. The next time the client connects to the server to make a request, the server has no memory of the prior interaction with this client.

HTTP, therefore, defines a connection oriented but stateless protocol.

> The astute reader will have noticed that a telephone conversation is not quite the best analogy for an HTTP interaction. While it is connection oriented, there is an element of state that is retained in the memories of both parties while the communication is in progress. On the other hand, the HTTP protocol is completely stateless.

Note that it is always the client that initiates the connection in this model. The server has no means to push content to the client. In this usage, the term client refers to the computer that initiates the communication. While this is usually a client's browser, it could also be a server host that initiates a web services type of connection. One way of simulating a push model, for a browser client, is to simply have the client reconnect, every so often, to refresh its content (say using the refresh meta tag or with JavaScript).

The underlying protocol used by HTTP is TCP/IP. While this protocol uses the well known TCP port 80, other ports may be used. For example, by default, your Tomcat installation will start up and listen on port 8080 for incoming requests.

Uniform Resource Locator, URL

A **Uniform Resource Locator (URL)** is described in RFC 3986 (`http://www.ietf.org/rfc/rfc3986.txt`) as a uniform way of uniquely identifying a resource such as an electronic document or an image. URLs are designed to implicitly provide a means of locating the resource by describing its 'location' on a network.

A generic URL is a hierarchical sequence of components, structured as follows:

`scheme://hostName:portNumber/path/to/resource?queryString#fragment`

An example of which is:

`http://www.swengsol.com:80/file.htm?name=bwayne&city=gotham#profile`

Here the scheme is `http`, the host name is `www.swengsol.com`, the port number is `80`, the path to the resource is `/index.html`, the query string is `name=bwayne&city=gotham`, and the fragment is `profile`.

The combination of host name and port number taken together is termed an **authority**.

A number of these parts are optional, including the port number (which defaults to the well known ports 80 and 443 for the `http` and `https` schemes respectively), the query string, and the fragment.

When present, a query string is a series of name-value pairs that are preceded with a question mark and with an ampersand (&) separating the pairs.

The hierarchical organization of a URL becomes apparent as you travel from left to right, with its components increasing in specificity the farther right you go. You start off with a server domain name, a port on that server, and finally an absolute path on that server. The portion that comes after '?' is additional information that is useful to process the located resource.

A URL is composed of characters that are taken from a very limited set—the letters of the basic Latin alphabet (ISO-8859-1), digits, and a few special characters ('-', '.', '_', '~'). All other characters are deemed to be reserved and must be percent-encoded before use. In other words, you must convert them to their hexadecimal representation and prefix them with a % sign. For example, a space character (32 in ISO-8859-1) is encoded as %20. Other characters that should be encoded include the percent itself (%25) as well as characters that are used as delimiters (such as '&', '$', and ':').

HTTP methods

An HTTP method, or request type, defines the actions that a client may request from a server. HTTP/1.1 specifies seven such methods.

GET (HTTP/0.9)

This is the oldest and most commonly used method. It is used to GET a resource (such as a document or an image file) from a server. It can also request dynamic content by passing in additional parameters in a **query string**. This method is intended to be used only for idempotent requests, that is requests that do not cause state changes on the server. For example, a retrieval of a resource from the server is considered idempotent.

The URL for a GET request is portable as it is a self contained unit that can be bookmarked or emailed. Typing it in over and over into a browser's address bar should return the same content.

There are some downsides to using this method. Though the protocol does not place any limit on the length of a URL, lengths should be limited to 255 bytes because some older browsers or proxies may not properly support greater lengths. As the query string is counted against this limit, this restricts the amount of information that can be passed using this mechanism. A security risk associated with this method is that the parameters that are passed to the web server appear on the address bar in plain text and so can be easily viewed by anyone. In addition, the URL along with its query string is often logged at the server and at other hops along its journey, leading to additional security risks.

Finally, while the specification recommends that a GET request is used only for idempotent requests, nothing prevents an errant application from violating this recommendation. It is therefore not at all uncommon to find, for example, a GET request that causes a shopping cart order to be saved, or a credit card to be charged.

POST (HTTP/1.0)

This method was introduced to handle non-idempotent requests, that is, requests that cause a state change on the server, such as inserting a record in the server's database.

Repeated submission of a non idempotent request is unsafe, as it may end up causing undesirable effects such as a shopping cart order being saved to the database multiple times. This method sends its parameters to the server as part of the request body, rather than in a plainly visible query string. This means that a large amount of data (even megabytes) can be sent from the client.

A key downside is that the URL is no longer self-sufficient, as the parameters are now part of the body's payload. As a result, the URL cannot be bookmarked or emailed to others.

PUT (HTTP/1.1)

The PUT method is used to place a document at the location specified by the URL on the server.

DELETE (HTTP/1.1)

This method is used to delete a document at the specified URL on the server.

TRACE (HTTP/1.1)

The TRACE method simply returns an exact copy of a request to a client. It is intended for debugging use and traces the path taken by a request.

OPTIONS (HTTP/1.1)

This method allows the client to query the server about the communication options that are available with regards to a particular resource without explicitly requesting that resource. The returned response would include header fields that indicate optional features that are implemented by the server which are applicable to that resource. For example, the `Allow` header lists the set of methods (GET, POST, and so on) that are supported for a given resource.

HEAD (HTTP/1.0)

The HEAD method is identical to GET, except that it asks the server to return only the headers of a response, without the message body. It is used when a client only wants to check the metadata of an entity, such as its last modified time.

HTTP requests

The simplest HTTP request is composed of the following elements:

```
[request-method] [/path/to/resource] [HTTP protocol version]
[request-header=value]+
[blank-line to indicate the end of the request headers]
[POST:request-payload]
```

The first line of the request contains the following:

- The type of the request, which is usually GET, POST, PUT, DELETE, OPTIONS, HEAD, and TRACE
- The name of the resource that is being requested
- The protocol that the browser wishes to use for this communication

Following this first line are the request headers, which in turn are followed by the request's payload (for a POST request).

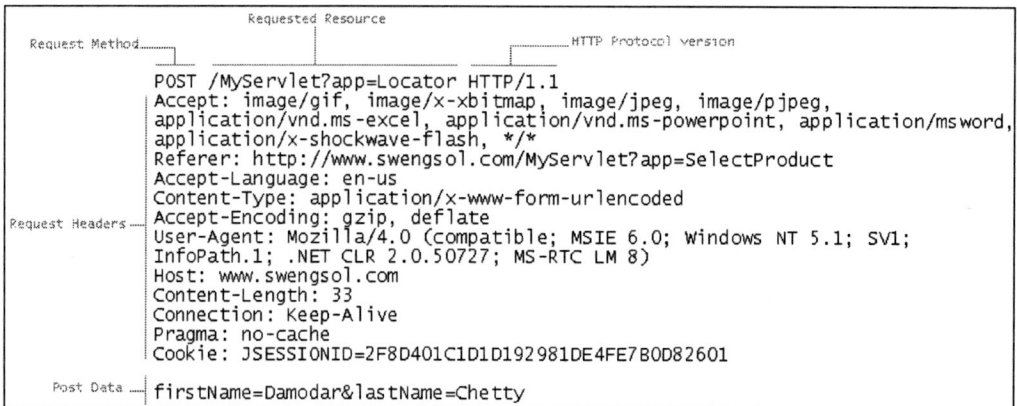

```
                              Requested Resource
         Request Method............
                                 |                      ............HTTP Protocol version
                          |      |              |
                          |      |              |
                          POST /MyServlet?app=Locator HTTP/1.1
                          Accept: image/gif, image/x-xbitmap, image/jpeg, image/pjpeg,
                          application/vnd.ms-excel, application/vnd.ms-powerpoint, application/msword,
                          application/x-shockwave-flash, */*
                          Referer: http://www.swengsol.com/MyServlet?app=SelectProduct
                          Accept-Language: en-us
                          Content-Type: application/x-www-form-urlencoded
         Request Headers ---- Accept-Encoding: gzip, deflate
                          User-Agent: Mozilla/4.0 (compatible; MSIE 6.0; Windows NT 5.1; SV1;
                          InfoPath.1; .NET CLR 2.0.50727; MS-RTC LM 8)
                          Host: www.swengsol.com
                          Content-Length: 33
                          Connection: Keep-Alive
                          Pragma: no-cache
                          Cookie: JSESSIONID=2F8D401C1D1D192981DE4FE7B0D82601
         Post Data ---- firstName=Damodar&lastName=Chetty
```

As shown, the browser is asking the server (specified by the Host: header) for the specified resource and is stating that it would like to use HTTP 1.1 for the communication.

Each request header conveys information either about the client's capabilities or about the request body. Each header is on a separate line, and the end of the headers is indicated by a blank line. The final section is the request's body, which contains form parameters for a POST request.

Request headers are name-value pairs, which take the form `Header-Name: value`. Headers allow the client to send optional metadata about the request. The information provided in these headers can be used by the server to tailor its response to the specific circumstances and capabilities of the requesting client.

Some commonly seen request headers include the following:

- `Accept`: This header specifies the MIME types that the client can handle. The server can query this request header to determine how to craft the response to the client.

- `Accept-Charset`: The character sets that the client can handle.

- `Accept-Encoding`: The encodings that the client can handle, such as the `gzip` or `compress` compression formats, which serve to save transmission time. On receiving the response, the browser first reverses this encoding. It then uses the `Content-Type` response header to determine how to handle the decoded content.

- `Accept-Language`: It allows the client to request a preferred language for the response. In the previous image, this request header indicates that the browser would prefer a response in English (United States), which is represented by the language code `en-us`.

- `Content-Length`: This header is applicable to POST requests and gives the size of the request body in bytes.

- `Content-Type`: This header is applicable to POST requests, and is used to communicate the type of the POST data.

- `Cookie`: This header is used to return a cookie that has been previously sent by a server.

- `Host`: This helps the server to determine the original host name and port for this request, which might otherwise be obscured due to request forwarding.

- `If-Modified-Since` and `If-Unmodified-Since`: These are used by the client to support caching of resources.

- `Referer`: This header indicates the URL of the referring web page.

- `User-Agent`: This header identifies the browser that is making the request. A server can use this to customize the content by the type of browser that is being used.

HTTP responses

The basic response that is returned by a server is comprised of a response line, headers, and a body.

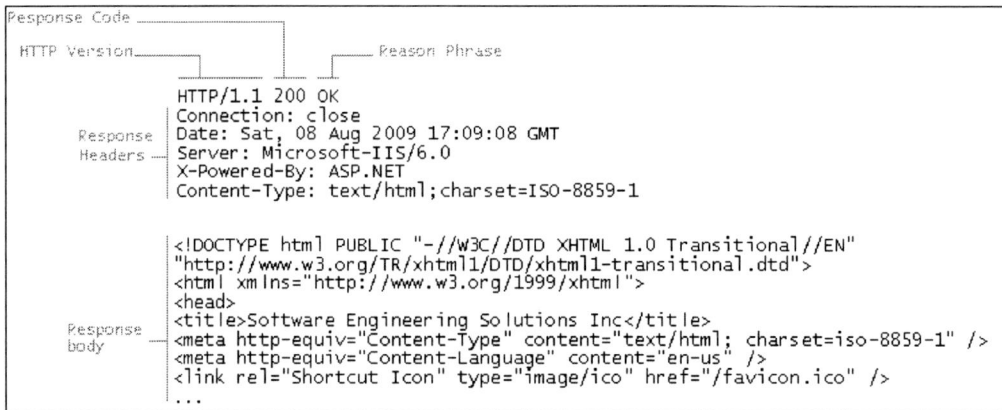

```
Response Code
  HTTP Version                        Reason Phrase

              HTTP/1.1 200 OK
              Connection: close
  Response    Date: Sat, 08 Aug 2009 17:09:08 GMT
  Headers     Server: Microsoft-IIS/6.0
              X-Powered-By: ASP.NET
              Content-Type: text/html;charset=ISO-8859-1

              <!DOCTYPE html PUBLIC "-//W3C//DTD XHTML 1.0 Transitional//EN"
              "http://www.w3.org/TR/xhtml1/DTD/xhtml1-transitional.dtd">
              <html xmlns="http://www.w3.org/1999/xhtml">
              <head>
  Response    <title>Software Engineering Solutions Inc</title>
  body        <meta http-equiv="Content-Type" content="text/html; charset=iso-8859-1" />
              <meta http-equiv="Content-Language" content="en-us" />
              <link rel="Shortcut Icon" type="image/ico" href="/favicon.ico" />
              ...
```

The first line of the response indicates the overall status of the request (for example, success or failure at a very specific level of detail). This is followed by response headers, which indicate control information to the browser (such as the length of the content being sent in the response's body). Finally, you have the response body, which is the response's main content—an HTML document, a graphical image, and so on.

The response line

The response line contains the HTTP version of the server, a response code, and a reason phrase that describes the response in a human readable format (such as 'OK' or 'Not Found').

A response code is a 3 digit number, where the first digit indicates a response category. The supported response categories include 1xx for informational messages, 2xx for successful requests, 3xx to indicate files that have moved to a different URL, 4xx for client browser errors, and 5xx for server errors.

Common examples of response codes are as follows:

- 200 (OK) indicates a successful response, and that a document is being returned for GET and POST requests.

- 302 (Found) indicates that the requested document has been moved, and that the new URL for that document is provided in the Location response header. A browser receiving a 302 response code will automatically request the new document.

- 404 indicates that the requested resource could not be found at the given URL, the dreaded 'File Not Found' error.

- 500 indicates that an internal server error has occurred. This is normally caused by a severe program error in your servlet code.

Response headers

The server sends response headers as name-value pairs to provide information to the client about the server and the content of the response body.

Some commonly seen response headers include the following:

- `Cache-Control`: This header tells the client whether a response may be cached. For example, setting it to `no-cache` indicates that the document should never be cached.

- `Content-Encoding`: This indicates how the page was encoded, say by compressing it using `gzip`, for transmission.

- `Content-Language`: It indicates the language in which the document was written (for example, `fr` or `es`).

- `Content-Length`: This is the number of bytes in the response.

- `Content-MD5`: This header provides an MD5 digest for the subsequent body content to allow clients to verify that the document was not modified in transit.

- `Content-Type`: This indicates the **Multipurpose Internet Mail Extension (MIME)** type of the response document. A MIME type is a universally accepted way of identifying the type of content when a file is transmitted over the Web. It serves as a standard way of associating content with the application that can be used to view/edit it, and is more portable than file extensions. The most common MIME types are `text/plain` or `text/html` that indicates a response payload that consists of ordinary text or HTML content. Other types include `image/gif` for GIF images, or `video/mpeg` for MPEG video clips.

- `Last-Modified`: This header indicates when this resource was last changed, enabling a client to cache the document, and to use caching request headers like `If-Modified-Since` to request efficient updates in later requests.

- `Location`: It provides the location of the new document that is set when the response status code is in the 300s.

- `Pragma`: This is used with a value of `no-cache` to prevent the caching of the response, and is recognized by older HTTP/1.0 clients.

- `Refresh`: This header indicates the seconds after which the client browser should ask the server for an updated version of this resource. You must continue to supply `Refresh` in all subsequent responses until the server returns a 204 response, which should stop the client browser from requesting further refreshes. Note that using the `Refresh` meta tag is a bit more powerful, as you can request a page other than the current page.
- `Set-Cookie`: It sets a given cookie on the client.
- `WWW-Authenticate`: This is used with a 401 (Unauthorized) status code to indicate to the client which authorization type the client should supply in its `Authorization` header.

Spying on HTTP

A couple of nifty tools allow you to eavesdrop on the HTTP communication that occurs between your browser and the server.

For Internet Explorer users, there is the amazingly featured Fiddler v2 HTTP Debugging proxy at `http://www.fiddlertool.com/fiddler/`.

For Firefox users, there's the `http://livehttpheaders.mozdev.org/` add-on.

Both these tools give you amazing insights into the request/response process and are an invaluable aid while debugging server-side applications.

What is the Servlet API?

Now that we've looked at the environment within which the Servlet API executes, the remainder of this chapter is pointed squarely at the Servlet API. This API is one of the oldest within the Java Enterprise Edition family — its first incarnation dates back to 1997.

In this section, we'll take a quick walk through JSR 154 for the Servlet 2.5 API.

The information in this section is applicable to all Java EE compliant servlet containers, including those contained in IBM WebSphere and BEA WebLogic, as well as to Apache Tomcat.

The word 'servlet' conjures up an image of a baby server, and that is exactly what it is. It is a play on the word 'applet', which represents a baby application.

A **servlet** is a web component, a pluggable piece of functionality that is written in Java and deployed to a web container to extend the container's functionality in a very custom way.

For all intents and purposes, a servlet functions in a very similar manner to its bigger sibling—the web server/container. It waits around for incoming requests, jumps up to process them, returns a response (most usually as HTML), and then returns to waiting for the next request.

What makes servlets attractive is that the average developer can quickly extend server functionality without being aware of low level network programming details like sockets and protocols and can instead focus on higher level abstractions such as requests, responses, and sessions.

Servlet container

As we have discussed earlier, the Java EE architecture is based on a containment hierarchy, where components that contain your application logic are deployed into containers that manage the life cycle of their contained components and provide those components with various enterprise services.

In the Servlet API, the central role is played by the servlet container into which web components, such as servlets, JSP pages, filters, and event listeners are deployed. The servlet container is responsible for managing their life cycles, and also provides access to Service APIs like JNDI and JAXP.

For example, in the case of a servlet component, the container's life cycle management process includes instantiating an instance of that servlet on first access, calling its `init()` method to allow it to initialize itself, calling its `service()` method once for each request that comes in for that servlet, and then when the servlet is ready to be taken out of service, calling its `destroy()` method to release its resources.

The following diagram depicts the typical process flow for a request for a given servlet:

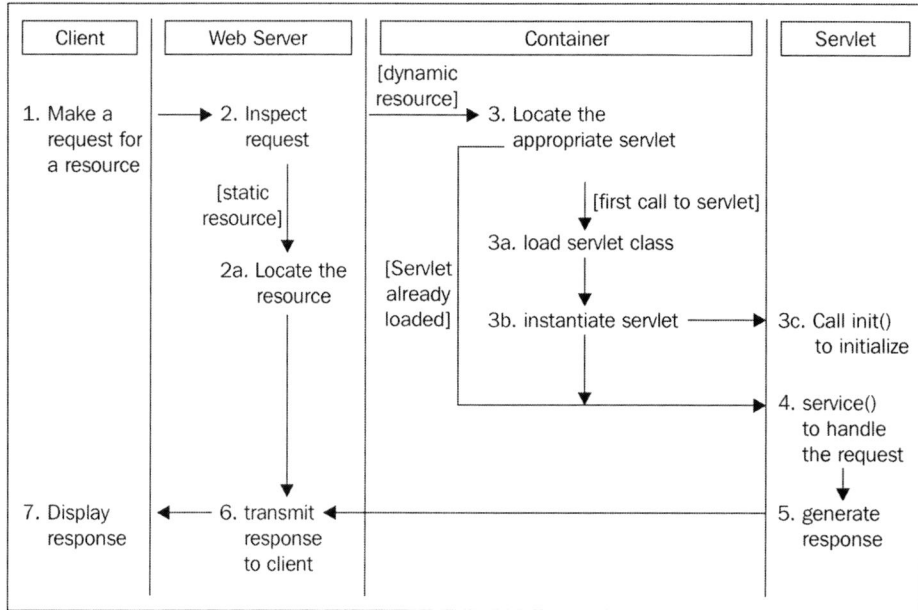

```
┌──────────┬──────────────┬────────────────────────────────────┬──────────┐
│  Client  │  Web Server  │             Container              │  Servlet │
└──────────┴──────────────┴────────────────────────────────────┴──────────┘

                              [dynamic
                              resource]
1. Make a        2. Inspect  ─────────────► 3. Locate the
   request for      request                    appropriate servlet
   a resource
                 [static                                  [first call to servlet]
                 resource]                     3a. load servlet class

                 2a. Locate the   [Servlet
                    resource      already
                                  loaded]    3b. instantiate servlet ──► 3c. Call init()
                                                                            to initialize

                                                                      ──► 4. service()
                                                                            to handle
                                                                            the request

7. Display   ◄── 6. transmit ◄──────────────────────────────────────── 5. generate
   response       response                                                 response
                  to client
```

From the previous diagram, the process flow may be explained as follows:

1. A client browser requests a resource on the web server.

2. The web server checks the request. If it is for a static resource, the web server locates the static resource and transmits it to the client. Skip to step 6.

> The Tomcat container, when deployed in standalone mode, can play the roles of both the web server and a servlet container and can serve up both static and dynamic resources.

3. If it is for a dynamic resource that is being served up by a servlet container, the web server delegates to the servlet container instead, which must locate the servlet that will process this request. It uses the request URI as well as the mappings declared in the deployment descriptor to locate the appropriate servlet. If the servlet is already loaded and initialized, then skip to step 4.

   Otherwise, the appropriate servlet class is located, loaded, and instantiated. The servlet's `init()` method is then called, to give it a chance to initialize itself.

4. It then invokes the `service()` method of the servlet to generate the appropriate response.

5. The response is generated.

6. The web server returns the completed response to the client browser.

7. The client browser renders the rendered response.

Core servlet classes

This diagram represents the classes that make up the core Servlet API.

This image provides a summary of key aspects of the Servlet API. As shown, the Servlet API is designed to be protocol agnostic. This design goal can be seen by the fact that GenericServlet deals with a generic ServletRequest and ServletResponse, whereas HttpServlet uses the HTTP protocol specific HttpServletRequest and HttpServletResponse.

However, the only protocol that is currently used with servlets is HTTP. As a result, you will normally always work with a javax.servlet.http.HttpServlet.

Servlets

The javax.servlet.Servlet interface defines key lifecycle methods that are invoked at appropriate points in a servlet's life by the container.

After a servlet is first loaded and instantiated, its init(ServletConfig) method is called, so as to provide it with its initialization parameters, as well as to allow it to access its runtime context through this ServletConfig parameter. Only after the init() method completes, will the servlet be asked to service any incoming requests. A servlet will typically use this opportunity to initialize any resources that it needs for its functioning.

The service() method is called once per incoming request for this servlet.

The destroy() method is called by the container just before the servlet is taken out of service and gives the servlet a chance to release any resources that it has acquired.

The GenericServlet abstract class defines an init() method that takes no parameters. This is a convenience method that is called by the default init(ServletConfig) method to execute any application-specific servlet initialization. The default implementation does nothing, and is provided for subclasses to override.

Though the service() method in this class is marked abstract, you will rarely, if ever, override the service() method. Instead, the service() method is implemented by javax.servlet.http.HttpServlet which inspects the incoming HTTP method and invokes the appropriate method for that request type. There are seven request methods defined by HTTP/1.1, and the HttpServlet class provides default implementations for each of these methods that you may choose to override. Most application developers write servlets that override only the doGet() and doPost() methods.

The HttpServlet also has a getLastModified() method that supports caching of resources. When a client browser is attempting to reload a resource, it can send in an If-Modified-Since request header to have the server check to see if a newer version of the resource is available.

The `getLastModified()` method lets the server query the servlet for the time that this servlet last modified its output. This method returns a `long` return value that indicates the time at which this resource was last modified.

The server can compare the returned time to the `If-Modified-Since` request header, and if the content has not changed, then it simply returns a response status to the client that indicates that the resource has not been changed from its previous state.

If the server indicates that a newer version is not available, the browser can simply use the resource in its cache.

ServletConfig interface

An instance of the `javax.servlet.ServletConfig` interface is little more than a holder for the servlet context, as well as per-servlet initialization parameters that are specified by the deployer in the deployment descriptor as `String` name-value pairs.

ServletContext interface

A `javax.servlet.ServletContext` instance represents the web application to which this servlet belongs. A servlet context represents the collection of web components (servlets, filters, listeners, and JSP files), utility classes, library JARs, static content (HTML, CSS, JavaScript, and so on), and other resources that are made available to clients under a specific context path within the servlet container. There is one context per web application that is deployed into the container.

The `ServletContext` provides access to attributes that are placed into the context scope (also known as, application scope). The `ServletContext` object is accessed through the `ServletConfig` object, which the container provides to the servlet when the servlet is initialized.

> A web application deployed to a container can usually be represented by a single `ServletContext` instance within a Java Virtual Machine. This ensures that attributes in the `ServletContext` are truly global variables for that JVM.
>
> However, it is to be noted that in a clustered environment, there will be many cooperating Java Virtual Machines in existence.
>
> The topic of deploying web application contexts in a clustered environment is out of scope for this book.

Multithreading in servlets

Servlets are inherently multithreaded. In other words, the servlet container will create only one instance per servlet declaration within the deployment descriptor. (Note that this is per declaration and not per servlet class.)

As a result, at any given time, multiple processor threads within the container may be executing within a servlet instance's `service()` method. It is the servlet developer's responsibility to ensure that this invocation is thread-safe.

> **Multithreading** is the mechanism by which multiple threads of execution can be started within a single process.
>
> Each thread of execution has its own copy of local variables but will see common state when executed within the context of an object or when considering global application state. This is where a lot of the problem begins.
>
> New programmers often make the mistake of assuming that their code will never be executed in a multithreaded context, and when it eventually is (as in any Java EE environment), strange and hard-to-reproduce bugs invariably result.
>
> A common solution is to make code that will be traversed by multiple threads stateless. In other words, all the information required by that code is passed in as arguments, resulting in reliance on local variables alone.
>
> However, this is not always possible. In such cases, we need to rely on the synchronization facilities that are provided by the Java programming language. These facilities allow us to mark critical sections of code to which the JVM will serialize any access by multiple concurrent threads.
>
> This topic is fairly involved, and the interested reader is referred to any number of texts on the Java programming language for additional details.

When we consider this possibility, the simple diagram that we saw earlier tends to get just a tiny bit more complicated. In the following diagram, the container now has three processor threads, and each thread is currently in the process of handling a request of a different client.

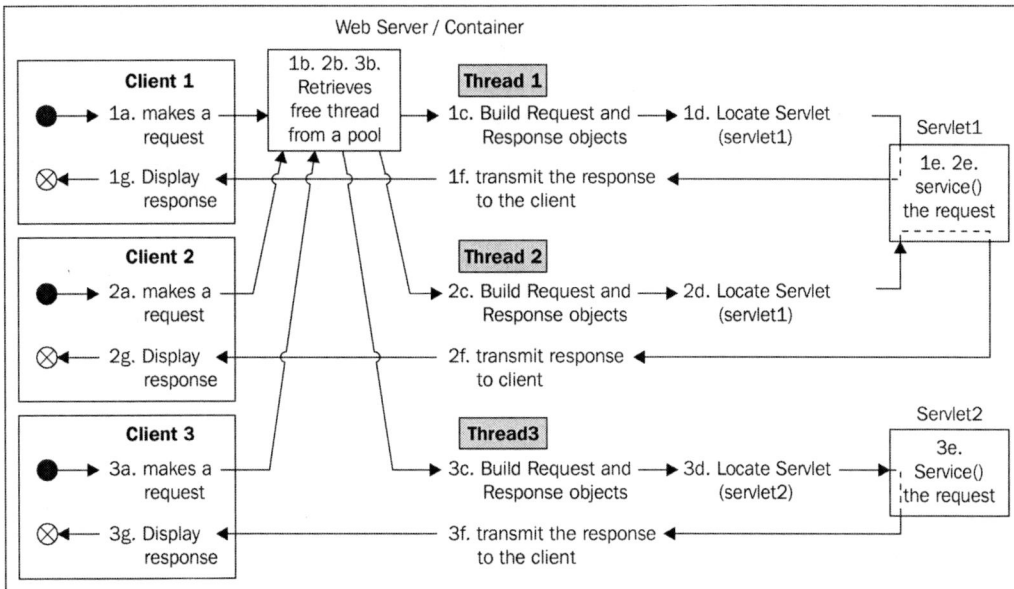

This container has two servlet instances, servlet1 of the class Servlet1 and servlet2 of the class Servlet2.

When Client1 makes a request (1a), the container retrieves a free thread, Thread1, from the thread pool (1b) and asks it to process the request. Thread1 begins by building the request and response objects (1c), locates the appropriate servlet that should process this request (1d), and invokes the servlet instance's service() method (1e). The response generated by the servlet is then returned to the client (1f), and is rendered by Client1 (1g).

The flows 2a through 2g and 3a through 3g follow a similar pattern.

Let us take a snapshot of this system while all three threads are executing within the appropriate service() methods. At this particular instant in time, both processor thread Thread1 and processor thread Thread2 are in the process of executing servlet1.service(), whereas processor thread Thread3 is in the process of executing servlet2.service().

Any instance variables of the `servlet1` instance are now being accessed concurrently by both `Thread1` and `Thread2`. Therefore, they must be protected against corruption. Likewise, any variables in context or session scope (which we'll see later) may be accessed simultaneously by all three threads, and so must also be protected against concurrent access.

Request

An incoming request is represented by an implementation of the `javax.servlet.http.HttpServletRequest` interface. This interface extends the protocol-agnostic `ServletRequest` with HTTP-specific characteristics.

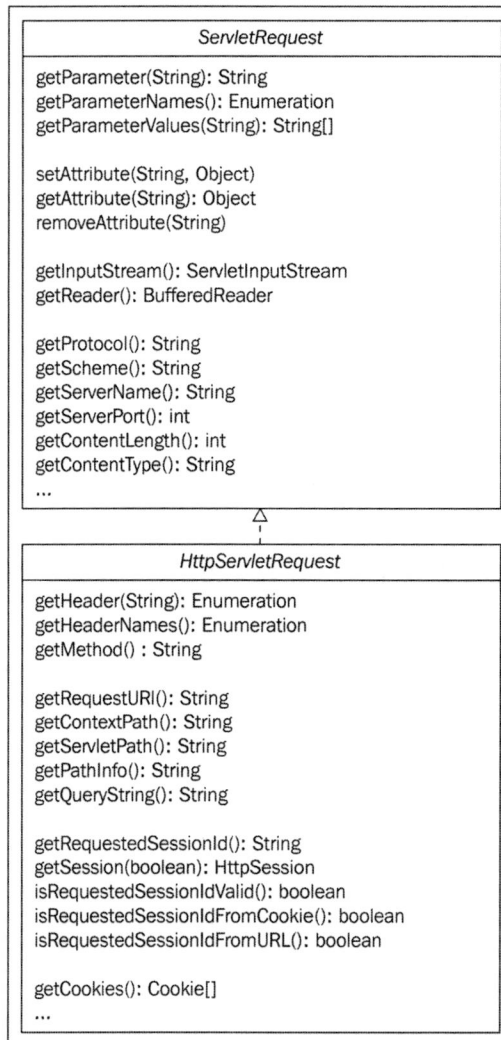

```
┌─────────────────────────────────────────────────┐
│              ServletRequest                       │
├─────────────────────────────────────────────────┤
│ getParameter(String): String                     │
│ getParameterNames(): Enumeration                  │
│ getParameterValues(String): String[]              │
│                                                   │
│ setAttribute(String, Object)                      │
│ getAttribute(String): Object                      │
│ removeAttribute(String)                           │
│                                                   │
│ getInputStream(): ServletInputStream              │
│ getReader(): BufferedReader                       │
│                                                   │
│ getProtocol(): String                             │
│ getScheme(): String                               │
│ getServerName(): String                           │
│ getServerPort(): int                              │
│ getContentLength(): int                           │
│ getContentType(): String                          │
│ ...                                               │
└─────────────────────────────────────────────────┘
                        △
                        ┊
┌─────────────────────────────────────────────────┐
│              HttpServletRequest                   │
├─────────────────────────────────────────────────┤
│ getHeader(String): Enumeration                    │
│ getHeaderNames(): Enumeration                     │
│ getMethod() : String                              │
│                                                   │
│ getRequestURI(): String                           │
│ getContextPath(): String                          │
│ getServletPath(): String                          │
│ getPathInfo(): String                             │
│ getQueryString(): String                          │
│                                                   │
│ getRequestedSessionId(): String                   │
│ getSession(boolean): HttpSession                  │
│ isRequestedSessionIdValid(): boolean              │
│ isRequestedSessionIdFromCookie(): boolean         │
│ isRequestedSessionIdFromURL(): boolean            │
│                                                   │
│ getCookies(): Cookie[]                            │
│ ...                                               │
└─────────────────────────────────────────────────┘
```

This image depicts key aspects of the request interfaces within the Servlet API.

The lifetime of a request object is intended to be the duration of a request. It is constructed by the container from the incoming HTTP request.

It exposes operations that allow a servlet to manipulate the incoming request and to extract various pieces of information from it.

Request parameters and attributes

Request parameters and request attributes are both name-value pairs, but the similarity ends there.

A request parameter represents a form parameter that comes in on the incoming request, either as part of the request's payload, or in the URL query string. The value of each named parameter is always a standard Java `String`.

On the other hand, a request attribute is a named object that is set on the `HttpServletRequest` by a web component, such as a filter or a servlet. The value of an attribute can be any Java object. A request attribute is meant to be used only during the current request processing cycle and is a convenient way to cache objects while processing a request or to transfer arbitrary objects to another servlet.

Path parameters, such as `;jsessionid=xxxx`, are not exposed, and you will need to parse the request URI to access them.

Protocol and URI details

The request instance provides methods to access all aspects of the request URI used to identify the requested resource:

```
requestURI = contextPath + servletPath + pathInfo
```

The context path represents the web application specific prefix (for the default root context, this is empty), the servlet path represents the `web.xml` servlet mapping that activated this request, and the path info is the remainder of the URI.

This object has methods that also let you query the protocol that has been used (for example, `HTTP/1.1`), the scheme (`http`, `https`, or `ftp`), and whether the request arrived over a secure channel (for example, `https`).

Reading request data

When data is sent to the server in the request entity's body, say using a POST, you can bring other methods to bear that help you to determine the type and length of the content that was sent.

You can also help the servlet container parse the content correctly by setting the appropriate character encoding.

If you choose to, you can directly read the request body, either as a binary stream (using a `ServletInputStream`) or using a reader, which applies the appropriate character conversions based on the character encoding in effect.

Connection information

It is possible to query the request object for the IP address, host name, and port of the remote client computer. In addition, you can also obtain the host name and port of the server to which the client computer made the original request, and the IP address, host name, and the port number of the host on which the request was actually received.

HTTP specific information

`HttpServletRequest` also allows you to access information that is specific to the HTTP protocol, such as request headers, session related information, and the request method. It also grants you access to any cookies that were set by the server on this client and which are now diligently being returned on each request from that client.

Response

An `HttpServletResponse` object represents a general HTTP response that was generated by the servlet, including the status code, any response headers, and the response entity body. This image depicts key aspects of the response interfaces within the Servlet API.

```
┌─────────────────────────────────────────────────┐
│  ┌───────────────────────────────────────────┐  │
│  │              ServletResponse              │  │
│  ├───────────────────────────────────────────┤  │
│  │  getContentType(): String                 │  │
│  │  setContentType(String)                   │  │
│  │  getContentLength(): int                  │  │
│  │  setContentLength(int)                    │  │
│  │                                           │  │
│  │  getOutputStream(): ServletOutputStream   │  │
│  │  getWriter(): PrintWriter                 │  │
│  │                                           │  │
│  │  flushBuffer()                            │  │
│  │  resetBuffer()                            │  │
│  │  reset()                                  │  │
│  │  isCommitted(): boolean                   │  │
│  │  ...                                      │  │
│  └───────────────────────────────────────────┘  │
│                      △                           │
│                      ┊                           │
│  ┌───────────────────────────────────────────┐  │
│  │            HttpServletResponse            │  │
│  ├───────────────────────────────────────────┤  │
│  │  setStatus(int)                           │  │
│  │                                           │  │
│  │  addHeader(String, String)                │  │
│  │  addCookie(Cookie)                        │  │
│  │  containsHeader(boolean): String          │  │
│  │                                           │  │
│  │  encodeURL(String): String                │  │
│  │  encodeRedirectURL(String): String        │  │
│  │                                           │  │
│  │  sendError(int, String)                   │  │
│  │  sendError(int)                           │  │
│  │  sendRedirect(String)                     │  │
│  │  ...                                      │  │
│  └───────────────────────────────────────────┘  │
└─────────────────────────────────────────────────┘
```

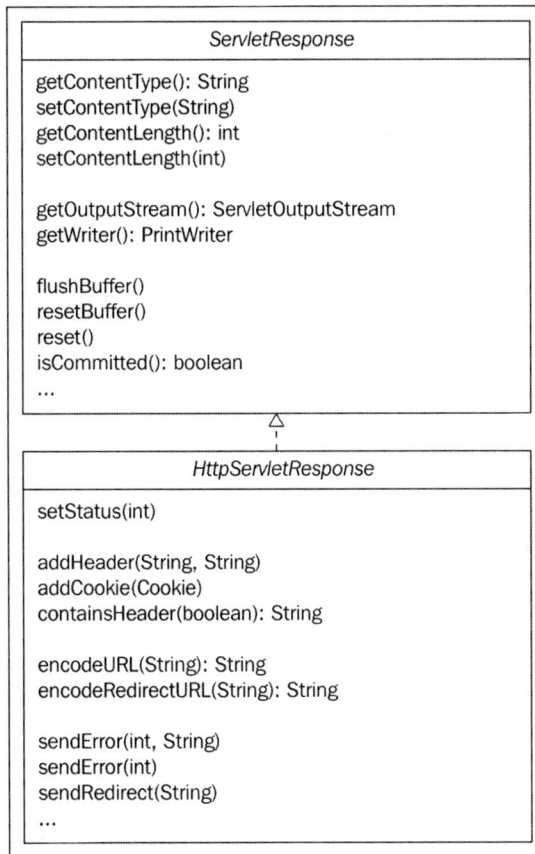

For efficiency considerations, a response may be buffered. You may write to it using a character oriented `Writer` or a byte oriented `ServletOutputStream`. You can also set the content type and length as appropriate.

Headers must be added to the response before the response is committed, in other words, before any part of the response has been flushed to the client.

This class supports convenience methods to send a redirect response, or an error response.

Sessions

As we have seen before, HTTP is a stateless protocol. In other words, every connection stands by itself and is not aware of any previous connection that was established between the client and the server.

However, for any kind of web application to function, it is necessary for a conversation to be established between a given client and the server.

The Servlet API achieves this by using the concept of a session. A `javax.servlet.http.HttpSession` instance is associated with a particular client, and a session identifier that represents this instance is transmitted to the client, either as a cookie or encoded onto a URL. When the next request from this client comes in, it is examined for either a cookie or a URL path parameter named `jsessionid` that holds the session identifier that describes the conversation with this client. If this parameter is found, the server is able to associate conversational state with this new request.

The specific session tracking mechanism used is transparent to the user, and cookies will be used by default. URL rewriting, which requires that each URL generated must have the `jsessionid` path parameter encoded into it, is used as a fallback mechanism.

It is interesting to note that sessions are scoped at the application context level. In other words, they are unique to a particular servlet context. If you forward a request to a servlet in another web application, then that servlet will use a session that is different from the session of the calling servlet.

Session scoped objects are particularly sensitive to multithreading issues. Care should be taken to ensure that any accesses to session attributes are done in a thread-safe manner, possibly by synchronizing on the user's session itself.

On the client, cookies are usually controlled by the web browser process and are not associated with any particular tab or window of the browser. As a result, requests from all the windows of a client application might be part of the same session. For maximum safety, you should always assume that this is the case.

Filters

Filters are web components that usually do not by themselves process requests. Instead, they are intended to act as assembly-line processors placed in front of the servlet. They pre-process the request, passing the request along to the next filter in line, until it finally arrives at the servlet, which does the actual processing. Then, the assembly line works in reverse, with each filter getting a chance to weigh in on the response that is generated by the servlet.

Any filter can short circuit the processing, simply by refusing to pass on the request and is then responsible for generating the response sent to the client.

The servlet container is responsible for instantiating the filters and deciding the order in which they must be invoked for a given request.

Filters are very selective, and you can configure them to be invoked for one or more of the following types of requests:

- Those that come directly from a client (the default)
- Those that arise out of a server-side forward, where one servlet hands off processing to another
- Those that arise out of an include, where one servlet delegates part of the processing to another servlet
- Those that arise when the error page mechanism is invoked

In all cases, the filter is invoked only if the web container finds a match between the URL-pattern or servlet name that is configured for that filter and the destination resource.

Listeners

Event listeners are classes that implement one or more of the standard servlet event listener interfaces. For example, a class that implements the `javax.servlet.ServletContextListener` interface will be notified when the servlet context has been started, and when the servlet context is about to be shut down.

Listener classes are declared in the web application's deployment descriptor. When the web application is deployed, the web container will automatically instantiate each listener that it finds in the deployment descriptor, and will register them with their subjects, according to the interfaces that they implement, and the order in which they appear in the deployment descriptor.

During web application execution, listeners are notified in the order of their registration.

Web applications

The web container makes the application available to the application's servlets in the form of a servlet context. In other words, a `javax.servlet.ServletContext` instance represents a running web application within a container.

A web application is a collection of servlets, JSPs, utility classes, static content (HTML, CSS, images, and so on), and other resources along with an application deployment descriptor that are arranged in a structured hierarchy of directories.

The root of this directory hierarchy maps to the context path for this web application and also serves as the document root for the files that are part of this application.

For example, for an application whose context path is `/products`, the file `/index.html`, which is at this document root, can be accessed in a browser as `/products/index.html`.

A special directory exists within this structured hierarchy named `WEB-INF`. This directory and its contents are not part of the document root of the web application, and no file contained within it may be served to a client. Any requests to files within this directory will be met with a `NOT_FOUND` (`404`) response. However, the contents of this folder are visible to server-side code.

The usual contents of `WEB-INF` include the web application's deployment descriptor, `web.xml`; a `classes` folder, which contains the servlets and utility classes for this application; and a `lib` folder, which contains the JAR files that are required by this application. As we will see in a later chapter, the class files in this folder are accessed using a special web application class loader that defies the laws of class loading, well at least those related to the standard delegation model. This class loader must load classes from `WEB-INF\classes` first, and then from the JARs in `WEB-INF\lib`.

Web applications may be packaged into a **Web Archive Format (WAR)** using the JAR tool. WAR files will usually have an additional `META-INF` folder, which contains an optional context fragment as well as a manifest file. The contents of this folder also cannot be directly requested by a client.

Deployment descriptors

Every web application must be accompanied by a deployment descriptor named `web.xml` that is placed directly in the application's `WEB-INF` folder. The root element in this document is named `web-app`, and its sub elements can be in an arbitrary order.

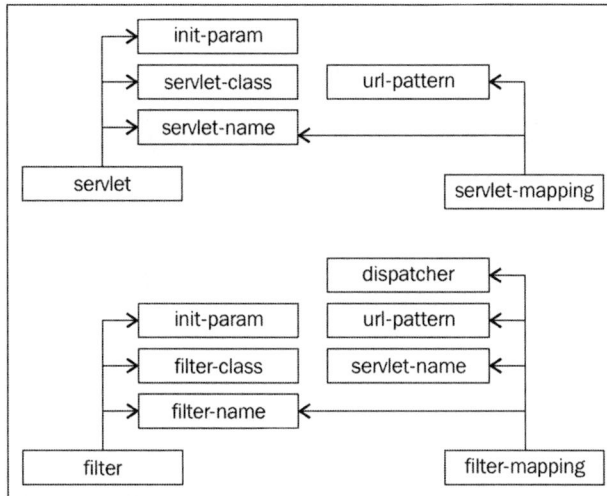

Its primary purpose is to link the various elements that we've described so far into a harmonious whole. For instance, the `<servlet>` element maps a fully qualified servlet class to a logical name that will be used to refer to that servlet. That logical name is then mapped using a `servlet-mapping` element to a given URL pattern.

Its `<filter>` element associates the fully qualified class name of a servlet filter with a logical name. This logical name can then be mapped to a given URL pattern or to a servlet's logical name using the `filter-mapping` element.

Both servlets and filters can be initialized using parameters that are provided within the deployment descriptor.

A `<context-param>` element lets you specify global servlet context initialization parameters, which are available to all servlets that run within this application context.

The `<listener>` element defines the fully qualified name of a class that is to be registered as a web application event listener.

Another key element is `<session-config>`, which lets you set the default session timeout interval for all sessions that are created in this web application.

Given its central role within a web application, we'll see a lot more of this deployment descriptor in later chapters. For now, this brief introduction should suffice.

Summary

The goal of this chapter was to provide you with a general background of the foundational elements upon which the servlet specification is built. As a result, we covered a significant amount of ground in the course of this chapter.

We began with a tour of the characteristics of an enterprise application that make it a particularly unique problem domain, requiring the special attention of an entire set of APIs, all of which are packaged conveniently in the Java Enterprise Edition Platform specification.

We then took a high level overview of the HTTP version 1.1 and noted that it was a connection oriented, stateless protocol. We saw the methods it defines, as well as with the structure of the request and response that form the core of the protocol.

Finally, we reviewed JSR 154, the Servlet 2.5 specification that forms the requirements that any Java EE compliant servlet container should implement. We looked at the core classes that form the basis of the Servlet API and the basic building blocks such as filters, sessions, and listeners. We ended with a quick tour of a basic web application and its deployment descriptor.

Servlet Container Overview

3

In the last chapter, we noted that the Java Enterprise Edition can be considered to be nothing more than a set of specifications, or interfaces, for which service providers are required to provide implementations.

While it is the actual implementation that does all the work, these specifications ensure that each implementation can assume that all its other collaborating pieces work as described by their interfaces. In theory, this allows complex software platforms (such as application servers) to be assembled from constituent implementations, each of which is sourced from a different vendor.

In practice, it is highly unlikely that you will interface an EJB container from WebSphere and a JMS implementation from WebLogic, with the Tomcat servlet container from the Apache foundation, but it is at least theoretically possible.

Note that the term 'interface', as it is used here, also encompasses abstract classes. The specification's API might provide a template implementation whose operations are defined in terms of some basic set of primitives that are kept abstract for the service provider to implement. For instance, in Chapter 2, we noted that the servlet hierarchy is made up of the `Servlet` interface, and the `GenericServlet` and `HttpServlet` abstract classes within the `javax.servlet` package.

A service provider is required to make available concrete implementations of these interfaces and abstract classes. For example, the `HttpSession` interface is implemented by Tomcat in the form of `org.apache.catalina.session.StandardSession`.

Let's return to the image of the Tomcat container that we saw in Chapter 1.

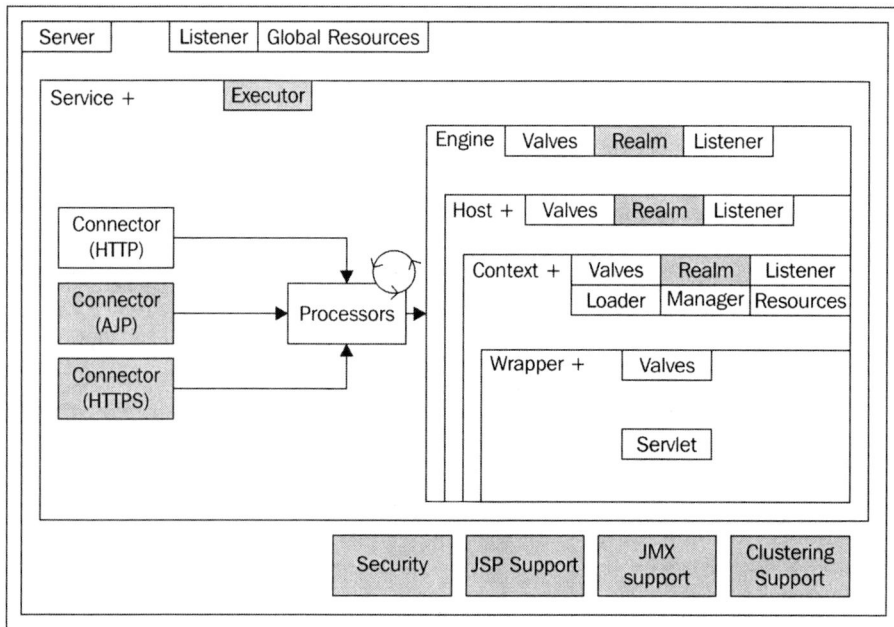

As was stated in Chapter 1, the objective of this book is to cover the primary request processing components that are present in this image. Advanced topics, such as clustering and security, are shown as shaded in this image and are not covered.

In this image, the '+' symbol after the `Service`, `Host`, `Context`, and `Wrapper` instances indicate that there can be one or more of these elements. For instance, a `Service` may have a single `Engine`, but an `Engine` can contain one or more `Hosts`. In addition, the whirling circle represents a pool of request processor threads.

In this chapter, we will fly over the architecture of Tomcat from a 10,000-foot perspective taking in the sights as we go.

Component taxonomy

Tomcat's architecture follows the construction of a Matrushka doll from Russia. In other words, it is all about containment where one entity contains another, and that entity in turn contains yet another.

In Tomcat, a 'container' is a generic term that refers to any component that can contain another, such as a `Server`, `Service`, `Engine`, `Host`, or `Context`.

Of these, the `Server` and `Service` components are special containers, designated as **Top Level Elements** as they represent aspects of the running Tomcat instance. All the other Tomcat components are subordinate to these top level elements.

The `Engine`, `Host`, and `Context` components are officially termed **Containers**, and refer to components that process incoming requests and generate an appropriate outgoing response.

Nested Components can be thought of as sub-elements that can be nested inside either Top Level Elements or other Containers to configure how they function. Examples of nested components include the `Valve`, which represents a reusable unit of work; the `Pipeline`, which represents a chain of `Valves` strung together; and a `Realm` which helps set up container-managed security for a particular container.

Other nested components include the `Loader` which is used to enforce the specification's guidelines for servlet class loading; the `Manager` that supports session management for each web application; the `Resources` component that represents the web application's static resources and a mechanism to access these resources; and the `Listener` that allows you to insert custom processing at important points in a container's life cycle, such as when a component is being started or stopped.

> Not all nested components can be nested within every container.

A final major component, which falls into its own category, is the **Connector**. It represents the connection end point that an external client (such as a web browser) can use to connect to the Tomcat container.

Before we go on to examine these components, let's take a quick look at how they are organized structurally.

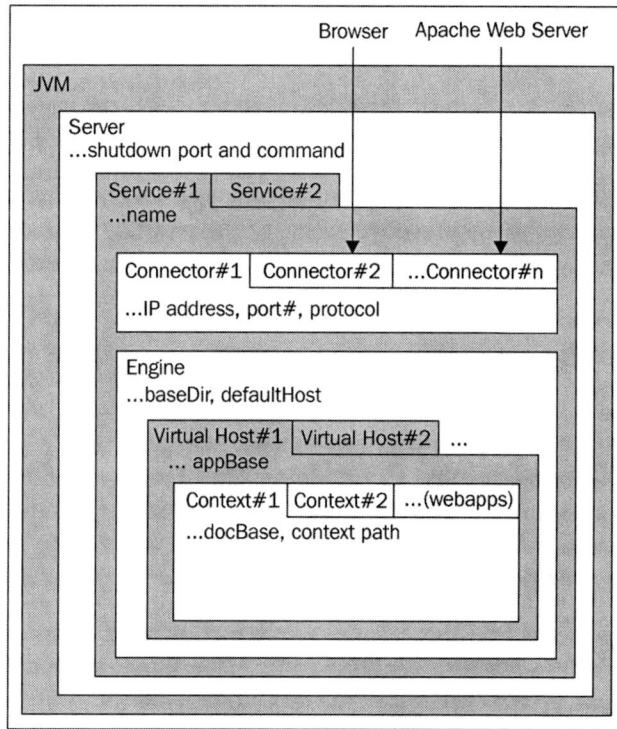

Note that this diagram only shows the key properties of each container.

When Tomcat is started, the **Java Virtual Machine (JVM)** instance in which it runs will contain a singleton `Server` top level element, which represents the entire Tomcat server. A `Server` will usually contain just one `Service` object, which is a structural element that combines one or more `Connectors` (for example, an HTTP and an HTTPS connector) that funnel incoming requests through to a single Catalina servlet `Engine`.

The `Engine` represents the core request processing code within Tomcat and supports the definition of multiple **Virtual Hosts** within it. A virtual host allows a single running Tomcat engine to make it seem to the outside world that there are multiple separate domains (for example, www.my-site.com and www.your-site.com) being hosted on a single machine.

Each virtual host can, in turn, support multiple web applications known as **Contexts** that are deployed to it. A context is represented using the web application format specified by the servlet specification, either as a single compressed **WAR (Web Application Archive)** file or as an uncompressed directory. In addition, a context is configured using a web.xml file, as defined by the servlet specification.

A context can, in turn, contain multiple servlets that are deployed into it, each of which is wrapped in a `Wrapper` component.

The `Server`, `Service`, `Connector`, `Engine`, `Host`, and `Context` elements that will be present in a particular running Tomcat instance are configured using the server.xml configuration file.

> Things are a bit more complicated than this. However, we'll defer the complexity until later chapters when we deal with each component in a lot more detail.

Architectural benefits

This architecture has a couple of useful features. It not only makes it easy to manage component life cycles (each component manages the life cycle notifications for its children), but also to dynamically assemble a running Tomcat server instance that is based on the information that has been read from configuration files at startup. In particular, the server.xml file is parsed at startup, and its contents are used to instantiate and configure the defined elements, which are then assembled into a running Tomcat instance.

> The server.xml file is read only once, and edits to it will not be picked up until Tomcat is restarted.

This architecture also eases the configuration burden by allowing child containers to inherit the configuration of their parent containers. For instance, a `Realm` defines a data store that can be used for authentication and authorization of users who are attempting to access protected resources within a web application. For ease of configuration, a realm that is defined for an engine applies to all its children hosts and contexts. At the same time, a particular child, such as a given context, may override its inherited realm by specifying its own realm to be used in place of its parent's realm.

Top Level Components

The `Server` and `Service` container components exist largely as structural conveniences. A `Server` represents the running instance of Tomcat and contains one or more `Service` children, each of which represents a collection of request processing components.

Server

A `Server` represents the entire Tomcat instance and is a singleton within a Java Virtual Machine, and is responsible for managing the life cycle of its contained services.

The following image depicts the key aspects of the `Server` component. As shown, a `Server` instance is configured using the `server.xml` configuration file. The root element of this file is `<Server>` and represents the Tomcat instance. Its default implementation is provided using `org.apache.catalina.core.StandardServer`, but you can specify your own custom implementation through the `className` attribute of the `<Server>` element.

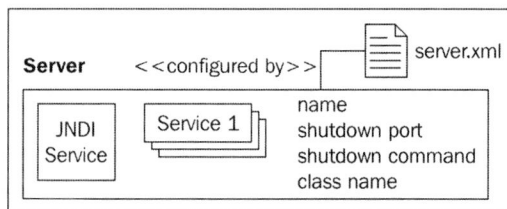

A key aspect of the `Server` is that it opens a server socket on port 8005 (the default) to listen a shutdown command (by default, this command is the text string `SHUTDOWN`). When this shutdown command is received, the server gracefully shuts itself down. For security reasons, the connection requesting the shutdown must be initiated from the same machine that is running this instance of Tomcat.

A `Server` also provides an implementation of the **Java Naming and Directory Interface (JNDI)** service, allowing you to register arbitrary objects (such as data sources) or environment variables, by name.

At runtime, individual components (such as servlets) can retrieve this information by looking up the desired object name in the server's JNDI bindings.

While a JNDI implementation is not integral to the functioning of a servlet container, it is part of the Java EE specification and is a service that servlets have a right to expect from their application servers or servlet containers. Implementing this service makes for easy portability of web applications across containers.

While there is always just one server instance within a JVM, it is entirely possible to have multiple server instances running on a single physical machine, each encased in its own JVM. Doing so insulates web applications that are running on one VM from errors in applications that are running on others, and simplifies maintenance by allowing a JVM to be restarted independently of the others. This is one of the mechanisms used in a shared hosting environment (the other is virtual hosting, which we will see shortly) where you need isolation from other web applications that are running on the same physical server.

Service

While the Server represents the Tomcat instance itself, a Service represents the set of request processing components within Tomcat.

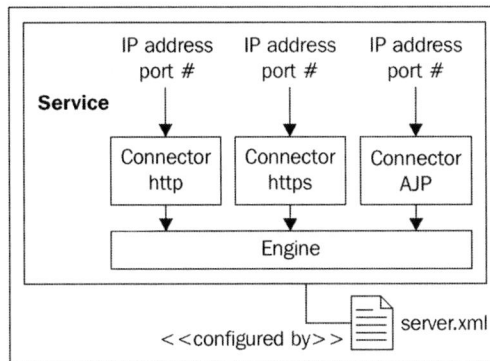

A `Server` can contain more than one `Service`, where each service associates a group of `Connector` components with a single `Engine`.

Requests from clients are received on a connector, which in turn funnels them through into the engine, which is the key request processing component within Tomcat. The image shows connectors for HTTP, HTTPS, and the Apache JServ Protocol (AJP).

There is very little reason to modify this element, and the default `Service` instance is usually sufficient.

A hint as to when you might need more than one `Service` instance can be found in the above image. As shown, a service aggregates connectors, each of which monitors a given IP address and port, and responds in a given protocol. An example use case for having multiple services, therefore, is when you want to partition your services (and their contained engines, hosts, and web applications) by IP address and/or port number.

For instance, you might configure your firewall to expose the connectors for one service to an external audience, while restricting your other service to hosting intranet applications that are visible only to internal users. This would ensure that an external user could never access your Intranet application, as that access would be blocked by the firewall.

The `Service`, therefore, is nothing more than a grouping construct. It does not currently add any other value to the proceedings.

> The server and service components are covered in more detail in Chapter 5, *The Server and Service Components*.

Connectors

A `Connector` is a service endpoint on which a client connects to the Tomcat container. It serves to insulate the engine from the various communication protocols that are used by clients, such as HTTP, HTTPS, or the **Apache JServ Protocol (AJP)**.

Tomcat can be configured to work in two modes—Standalone or in Conjunction with a separate web server.

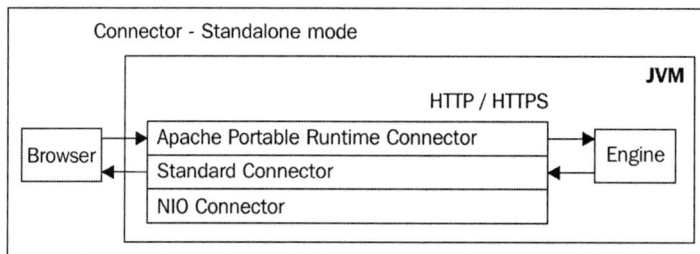

In standalone mode, Tomcat is configured with HTTP and HTTPS connectors, which make it act like a full-fledged web server by serving up static content when requested, as well as by delegating to the Catalina engine for dynamic content.

Out of the box, Tomcat provides three possible implementations of the HTTP/1.1 and HTTPS connectors for this mode of operation.

The most common are the standard connectors, known as **Coyote** which are implemented using standard Java I/O mechanisms.

You may also make use of a couple of newer implementations, one which uses the non-blocking NIO features of Java 1.4, and the other which takes advantage of native code that is optimized for a particular operating system through the Apache Portable Runtime (APR).

Note that both the `Connector` and the `Engine` run in the same JVM. In fact, they run within the same `Server` instance.

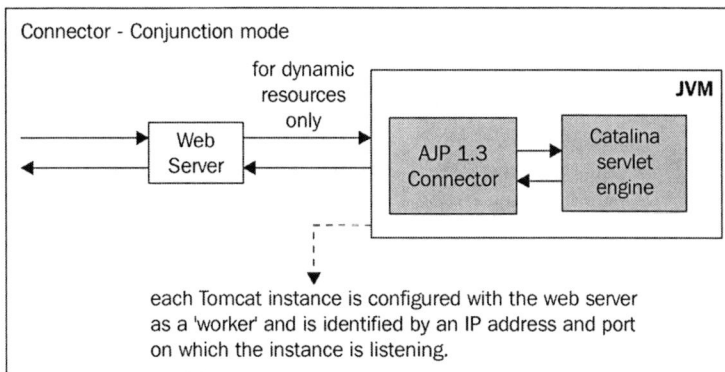

In conjunction mode, Tomcat plays a supporting role to a web server, such as Apache `httpd` or Microsoft's IIS. The client here is the web server, communicating with Tomcat either through an Apache module or an ISAPI DLL. When this module determines that a request must be routed to Tomcat for processing, it will communicate this request to Tomcat using AJP, a binary protocol that is designed to be more efficient than the text based HTTP when communicating between a web server and Tomcat.

On the Tomcat side, an AJP connector accepts this communication and translates it into a form that the Catalina engine can process.

In this mode, Tomcat is running in its own JVM as a separate process from the web server.

In either mode, the primary attributes of a `Connector` are the IP address and port on which it will listen for incoming requests, and the protocol that it supports. Another key attribute is the maximum number of request processing threads that can be created to concurrently handle incoming requests. Once all these threads are busy, any incoming request will be ignored until a thread becomes available.

By default, a connector listens on all the IP addresses for the given physical machine (its `address` attribute defaults to 0.0.0.0). However, a connector can be configured to listen on just one of the IP addresses for a machine. This will constrain it to accept connections from only that specified IP address.

Any request that is received by any one of a service's connectors is passed on to the service's single engine. This engine, known as Catalina, is responsible for the processing of the request, and the generation of the response.

The engine returns the response to the connector, which then transmits it back to the client using the appropriate communication protocol.

> This component is covered in more detail in Chapter 6, *The Connector Component.*

Container components

In this section, we'll take a look at the key request processing components within Tomcat; the engine, virtual host, and context components.

Engine

An `Engine` represents a running instance of the Catalina servlet engine and comprises the heart of a servlet container's function. There can only be one engine within a given service. Being a true container, an `Engine` may contain one or more virtual hosts as children.

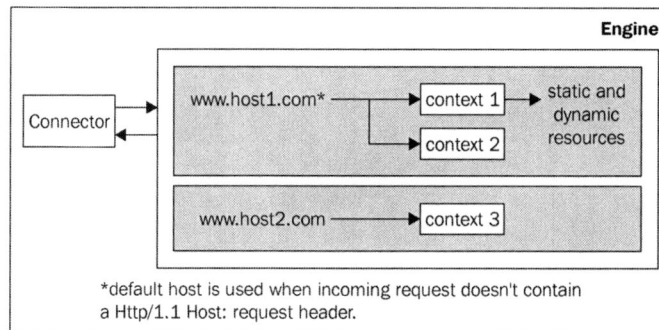

*default host is used when incoming request doesn't contain a Http/1.1 Host: request header.

Being the primary request processing component, it receives objects that represent the incoming request and the outgoing response. Its main function is to delegate the processing of the incoming request to the appropriate virtual host. If the engine has no virtual host with a name matching the one to which the request should be directed, it consults its `defaultHost` attribute to determine the host that should be used.

Virtual host

A virtual host in Tomcat is represented by the `Host` component, which is a container for web applications, or, in Tomcat parlance, contexts.

Two key concepts come into play when working with virtual hosts—the host's domain name and its application base folder.

- **Domain name**: Each virtual host is identified by the domain name that you registered for use with this host. This is the value that you expect the client browser to send in the `Host:` request header. A host's name is required to be unique within its containing engine.

- **Application base folder**: This folder is the location that contains the contexts that will be deployed to this host. This folder location can either be specified as an absolute path or as a path relative to CATALINA_BASE.

> CATALINA_HOME is an environment variable that references the location of the Tomcat binaries. The CATALINA_BASE environment variable makes it possible to use a single binary installation of Tomcat to run multiple Tomcat instances with different configurations (which are primarily determined by the contents of the `conf` folder).
>
> In addition, the use of a CATALINA_BASE location that is separate from CATALINA_HOME keeps the standard binary distribution separate from your installation. This has the beneficial effect of making it easy to upgrade to a newer Tomcat version, without having to worry about clobbering your existing web applications and related configuration files.
>
> This component is covered in more detail in Chapter 7, *The Engine Component*.

Basic concepts

When it comes to mapping host names to Internet Protocol addresses, the simplest scenario is one in which a given **Fully Qualified Host Name (FQHN)**, such as www.swengsol.com, is associated with the IP address that maps to a particular physical host.

The downside with this approach is that connecting a host to the Internet is fairly expensive. This is especially true when you consider the costs related to bandwidth, infrastructure (such as database/mail servers, firewalls, uninterruptible power supplies, fault tolerance, and so on), and maintenance (including staffing, administration, and backups), not to mention having to obtain an IP address in the first place.

As a result, many small businesses find it preferable to lease space and infrastructure from hosting service providers. The hosting service may have a single physical server that is connected to the Internet and is identified with a specific IP address. This physical server could host several domains on behalf of the provider's customers.

For example, consider the case where Acme Widgets Inc. and Vertico LLC have their domains, www.acme-widgets.com and www.vertico.com, hosted on a single physical machine at a hosting service. The applications that are deployed to both these domains must be able to function without any interference from the other.

In this case, both these domains are termed 'virtual' hosts, in the sense that they appear to be represented by separate physical hosts. However, in reality, they exist simply as a logical partitioning of the address space on a single physical host.

Virtual host techniques

There are two common ways to set up virtual hosting:

- IP-based virtual hosting
- Name-based virtual hosting

IP-based virtual hosting

With this technique, each FQHN resolves to a separate IP address. However, each of these IP addresses resolves to the same physical machine.

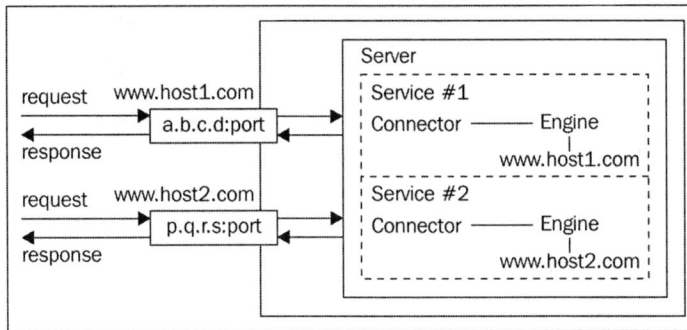

You can achieve this by using either of the following mechanisms:

- A multi-homed server, that is, a machine that has multiple physical Network Interface Cards (NICs) installed, each of which has an assigned IP address.

- Using operating system facilities to set up virtual network interfaces by dynamically assigning multiple IP addresses to a single physical NIC.

In either case, the downside is that we need to acquire multiple IP addresses, and these addresses (at least for IPv4) are a limited resource.

The web server is configured to listen on ports that are assigned to each of these IP addresses, and when it detects an incoming request on a particular IP address, it generates the response appropriate for that address.

For example, you can have a web server that is running on a particular physical host that is monitoring port 80 on both 11.156.33.345 and 11.156.33.346. It is configured to respond to requests that are coming in on the former IP address with content that is associated with a particular host name, say www.host1.com, whereas it is www.host2.com for the latter.

When a request comes in on 11.156.33.346, the server knows that it should serve content from the www.host2.com, and does so. To the user, this is indistinguishable from an entirely separate physical server.

Name-based virtual hosting

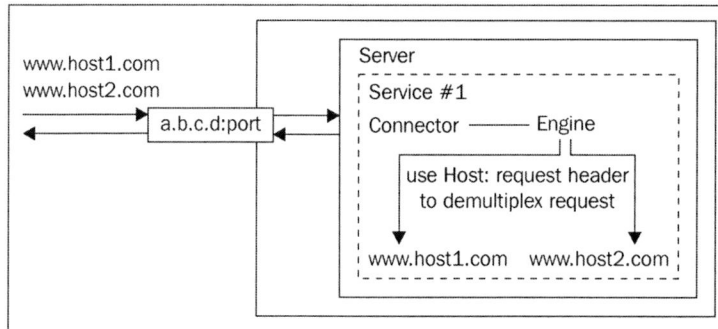

This is a newer technique that lets you map different domain names to the same IP address. The domain names are registered as normal, and multiple DNS entries exist to map these domain names to the same IP address.

The HTTP/1.1 protocol requires that every request must contain a Host: header that carries the fully qualified host name, as well as the port number (if specified) to which the user wishes to connect. The web server that runs on the host at the IP address will receive this request and will read this header to determine the specific virtual host that should handle this request.

Name-based virtual hosting is preferred for its simplicity and for the fact that it does not use up IP addresses needlessly.

However, you may have to use IP-based virtual hosting when you are using virtual hosts together with SSL. The reason is that the negotiation protocol commits to a certificate before it pays heed to the specific virtual host for which the request is being made. This is because the SSL protocol layer works at a lower level than the HTTP protocol, and the module negotiating this handshake with the client cannot read the HTTP request header until the handshake is complete.

> You may be able to use name-based virtual hosting with SSL if your web server and client supports the Server Name Indication extension as specified in RFC 3546—Transport Layer Security Extensions (http://www.ietf.org/rfc/rfc3546.txt). Using this extension, during the SSL negotiation, the client also transmits the host name to which it is trying to connect, thereby allowing the web server to handle the handshake appropriately by returning the certificate for the correct host name.

Virtual host aliasing

Aliasing works by informing the web server that if it sees the aliased domain name in the Host: header, it should be treated in exactly the same manner as the virtual host's domain name.

For example, if you set up swengsol.com as an alias for the www.swengsol.com virtual host, then typing either domain name in the URL will result in the same virtual host being used to process the request.

This works well when a particular host may be known by more than one domain name, and you don't want to clutter your configuration file by creating one set of entries per alias that a user may use to connect to that host.

> This component is covered in more detail in Chapter 8, *The Host Component.*

Context

A Context, or web application, is where your application specific code (servlets and JSPs) live. It provides a neat way to organize the resources that comprise a given web application.

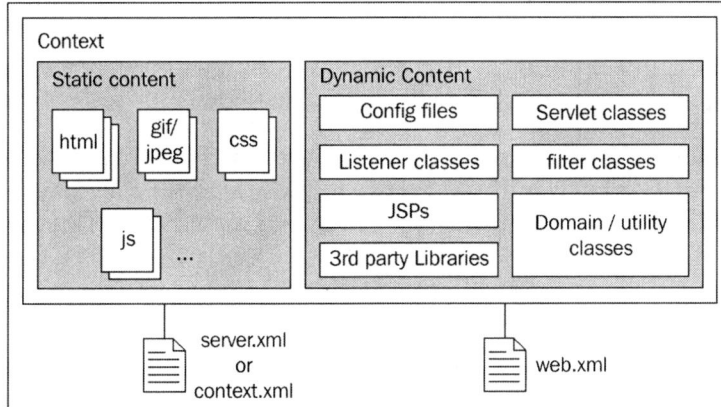

A context maps to a ServletContext instance within the servlet specification. In many ways, the servlet specification is primarily concerned with this context component. For instance, it mandates the format for deploying a context, and dictates the contents of the deployment descriptor.

Important attributes for a context include:

- **Document base**: This is the path name, either absolute or relative to its containing host's application base, to where its WAR file or exploded folder (its content root) are located.

- **Context path**: It represents the portion of the URL that uniquely identifies a web application within a given host. It helps the host container to determine which of its deployed contexts should be responsible for handling an incoming request.

  One of your contexts may be identified as the default context. This context is then the application that will be invoked when no context path is specified on the URL. This default context is identified by specifying an empty string as its context path, and as such, can be referenced by using a URL that only specifies a hostname. The default application is identified in Tomcat by a folder named ROOT in the application base folder for a given host.

- **Automatic reload**: A context's resources can be monitored for changes, and the context reloaded automatically when any changes are detected. While this is remarkably useful during development, this is an expensive operation and should be turned off in production.

Context configuration

A Context is unique because it has multiple options when it comes to its configuration. We have already noted the presence of the conf/server.xml file that is used to set up the overall structure of the Tomcat instance. While this file's <Context> element can be used to configure a context, this is no longer recommended.

Instead, Tomcat lets you configure a Context by letting you extract the <Context> element from the server.xml file and move it into a separate file called a **context fragment file**. Context fragments are monitored and reloaded by Tomcat at runtime.

> Note that the server.xml file is only ever loaded once at startup.

To ensure a clear separation of contexts by host and engine, Tomcat expects to find context fragments using a specific directory path CATALINA_HOME/conf/ <EngineName>/<HostName>/. The context fragments for contexts deployed into this host are found within this folder and are named <ContextPath>.xml.

For the default case, that is, an engine named `Catalina` and a host named `localhost`, this works out to be the folder `CATALINA_HOME/conf/Catalina/localhost`. However, the name of the host could be any valid domain name, for example, `www.swengsol.com`, resulting in a folder named `CATALINA_HOME/conf/Catalina/www.swengsol.com`.

In addition, context fragments may also be found embedded within the META-INF folder of a web application's WAR file or exploded directory. In such cases, the fragment must be named `context.xml`.

Contexts can also be configured using the web application deployment descriptor, `web.xml`. While the fragment file is proprietary to Tomcat, the deployment descriptor is described by the servlet specification, and therefore is portable across Java EE compliant servlet containers.

We will consider both of these in much greater detail in later chapters.

> This component is covered in more detail in Chapter 9, *The Context Component*.

Wrapper

A `Wrapper` object is a child of the context container and represents an individual servlet (or a JSP file converted to a servlet). It is called a `Wrapper` because it wraps an instance of a `javax.servlet.Servlet`.

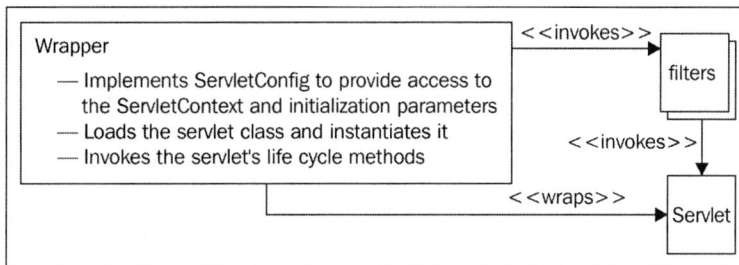

This is the lowest level of the `Container` hierarchy, and any attempt to add a child to it will result in an exception being thrown.

A wrapper is responsible for the servlet that it represents, including loading it, instantiating it, and invoking its lifecycle methods such as `init()`, `service()`, and `destroy()`.

It is also responsible, through its basic valve, for the invocation of the filters that are associated with the wrapped servlet.

[✎   This component is covered in more detail in Chapter 10,
      The Wrapper Component.]

Nested components

These components are specific to the Tomcat implementation, and their primary purpose is to enable the various Tomcat containers to perform their tasks.

Valve

A valve is a processing element that can be placed within the processing path of each of Tomcat's containers—engine, host, context, or a servlet wrapper. A `Valve` is added to a container using the `<Valve>` element in `server.xml`. They are executed in the order in which they are encountered within the `server.xml` file.

The Tomcat distribution comes with a number of pre-rolled valves. These include:

- A valve that logs specific elements of a request (such as the remote client's IP address) to a log file or database
- A valve that lets you control access to a particular web application based on the remote client's IP address or host name
- A valve that lets you log every request and response header
- A valve that lets you configure single sign-on access across multiple web applications on a specific virtual host

If these don't meet your needs, you can write your own implementations of `org.apache.catalina.Valve` and place them into service.

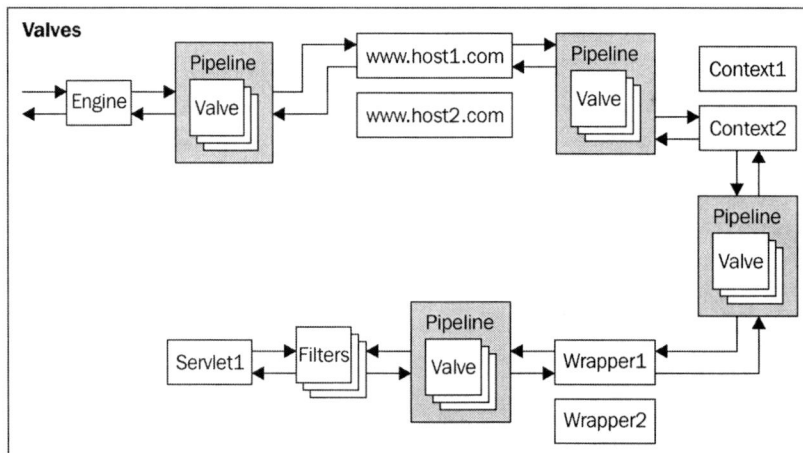

A container does not hold references to individual valves. Instead, it holds a reference to a single entity known as the `Pipeline`, which represents a chain of valves associated with that container.

When a container is invoked to process a request, it delegates the processing to its associated pipeline.

The valves in a pipeline are arranged as a sequence, based on how they are defined within the `server.xml` file. The final valve in this sequence is known as the pipeline's basic valve. This valve performs the task that embodies the core purpose of a given container.

Unlike individual valves, the pipeline is not an explicit element in `server.xml`, but instead is implicitly defined in terms of the sequence of valves that are associated with a given container.

Each `Valve` is aware of the next valve in the pipeline. After it performs its pre processing, it invokes the next `Valve` in the chain, and when the call returns, it performs its own post processing before returning.

This is very similar to what happens in filter chains within the servlet specification.

In this image, the engine's configured valve(s) fire when an incoming request is received. An engine's basic valve determines the destination host and delegates processing to that host. The destination host's (`www.host1.com`) valves now fire in sequence. The host's basic valve then determines the destination context (here, `Context1`) and delegates processing to it. The valves configured for `Context1` now fire and processing is then delegated by the context's basic valve to the appropriate wrapper, whose basic valve hands off processing to its wrapped servlet.

The response then returns over the same path in reverse.

> A `Valve` becomes part of the Tomcat server's implementation and provides a way for developers to inject custom code into the servlet container's processing of a request. As a result, the class files for custom valves must be deployed to `CATALINA_HOME/lib`, rather than to the `WEB-INF/classes` of a deployed application.

As they are not part of the servlet specification, valves are non-portable elements of your enterprise application. Therefore, if you rely on a particular valve, you will need to find equivalent alternatives in a different application server.

It is important to note that valves are required to be very efficient in order not to introduce inordinate delays into the processing of a request.

[The valve and pipeline components are covered in more detail in Chapter 7, *The Engine Component*.]

Realm

Container managed security works by having the container handle the authentication and authorization aspects of an application.

Authentication is defined as the task of ensuring that the user is who she says she is, and **authorization** is the task of determining whether the user may perform some specific action within an application.

The advantage of container managed security is that security can be configured declaratively by the application's deployer. That is, the assignment of passwords to users and the mapping of users to roles can all be done through configuration, which can then be applied across multiple web applications without any coding changes being required to those web applications.

[**Application Managed Security**

The alternative is having the application manage security. In this case, your web application code is the sole arbiter of whether a user may access some specific functionality or resource within your application.]

For Container managed security to work, you need to assemble the following components:

- **Security constraints**: Within your web application's deployment descriptor, web.xml, you must identify the URL patterns for restricted resources, as well as the user roles that would be permitted to access these resources.

- **Credential input mechanism**: In the web.xml deployment descriptor, you specify how the container should prompt the user for authentication credentials. This is usually accomplished by showing the user a dialog that prompts the user for a user name and password, but can also be configured to use other mechanisms such as a custom login form.

- **Realm**: This is a data store that holds user names, passwords, and roles, against which the user-supplied credentials are checked. It can be a simple XML file, a table in a relational database that is accessed using the JDBC API, or a Lightweight Directory Access Protocol (LDAP) server that can be accessed through the JNDI API. A realm provides Tomcat with a consistent mechanism of accessing these disparate data sources.

All three of the above components are technically independent of each other. The power of container based security is that you can assemble your own security solution by mixing and matching selections from each of these groups.

Now, when a user requests a resource, Tomcat will check to see whether a security constraint exists for this resource. For a restricted resource, Tomcat will then automatically request the user for her credentials and will then check these credentials against the configured realm. Access to the resource will be allowed only if the user's credentials are valid and if the user is a member of the role that is configured to access that resource.

Executor

This is a new element, available only since 6.0.11. It allows you to configure a shared thread pool that is available to all your connectors. This places an upper limit on the number of concurrent threads that may be started by your connectors. Note that this limit applies even if a particular connector has not used up all the threads configured for it.

Listener

Every major Tomcat component implements the `org.apache.catalina.Lifecycle` interface. This interface lets interested listeners to register with a component, to be notified of lifecycle events, such as the starting or stopping of that component.

A listener implements the `org.apache.catalina.LifecycleListener` interface and implements its `lifecycleEvent()` method, which takes a `LifecycleEvent` that represents the event that has occurred.

This gives you an opportunity to inject your own custom processing into Tomcat's lifecycle.

Manager

Sessions allows 'applications' to be made possible over the stateless HTTP protocol. A session represents a conversation between a client and a server and is implemented by a `javax.servlet.http.HttpSession` instance that is stored on the server and is associated with a unique identifier that is passed back by the client on each interaction.

A new session is created on request and remains alive on the server either until it times out after a period of inactivity by its associated client, or until it is explicitly invalidated, for instance, by the client choosing to log out.

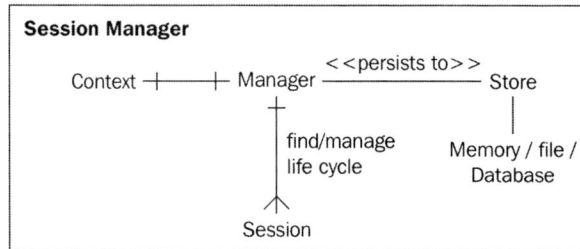

The above image shows a very simplistic view of the session mechanism within Tomcat.

An `org.apache.catalina.Manager` component is used by the Catalina engine to create, find, or invalidate sessions. This component is responsible for the sessions that are created for a context and their life cycles.

The default `Manager` implementation simply retains sessions in memory, but supports session survival across server restarts. It writes out all active sessions to disk when the server is stopped and will reload them into memory when the server is started up again.

A `<Manager>` must be a child of a `<Context>` element and is responsible for managing the sessions associated with that web application context.

The default `Manager` takes attributes such as the *algorithm* that is used to generate its session identifiers, the frequency in seconds with which the manager should check for expired sessions, the maximum number of active sessions supported, and the file in which the sessions should be stored.

Other implementations of `Manager` are provided that let you persist sessions to a durable data store such as a file or a JDBC database.

This component is covered in more detail in Chapter 11, *The Manager Component*.

Loader

This element represents the *class loader* for a given web application. A class loader is a very sacred entity in Java. In its most basic form, it is responsible for locating the bytecode that represents a compiled Java class and interpreting it.

The bytecode for a given class may be found in a variety of locations, the most common being either on the local file system or over the network. A class loader's primary goal is to abstract away the process of how the bytes are obtained and reconstituted into a class in memory.

Delegation model

Since Java 2, the class loading mechanism has used a delegating model, where the class loaders within a JVM are organized in a parent-child hierarchy. It is recommended that each class loader first delegate the task of finding and loading a class to its parent before it may attempt to do so itself.

This delegation mechanism ensures that no application can load in a malicious version of a system class (such as `java.lang.Object`) that may then compromise the integrity of the applications that are running in the JVM.

At the top of this class loader hierarchy is the *Bootstrap class loader*, called the primordial class loader, which is written in native code and is part of the JVM itself. Being part of the JVM ensures that there is at least one class loader that can be relied upon to load the core Java classes, such as `java.lang.Object`. This class loader is responsible for loading classes from the core Java packages (such as `java.lang` or `java.util`). In the Sun JVM implementation, these classes are found in `JAVA_HOME/jre/lib/rt.jar`. The Bootstrap class loader is unique in that, it is at the top of the tree, and so has no parent class loader.

Next down the hierarchy is the *Extension class loader* which, in the Sun JVM, is a `java.net.URLClassLoader` that monitors the `JAVA_HOME/jre/lib/ext` folder for extension JARs. Any JARs placed in this folder are automatically loaded without needing to be on the class path.

Finally, there is the *System class loader* (or Application class loader), which is also a `URLClassLoader` in the Sun JVM implementation. It monitors the folders and JARs that are described in the `CLASSPATH`. This class loader is responsible for loading the application's main class.

If a normal application needs to load a class (such as `java.lang.String`), it will first ask the System class loader for it. The System class loader delegates to the Extension class loader, which in turn delegates to the Bootstrap class loader, which locates the `String.class` file in `rt.jar`, loads the class and makes it available as an instance of `java.lang.Class`.

If an application-specific class file, such as com.swengsol.UserModel.class, is requested, the delegation process works just as before. However, this time the Bootstrap class loader is unable to locate this class in rt.jar. Next, it is the turn of the Extension class loader, and it too is unsuccessful. Finally, the System class loader has a go, and locates the class on its CLASSPATH. This class is then loaded and made available for the JVM to use.

Caching occurs within each class loader, so each must first check its own cache to see if the class was loaded earlier. If a hit is found, then the class is returned right away.

In our previous example, if the application needed to use another String, then the Bootstrap class loader would return its cached instance of the String class.

> **Endorsed Standards Override Mechanism**
>
> Both J2SE 1.4 and 1.5 include a Java API for XML Processing Parser. The classes for this parser are loaded by the Bootstrap class loader, and so take precedence over any parser that you might have installed on your classpath, even if you have a newer version of the parser classes installed.
>
> The Endorsed Standards Override Mechanism lets you place overrides to certain classes (CORBA and JAXP classes) in the JAVA_HOME/lib/endorsed folder. The Bootstrap loader will then load these preferentially over any classes that it might otherwise find. For details on this mechanism, see http://java.sun.com/j2se/1.5.0/docs/guide/standards/.

Some interesting points to note about class loading are as follows:

- A class is considered fully qualified only when it is described in terms of its package name, its class name, and the class loader instance that was used to load that class. In other words, the same class loaded by two different class loaders is treated as two distinct classes. This has implications for the assignment of instances of this class and treatment of static fields or singletons, even within a single JVM.

- Each class loader can only see the class locations that are above it in the hierarchy. For example, a JAR in the Extension folder cannot use a class file on the application's CLASSPATH. This is because the classes in the Extension folder can only see classes that are served up by either the Extension class loader or the Bootstrap class loader.

- When code in a class references another class, the referenced class is loaded using the same class loader that loaded the referencing class, called its *defining class loader*. The defining class loader for a class can be obtained using `Class.getClassLoader()`.

- Every thread has a context class loader that can be accessed using `Thread.currentThread().getContextClassLoader()`. Every time a thread is created, its context class loader is set to that of its creating thread. The class loader for the `main()` thread is the System class loader, which is automatically propagated down to each worker thread, unless you intervene by invoking `Thread.currentThread().setContextClassLoader()`.

Java EE class loading

The Java EE world throws in a bit of a twist into this model.

A servlet container is required to provide a restricted environment for its web applications.

If a servlet were to directly use the System class loader, then it would be able to see every class that was on the class path for the JVM command that was used to start Tomcat. This is potentially a security risk, as a malicious web application (as in a hosting vendor's deployment) may be able to load classes of its sibling web applications.

As a result, each web application must be given its very own class loader, which is placed at the bottom of the tree and preferentially loads classes that are found in the `WEB-INF/classes` and `WEB-INF/lib` folders of the web application directory.

This custom class loader will only delegate to its parent class loader when the class that is being requested is one of the standard Java classes.

When a web application needs any other class, instead of delegating to its parent, this custom class loader will first check within the `WEB-INF\classes` and `WEB-INF\lib` folders.

Only if it is not found there will it delegate to its parent class loader, which will then follow the standard delegating pattern.

Tomcat's additional class loaders

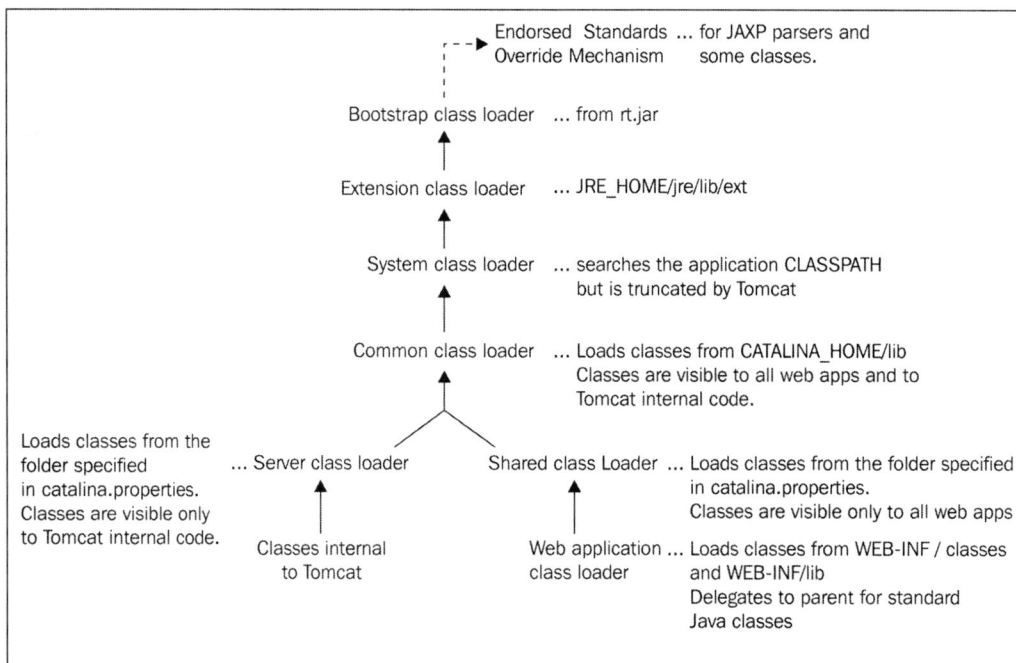

```
                                          Endorsed  Standards ... for JAXP parsers and
                                 - - -►    Override Mechanism     some classes.

                     Bootstrap class loader   ... from rt.jar
                                   ▲
                                   │
                 Extension class loader     ... JRE_HOME/jre/lib/ext
                               ▲
                               │
                     System class loader  ... searches the application CLASSPATH
                                ▲                but is truncated by Tomcat
                                │
                 Common class loader   ... Loads classes from CATALINA_HOME/lib
                              ▲            Classes are visible to all web apps and to
                              │            Tomcat internal code.
 Loads classes from the      │
 folder specified          ╱   ╲
 in catalina.properties.  ... Server class loader    Shared class Loader ... Loads classes from the folder specified
 Classes are visible only    ▲                          ▲                    in catalina.properties.
 to Tomcat internal code.    │                          │                    Classes are visible only to all web apps
                         Classes internal          Web application ... Loads classes from WEB-INF / classes
                           to Tomcat               class loader       and WEB-INF/lib
                                                                      Delegates to parent for standard
                                                                      Java classes
```

During startup, Tomcat first neutralizes the System class loader by clearing out the CLASSPATH and resetting it to point to CATALINA_HOME/bin/bootstrap.jar (for the classes required for Tomcat to start up), tomcat-juli.jar (for logging), and tools.jar (for the JSP compiler). This leaves the System class loader useful only for loading a minimal set of Tomcat-specific classes.

Tomcat also changes the endorsed directory to point to CATALINA_HOME/endorsed.

Below it, Tomcat establishes its own hierarchy of class loaders by appending the Server class loader, the Shared class loader, the Common class loader, and one web application class loader per deployed application.

When a web application needs to load a class, the request first comes to the web application class loader, which is responsible (as described above) for loading the classes in the web application's WEB-INF/classes and WEB-INF/lib folders.

This class loader first delegates to the System class loader to allow the delegation hierarchy to locate any core Java classes. If the requested class cannot be found, then the web application class loader attempts to locate the class within its own repositories. If the class is still not found, it will delegate to the Common class loader, or to the Shared class loader if it is installed.

The Shared class loader and the Server class loader are not instantiated by default. You can enable them by editing the CATALINA_HOME/conf/catalina.properties file and adding the shared.loader and server.loader entries.

The Common class loader monitors the contents of the CATALINA_HOME/lib folder, which contains commonly used JARs such as servlet-api.jar, jasper.jar, coyote.jar, and jsp-api.jar.

Classes that are placed in the Shared loader directory will be available to all web applications, but not to Tomcat's internal classes, whereas classes that are placed in the Server loader directory will be available only to Tomcat's internal classes.

Class reloading in web applications

Having a web application-specific class loader enables Tomcat to support class reloading.

When a context needs to be redeployed or when a class needs to be reloaded (such as when a recompiled class file is copied into WEB-INF\classes), the entire web application class loader is discarded, and a brand new instance is created to load all the classes for this web application.

This new class loader is now used to service all future requests.

> This component is covered in more detail in Chapter 9, *The Context Component.*

Logger

The Logger element in server.xml has been deprecated since Tomcat 5.5. Instead, logging in Tomcat 6 is based on the Java Logging API that was introduced in Java 1.4.

Java Logging could only be configured at the entire JVM level and not at the per class loader level. To allow a different configuration file per web application, Tomcat implemented its own **Java Logging implementation**, known as **JULI** and implemented in CATALINA_HOME/bin/tomcat-juli.jar.

The global `CATALINA_HOME/conf/logging.properties` file controls the debug log settings. In addition, each web application can have its own logging configuration file, `WEB-INF/classes/logging.properties`.

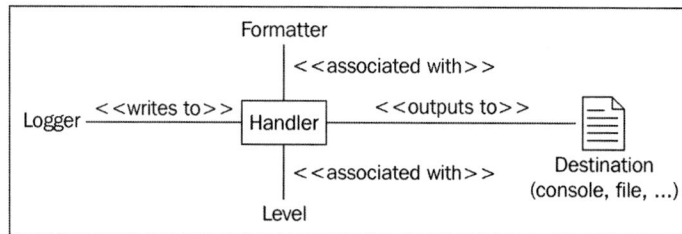

As shown in the image above, logging is comprised of the following components:

- **Logger**: All logging requests are made to Logger objects. These objects are arranged in a hierarchy, rooted at a root logger. This hierarchy mirrors the package hierarchy of classes. Properties can be tied to any level within this hierarchy, and a child Logger inherits properties from its parent.

- **Handler**: It specifies the location where log messages should be sent. Options include a `ConsoleHandler` (which writes to the console), a `FileHandler` (which writes to a file), and a `SocketHandler` (which writes to a TCP socket).

- **Level**: This is one of seven levels, `SEVERE`, `WARNING`, `INFO`, `CONFIG`, `FINE`, `FINER`, `FINEST`, `OFF` (disabled), and `ALL` (all messages logged), that define which message types are logged.

- **Formatter**: This element determines how the information is formatted for display. Tomcat provides both a `SimpleFormatter` and an `XMLFormatter` for this purpose.

Resources

The resources associated with a web application context include static resources such as classes, HTML, JSP, and CSS files. These resources may exist in a variety of storage formats. By default, Tomcat supports retrieval of resources from either a compressed WAR file, or from an exploded folder laid out in the WAR format.

It is conceivable that a context's resources may also be accessed from alternative storage mechanisms, such as a JDBC database. The `Resources` component makes this possible.

Tomcat provides a directory service implementation of the JNDI API, that supports access of resources in a storage-agnostic manner.

> This mechanism is covered in more detail in Chapter 9, *The Context Component*.

Summary

That was a lot to take in, but now that you are done, rest assured that you understand the overall architecture of Tomcat. We looked at some of the core building blocks of Tomcat and saw how a running Tomcat instance was composed of the various Top Level Components, Connectors, and Nested Components. In the next few chapters, we will take the request processing components that were identified in this chapter and examine them in a lot more detail. But before we get there, we have one more stop to make. In the next chapter, we will explore the bootstrapping process for Tomcat.

4
Starting Up Tomcat

In this chapter, we explore the process of starting up a Tomcat server.

In the course of our adventures, we've already seen two different ways of starting up Tomcat. In Chapter 1, we started a new build of Tomcat using the `startup.bat` script after a fresh Ant build of the Tomcat source, and we also started Tomcat from within the Eclipse IDE.

The former is how you will typically start Tomcat in a production environment, whereas the latter lets you start Tomcat in its dissected experimental form.

In this chapter, I'll present a quick overview of the script-based approach before getting down to the business of starting up Tomcat in the usual scenario that is dealt with in this book, where we have it lying cut open in our favorite development environment, and where we get to watch the process unfold before our eyes.

Using scripts

The Tomcat startup scripts are found within your project under the `bin` folder. Each script is available either as a Windows batch file (`.bat`), or as a Unix shell script (`.sh`). The behavior of either variant is very similar, and so I'll focus on their general structure and responsibilities, rather than on any operating system differences. However, it is to be noted that the Unix scripts are often more readable than the Windows batch files.

> In the following text, the specific extension has been omitted, and either `.bat` or `.sh` should be substituted as appropriate. Furthermore, while the Windows file separator '\' has been used, it can be substituted with a '/' as appropriate.

The overall structure of the scripts is as shown—you will most often invoke the
`startup` script.

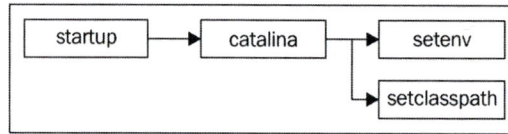

Note that the `shutdown` script has a similar call structure. However, given its
simplicity, it lends itself to fairly easy investigation, and so I leave it as an exercise
for the reader.

Both `startup` and `shutdown` are simple convenience wrappers for invoking the
`catalina` script. For example, invoking `startup.bat` with no command line
arguments calls `catalina.bat` with an argument of `start`. On the other hand,
running `shutdown.bat` calls `catalina.bat` with a command line argument of `stop`.
Any additional command line arguments that you pass to either of these scripts are
passed right along to `catalina.bat`.

The `startup` script has the following three main goals:

- If the CATALINA_HOME environment variable has not been set, it is set to the
  Tomcat installation's root folder. The Unix variant defers this action to the
  `catalina` script.
- It looks for the `catalina` script within the CATALINA_HOME\bin folder.
  The Unix variant looks for it in the same folder as the `startup` script. If the
  `catalina` script cannot be located, we cannot proceed, and the script aborts.
- It invokes the `catalina` script with the command line argument `start`
  followed by any other arguments supplied to the `startup` script.

The `catalina` script is the actual workhorse in this process. Its tasks can be broadly
grouped into two categories. First, it must ensure that all the environment variables
needed for it to function have been set up correctly, and second it must execute the
main class file with the appropriate options.

Setting up the environment

In this step, the catalina script sets the CATALINA_HOME, CATALINA_BASE, and CATALINA_TMPDIR environment variables, sets variables to point to various Java executables, and updates the CLASSPATH variable to limit the repositories scanned by the System class loader.

1. It ensures that the CATALINA_HOME environment variable is set appropriately. This is necessary because catalina can be called independently of the startup script.

2. Next, it calls the setenv script to give you a chance to set any installation-specific environment variables that affect the processing of this script. This includes variables that set the path of your JDK or JRE installation, any Java runtime options that need to be used, and so on. If CATALINA_BASE is set, then the CATALINA_BASE\bin\setenv script is called. Else, the version under CATALINA_HOME is used.

3. If the CATALINA_HOME\bin\setclasspath does not exist, processing aborts. Else, the BASEDIR environment variable is set to CATALINA_HOME and the setclasspath script is invoked. This script performs the following activities:

    a. It verifies that either a JDK or a JRE is available. If both the JAVA_HOME and JRE_HOME environment variables are not set, it aborts processing after warning the user.

    b. If we are running Tomcat in debug mode, that is, if '-debug' has been specified as a command line argument, it verifies that a JDK (and not just a JRE) is available.

    c. If the JAVA_ENDORSED_DIRS environment variable is not set, it is defaulted to BASEDIR\endorsed. This variable is fed to the JVM as the value of the -Djava.endorsed.java.dirs system property.

    d. The CLASSPATH is then truncated to point at just JAVA_HOME\lib\tools.jar. This is a key aspect of the startup process, as it ensures that any CLASSPATH set in your environment is now overridden.

       Note that tools.jar contains the classes needed to compile and run Java programs, and to support tools such as Javadoc and native2ascii. For instance, the class com.sun.tools.javac.main.Main that is found in tools.jar represents the javac compiler. A Java program could dynamically create a Java class file and then compile it using an instance of this compiler class.

e. Finally, variables are set to point to various Java executables, such as java, javaw (identical to java, but without an associated console window), jdb (the Java debugger), and javac (the Java compiler). These are referred to using the _RUNJAVA, _RUNJAVAW, _RUNJDB, and _RUNJAVAC environment variables respectively.

4. The CLASSPATH is updated to also include CATALINA_HOME\bin\bootstrap. jar, which contains the classes that are needed by Tomcat during the startup process. In particular, this includes the org.apache.catalina.startup. Bootstrap class. Note that including bootstrap.jar on the CLASSPATH also automatically includes commons-daemon.jar, tomcat-juli.jar, and tomcat-coyote.jar because the manifest file of bootstrap.jar lists these dependencies in its Class-Path attribute.

5. If the JSSE_HOME environment variable is set, additional *Java Secure Sockets Extension* JARs are also appended to the CLASSPATH.

    Secure Sockets Layer (SSL) is a technology that allows clients and servers to communicate over a secured connection where all data transmissions are encrypted by the sender. SSL also allows clients and servers to determine whether the other party is indeed who they say they are, using certificates. The JSSE API allows Java programs to create and use SSL connections.

    Though this API began life as a standalone extension, the JSSE classes have been integrated into the JDK since Java 1.4.

6. If the CATALINA_BASE variable is not set, it is defaulted to CATALINA_HOME. Similarly, if the Tomcat work directory location, CATALINA_TMPDIR is not specified, then it is set to CATALINA_BASE\temp. Finally, if the file CATALINA_BASE\conf\logging.properties exists, then additional logging related system properties are appended to the JAVA_OPTS environment variable.

> All the CLASSPATH machinations described above have effectively limited the repository locations monitored by the System class loader. This is the class loader responsible for finding classes located on the CLASSPATH.

At this point, our execution environment has largely been validated and configured.

The script notifies the user of the current execution configuration by writing out the paths for CATALINA_BASE, CATALINA_HOME, and the CATALINA_TMPDIR to the console. If we are starting up Tomcat in debug mode, then the JAVA_HOME variable is also written, else the JRE_HOME is emitted instead.

These are the lines that we've grown accustomed to seeing when starting up Tomcat.

```
C:\tomcat\TOMCAT_6_0_20\output\build\bin>startup
Using CATALINA_BASE:   C:\tomcat\TOMCAT_6_0_20\output\build
Using CATALINA_HOME:   C:\tomcat\TOMCAT_6_0_20\output\build
Using CATALINA_TMPDIR: C:\tomcat\TOMCAT_6_0_20\output\build\temp
Using JRE_HOME:        C:\java\jdk1.6.0_14
```

With all this housekeeping done, the script is now ready to actually start the Tomcat instance.

Executing the requested command

This is where the actual action begins. This script can be invoked with the following commands:

- debug [-security], which is used to start Catalina in a debugger
- jpda start, which is used to start Catalina under a JPDA debugger
- run [-security], which is used to start Catalina in the current window
- start [-security], which starts Catalina in a separate window
- stop, which is used to stop Catalina.
- version, which prints the version of Tomcat

> The use of a security manager, as determined by the optional -security argument, is out of scope for this book.

The easiest way to understand this part of catalina.bat is to deconstruct the command line that is executed to start up the Tomcat instance.

This command takes this general form (all in one line):

```
_EXECJAVA
   JAVA_OPTS
   CATALINA_OPTS
   JPDA_OPTS
   DEBUG_OPTS
   -Djava.endorsed.dirs="JAVA_ENDORSED_DIRS"
   -classpath "CLASSPATH"
   -Djava.security.manager
   -Djava.security.policy=="SECURITY_POLICY_FILE"
```

```
-Dcatalina.base="CATALINA_BASE"
-Dcatalina.home="CATALINA_HOME"
-Djava.io.tmpdir="CATALINA_TMPDIR"
MAINCLASS
CMD_LINE_ARGS
ACTION
```

Where:

- `_EXECJAVA` is the executable that should be used to execute our main class. This defaults to the Java application launcher, `_RUNJAVA`. However, if `debug` was supplied as a command-line argument to the script, this is set to `_RUNJDB` instead.

- `MAINCLASS` is set to `org.apache.catalina.startup.Bootstrap`.

- `ACTION` defaults to `start`, but is set to `stop` if the Tomcat instance is being stopped.

- `CMD_LINE_ARGS` are any arguments specified on the command line that follow the arguments that are consumed by `catalina`.

- `SECURITY_POLICY_FILE` defaults to `CATALINA_BASE\conf\catalina.policy`.

- `JAVA_OPTS` and `CATALINA_OPTS` are used to carry arguments, such as maximum heap memory settings or system properties, which are intended for the Java launcher. The difference between the two is that `CATALINA_OPTS` is cleared out when `catalina` is invoked with the `stop` command. In addition, as indicated by its name, the latter is targeted primarily at options for running a Tomcat instance.

- `JPDA_OPTS` sets the **Java Platform Debugger Architecture (JPDA)** options to support remote debugging of this Tomcat instance. The default options are set in the script. It chooses TCP/IP as the protocol used to connect to the debugger (`transport=dt_socket`), marks this JVM as a server application (`server=y`), sets the host and port number on which the server should listen for remote debugging requests (`address=8000`), and requires the application to run until the application encounters a breakpoint (`suspend=n`).

- `DEBUG_OPTS` sets the `-sourcepath` flag when the Java Debugger is used to launch the Tomcat instance.

- The other variables are set as seen in the previous section.

- At this point, control passes to the `main()` method in `Bootstrap.java`. This is where the steps that are unique to script-based startup end. The rest of this chapter follows along with the logic coded into `Bootstrap.java` and `Catalina.java`.

Setting up your project

Our Eclipse Run/Debug configuration, that we set up in Chapter 1, directly invokes the `main()` method on the `org.apache.catalina.startup.Bootstrap` class. As is evident from its name, this class is responsible for starting up and initializing, or bootstrapping, Tomcat. This class exists as a single global singleton instance, there's a single static member named `daemon`, which is instantiated and initialized by the `main()` method. This instance holds references to three class loaders, and to an instance of the `org.apache.catalina.startup.Catalina` class, which serves as the primary means by which all the components that comprise Tomcat are assembled into a running whole.

> The `Catalina` class extends `org.apache.catalina.startup.Embedded`, which you can use directly to embed a running Tomcat instance into any standard Java application that you might write. This class provides a programmatic means to setting up your own Tomcat instance.

The `Bootstrap` and `Catalina` classes that we discuss in this chapter simply provide a convenient means to do the same when running Tomcat in a traditional manner.

Modifying the Run/Debug configuration

In this section, we will modify the project that we setup in Chapter 1 to make it look more like a real world instance. First, ensure that you have built our project using Ant, as described in Chapter 1.

Next, in the debug configuration that was set up to run Tomcat from within Eclipse, set the arguments for the JVM as shown (all in one line):

```
-Dcatalina.home="${project_loc}\output\build"
-Dcatalina.base="${project_loc}\output\build"
```

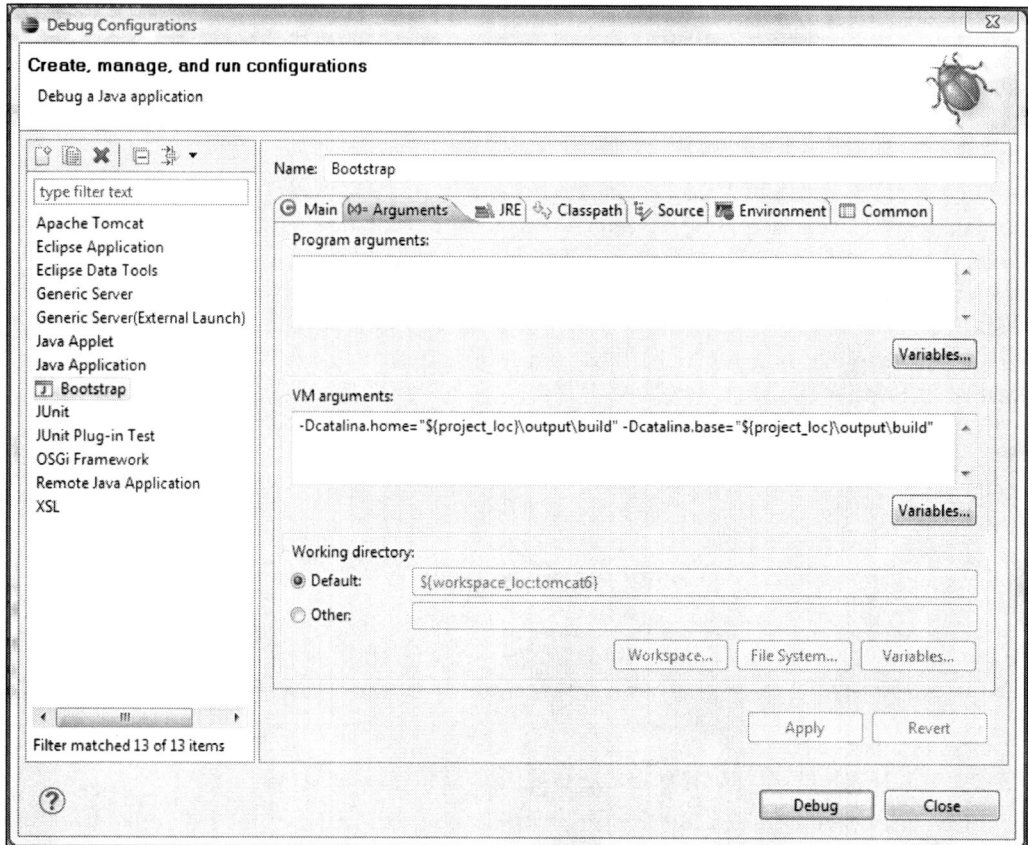

Next, limit your System class loader to only consider the following paths:

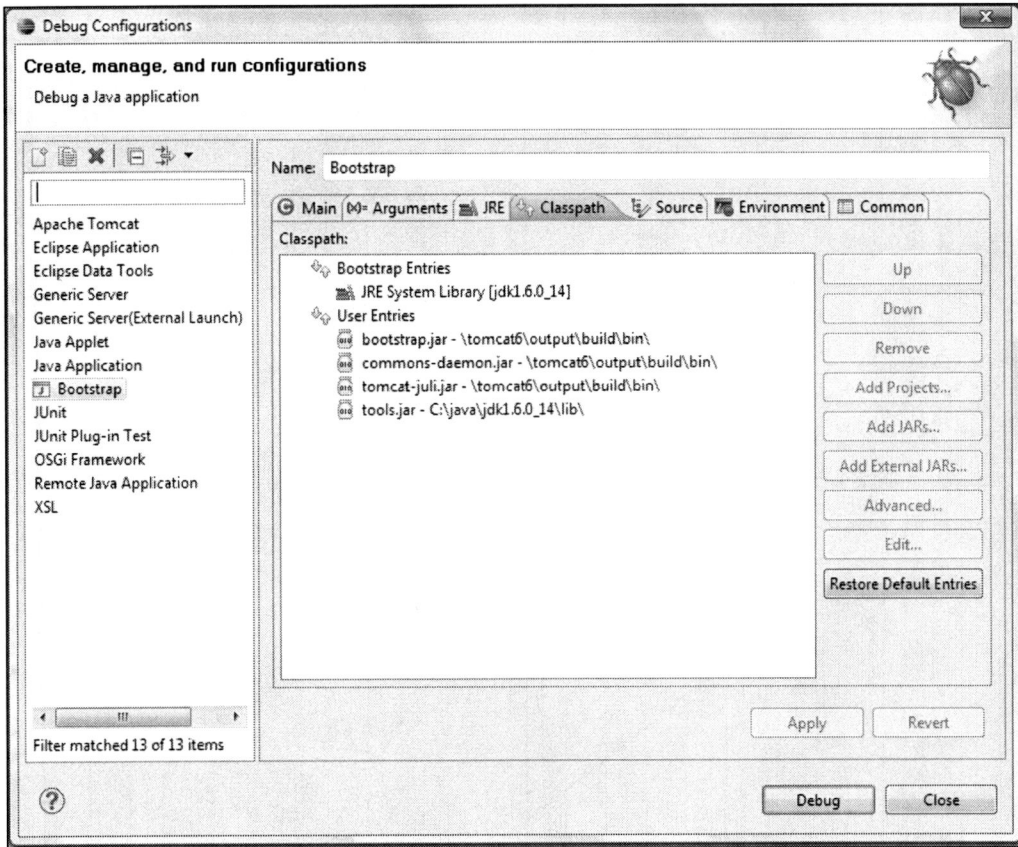

Finally, reattach your project source by setting the **Source** tab as shown:

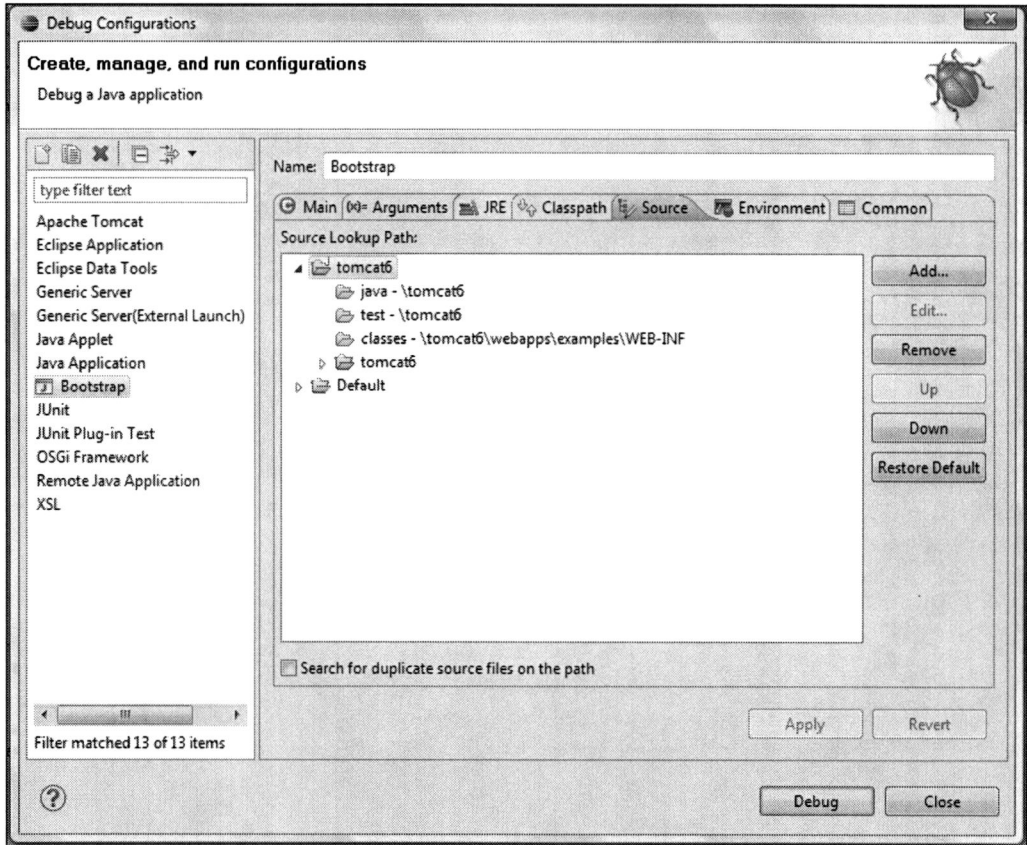

Now, launch your Debug configuration.

What we have done here is to set up a configuration that runs Tomcat in a mode that is as close to a standard deployment as possible. However, you should note that any file that you modify and compile will not automatically make it to the output folder. As a result, rather than doing a standard Eclipse build, you will need to do an Ant build from within Eclipse. This will ensure that the output\build folders are updated with your changes, allowing them to be picked up by this Debug configuration.

> Executing a Run configuration sometimes results in a cryptic message that claims the following:
>
> ```
> Variable references empty selection: ${project_loc}
> ```
>
> The workaround is fairly simple. Before you execute your configuration, ensure that the `tomcat6` project has been selected in the Eclipse browser view.

Bootstrapping Tomcat

The bootstrapping process is actually rather simple. All we have to do is:

- Set up the environment variables required by this Tomcat instance
- Instantiate the general class loaders that will be used for our running Tomcat instance
- Initialize this Tomcat instance
- Parse the main configuration file for a Tomcat instance, `server.xml`, converting each configuration element into the appropriate Tomcat component
- Start up our outermost Top Level Element—the `Server` instance
- Set up a shutdown hook

In this section, we'll explore each aspect of this bootstrap process.

Bootstrapping environment variables

The first step is to set the CATALINA_HOME and CATALINA_BASE environment variables.

As we saw earlier, CATALINA_HOME identifies the location of the Tomcat binaries, whereas CATALINA_BASE sets the root location of a given running Tomcat instance. The reason for keeping these separate is to allow multiple Tomcat instances to be started (with independent configurations), while relying on a single set of binaries.

The `catalina.bat` startup script automatically obtains the values of the CATALINA_BASE and CATALINA_HOME environment variables, and then sets these as system properties for the JVM.

However, when starting the server using a debug configuration, these are empty, unless you have updated the JVM arguments as indicated in the previous section.

If these are uninitialized, Bootstrap determines the catalina.home system property from the user's current directory. It sets catalina.home to the user's current directory, unless the current directory contains a bootstrap.jar file, in which case, it is set to the parent folder of the user's current directory.

Next, if the catalina.base system property is not set, it is simply set to the catalina.home property.

Bootstrapping class loading

Remember that unlike a typical execution scenario, where the System class loader is responsible for loading all the classes found on the classpath, the startup process has neutered our System class loader so that it is able to only locate startup or utility classes.

Instead, the burden of finding Tomcat implementation classes, as well as common libraries that are used across all web applications, is handled by a separate hierarchy of three class loaders that are initialized by the bootstrap process.

Our Bootstrap instance holds references to the following three class loaders:

- commonLoader, which loads classes that are common across Tomcat, as well as all the web applications.
- catalinaLoader, or serverLoader, which loads classes that are used just by Tomcat.
- sharedLoader, which loads classes that are common just across all the web applications within a Tomcat instance.

The sharedLoader is the ideal place to place common JAR files, rather than placing them in the WEB-INF\lib of each web application in a Tomcat instance.

The repositories watched by each of these class loaders are defined in the catalina.properties file that is located in the CATALINA_BASE/conf folder. This file is read in by the org.apache.catalina.startup.CatalinaProperties class, which converts the entries into system properties.

This file has one property key per class loader. The common.loader key defaults to ${catalina_home}/lib, ${catalina_home}/lib/*.jar, whereas the server.loader and shared.loader keys are both left empty. These properties point to repository locations that define the locations from where a class loader will load its classes.

Valid repository locations for a class loader may be:

- A URL location with a known protocol, usually a directory in which `.class` files can be found, such as `${catalina_home}/lib`
- A single JAR file
- A directory that contains JAR files, where the individual JAR files need to be added to the list of repository locations, such as `${catalina_home}/lib/*.jar`

This information is converted by the static `createClassLoader()` method of `org.apache.catalina.startup.ClassLoaderFactory` into a class loader that monitors these repositories. This class loader is an instance of `org.apache.catalina.Loader.StandardClassLoader`.

This method verifies that the specified repositories exist and that they can be accessed. Wildcard-based repository locations are expanded into individual file names. These file paths are converted into URLs with a `file:` protocol (such as `file:/C:/tomcat/TOMCAT_6_0_20/output/build/lib/`).

The `StandardClassLoader` is a subclass of `java.net.URLClassLoader`, and there are no real functional differences between these two classes. The `commonLoader` is created with the System class loader as its parent. The `serverLoader` and `sharedLoader` class loaders are created with the `commonLoader` as their parent.

The `serverLoader` and `sharedLoader` class loaders are not instantiated if the `server.loader` and `shared.loader` properties are empty, respectively, in `catalina.properties`. In this case, both of these loaders are simply set to reference the `commonLoader` itself.

The general class loader model can thus be depicted as follows:

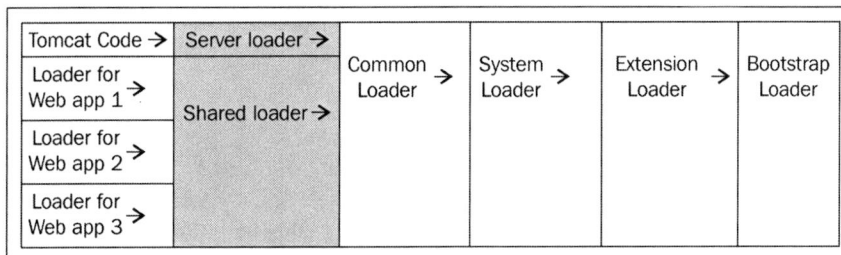

Tomcat Code →	Server loader →				
Loader for Web app 1 →		Common Loader →	System Loader →	Extension Loader →	Bootstrap Loader
Loader for Web app 2 →	Shared loader →				
Loader for Web app 3 →					

The grayed out class loaders indicate that the `serverLoader` and `sharedLoader` loaders are optional. If they are omitted, the Tomcat code as well as the individual web application class loaders directly delegate to the `commonLoader`.

The `serverLoader` (or the `commonLoader`, when there is no `serverLoader` instantiated) is set up as the context class loader for the current thread.

A context class loader is set as a `ThreadLocal` variable in the current thread, and provides a convenient mechanism for the Java EE container to propagate an appropriate class loader that can be used by class loaders higher in the hierarchy to load Tomcat related classes.

> This is done to solve the *class loader inversion problem* that occurs often in the Java EE world. Here, classes from an API (such as the JDBC API) are often loaded by class loaders high up in the delegation hierarchy—such as the Bootstrap loader. Code within such an API class often needs to work with implementation classes (such as a JDBC driver) that are provided by some service provider, and whose names are exposed to the API class either through system properties or configuration files. The problem is that these implementation classes are often not visible to the higher class loader.
>
> When code within the API class must load an implementation class, it simply delegates the task to the context class loader found in the current thread. This context class loader is set by the container to a class loader that can load the Tomcat server's code (either the `serverLoader` or the `commonLoader`). This context class loader is low enough in the hierarchy to be able to see the appropriate implementation classes.

Bootstrapping the embedded container

As we saw earlier, `Bootstrap` is simply a convenience class that is used to run the `Embedded` class, or rather to run `Catalina`, which subclasses `Embedded`. The `Catalina` class is intended to add the ability to process a `server.xml` file to its parent class. It even exposes a `main()` method, so you can invoke it directly with appropriate command-line arguments.

`Bootstrap` uses its newly constructed `serverLoader` to load the `Catalina` class, which is then instantiated.

It delegates the loading process to this `Catalina` instance's `load()` method. This method updates the `catalina.base` and `catalina.home` system properties to absolute references, verifies that the working directory is set appropriately, and initializes the naming system, which is Tomcat's implementation of the JNDI API. We will see more about this in Chapter 5. For now, all we need to note is that it indicates that JNDI is enabled by setting the `catalina.useNaming` system property to true, and prefixing the `Context.URL_PKG_PREFIXES` system property with the package `org.apache.naming` using a colon delimiter.

The `Context.URL_PKG_PREFIXES` property indicates a list of fully qualified package prefixes for URL context factories. Setting `org.apache.naming` as the first entry makes it the first URL context factory implementation that will be located.

For the `java:comp/env` **Environment Naming Context (ENC)**, the actual class name for the URL context factory implementation is generated as `org.apache.naming.java.javaURLContextFactory`. If the `Context.INITIAL_CONTEXT_FACTORY` is currently not set for this environment, then this is set as the default `INITIAL_CONTEXT_FACTORY` to be used.

Bootstrapping the Tomcat component hierarchy

The configuration for a Tomcat instance is found in the `conf\server.xml` file. This file is now processed, converting each element found into a Java object. The net result at the end of this processing is a Java object tree that mirrors this configuration file.

This conversion process is facilitated by the use of the *Apache Commons Digester* project (`http://commons.apache.org/digester/`), an open source `Commons` project that allows you to harness the power of a SAX parser while at the same time avoiding the complexity that comes with event driven parsing.

Commons Digester

The `Digester` project was originally devised as a way of unmarshalling the `struts-config.xml` configuration file for `Struts`, but was moved out to a `Commons` project due to its general purpose usefulness.

The basic principle behind the `Digester` is very simple. It takes an XML document and a `RuleSet` document as inputs, and generates a graph of Java objects that represents the structure that is defined in the XML instance document.

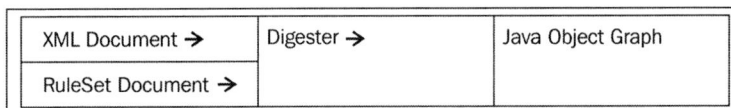

XML Document →	Digester →	Java Object Graph
RuleSet Document →		

There are three key concepts that come into play when using the `Digester` — a pattern, a rule, and an object stack.

The pattern

As the digester parses the input XML instance document, it keeps track of the elements it visits. Each element is identified by its parent's name followed by a forward slash ('/') and then by its name.

For instance, in the example document below, the root element is represented by the pattern rolodex. two <contact> elements are represented by the pattern rolodex/contact, the <company> elements are represented by the pattern rolodex/contact/company, and so on.

```
<rolodex type=paperSales>
  <contact id="1">
    <firstname>Damodar</firstname>
    <lastname>Chetty</lastname>
    <company>Software Engineering Solutions, Inc.</company>
  </contact>
  <contact id="2">
    <firstname>John</firstname>
    <lastname>Smith</lastname>
    <company>Ingenuitix, Inc.</company>
  </contact>
</rolodex>
```

The rule

A rule specifies the action(s) that the Digester should take when a particular pattern is encountered.

The common rules you will encounter are:

- Creational actions (create an instance of a given class to represent this XML element)
- Property setting actions (call setters on the Java object representing this XML element, passing in the value of either a child element or an attribute)
- Method invocation actions (call the specified method on the Java object representing this element, passing in the specified parameters)
- Object linking actions (set an object reference by calling a setter on one object while passing in the other as an argument)

The object stack

As objects are created, using the creational actions discussed above, Digester pushes them to the top of its internal stack. All actions typically affect the object at the top of the stack.

A creational action will automatically pop the element on the top of the stack when the end tag for the pattern is detected.

Using the Digester

The typical sequence of actions is to create an object using a creational action, set its properties using a property setting action, and once the object is fully formed, to pop it off the top of the stack by linking it to its parent, which is usually just below it on the stack. Once the child has been popped off, the parent is once again at the top of the stack. This repeats as additional children objects are created, initialized, linked, and popped. Once all the children are processed and the parent object is fully initialized, the parent itself is popped off the stack, and we are done.

You instantiate an `org.apache.commons.digester.Digester` by invoking the `createDigester()` method of `org.apache.commons.digester.xmlrules.DigesterLoader` and passing it the URL for the file containing the patterns and rules.

Patterns and rules can also be specified programmatically by calling methods directly on the digester instance. However, defining them in a separate XML `RuleSet` instance document is much more modular, as it extracts rule configuration out of program code, making the code more readable and maintainable.

Then, you invoke the `parse()` method of a `Digester` instance and pass it the actual XML instance document. The digester uses its configured rules to convert elements in the instance document into Java objects.

The server.xml Digester

The `Catalina` instance creates a `Digester` to process the `server.xml` file. Every element in this file is converted into an instance of the appropriate class, its properties are set based on configuration information in this file, and connections between the objects are set up, until what you are left with is a functioning framework of classes.

This ability to configure the structure of cooperating classes using a declarative approach makes it easy to customize a Tomcat installation with very little effort.

The `createStartDigester()` method in `Catalina` does the work of instantiating a new `Digester` and registering patterns and rules with it. The `Catalina` instance is then pushed to the top of the `Digester` stack, making it the root ancestor for all the elements parsed from the `server.xml` document.

The rules can be described as follows:

Pattern	Rule
Server	**Creational action:** Instantiates an `org.apache.catalina.core.StandardServer`
	Set properties action: Copies attribute values over to the topmost object of the stack using mutator methods that are named similarly to the attribute
	Object linking action: Invokes `setServer()` to set this newly minted `Server` instance on the `Catalina` instance found on the stack.
Server/ GlobalNamingResources	**Creational action:** Instantiate an `org.apache.catalina.deploy.NamingResources`
	Set properties action: Copies attribute values from this element over to the topmost object on the stack
	Object linking action: Sets this newly instantiated object on the `StandardServer` instance at the top of the stack, by invoking its `setGlobalNamingResources()`.
Server/Listener	**Creational action:** Instantiate the class specified by the fully qualified class name provided as an attribute.
	Set properties action: Copy attributes from this element.
	Object linking action: Sets this instance on the `StandardServer` instance at the top of the stack, by invoking its `addLifecycleListener()` method with this new intance.
Server/Service	**Creational action:** Instantiates an `org.apache.catalina.core.StandardService`.
	Set properties action: Copy attributes from this element
	Object linking action: Invokes `addService()` on the `StandardServer` instance at the top of the stack passing in this newly minted instance
Server/Service/ Listener	**Creational action:** Instantiate the class specified by the fully qualified class name provided as the `className` attribute
	Set properties action: Copy attributes from this element
	Object linking action: Invokes `addLifecycleListener()` on the `StandardService` instance at the top of the stack, passing in this listener instance

Pattern	Rule
Server/Service/ Executor	**Creational action**: Instantiate the class `org.apache.` `catalina.core.StandardThreadExecutor`
	Set properties action: Copy attributes for this element
	Object linking action: Invokes `addExecutor()` with this instance, on the `StandardService` instance at the top of the stack
Server/Service/ Connector	**Creational action**: Instantiate the class `org.apache.` `catalina.startup.ConnectorCreateRule`
	Set properties action: Copy all attributes for this element except for the executor property
	Object linking action: Invokes `addConnector()`, passing in this instance, on the `StandardService` instance at the top of the stack
Server/Service/ Connector/Listener	**Creational action**: Instantiate the class specified by the fully qualified class name provided as the `className` attribute
	Set properties action: Copy attributes from this element
	Object linking action: Invokes `addLifecycleListener()`, passing in this instance, on the `Connector` instance at the top of the stack
Server/Service/Engine	Set the `Engine` instance's parent class loader to the `serverLoader`

In addition to setting rules individually on the digester, you can also define sets of rules, known appropriately as `RuleSets`. The rule sets we add to our digester include a `NamingRuleSet`, `EngineRuleSet`, `HostRuleSet`, and a `ContextRuleSet`.

The `NamingRuleSet` is constructed for the patterns that begin with `Server/GlobalNamingResources/` and which match naming resource elements, such as `Resource`, `ResourceEnvRef`, and `Environment`.

For each pattern matched, we create the appropriate instance of `org.apache.`
`catalina.deploy.Context<patternName>`, for example, `ContextResource`,
`ContextResourceEnvRef`, and `ContextEnvironment`. We then set the instance's
properties from the XML element, and finally we set this instance on the
`GlobalNamingResources` instance using the appropriate `add<patternName>()`
method, such as `addResource()`, `addResourceEnvRef()`, and `addEnvironment()`.

The EngineRuleSet is constructed for patterns that begin with Server/
Service/Engine. It instantiates an org.apache.catalina.core.
StandardEngine to represent an Engine element, sets its properties, and
invokes addLifecycleListener() on the Engine instance to add an org.
apache.catalina.startup.EngineConfig instance as a listener. It also invokes
setContainer() on the Service with this Engine instance to indicate the container
that will handle all requests that come in on all connectors that are associated
with this Service. It also adds other lifecycle listeners that are specified using
the <Listener> element for this Engine and adds any valves specified using the
<Valve> element within this Engine.

The HostRuleSet does the same for virtual hosts. It instantiates an org.apache.
catalina.core.StandardHost to represent each host, and sets its properties from the
element's attributes. By default, it sets an instance of org.apache.catalina.startup.
HostConfig as a lifecycle listener, invokes addChild() on its Engine to register itself
as a child, invokes addAlias() on the host instance with the <Alias> element's body
as an argument, and adds any registered listeners and valves for this host.

The ContextRuleSet works in a similar fashion to process the Context elements for
a given Host. It instantiates a new org.apache.catalina.core.StandardContext,
and sets its properties from the element. It also sets up an org.apache.catalina.
startup.ContextConfig as a lifecycle listener, add invokes the addChild() method
of its Host to add this context instance as a child. A WatchedResource child element
is added to the Context instance using its addWatchedResource() method with the
element's body as an argument. Similarly, any Valve child elements are instantiated
using the class name specified in the element, the properties are set from the element,
and then the Valve instance is added to the context using the addValve() method.
Rules are also defined for child elements that are naming resources, lifecycle
listeners, loaders, session managers, stores, and context parameters.

Parsing the server.xml file

Once the digester is completely set up with all its rules, we are ready to begin.

The conf/server.xml file under catalina.base is located, the current Catalina
instance is set as the top object on the digester's stack, and the digester's parse()
method is invoked to parse the server.xml file using its configured rules.

The digester parses the input stream, constructing objects, setting properties, and
linking objects as it works through the server.xml file.

Normally, the parse() method returns the first object in the stack, all configured with the appropriate relationships. Interestingly, we don't bother with that fully configured object. This is because we have added the Catalina instance as the first object in the stack, and the process of constructing a fully configured Tomcat instance culminates in invoking setServer() on the Catalina instance with that configured Server instance.

Initializing the Server

Next, the newly constructed Server instance is initialized by invoking its initialize() method. This causes initialize() to be invoked on each service. Initialization events are fired before, during, and after the server is initialized to allow server lifecycle listeners to react. Initialization of a service causes its associated connectors to be initialized as well.

The start() method on the Bootstrap instance is invoked as the last step of the bootstrapping process. This method turns around and invokes start() on the Catalina instance. This method has two main purposes. First, it starts up its server instance, by invoking start() on its topmost StandardServer instance, and second, it sets up a shutdown hook.

The Server instance's start() method fires startup notification lifecycle events to notify all listeners that the server is starting up, and then invokes start() on each of its registered services. The services in turn invoke start() on their components, and so on, until the entire server has been started. We will see the specific actions that are taken in these methods in later chapters.

In an ideal world, a server is always shutdown by the receipt of a shutdown command on the port that it monitors. However, the real world is not quite so orderly, and the JVM may be shutdown for other reasons, such as the computer having been shutdown or the process having been killed.

In such cases, you can ask the JVM to notify your program of the shutdown request. You do this by registering a shutdown hook with the Java runtime system.

A **shutdown hook** is a standard Thread that encapsulates cleanup actions that should be taken before the Java runtime exits. All shutdown hooks are called by the runtime when the JVM is shutting down.

Therefore, the last task that we perform is to install a shutdown hook, as implemented by CatalinaShutdownHook. This hook is registered with the Java Runtime by invoking its addShutdownHook() method:

```
Runtime.getRuntime().addShutdownHook()
```

CatalinaShutdownHook is an inner class of Catalina and so has access to all the data members of Catalina. Its run() method is very simple. It just ensures that stop() is called on this instance of Catalina. This method invokes stop() on the StandardServer instance, which in turn performs a cascaded invocation of stop() on all its child components. Each child does the same for its children, until the entire server has been cleanly stopped.

With this, the server is now up and running, and is ready to serve requests.

Adding a new web application to Tomcat in Eclipse

In this section, we'll create a brand new web application, which will be made available at the context path, /devguide. This context can be accessed at the URL http://localhost:8080/devguide. We will add a single servlet to this web application called HelloWorldServlet.java, which will simply print a **Hello World** message when requested.

Our main objectives with this example are to see how we might deploy a new web application context into our Tomcat installation and to have all code (both Tomcat itself as well as our web application) run within the same Eclipse project so that we can debug it by seamlessly stepping through both the Tomcat source as well as your application source.

Let us begin by adding a new directory called devguide under the webapps folder within our project. This folder will hold our new context's resources.

Add the following deployment descriptor as webapps/devguide/WEB-INF/web.xml:

WEB.XML

```xml
<?xml version="1.0" encoding="ISO-8859-1" ?>
<web-app xmlns="http://java.sun.com/xml/ns/javaee"
         xmlns:xsi="http://www.w3.org/2001/XMLSchema-instance"
         xsi:schemaLocation="http://java.sun.com/xml/ns/javaee
            http://java.sun.com/xml/ns/javaee/web-app_2_5.xsd"
         version="2.5">
  <description>Tomcat Developer's Guide</description>
  <display-name>Tomcat Developer's Guide</display-name>
  <servlet>
    <servlet-name>HelloWorld</servlet-name>
    <servlet-class>com.swengsol.HelloWorldServlet</servlet-class>
  </servlet>
  <servlet-mapping>
    <servlet-name>HelloWorld</servlet-name>
    <url-pattern>/HelloWorld</url-pattern>
  </servlet-mapping>
</web-app>
```

This is a fairly minimal deployment descriptor and indicates that we have a single servlet, `com.swengsol.HelloWorldServlet` that we will map to the path `/HelloWorld`.

Our static content consists of the single file, `webapps/devguide/index.html`:

```
<!DOCTYPE HTML PUBLIC "-//W3C//DTD HTML 4.0 Transitional//EN">
<HTML>
  <HEAD>
    <TITLE>Hello World</TITLE>
    <META http-equiv = Content-Type content = "text/html">
  </HEAD>
  <BODY>
    <H3>Tomcat Developer's Guide</H3>
    <ul>
      <li><a href = "HelloWorld">Hello World Example Servlet</a></li>
    </ul>
  </BODY>
</HTML>
```

This file provides a launching point for our `HelloWorld` servlet.

Create a new servlet class, `com.swengsol.HelloWorldServlet.java`, and place it in `webapps/devguide/WEB-INF/classes`:

```
package com.swengsol;
import java.io.IOException;
import java.io.PrintWriter;
import javax.servlet.ServletException;
import javax.servlet.http.HttpServlet;
import javax.servlet.http.HttpServletRequest;
import javax.servlet.http.HttpServletResponse;
public class HelloWorldServlet extends HttpServlet {
  private static final long serialVersionUID = 1L;
  public void doGet(HttpServletRequest request, HttpServletResponse
response)
    throws IOException, ServletException {
      response.setContentType("text/html");
      PrintWriter out = response.getWriter();
      out.println("<html>");
      out.println("<head>");
      String title = "Hello World - Tomcat Developer's Guide";
      out.println("<title>" + title + "</title>");
      out.println("</head>");
      out.println("<body bgcolor = \"white\">");
      out.println("<h1>Hello World from the Developer's Guide!</h1>");
      out.println("</body>");
      out.println("</html>");
    }
}
```

This servlet class extends `HttpServlet` and overrides the `doGet()` method to print out a welcoming message.

Now, add the `webapps/devguide/WEB-INF/classes` as a source folder to the build path. You can do this by right clicking on the folder, picking **Build Path**, and then **Use as Source Folder** from the context menu.

Next, let us add a new context fragment, `webapps/devguide/META-INF/context.xml`, for this web application.

```
<?xml version = "1.0" encoding = "UTF-8"?>
<Context antiResourceLocking = "false" reloadable = "true" privileged
= "false" />
```

With this step, the application is complete.

The final step is to make sure that Ant is aware of this new web application so that it is deployed to the output folders along with the other example applications.

To do this, we edit the project's `build.xml` file (found in the project's root folder) to enhance the `deploy` target to make it aware of our new web application.

The first section that we will edit is the `copy` task, which copies the `webapps\devguide` folder tree out to the `output\build` folder.

```
<!-- Copy other regular webapps -->
<copy todir = "${tomcat.build}/webapps">
  <fileset dir = "webapps">
    <include name = "ROOT/**"/>
    <include name = "examples/**"/>
    <include name = "manager/**"/>
    <include name = "host-manager/**"/>
    <include name = "devguide/**"/>
  </fileset>
</copy>
```

Second, we add a new `javac` task to the same `deploy` target, to compile the servlets that are part of this new web application.

```
<!-- Build classes for devguide webapp -->
<javac srcdir = "webapps/devguide/WEB-INF/classes"
       destdir = "${tomcat.build}/webapps/devguide/WEB-INF/classes"
       debug = "${compile.debug}" deprecation = "${compile.
deprecation}"
       source = "${compile.source}" target = "${compile.target}"
       optimize = "${compile.optimize}" classpath = "${tomcat.
classes}"
       excludes = "**/CVS/**,**/.svn/**">
</javac>
```

These edits to `build.xml` register our new web application as an additional web application that can be potentially distributed along with Tomcat.

All the pieces are in place now, and all that remains is to run an Ant build. Once the build completes, run the usual Debug configuration that we have set up for this project. Experiment by setting breakpoints in your servlet and by editing the servlet class. Any edits that you make will need to be followed by an Ant build for the changes to be picked up.

> As a convenience, you can set up a new Ant builder for your project to automatically start an Ant build whenever a file in the project is changed.

Summary

In this chapter, we looked at how a Tomcat instance can be started using either the standard script-based mechanism or the alternative Run/Debug configuration. We looked at the various class loader hierarchies that are set up during the initialization process. We also looked at how the Apache Commons Digester library provides a convenient way of converting an XML file into a Java object graph. We ended this chapter with an example of a web application that was deployed into our Tomcat instance.

5

The Server and Service Components

In the last chapter, we noted that a `Server` instance is created during the bootstrap process and watched its `initialize()` and `start()` methods being called. However, we glossed over quite a bit of what happens during these invocations.

In this chapter, we'll take a closer look at the `StandardServer` instance and its operations.

The `Server` component is a Top Level Component that has two primary roles:

- It serves as the outermost element of a running Tomcat instance.
- It provides an implementation of the JNDI API, allowing resources and environment variables to be made available to the container's components through configuration.

In this chapter we'll explore both these roles.

As we saw in Chapter 3, a `Server` component can contain one or more `Service` components. Each `Service` component is purely a structural entity, that aggregates one or more `Connector` components with a single `Engine` component. The connectors provide the server end points at which clients may connect, and the engine is the primary request processor within Tomcat.

We consider the `Connector` component in Chapter 6 and the `Engine` component in Chapter 7.

Setting up your project

The topic of JNDI can be quite overwhelming to the uninitiated, and so we begin this chapter with a simple example to properly demonstrate Tomcat's JNDI support. We'll use JNDI to obtain a `javax.sql.DataSource` that can be used to access a database, as well as to obtain an environment variable that is configured into the container.

In order to access a database, we first need a database to access, so our first order of business will be to install some additional software.

Installing MySQL

[![note icon] If you already have MySQL or other database software installed, you can omit this installation step.]

To install the MySQL database server, first download the appropriate binary distribution for your operating system from `http://dev.mysql.com/downloads/mysql/5.1.html#downloads`. The *Essentials* version of MySQL has all the functionality that we will need for this example. For 64-bit Vista, this file is named `mysql-essential-5.1.37-win32.msi`.

Once the installation has completed, run the **MySQL Server Instance Configuration Wizard**, which lets you configure your new MySQL server instance. In the interests of simplicity, we'll pick the **Standard Configuration** option, which skips the scenic route and uses reasonable defaults.

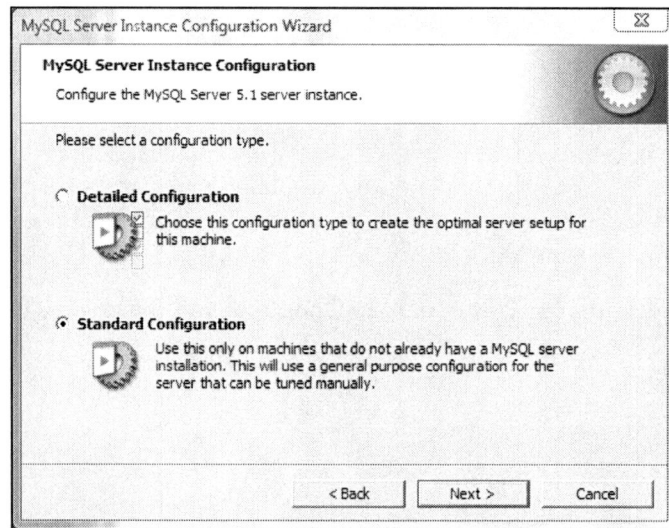

Next, we will install MySQL as a service that launches automatically at startup.

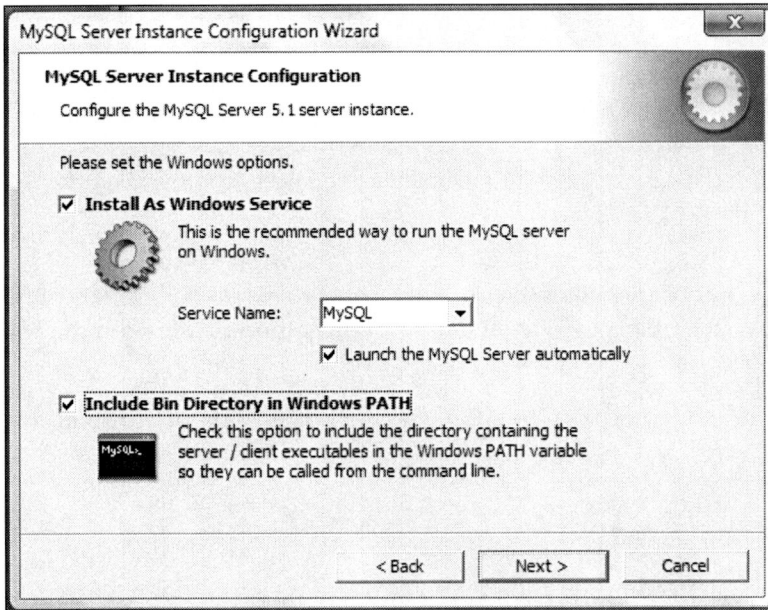

Finally, we pick a password, which I'll just set to **changeme**.

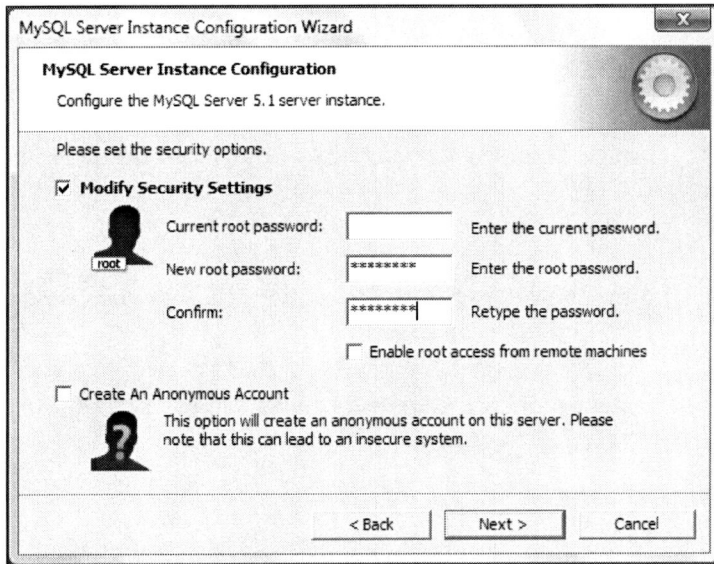

On the final wizard dialog, click the **Execute** button to begin the configuration of your MySQL instance.

> There are a number of excellent resources on MySQL available. I recommend starting with the developer's reference manual that can be found at http://dev.mysql.com/doc/refman/5.1/en/.
>
> Rest assured that I will cover all that you need to know about MySQL for this chapter.

Once MySQL has been installed, you will be able to access a command-line utility, mysql.exe, which opens up a shell that lets you communicate with the MySQL Server Instance.

To start up the command-line client, open up a normal command shell, and enter the command shown:

```
c:> mysql -u root -p
Enter password:
```

As before, you are prompted for a password, and on supplying it correctly, you will be taken to the mysql prompt.

> Alternatively, use the following command:
> ```
> c:>mysql --host=localhost --port=3306 --user=root --password=changeme
> ```

At this prompt, your best friend will soon become the help command. Some ways of invoking this include:

```
mysql> help contents;
```

This command displays the categories of instructions that you can send to the server.

```
mysql> help Data Definition;
```

The *Data Definition* category includes the various ALTER, CREATE, and DROP SQL **Data Definition Language (DDL)** statements.

```
mysql> help Create Database;
```

This command lets you obtain more detailed help on a particular statement, in this case, *Create Database*. The help text also provides you with the URL to the Developer's Reference Manual, at which more detailed information can be found.

Next, we'll create our data structures, beginning with the database instance that we will use in this example:

```
mysql> create database swengsol;
Query OK, 1 row affected (0.01 sec)
```

To verify that things look good, run the following command:

```
mysql> show databases;
+--------------------+
| Database           |
+--------------------+
| information_schema |
| mysql              |
| pim                |
| swengsol           |
+--------------------+
4 rows in set (0.00 sec)
```

Next, let's add a new table called `contacts` into our `swengsol` database.

```
mysql> use swengsol;
Database changed
mysql> create table contacts (
    ->     id bigint not null auto_increment,
    ->     firstName      varchar(35),
    ->     lastName       varchar(35),
    ->     email          varchar(100),
    ->     primary key (id)
    -> );
Query OK, 0 rows affected (0.10 sec)
```

Now, execute the `show tables` command, to verify that the table was created successfully.

```
mysql> show tables;
+--------------------+
| Tables_in_swengsol |
+--------------------+
| contacts           |
+--------------------+
1 row in set (0.00 sec)
```

For more detail, use the `describe` command as shown:

```
mysql> describe contacts;
+-----------+--------------+------+-----+---------+----------------+
| Field     | Type         | Null | Key | Default | Extra          |
+-----------+--------------+------+-----+---------+----------------+
| id        | bigint(20)   | NO   | PRI | NULL    | auto_increment |
| firstName | varchar(35)  | YES  |     | NULL    |                |
| lastName  | varchar(35)  | YES  |     | NULL    |                |
| email     | varchar(100) | YES  |     | NULL    |                |
+-----------+--------------+------+-----+---------+----------------+
4 rows in set (0.01 sec)
```

Finally, we are ready to insert a contact into our table.

```
mysql> insert into contacts
    -> (firstName, lastName, email)
    -> values
    -> (
    -> 'Damodar', 'Chetty', 'dc@swengsol.com'
    -> );
Query OK, 1 row affected (0.06 sec)

mysql> select * from contacts;
+----+-----------+----------+-----------------+
| id | firstName | lastName | email           |
+----+-----------+----------+-----------------+
|  1 | Damodar   | Chetty   | dc@swengsol.com |
+----+-----------+----------+-----------------+
1 row in set (0.00 sec)
```

Go ahead and add a few more records into this table if you feel like it. When you are done, exit the command-line utility using the following command:

```
mysql> quit;
```

That's all you need to know about MySQL.

Installing the MySQL driver

In order to access MySQL from within a Java program, we need the JDBC driver for MySQL, which can be found at `http://dev.mysql.com/downloads/connector/j/5.1.html`. From the downloaded file, extract the driver, which is named `mysql-connector-java-5.1.8-bin.jar`.

The JDBC driver needs to be available to internal Tomcat classes, and so the ideal place for this JAR is in the location monitored by the `common` loader. In the deployment scenario that we set up in the last chapter, this location is the `${tomcat6}\output\build\lib` folder, where `${tomcat6}` is the location of your project file.

The only downside is that this location is cleaned out after each `ant clean` invocation. In order to ensure that it is restored after `ant deploy`, the `build.xml` file would have had to be modified. However, that would be a non-reusable change to the build file, and so we'll take the manual route of copying this file over, after each `ant deploy` build.

> If this JAR were to be placed inside a web application's `WEB-INF\lib` folder, then the JDBC driver class, `com.mysql.jdbc.Driver` would not be available to the Tomcat classes. This is because Tomcat's internal classes can see classes loaded by the `common` loader, but not those served up by the class loaders of individual web applications.

With this, we are now done with the setup steps, and are ready to begin with our example application.

Enhancing the devguide web application

In this section, we will enhance the `devguide` application that we had started in Chapter 4. The star servlet in this chapter is `com.swengsol.ContactListServlet.java`, which prints out the contacts in our database table.

server.xml

Global JNDI resources are resources that are available throughout a given `Server` instance. As a result, it is appropriate for these resources to be defined in the `server.xml` file, within the appropriately named `<GlobalNamingResources>` child of the `<Server>` element.

```
<GlobalNamingResources>
  <Environment name = "contactsCaption" Type = "java.lang.String"
            value = "Contact List -- MySQL"/>
  <Resource name = "jdbc/swengsolDB" auth = "Container"
          type = "javax.sql.DataSource"
          driverClassName = "com.mysql.jdbc.Driver"
          url = "jdbc:mysql://localhost:3306/swengsol"
          username = "root" password = "changeme"
          maxActive = "30" maxIdle = "20000"
          maxWait = "120"/>
</GlobalNamingResources>
```

Here, we have defined a global environment variable, named `contactsCaption`, that is now available for use within any context associated with this server. In addition, we have also defined a resource named `"jdbc/swengsolDB"` which is an instance of `javax.sql.DataSource`. This resource is also configured with parameters that can be used to establish a connection with the external database. In our case, these parameters allow you to connect with our MySQL database server instance.

> The `root` username is used along with the default password, purely for expediency.

Context fragment

We add a new element to our context fragment, `META-INF\context.xml`, as highlighted in the following code snippet:

CONTEXT.XML

```
<?xml version="1.0" encoding="UTF-8"?>
<Context antiResourceLocking = "false" reloadable = "true" privileged
= "false">
    <ResourceLink name = "contactsTableCaption"
                  global = "contactsCaption"
                  type = "java.lang.String"/>
    <ResourceLink name = "jdbc/swengsolDB"
                  global = "jdbc/swengsolDB"
                  type = "javax.sql.DataSource"/>
</Context>
```

The `ResourceLink` element allows a context to express an interest in a global JNDI resource. It makes a global resource available for use within that context.

Web application deployment descriptor

We also modify our `WEB-INF\web.xml` deployment descriptor, as highlighted in the following code snippet:

WEB.XML

```
<?xml version="1.0" encoding="ISO-8859-1"?>
<web-app xmlns="http://java.sun.com/xml/ns/javaee"
         xmlns:xsi="http://www.w3.org/2001/XMLSchema-instance"
         xsi:schemaLocation="http://java.sun.com/xml/ns/javaee
           http://java.sun.com/xml/ns/javaee/web-app_2_5.xsd"
         version="2.5">
    <description>Tomcat Developer's Guide</description>
    <display-name>Tomcat Developer's Guide</display-name>

  <resource-ref>
    <res-ref-name>jdbc/swengsolDB</res-ref-name>
    <res-type>javax.sql.DataSource</res-type>
    <res-auth>Container</res-auth>
  </resource-ref>
```

```
<resource-env-ref>
  <resource-env-ref-name>
    contactsTableCaption
  </resource-env-ref-name>
  <resource-env-ref-type>java.lang.String</resource-env-ref-type>
</resource-env-ref>
  <servlet>
    <servlet-name>HelloWorld</servlet-name>
    <servlet-class>com.swengsol.HelloWorldServlet</servlet-class>
  </servlet>

  <servlet-mapping>
    <servlet-name>HelloWorld</servlet-name>
    <url-pattern>/HelloWorld</url-pattern>
  </servlet-mapping>
  <servlet>
    <servlet-name>ContactList</servlet-name>
    <servlet-class>com.swengsol.ContactListServlet</servlet-class>
  </servlet>

  <servlet-mapping>
    <servlet-name>ContactList</servlet-name>
    <url-pattern>/ContactList</url-pattern>
  </servlet-mapping>
</web-app>
```

The contact list servlet

This servlet retrieves a connection to the MySQL database server and uses it to
execute a simple SELECT statement.

```
package com.swengsol;

import java.io.*;
import java.sql.Connection;
import java.sql.ResultSet;
import java.sql.Statement;

import javax.naming.Context;
import javax.naming.InitialContext;
import javax.servlet.*;
import javax.servlet.http.*;
import javax.sql.DataSource;

public class ContactListServlet extends HttpServlet {
  private static final long serialVersionUID = 1L;
```

```
public void doGet
  (HttpServletRequest request, HttpServletResponse response)
    throws IOException, ServletException {
  response.setContentType("text/html");
  PrintWriter out = response.getWriter();
  out.println("<html>");
  out.println("<head>");
  out.println("<title>" + "Contacts List-MySQL" + "</title>");
  out.println("</head>");
  out.println("<body bgcolor = \"white\">");
  out.println("<a href = \"index.html\">");
  out.println("Return</a>");
  try {
    String caption =
      (String) new InitialContext().
        lookup("java:comp/env/contactsTableCaption");
    out.println("<h1>" + caption  + "</h1>");
    out.println("<p>");

    Context myctx = new InitialContext();
    DataSource myDS = (DataSource)
      myctx.lookup("java:comp/env/jdbc/swengsolDB");
    Connection myConnection = myDS.getConnection();
    myConnection.setAutoCommit(false);
    Statement stmt = myConnection.createStatement();
    ResultSet rs = stmt.executeQuery
      ("SELECT firstname, lastname, email FROM contacts");
    out.println("<table>");
    while (rs.next()) {
      out.println("<tr>");
      String firstname = rs.getString("firstname");
      String lastname = rs.getString("lastname");
      String email = rs.getString("email");
      out.println("<td>" + firstname + "</td> <td>"
        + lastname + "</td><td> " + email + "</td>");
      out.println("</tr>");
    }
    out.println("</table>");
    myConnection.close();
  } catch (Exception e) {
    e.printStackTrace();
  }
  out.println("<p>");
  out.println("</body>");
  out.println("</html>");
  }
}
```

This servlet performs three key operations:

1. It obtains an `InitialContext` and uses it to look up the environment variable as well as the data source.

2. It uses the `DataSource` to obtain an actual connection to the external database server.

3. It uses that connection to execute a query against that server.

Run up this project, and navigate to `http://localhost:8080/devguide/ContactList`. The page displayed will contain the rows that you added to the `contacts` table in the `swengsol` database.

Additional notes

When a web application with a context fragment in the `META-INF` folder is deployed, that context fragment is renamed using the context path and is copied below the `CATALINA_BASE\conf` folder into a folder hierarchy that represents its `Engine` and `Host`. For example, the `META-INF\context.xml` of the `devguide` web application is copied out to `CATALINA_BASE\Catalina\localhost\devguide.xml`.

Unfortunately, when a change is made to the `context.xml` file of `devguide` and the `deploy` target is run, this target does not clean out the `output\build\conf` folder. This causes Tomcat to use the outdated version of `devguide.xml`, rather than deploying the latest version of `META-INF\context.xml`.

To force this to happen, we will edit `build.xml` and change the `build-prepare` target to also delete this folder, as shown in the following code snippet:

```
<!-- Just build Tomcat -->
<target name = "build-prepare">

  <available classname = "junit.framework.TestCase"
    property = "junit.present" />
  <mkdir dir = "${tomcat.classes}"/>

  <delete dir = "${tomcat.build}/temp" />
  <delete dir = "${tomcat.build}/work" />
  <delete dir = "${tomcat.build}/conf" />

  <mkdir dir = "${tomcat.build}"/>
  <mkdir dir = "${tomcat.build}/bin"/>
  <mkdir dir = "${tomcat.build}/conf"/>
  <mkdir dir = "${tomcat.build}/lib"/>
  <mkdir dir = "${tomcat.build}/logs"/>
  <mkdir dir = "${tomcat.build}/temp"/>
  <mkdir dir = "${tomcat.build}/webapps"/>

</target>
```

This example was a whirlwind tour of how an administrator could define resources for a server, and how those resources could then be used within the contexts deployed into that server. We'll now take a step back to look at how the `Server` component implements this JNDI mechanism.

JNDI service

A naming service's primary functions are to provide an application deployer or assembler with a mechanism to set up a mapping (known as a **binding**) of an object to a logical name, and to provide a mechanism by which an application component, such as a servlet, may retrieve an object by presenting the naming service with the object's logical name.

The objects registered with a naming service include environment variables, application components (such as EJBs), and resources (such as a factory object that constructs connections to an external resource, or even a plain old Java object.)

At runtime, an application component, such as a servlet, would use JNDI to ask its container to resolve these logical references to the environment variables, components, or resources, that it needs.

> A web application is required to publish its dependencies by registering these logical references in its web.xml deployment descriptor. It is up to the application deployer to ensure that all of these dependencies can be resolved at runtime.

This has a couple of beneficial effects:

- Instead of directly instantiating these resources in application code, components such as servlets instead contain logical references to these objects. This removes any hardcoded resource references from the web application components, and moves these to configuration files instead. This allows a resource to be reconfigured at runtime, simply by changing the binding for a logical name, without requiring any changes to the component's code.

- The fact that a component may no longer directly instantiate a resource, and instead must go through the container, allows the container to:
    - Influence the resource's life cycle (for example, by supporting the pooling of limited resources)

- ° Interpose itself into method calls by the component (say, to support transactions)
- ° Make decisions about how components should access one another in the interest of efficiency

Basic JNDI concepts

Before we go any deeper, let us discuss some of the foundational concepts of the Java Naming and Directory Interface.

Context

A JNDI context is a named set of bindings, where each binding maps a logical reference to an instance of some object. A JNDI context serves as a namespace for the logical references, and each logical reference must be unique within its JNDI context.

Additionally, JNDI contexts can be arranged in a hierarchical structure, using child JNDI context nodes known as **subcontexts**.

Each JNDI context (or subcontext) has methods to look up names from its set of bindings, and to manage its contained bindings as well as any children subcontexts.

These nodes bear a passing resemblance to a file system, where named folders organize related files and exist in a hierarchical tree. However, this analogy can only be taken so far, as a JNDI context is nothing like a folder, either in form or function. For instance, each JNDI context is pretty much standalone, and cannot be queried for its parent.

> A JNDI Context is an implementation of `javax.naming.Context`, and is not the same as a Tomcat web application context component. In this text, I will refer to the former as 'JNDI contexts'.

InitialContext

All access to the naming service is required to be relative to some JNDI context. In order to look up any object within the service, you are required to establish a JNDI context from where the look up will proceed. This initial context is appropriately termed the `InitialContext`.

The InitialContext is a special JNDI context in that it is usually used to set the root of the JNDI hierarchy, as well as to encapsulate the process of connecting to the container's JNDI service. As a result, instantiating an InitialContext is a prerequisite to using the JNDI API in your application.

Your InitialContext determines the subset of the JNDI context tree that you can navigate around. As you traverse the JNDI context hierarchy, your current context will change to reflect your position within the hierarchy. You may only navigate to a subcontext that is some descendant of the initially established InitialContext.

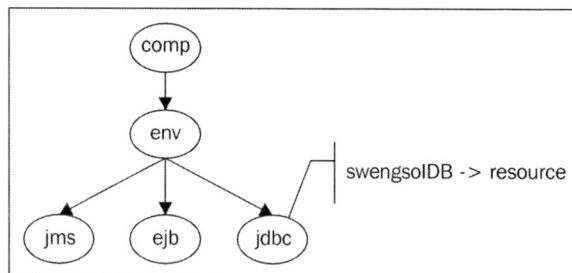

In this image, if you establish your InitialContext at the jdbc Context, you will not be able to access any of the other contexts or their bindings. However, you would be able to look up the swengsolDB binding that is associated with your current context.

On the other hand, if your InitialContext was established at the env context, then you would be able to access any of its subcontexts, as well as their associated bindings.

It is important to note that there is no absolute root in the JNDI hierarchy. This root happens to be whatever JNDI context that you start out with as your InitialContext.

Environment naming context

According to the Java EE and servlet specifications, the naming service should support the referencing of elements in the JNDI context tree with URLs that use the java: scheme. In addition, the topmost JNDI context (a child of the root) is named comp, and it in turn contains the subcontext env. All application-specific subcontexts and bindings are required to appear below this in the JNDI context hierarchy.

The comp JNDI context is reserved for resources that are tied to application *components*. The presence of this JNDI context allows for the possibility that additional sibling subcontexts may be added to the naming service's root in the future to store other types of resources.

In turn, the `env` subcontext holds the bindings that an application component expects to find in its container's *environment*.

It is possible for all your application's resources to reside directly within the `env` subcontext. However, it is strongly recommended that you place them within further subcontexts of `env` in order to organize your resources by type. For example, create a subcontext `ejb` to hold EJB components, a `jdbc` subcontext for JDBC `DataSource` references, a `jms` subcontext for JMS connection factories, a `mail` subcontext for `JavaMail` connection factories, a `url` subcontext for URL connection factories, and so on.

This `java:comp/env` JNDI context hierarchy is termed the **Environment Naming Context (ENC)** in the Java EE specification. As everything of interest to the application is below this context in the JNDI tree, you will often start with your `InitialContext` set at the ENC.

JNDI URLs

When working with JNDI, you will reference contexts and bindings using either absolute or relative URLs.

- An absolute URL begins with the scheme, `java`, starts at the root JNDI context, `comp`, and enumerates all the intermediate subcontexts in the hierarchy (if any) up until the leaf JNDI context or binding. For example, in the sample application, the absolute URL `java:comp/env/jdbc/swengsolDB` refers to the resource named `swengsolDB`.

- A relative URL starts at the current JNDI context and lists all the intermediate subcontexts in the hierarchy (if any) until the leaf JNDI context or binding is identified. For example, if the current JNDI context is `java:comp/env`, then the relative URL `jdbc/swengsolDB` would refer to the same resource as our earlier absolute URL. However, if the current context were `java:comp/env/jdbc`, then the equivalent relative URL would simply be `swengsolDB`.

Initializing an InitialContext

Instantiating an `InitialContext` establishes a connection to the JNDI service and provides you with a JNDI context that you can now query or manipulate.

To instantiate an `InitialContext`, you need to provide details about the service provider's implementation. This includes the fully qualified name of the factory class that will create the initial context, as well as the location of the JNDI service on the network, which is specified as a complete URL with protocol, host name, and port.

You can supply this information either to the constructor of an `InitialContext` through its `Hashtable` parameter, or you can specify it implicitly in the environment and use the default constructor. The latter approach is by far the easiest and most reusable way of obtaining an `InitialContext`.

```
Context context = new InitialContext();
```

The default constructor relies on the deployer making connection details available declaratively, either as system parameters supplied to the Java interpreter using the –D command line option, or through a properties file (such as `jndi.properties`) located either on the application's classpath or in `JAVA_HOME/lib`.

The names of these properties are defined as constants in the `javax.naming.Context` interface. For example, the fully qualified class name of the factory class that will create an initial context, is specified using the system property named `java.naming.factory.initial`, and the URL at which the naming service is available is specified using the `java.naming.provider.url` system property.

By moving these environmental specifics into configuration and out of the application code, we make programs easier to write and systems easier to maintain.

Looking up names

In our earlier example, a JDBC `DataSource`, `swengsolDB`, was bound to the `java:comp/env/jdbc` subcontext. A servlet needing to look up this resource would first instantiate an initial context as shown:

```
Context context = new InitialContext();
```

It would then look up the logical binding by specifying an absolute URL string.

```
DataSource jdbcDS = (DataSource)context.lookup("java:/comp/env/jdbc/
swengsolDB");
```

Alternatively, it might first set its working context to the ENC, and then specify a relative reference as shown:

```
Context myCtx = context.lookup("java:/comp/env");
DataSource jdbcDS = (DataSource) myCtx.lookup("jdbc/swengsolDB");
```

Using multiple naming implementations

When a relative URL is used, the scheme is assumed to be that associated with the current JNDI context. In other words, the factory specified in the `java.naming.factory.initial` system property determines the naming service within which the requested operation will be performed.

As a result, if this property is set to some provider implementation, then the default `InitialContext` will always look up the binding for a name only within that default naming service.

In such a case, how would you access a different naming service within an application?

The answer is simple — you use an absolute URL instead.

Using an absolute URL string causes JNDI to locate a URL Context Factory implementation appropriate for the requested scheme. In this case, you can perform naming operations, such as lookups or binds, within any namespace for which an implementation is available.

As long as you specify an absolute URL, you can use the very same `InitialContext` to look up names in a CORBA namespace, within the container's naming service implementation, or within some other naming service.

URL context factory lookup implementation details

The methods of a JNDI context take either a `String` or a `javax.naming.Name` instance. In either case, this is the logical name of the object that is stored in the naming service, and the method uses it to locate the appropriate binding. If a relative URL is being used, it uses the `java.naming.factory.initial` system property which is set to the fully qualified name of the class that implements the `InitialContext` for a given JNDI service provider.

However, when the `InitialContext` receives a naming service request with an absolute URL string as a logical name argument, it ignores this property, and instead looks for the implementation for that URL scheme.

Instead, the absolute URL is handed off to the URL context factory that is defined for the scheme associated with that absolute URL. That factory is then responsible for returning an `InitialContext` implementation.

The URL context factory to be used to instantiate the `InitialContext` is determined using the name of the URL's scheme, as well as the colon-separated list of package prefixes defined in the `java.naming.factory.url.pkgs` system property. This property lists the packages that may contain this scheme's context factory implementation as a list of fully qualified package name prefixes, delimited by colons. This property takes the form `package_prefix1:package_prefix2:com.sun.jndi.url`, where the final `com.sun.jndi.url` package name is implicitly included. In addition, during startup the `org.apache.naming` package is added to this property.

For each package name in this property, the fully qualified URL context factory implementation class name is generated as `[package_prefix].[scheme].[scheme]URLContextFactory`. For instance, the actual URL context factory implementation class for the `java:` scheme in Tomcat is `org.apache.naming.java.javaURLContextFactory`.

For a given scheme, an attempt is made to instantiate each class name generated by this process, and to invoke its `getObjectInstance()` method to retrieve a context for that scheme's implementation. The first valid non-null JNDI context that is returned is then used to carry out the originally intended naming service method, using the URL string as the name argument.

If none of the discovered URL context factories returns a valid JNDI `Context`, then the `java.naming.factory.initial` system property is consulted to determine the `InitialContext` implementation, which is then instantiated, and is passed the input URL string.

References

Even a physical entity such as a printer can be bound into a naming service, by first converting it into a logical representation, a `javax.naming.Reference`, which is then bound to the naming service. You would use the reference to establish contact with the physical device, and then query it for any additional information that you need.

A logical reference for a printer device could include information on how you might access that printer, such as its IP address and printing protocol.

The conversion between a logical reference and an object that represents the physical device is done using factories configured into the naming service itself. This makes the whole process transparent to the application program.

A state factory converts a physical object reference into a logical reference that is suitable for binding into a naming service. The service provider's JNDI context implementation will use the state factory for that physical object to transform the physical object into a more compact object, the `Reference` that can then be stored in the naming service. The `NamingManager.getStateToBind()` loads in state factories and then invokes the `getStateToBind()` method on each `StateFactory` until one produces a non-null answer. If a factory cannot create an object using the arguments that are supplied, it should return null. A factory that is the only intended factory for a particular object can throw an exception to abort the process.

An object factory performs the reverse operation of converting a bound logical reference into a reference to the physical object.

JNDI resources

We're almost done with the coverage of general JNDI concepts. We just have one final stop to view the terminology that you will encounter often when dealing with resources that are made available through a naming service.

A **resource** is the external software system or component being accessed, such as a relational database or a messaging destination. A *resource* therefore is not part of the Java EE container, and often runs on a separate machine.

A **resource manager** is the software that manages an external *resource*. For example, it is the database server software, a `JavaMail` implementation, or even a messaging service. Like the *resource* that it manages, a *resource manager* is also not part of the Java EE container, and often runs on a separate machine.

A **resource adapter** is the driver that is used by application components and containers to connect to an external *resource*. For example, a JDBC driver is used to access a relational database.

A **factory** is an object that implements the **Factory** Gang of Four pattern and is used to create other objects. It encapsulates the instantiation of the object, and replaces the function of the constructor. A *factory* need not always instantiate a new object, and could instead return an object from its cache.

A **connection** object represents an active *connection* to an external *resource*, such as a relational database. It encapsulates the authentication credentials required to establish communication with, as well as the mechanisms to interact with, an external *resource*.

A **resource manager connection factory (RMCF)** class is provided by the container, and is used as a *factory* to create *connection* objects that allow an application component to access a *resource manager*. The objects returned by this factory are termed **managed resources**. For example, an object that implements `javax.sql.DataSource` is a RMCF for instances of `java.sql.Connection` that represent connections to database management systems. Similarly, an object that implements `javax.mail.Session` is a RMCF for `JavaMail` API connections. The use of the Factory design pattern, allows the container to support pooling of connections, automatic enlistment of the connection with a transaction, and other optimizations.

A **resource manager connection factory reference** is a logical JNDI name that an application deployer binds to the actual *resource manager connection factory* as implemented by a container.

A **managed resource** is a software component which a Java EE container chooses to manage in terms of how it is instantiated, how it is shared among application components, and how it participates in a transaction. This is particularly true for resources that are expensive to create and remove, such as database *connections*. It is not a scalable proposition to expect that every request for a *connection* will result in a new *connection* being instantiated. In particular, an external *Resource Manager* will often limit the number of *connections* that may be open at a given time. Therefore, Java EE containers and application servers support connection pooling to allow *connections* to be shared across various clients.

Managed resources are typically acquired through a *Resource Manager Connection Factory*. For instance, each time an application component needs a database connection, it will request the container's RMCF for it. Once an application component is done with its connection, it should call `Connection.close()` to enable the container to return the connection to the pool.

A *managed resource* may also be a plain old `JavaBean` object that is instantiated by the container and made available to application components through a logical reference.

Using JNDI

There are three sets of responsibilities that come into play when you need to set up and use JNDI in your web application. There are tasks for the component's developer, for the application's assembler/deployer, and for the Java EE container.

Component developer responsibilities

A web component developer is responsible for coding all application components to use logical references, rather than directly instantiating the required resources. In addition, the developer must advertise all these logical references in the application's deployment descriptor, `web.xml`.

Using JNDI within a web application component

In servlet code, you can look up a JNDI resource using code that looks like this:

```
Context myCtx = (Context) new InitialContext().
                lookup("java:comp/env");
Integer maxDiscount = (Integer)myCtx.lookup("maxDiscountPercent")
if ( discountPercent < maxDiscount.intValue() ) {
  // do something
}
```

Or:

```
Context initCtx = new InitialContext();
DataSource ds = (DataSource)initCtx.
                lookup("java:comp/env/jdbc/swengolDB");
Connection connection = ds.getConnection();
// access the database and close the connection
```

Individual application components such as servlets no longer need to have resource references hardcoded into them. Instead, the component can ask the JNDI service for that resource. The most common operation that a client will use to interact with a JNDI context is `lookup()` which will return the object associated with a given name.

In the first case, we've looked up an environment variable named `maxDiscountPercent` that was stored directly in the ENC—`java:comp/env`.

In the second, we looked up a Resource Manager Connection Factory using a RMCF Reference named `swengsolDB` that was bound to the `java:comp/env/jdbc` context.

When a component needs a connection to a resource, it will do the following:

- Pass the logical RMCF Reference to JNDI to look up the RMCF object that the deployer had bound to this logical name in the container environment.

- Invoke the appropriate factory method on the returned factory to obtain a connection to the resource.

Publishing logical references

The logical references used by an application component should be published in the application's deployment descriptor. This makes the application assembler and deployer aware of the environmental resources needed by an application.

A developer publishes dependencies using `web.xml` elements such as `<resource-ref>`, `<resource-env-ref>`, and `<env-entry>`. In this section we will only focus on the most commonly used resource types.

\<resource-ref\>

This element is used to publish *Resource Manager Connection Factory References,* and denotes a logical *reference* to a *factory* that returns a *connection* to an external *resource,* rather than returning the target *resource* itself. This element has the following child elements:

- \<res-ref-name\>: This is the logical name (the *reference*) by which an application component will look up the *resource manager connection factory.* The ENC name is implicit, and does not need to be specified. In other words, instead of java:comp/env/jdbc/myDS, you use jdbc/myDS.

- \<res-type\>: This is the type of the *factory* itself and not of the type of *connection* that this factory will produce. Only the following types are allowed — javax.sql.DataSource, javax.jms.QueueConnectionFactory, javax.net.URL, javax.mail.Session, and javax.jms. TopicConnectionFactory. In our example, we used the javax.sql. DataSource type to obtain an RMCF for JDBC Connection instances.

- \<res-auth\>: If the process of obtaining a connection to a resource involves authentication of the user, this process may be handled either by the application component itself, or by the container acting on behalf of the component. The former case is indicated by setting this element to Application and having the application component pass the authentication credentials via additional method parameters, while for the latter this element is set to Container which automatically presents credentials configured as its parameters by a deployer. Having the container handle authentication is easier since authentication can now be managed via configuration rather than using hard coded logic within applications.

- \<res-sharing-scope\>: By default, other application components that use the same resource (say, a database) in the same transaction context can share a connection. In general, this is a good idea and allows the container to optimize accesses to a resource, and so it should be set to Shareable. However, connections that are session based or stateful should not be shared, to minimize interference by other components. In such cases, set this to Unshareable.

A deployment descriptor could therefore specify a resource as follows:

```
<resource-ref>
  <res-ref-name>jdbc/swengsolDB</res-ref-name>
  <res-type>javax.sql.DataSource</res-type>
  <res-auth>Container</res-auth>
</resource-ref>
```

<resource-env-ref>

This element is used to publish a reference to an actual resource that is found within the container such as a plain JavaBean object or a JMS Queue. This element has the following children:

- `<resource-env-ref-name>`: This is a logical name that resolves to the resource.

- `<resource-env-ref-type>`: This is the type of the resource that is referenced by this logical name. It is the actual resource's type, not that of a factory that generates these resources.

A deployment descriptor would specify a resource such as a JavaBean object that you create, as follows:

```
<resource-env-ref>
  <description>My custom JavaBean</description>
  <resource-env-ref-name>bean/myBean</resource-env-ref-name>
  <resource-env-ref-type>com.swengsol.MyBean</resource-env-ref-type>
</resource-env-ref>
```

<env-entry>

This element is used to override an environment variable that is marked as overrideable by the deployer. It takes the following child elements:

- `<description>`: A descriptive entry

- `<env-entry-name>`: The name of the environment variable relative to the ENC

- `<env-entry-type>`: The type of the variable, which is either a standard Java wrapper type (Byte, Boolean, Character, Integer, Short, Long, Float, Double) or a String

- `<env-entry-value>`: The value associated with this environment variable

An example entry would look as shown:

```
<env-entry>
  <description>Max discount allowed on an order.</description>
  <env-entry-name>maxDiscountPercent</env-entry-name>
  <env-entry-type>java.lang.Integer</env-entry-type>
  <env-entry-value>30</env-entry-value>
</env-entry>
```

Application deployer responsibilities

An application deployer must walk through each web application's deployment descriptor looking for all references to resources, components, and environment variables.

The deployer must first determine the level at which the resource should be defined, either globally at the Server level or more narrowly at the Context level. Next, the deployer defines the resource and binds it to the appropriate logical reference used by the application component.

Resource definition levels

Resources available to application components may be defined at one of the following two levels:

- **Server level**: A resource that is defined at this level is available globally throughout the server. In other words, it is visible within every service (and its contained engine, hosts, and contexts) defined for this server. Resources are defined at the server level using the `<GlobalNamingResources>` element in `server.xml`. Contexts that wish to use these resources must first declare an interest through `<ResourceLink>` elements.
- **Context level**: Resources defined in a `<Context>` element are available only within that specific web application.

Binding logical references

In this step, the deployer must actually bind the logical reference found in the deployment descriptor to an actual resource within the container.

<Environment>

This element creates environment variables.

```
<Environment name = "maxDiscount" type = "java.lang.Integer"
             value = "30" />
```

This element takes the JNDI `name`, the data type of this variable, and its `value`. If its `override` attribute is true, then a web application may override this value in its web deployment descriptor.

<Resource>

The deployer must bind each Resource Manager Connection Factory Reference to an actual connection factory implementation that is provided by the container. The implementation must be compatible with the type that is declared in the `<res-type>` element of the web application deployment descriptor.

The deployer must provide any configuration information that the resource manager needs, such as the URL of the server where the resource manager is located.

If the `<res-auth>` element in the web application's deployment descriptor is set to `Container`, then the deployer must also provide the information required for the `Container` to authenticate with the resource manager, such as the user name and password.

```
<Resource name = "jdbc/swengsolDB" type = "javax.sql.DataSource"
        auth = "Container" username = "myname"
        password = "mypass"
        driverClassName = "com.mysql.jdbc.Driver"
        url = "jdbc:mysql://localhost:3306/mydb?autoReconnect=true"/>
```

This element defines a connection factory of type `javax.sql.DataSource` and binds it to the logical name `jdbc/swengsolDB`. It configures it for `Container` authentication, by providing authentication credentials. It also supplies the fully qualified class name of the JDBC driver, as well as the URL on which the database server is running.

The `javax.sql.DataSource` implementation in Tomcat is `org.apache.tomcat. dbcp.BasicDataSourceFactory`.

Tomcat uses the `Jakarta Commons Database Connection Pool` mechanism—so database connections can be recycled.

This element can also be used to bind logical resource references to actual resources within the container—to satisfy the dependency published using `<resource-env-ref>` elements.

```
<Resource name = "bean/myBean" type = "com.swengsol.MyBean"
        auth = "Container" description = "My Managed Bean"
        factory = "org.apache.naming.factory.BeanFactory" />
```

<ResourceLink>

This element is used with a `Context` container to reference a previously defined global resource (in the `<GlobalNamingResources>` element) and links the global name to a local name. The local name then acts as an alias and can be used by the web application to request this resource through JNDI.

```
<ResourceLink name = "bean/localBean" global = "bean/myBean"
            type = "com.swengsol.MyBean"/>
```

StandardServer

The default implementation of the `org.apache.catalina.Server` interface is `org.apache.catalina.core.StandardServer`. This is the implementation that you get if your `server.xml` does not specify a different class through the `className` attribute of the `<Server>` element.

The primary responsibilities of a `Server` are to act as a container for one or more `Service` instances and to open a server socket on a port on which to listen for a shutdown command. This port number and the shutdown command are specified using the `port` and `shutdown` attributes of the `<Server>` element respectively.

Its `initialize()` and `start()` methods are called during the startup process that is kicked off by the `Bootstrap` class's `main()` method. These methods simply call the similarly named methods on each `Service` instance that is contained by this `Server`. The `start()` method also notifies its listeners at various points in the startup process.

Its `stop()` method should be the last method called on a `Server` instance and is just as simple as `start()`. Its main responsibility is to notify listeners and to loop through its `Service` instances, calling `stop()` on each service.

Lifecycle

Every major Tomcat component, including the `Server` component, implements the `org.apache.catalina.Lifecycle` interface.

This interface is an application of the **Observer** design pattern (Gang of Four) that allows multiple observers to be notified of interesting events in the life of a given subject.

This interface defines static String constants that identify the following common lifecycle events: INIT_EVENT, BEFORE_START_EVENT, START_EVENT, AFTER_START_EVENT, BEFORE_STOP_EVENT, STOP_EVENT, AFTER_STOP_EVENT, DESTROY_EVENT, and PERIODIC_EVENT. We will examine these events in more detail as we progress through this book.

It also declares methods that manage listeners that wish to be notified when the component is at the appropriate lifecycle stage.

```
public void addLifecycleListener(LifecycleListener listener);
public LifecycleListener[] findLifecycleListeners();
public void removeLifecycleListener(LifecycleListener listener);
```

An interested listener is required to implement `org.apache.catalina.LifecycleListener`, which only defines a single method:

```
public void lifecycleEvent(LifecycleEvent event);
```

The `org.apache.catalina.LifecycleEvent` class contains the component that raised the event (as an instance of `Lifecycle`), the type of event being fired (for example, `START_EVENT`) as well additional information deemed necessary for the listener.

In order to make it convenient for a component to implement this interface, the helper class `org.apache.catalina.util.LifecycleSupport` is provided. This class maintains references to the subject component, as well to the interested observing `LifecycleListener` instances. It implements the listener management methods of the `Lifecycle` interface, and also throws in a `fireLifecycleEvent()` method that is invoked by the subject component when it wishes to notify all its listeners about an event.

A secondary benefit is that the `Lifecycle` interface also provides a consistent way for a parent component to start and stop its child component.

```
public void start() throws LifecycleException;
public void stop() throws LifecycleException;
```

Shutdown

The `await()` method of `StandardServer` opens a `ServerSocket` listening on the localhost port 8005. This is done for security purposes to ensure that the server can be shut down only from the local server.

It waits in a continuous loop for an incoming connection on this port. When a socket connection is detected, it reads the socket's input stream and if the incoming string matches the `shutdown` attribute configured in the `<Server>` element, the socket is closed, and the server exits.

JNDI implementation

We have already seen how JNDI is configured within the Tomcat container. Now it's time for us to look at how JNDI is implemented by the Tomcat container.

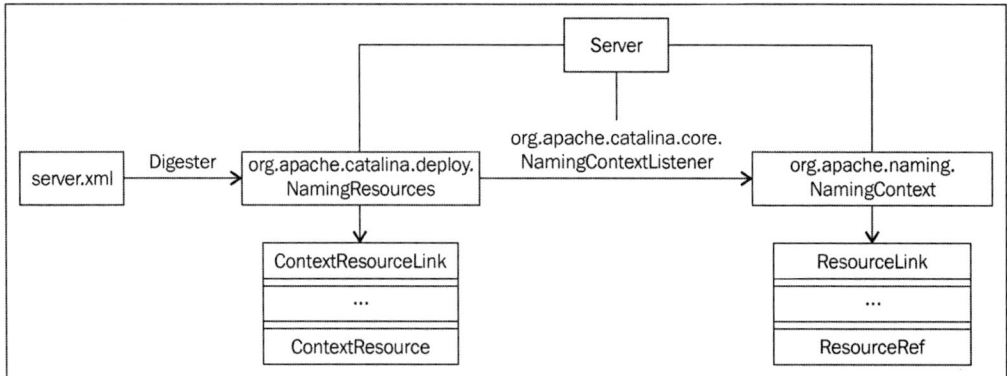

To recap our discussion from Chapter 4, the `Digester` is populated with rules that can process JNDI resource definitions that reside in the `<GlobalNamingResources>` element for a `<Server>`.

These rules convert each resource definition into an instance of the class that represents that resource type. For instance, the `<Environment>`, `<Resource>`, `<ResourceEnvRef>`, and `<ResourceLink>` elements are converted into instances of `ContextEnvironment`, `ContextResource`, `ContextResourceEnvRef`, and `ContextResourceLink` respectively. These classes reside in the `org.apache.catalina.deploy` package.

These instances are stored in the `Server`'s `NamingResources` data member, which represents the `<GlobalNamingResources>` element.

However, this is just a waypoint in the journey of these elements. The final stop for all resources is a binding within a naming service's JNDI context.

The next step is kicked off by the `NamingContextListener`, which is registered as a life cycle listener on the `Server` instance. This listener waits until it is notified of the `Server`'s start event, at which point it springs into action.

It begins by converting each resource instance stored in the `NamingResources` instance that represents the `Server`'s global resources into a type that is more suitable for binding to a JNDI context. Instances of `ContextResource` and `ContextResourceEnvRef` are converted into instances of `ResourceRef` and `ResourceEnvRef` respectively, from the `org.apache.naming` package.

An instance of ContextEnvironment is treated differently, and has its value converted to the appropriate wrapper type, which is then bound to the target JNDI context.

Depending on the name of the resource, additional subcontexts will be created as appropriate. For instance, the jdbc/swengsolDB resource is created by binding the jdbc context as a subcontext of the ENC and then binding the swengsolDB resource to that subcontext.

A key task of this NamingContextListener is to register the ENC NamingContext that it creates within maps that are maintained by the org.apache.naming. ContextBindings class. This class has multiple Hashtable instances as static data members. The members of particular interest are threadBindings and clBindings, which map either a Thread instance or a ClassLoader instance to a NamingContext instance respectively.

This is of importance to us as it is used by the context factory implementation that we will discuss later, to zero in on the specific NamingContext instance that is to be used for a given JNDI Context operation, such as a lookup. For instance, when we need to look up the global naming context, we use the Catalina Loader instance as a key into the clBindings map, which returns us the appropriate ENC context.

Structural relationships

The following image describes the overall structural relationships between the various classes. Note that the images in this section highlight only the key relationships between these classes.

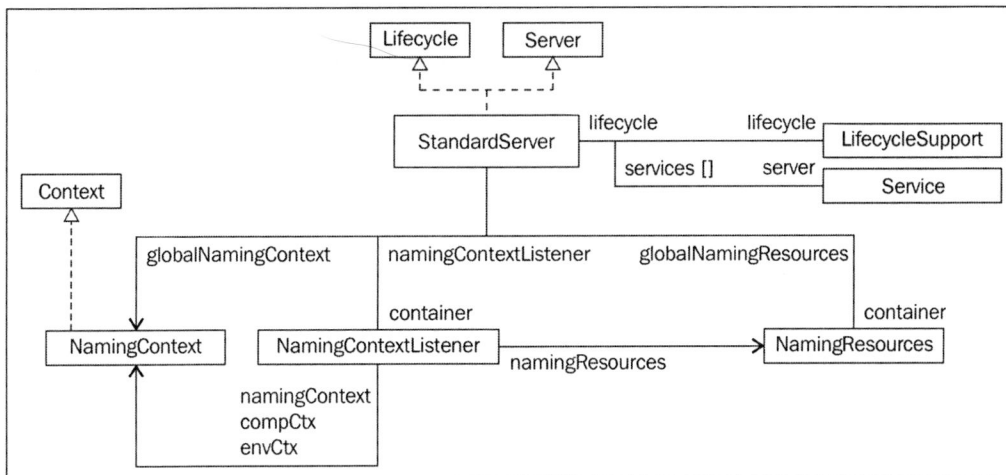

As shown, the `StandardServer` instance holds references to a `NamingResources` member that is initialized by the digester, to a `NamingContext` that represents the JNDI ENC, and to a `NamingContextListener` that converts the former into the latter. Note also that the `compCtx` and `envCtx` instance members of the `NamingContextListener` point to the same `NamingContext` instance. This works as an optimization, as the Java EE specification only ever requires that resources be available from below the `env` subcontext.

In addition, a server also holds an array of `Service` instances. The `LifecycleSupport` instance is used to manage the listeners that are interested in the lifecycle events of the `Server` instance.

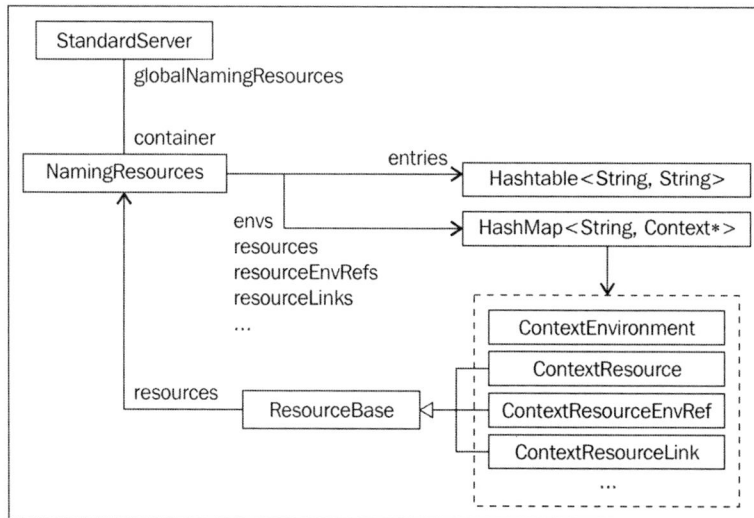

This image displays a close up view of the `NamingResources` class and its relationships. As described, this instance represents the `<GlobalNamingResources>` element in `server.xml`.

The `NamingResources` instance contains nothing more than a number of `Map` members, each of which maps a resource name to an instance that represents that resource's definition in `server.xml`. The `NamingResources` class provides a number of methods to manage each resource type. For example, the `addResource()` method adds a new `ContextResource` instance to the `resources` map, the `findResource()` method looks up a resource by name from this map, while the `removeResource()` method removes a resource from this map. The methods for the other resources work in a similar fashion.

The `org.apache.catalina.deploy.ResourceBase` class is a common class for most resource types. It defines a generic resource, with a `description`, `name`, `type`, and optional `properties`. The subclasses add attributes that are relevant to that resource type. For example, the `ContextResource` class adds the `authorization` and `scope` attributes, while the `ContextResourceLink` adds the `global` attribute that represents the global name for this resource.

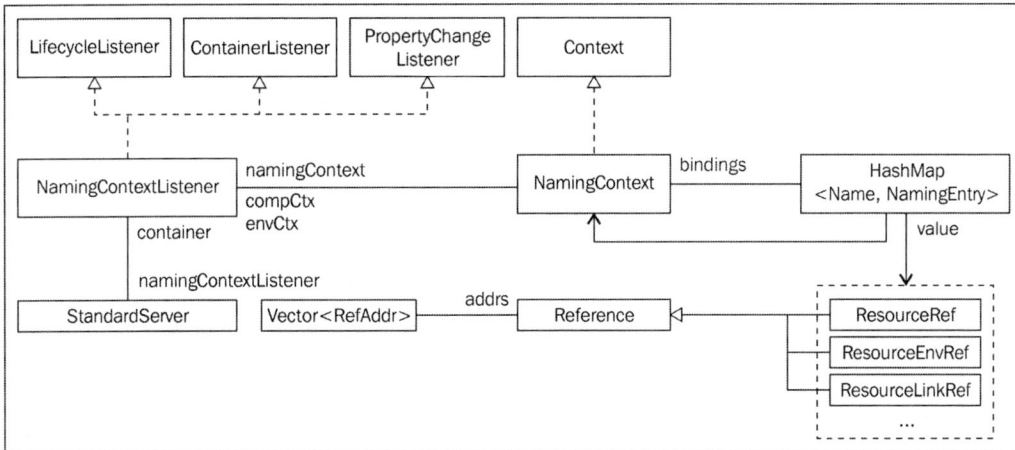

The context hierarchy of the JNDI naming service is set up as a hierarchical graph of `javax.naming.Context` nodes. This image takes a closer look at the construction of this hiearchy using the JNDI `org.apache.naming.NamingContext` class, which implements a JNDI context.

NamingContext

A `NamingContext` instance represents a node in the JNDI naming hierarchy. Its `bindings` map contains a binding of a name to an entity, as a `NamingEntry` instance. The entity bound to a name, within a given context, may represent either a subcontext, a resource reference, or even just a plain value.

The methods of a `NamingContext` are geared around these bindings. For example, a `bind()` method takes a `javax.naming.Name` instance, an object to be bound to that `Name` instance, and converts that object into an appropriate `NamingEntry` instance before adding it to the `bindings` Map. Similarly, a `lookup()` method takes a `Name` instance and retrieves the appropriate binding. Both methods parse the `Name` instance in order to navigate the context hierarchy to get to the appropriate subcontext that contains the bindings from which the requested resource is to be retrieved.

In addition, the lookup method invokes the object factory, whereas the bind method invokes the state factory to make the process seamless to the user.

References

Of the bindings made for a JNDI context, the most interesting one is the `javax.naming.Reference` instance. The binding of a subcontext or a plain value to a context are fairly trivial and are left as exercises for the reader.

When an object cannot be directly bound to a naming service, a logical reference to it is bound instead. This logical reference contains the information that can be used to communicate with that object, such as a network address and protocol. This information is maintained using `RefAddr` instances, each of which implements a key-value pair. For instance, a concrete implementation of this abstract class, `StringRefAddr`, maps a `String` key to a `String` value.

In addition, a `Reference` instance also contains the information that is required to instantiate it, in terms of the names of its implementation class, as well as its factory class.

The individual `Reference` subclasses add data members that are specific to the resource to which they refer. For example, an `org.apache.naming.ResourceRef` instance registers the `description`, `scope`, and `auth` properties as `StringRefAddr` instances. It also advertises its implementation class as well as its factory class (`org.apache.naming.factory.ResourceFactory`).

Factories

A reference is only useful if the mechanism of converting it to and from the referent is as painless as possible. This is achieved by the presence of factory classes — a state factory that converts the referent into its dormant form for storage in a naming service and an object factory that converts the dormant reference back into the referent. Each child class of `Reference` holds the name of the object factory class that should be used to convert the reference back into the original referent instance.

In the case of the `ResourceFactory`, the `getObjectInstance()` method takes the reference as an instance of `ResourceRef`, its JNDI `Name`, the JNDI `Context` into which it is bound, and the environment parameters that are used to configure the context. This factory attempts to locate a `RefAddr` that has a factory class name specified. If no such factory is found, then it uses default factory classes for well known resource references. For instance, for a resource of type `javax.sql.DataSource`, the default factory is `org.apache.tomcat.dbcp.dbcp.BasicDataSourceFactory`. The `getObjectInstance()` method is then invoked on this factory by passing it the incoming parameters to instantiate the referent.

URL context factory

A common way of accessing JNDI resources in a Java EE application is as shown here:

```
Context myctx = new InitialContext();
DataSource myDS = (DataSource) myctx.lookup("java:comp/env/jdbc/
swengsolDB");
```

This can also be used in an abbreviated version as shown:

```
DataSource myDS =
    (DataSource) new InitialContext().lookup("java:comp/env/jdbc/
    swengsolDB");
```

Both forms result in the creation of a throwaway `InitialContext` that is used simply to give us access to its `lookup()` method, which does the real magic. This method obtains the `URLContextFactory` implementation for the scheme that is specified in the URL. In this case, this is the `java:` scheme and results in the `org.apache.naming.java.javaURLContextFactory` class being instantiated and made available for the lookup. Its `getObjectInstance()` method is called to obtain the appropriate `javax.naming.Context` instance that will be used for the lookup.

Interestingly, the returned `Context` is not a `NamingContext`, but instead is an `org.apache.naming.SelectorContext` instance.

A `SelectorContext` isn't a true JNDI `Context` implementation. Instead, it serves as a proxy for a `NamingContext`. The specific `Context` instance that it proxies is determined by looking it up in the `ContextBindings` members, either by the current `Thread` instance or by the current context `ClassLoader` instance. Once the appropriate `NamingContext` instance has been located, this class delegates the call to the corresponding method in the actual `NamingContext`. This mechanism makes it easy to determine the JNDI context to be used from anywhere within the Tomcat instance.

StandardService

The default implementation of the `org.apache.catalina.Service` interface that is used, if no class name override is specified in the `server.xml` file, is `org.apache.catalina.core.StandardService`. This instance does nothing more than provide an organizational mechanism to hook multiple `Connector` instances to a single `Engine` instance. It is also responsible for the lifecycle invocations on its contained children. For instance, its `start()` method invokes `start()` on its single `Engine` instance, on all of its `Executor` instances, as well as on all of its `Connector` instances.

Similarly, it supports methods that support the registration and removal of its children from its containment structure. For example, the `addConnector()`, `removeConnector()`, and `findConnectors()` methods let you manage the `Connector` instances that are associated with a given `Service`.

By default, no listeners are registered with a given `Service` instance.

Summary

In this chapter, we took an up close and personal look at the roles that the `Server` top level container plays in a Tomcat instance. The `Server` serves its containment role by acting as a container for one or more `Service` instances that are configured in the Tomcat instance. It takes its responsibilities as a container seriously by invoking the appropriate life cycle methods on its services.

In addition, it initializes the global JNDI naming context from the elements that are configured into the `<GlobalNamingResources>` element of the `server.xml` configuration file. It also plays an active role in bootstrapping the JMX registration process. It then waits, listening patiently on a configured port, for a command to shut down the Tomcat instance.

The `Service` instance, on the other hand, is fairly trivial and does nothing more than serve as a structural construct that associates one or more Connectors with an Engine.

6
The Connector Component

In Tomcat, the `Connector` component provides the protocol-specific implementation of a web server. At its most basic level, this component monitors a particular port for incoming requests, receives requests that conform to a given protocol such as HTTP 1.1 or AJP 1.3, translates these requests into a canonical form that conforms to the servlet specification, hands these requests to the engine for processing, and returns the generated response to the client. In doing so, it insulates the remainder of the Catalina request processing engine from the specifics of any given protocol.

This component is composed of so many cooperating classes that it may be termed more correctly as the connector *subsystem*. The `Connector` class itself is only responsible for the bootstrapping of this subsystem. The remainder of this subsystem is comprised of the following:

- An endpoint connection acceptor that receives all incoming connections
- A protocol handler that implements a protocol to which the incoming requests will conform
- A connection handler that delegates the processing of an accepted connection to a request processor
- A request processor that implements the protocol-specific aspects of request processing
- An adapter that connects the connector subsystem to the Catalina request processing engine

Given the number of cooperating classes that are required to make this magic happen, this chapter is easily one of the most complex topics you will come across in this book.

However, there is no need to fear. We're going to take this topic slow and easy, looking at this subsystem from various high level perspectives before we dive into the details.

The best way to eat an elephant, one is told, is to simply do it one bite at a time.

So, let's dig in!

Connector classification

A good starting point is to establish a taxonomic basis for the connectors supported by Tomcat. In the wild, each connector can be completely described along three distinct axes—by usage scenario, by protocol, and by implementation technology. This is as demonstrated in the following table.

Usage scenario	Protocol	Implementation
Tomcat with external web server	AJP	`java.io`
	HTTP	`java.nio`
	HTTPS	APR
Tomcat standalone	HTTP	`java.io`
	HTTPS	`java.nio`
		APR

Usage scenario

As we have seen in earlier chapters, Tomcat can run either in conjunction with an external web server, such as Apache's `httpd`, or it can run in standalone mode.

In conjunction mode, the external web server delegates to Tomcat for dynamic content that will be generated by its contained servlets and JSPs. Whereas, in standalone mode, Tomcat serves up both the static as well as dynamic content for the site.

Tomcat with external web server

Here the actual client is a web server connector module (for Microsoft's IIS, this is an ISAPI filter) that communicates with Tomcat on behalf of the external web server.

These modules are loaded into, and run, as part of the external web server, and decide which requests will be routed to Tomcat, and to which Tomcat instance they will be sent.

Note that the module itself is not part of the connector subsystem.

mod_jk

The `mod_jk` module was developed by the Apache Tomcat project and implements the Apache JServ Protocol (AJP), which we'll visit in more detail shortly.

It is a stable module that supports a large number of web servers and Tomcat versions. For example, there is a version of this module available for Microsoft's IIS in the form of `isapi_redirect.dll`, which makes it easy to port your `mod_jk` settings over from an Apache to an IIS setup.

mod_proxy

The `mod_proxy` module that supports the AJP protocol is `mod_proxy_ajp`. It is derived from `mod_jk` and so has similar features. It connects through the **Transmission Control Protocol (TCP)** to Tomcat's AJP server port, sends requests on to Tomcat using the AJP protocol, waits for Tomcat's responses, which are returned to `httpd` which then forwards the responses out to the web client.

The `mod_proxy` module that supports the HTTP/HTTPS protocol is `mod_proxy_http`.

Tomcat in standalone mode

When used in standalone mode, the client is the user's web browser, which communicates directly with Tomcat using the HTTP/HTTPS protocols.

Protocol

The primary protocols that Tomcat supports are HTTP, HTTPS, and AJP.

The **Hypertext Transfer Protocol (HTTP)** and its secure version (HTTPS) are both text oriented application level protocols. A connector that supports these protocols will allow connections from browsers using HTTP/1.1 and will fall back to HTTP/1.0 if necessary.

On the other hand, AJP is a TCP packet-based binary protocol that is used for communications between an external web server and Tomcat. It dates back to the obsolete Apache JServ servlet engine.

AJP is more efficient than HTTP for system-to-system communications because it minimizes the network communications overhead by relaying already-parsed text strings of the requests over to Tomcat. This lets us avoid the parsing that would have otherwise been required on the Tomcat side of the connection.

AJP 1.3 is the current version of this protocol and supports a wide range of features, including SSL, client certificates, and clustering. It also has good performance on fast networks by compressing protocol elements that are transmitted between the cooperating servers.

Implementation architecture

This dimension describes how the connector is implemented.

Apache Portable Runtime Connector

The **Apache Portable Runtime (APR)** is a set of dynamic libraries, written in the C programming language, whose primary goal is to provide a platform-independent way of accessing low level operating system services. The APR wraps all the low level aspects that are unique to a platform, and by doing so, provides a unified view of these services to the applications that are written to it. Interestingly, even if an operating system does not support a particular function, the APR may provide a replacement—allowing your program to be truly portable. Implementations of the APR exist for operating systems such as Windows, Linux, and the Mac OS X.

Tomcat's APR-based connector is written in Java, but uses the APR for network communications rather than using the standard portable mechanisms provided by the **Java Runtime Environment (JRE)**. The assumption being that the implementations provided by the APR are more efficient than the equivalents provided by the JRE.

For Windows, the APR comes conveniently packaged in a dynamic library. For other environments, administrators must build it using a compiler. This connector supports the HTTP, HTTPS, and AJP protocols.

JIO Connector aka Coyote

This is a pure Java connector—it is written in Java and uses classes from the `java.io` package along with Java's Socket API. It supports the HTTP, HTTPS, and AJP protocols.

It is codenamed **Coyote** and is the fallback connector if the APR libraries are not found at Tomcat startup.

The use of standard Java constructs makes it portable across all platforms for which a compliant JRE exists. It is the most mature of the Tomcat connectors, is very stable, and is a decent performer.

> Benchmarks done by Brittain and Darwin in *Tomcat: The Definitive Guide* indicate that the standard Java IO based connector compares very favorably to the newer connectors.

NIO connector

This connector is also written in pure Java and uses the newer `java.nio` network classes. The major benefit here is that it supports non-blocking TCP sockets. This allows a smaller thread pool to be used to handle the same number of concurrent requests.

Connector configuration

Rather than cover all aspects of all connectors, in the interests of brevity (and sanity), I will cut a swath through the most common and popular usage of connectors – the use of a JIO HTTP connector in standalone mode.

As we have seen in the last chapter, a service component associates one or more connectors with an engine. It is therefore perfectly natural to have an HTTP connector, as well as an HTTPS connector feeding the same engine.

Examining the configuration entries for the two connectors registered within the default `server.xml` gives us important clues about its function.

```
<Connector port = "8080" protocol = "HTTP/1.1"
           redirectPort="8443" connectionTimeout="20000" />
<Connector port = "8009" protocol = "AJP/1.3"
           redirectPort = "8443" />
```

First, it defines the port on which this connector will listen for incoming connections. Second, it defines the protocol that this connector is designed to handle, such as HTTP/1.1. In addition, a connection timeout attribute indicates that you can set socket options using this declarative mechanism.

One aspect of the Tomcat documentation that is done exceedingly well is the **Apache Tomcat Configuration Reference** at `http://tomcat.apache.org/tomcat-6.0-doc/config/index.html`. This reference enumerates the attributes accepted by an HTTP connector in careful detail, and for the most part, I will defer to it. Here we only cover a few interesting attributes that you need to be aware of in your exploration of the standard HTTP/1.1 connector component.

Binding attributes

These attributes relate to how a connector is accessed.

`address`	When a host has multiple IP addresses, the server socket will, by default, listen for connections on (bind to) all IP addresses, allowing connections from all network devices. In IPv4, this wildcard address is 0.0.0.0.
	You may specify a single IP address if you choose to only allow connections from a single network device.
`port`	The port number on which this connector listens for requests. The default HTTP/1.1 Connector listens on port 8080.
`protocol`	The name of the protocol supported by a given Connector, for example, `HTTP/1.1` or `AJP/1.3`.
	It can also specify the Fully Qualified class name of the protocol handler class that should be used. For the standard HTTP/1.1 JIO Connector, this would be: `org.apache.coyote.http11.Http11Protocol`.

Socket attributes

These attributes deal with the characteristics of the socket connection.

The `connectionLinger`, `tcpNoDelay`, and the `connectionTimeout` attributes correspond to the standard socket options `soLinger`, `tcpNoDelay`, and `soTimeout`, respectively.

connection Linger	When the connector closes the client request socket connection, the connection will linger for the given milliseconds. (The default of -1 disables lingering).
connection Timeout	This attribute sets the milliseconds to wait from the time a TCP socket is accepted until the request method line is read. This attribute defaults to 60,000.
tcpNoDelay	This attribute controls whether Nagle's algorithm is in effect for this connector's socket connections. Setting this to true improves performance, at the expense of bandwidth. The default is true.
acceptCount	When all of the request processor threads are busy handling requests, and more request connections are made to Tomcat's server port, the connections wait in an accept queue until one or more threads is free. This attribute sets the size of that queue.
	Once the queue is full, any further connection attempts to this connector are ignored until the queue is no longer full.
	This attribute is better known as the *backlog* in the socket programming API.
	The JIoEndpoint class defaults this to 100.

See the *Socket options* section later in this chapter for more details.

Thread parameters

These attributes control the nature of the pool of the request processing threads maintained for a connector.

maxThreads	This attribute sets the maximum number of request handling threads that the connector will run concurrently. By default, the JIoEndpoint class sets this to 200.

The connector subsystem—a structural perspective

This subsystem's identity is forged by the collaboration of a number of classes, many of which are nested classes.

Note that the diagrams in this chapter only depict the key aspects of the subject under discussion.

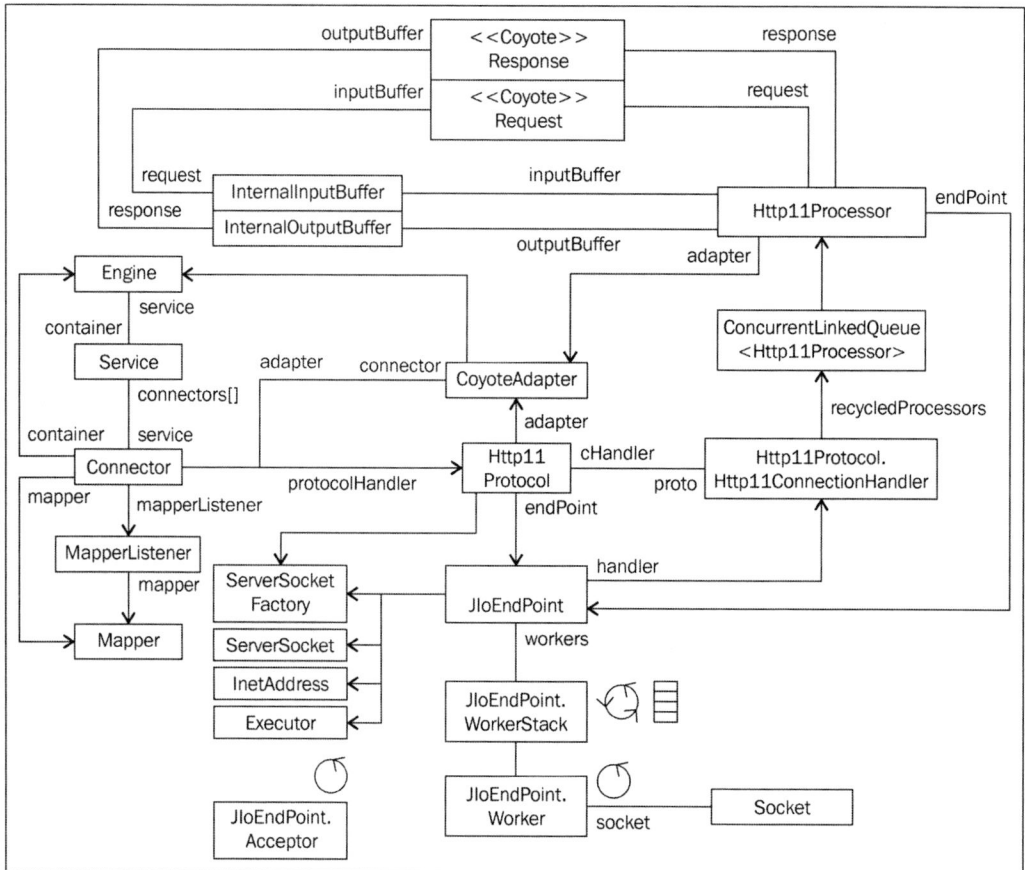

Don't let this diagram scare you away. Yes, it does look rather alarming at first glance, but as we peel away the layers of complexity, rest assured that this will soon make sense. Let us begin by taking a stroll through the structural aspects of this diagram.

The primary objectives of this subsystem are to:

- Establish the structural relationships between all these cooperating classes as appropriate for the selected protocol and implementation.
- Serve as a collection point for all the incoming requests for a given service.
- Maintain a pool of worker threads that are responsible for processing incoming requests.
- Determine the request processing components that should be asked to process an incoming request.
- Encapsulate the protocol-specific aspects of the request, in order to hide these from the request processing engine.

Let us begin by looking at the structural aspects of this diagram and consider how the classes in the diagram above help achieve our list of objectives.

Objective 1: Collection point

At server startup, the `server.xml` is digested, and the `Service` top level component is instantiated with any configured connectors, and its single configured engine instance.

An instance of the `org.apache.catalina.Connector` class serves as the collection point for all incoming requests associated with a `Service`. All `Connector` instances feed the single engine associated with their service with the requests that they receive.

In reality, the `Connector` class by itself is simply a configuration construct, and does not have much functional responsibility.

It is used as a convenient holding place for all the attributes that a user might specify that affect the manner in which requests are accepted and processed.

Objective 2: Establishing relationships

A connector's key role is to identify the handler class that is appropriate for the protocol configured for it in the `server.xml` file. This handler class is determined by the `Connector`'s constructor. For the HTTP/1.1 protocol, this defaults to an instance of the `org.apache.coyote.http11.Http11Protocol` class.

The `Connector` links the protocol handler to the rest of the request processing machinery by providing it with an adapter, `org.apache.catalina.connector.CoyoteAdapter`.

A protocol handler is aware of the classes that need to participate in the handling of a request for a given protocol. For instance, the protocol handler for the HTTP protocol knows about the end point and request processor implementations for the HTTP protocol, which are `org.apache.tomcat.util.net.JIoEndpoint` and `org.apache.coyote.http11.Http11Processor`, respectively.

An end point implementation, as shown in the diagram, is multithreading central. It provides the standard Java IO implementation of how incoming connection requests will be accepted and handed off for processing.

An `Http11Processor` instance handles the protocol-specific aspects of request processing before delegating to the adapter. This processor is responsible for parsing the request and for preparing the response in a format that is compatible with the HTTP/1.1 protocol.

The protocol handler instantiates and initializes the end point implementation for a given protocol, and connects it to a suitable request processor. This connection is actually made indirectly, through an instance of the `Http11Protocol.Http11ConnectionHandler` class, which maintains a queue of `Http11Processor` instances.

The `Connector` class defines standard attributes that are supported by all connectors, irrespective of protocol. This includes the `protocol`, `redirectPort`, and the `maxPostSize` attributes. Attributes that are unique to a protocol are passed through to the specific protocol handler instance instead. These include attributes such as the `compressableMimeType`, `maxThreads`, and `tcpNoDelay`.

Objective 3: Accept incoming connections

The actual work of listening for an incoming request, and for invoking the request processor, is performed by the `JIoEndpoint` class and its nested classes. The `JIoEndpoint.Acceptor` class is an active object (represented by the whirling circle in the image), that instantiates a server socket, and uses it to wait for incoming connections.

The network bindings configured for the `<Connector>` element are actually used by this instance.

Objective 4: Maintain a pool of worker threads

The `JIoEndpoint.WorkerStack` class manages a pool of `JIoEndpoint.Worker` instances (represented in the image by a furiously whirling circle next to a stack), where each instance represents a `Thread` that can be assigned a socket to process.

When a worker is assigned a socket, that worker sets the appropriate socket options as specified by the socket-related attributes of the `<Connector>` element, before obtaining an `Http11Processor` from its connection handler. It then delegates request processing to this processor.

The processor, in turn, performs some protocol-specific tasks (such as honoring keep alive requests), and then hands off the actual request processing to its associated adapter, which as we have seen earlier, connects the connector subsystem to the rest of the request processing machinery.

Objective 5: Maintain a mapping of request processing components

How do we determine the request processing components that should be involved in the processing of a given request? That's the job of the `org.apache.tomcat.util.http.mapper.Mapper`, which makes it convenient to determine the specific host, context, and optionally, wrapper components that will respond to a given incoming request.

The adapter obtains this `Mapper` instance from its connector, and uses it to determine the request processing components that will be tasked with processing a given request.

Objective 6: Insulate the engine from the outside world

By the time the `Engine` component receives the request for processing, all the dust has settled quite nicely, and it is presented with just the basic information that it needs to do its job. The engine and its subordinate containers are therefore pretty oblivious to all the protocol-specific action that has occurred in getting to this point. This allows the same engine to be used with different protocols.

That's it! With this, we have covered the most important classes in the connector subsystem. These classes comprise the collaborative workflow aspects of this subsystem.

Hopefully, the diagram is swimming into focus now. We're not done yet, however. Let's consider these classes in a bit more detail before revisiting this from a different perspective.

The `Executor` is not covered in this book, but its operation is fairly straightforward and amenable to self investigation.

Modeling the Request and Response

A request or a response in Tomcat presents two facets to the world. There is the internal representation used solely by Tomcat's implementation classes, and there is the public representation that conforms to the servlet specification.

In this text, I refer to the former as the Coyote `Request` or `Response`, and to the latter as the Catalina `Request` or `Response`.

Coyote and Catalina

The reason this distinction is important is because the Coyote classes, `org.apache.coyote.Request` and `org.apache.coyote.Response`, are intended for internal use, and are primarily used within the processor and adapter components.

On the other hand, the Catalina classes, `org.apache.catalina.connector.Request` and `org.apache.catalina.connector.Response`, are for more general use within the request processing components, such as the engine and its contained components.

The first thing to note about the Catalina classes is that they implement the `HttpServletRequest` and `HttpServletResponse` interfaces in the `javax.servlet.http` package. This brings them squarely within the realm of the servlet specification and hints that they are intended for consumption by user classes.

The second thing to note is that the Catalina classes have sibling implementations, `RequestFacade` and `ResponseFacade`, which also implement these servlet interfaces.

These facades are used to prevent rogue developers (you know who you are) from upcasting an `HttpServletRequest` passed into a servlet's `service()` method into a Catalina `Request`. Doing so would allow a servlet to access internal Tomcat implementation details, and create a potentially dangerous situation, if done with malicious intent.

Instead, whenever an `HttpServletRequest` implementation must be provided to a user-specified request processing component (such as a servlet), the `RequestFacade` is handed out instead. This facade implements all `HttpServletRequest` methods by delegating to its wrapped Catalina `Request`.

This ensures that user classes can get at all the functionality and information as promised by the Servlet API, while at the same time ensuring that user classes cannot violate any access constraints. It also simplifies the design of the Catalina `Request` since we don't need to concern ourselves with the visibility modifiers of its members, none of which will be directly accessible from user classes.

The same is true for the Catalina `Response`.

Request classes

In this section, we'll take a closer look at how a `Request` is modeled in Tomcat.

This diagram represents the key components of a Tomcat request. In particular, note the Coyote `Request` to the left of the diagram and the Catalina `Request` to the right.

Coyote Request

The Coyote `Request` is an efficient internal representation of a request. For example, it is intended to have a minimal garbage collection footprint. To achieve this it defines a `recycle()` method that resets its members, and readies the object for reuse, rather than simply discarding it. In addition, instead of using immutable `String` instances for its data members, such as the scheme, request URI, query string, and protocol, it uses instances of `MessageBytes`. This class is described further in the *Helper classes* section.

When this instance is created (by the `Http11Processor`), it is given an `org.apache.coyote.http11.InternalInputBuffer` instance that can be used to read bytes directly from the `InputStream` associated with the client `Socket`. The `InternalInputBuffer` can read in the request line and request headers and updates the Coyote `Request` appropriately.

Each header is represented using an `org.apache.tomcat.util.http.MimeHeaderField`, and a collection of headers is held by an `org.apache.tomcat.util.http.MimeHeaders` instance.

The `org.apache.tomcat.util.http.Parameters` class represents a data structure that maps a parameter name to an array of values. These parameters are parsed out from the query string associated with the Coyote `Request`.

The `org.apache.tomcat.util.http.Cookies` class retrieves any cookies present in the headers of the Coyote `Request`. The actual cookie is represented using an `org.apache.tomcat.util.http.ServerCookie`. This instance is where you will see attributes that are recognizable as belonging to a cookie, such as its name, value, age, and domain.

Catalina Request

The Catalina `Request` works with standard servlet specification classes such as the `javax.servlet.http.Cookie`. In addition, the `org.apache.catalina.util.ParameterMap` enforces the rule that the set of request parameters may not be modified by client components, once initialized.

The Catalina `Request` needs to be able to access the socket's input stream to get at the request's body, which includes parameters when using the POST HTTP method. This is accomplished using an `org.apache.catalina.connector.InputBuffer` instance that delegates the actual reading of bytes to the associated Coyote `Request`, which in turn obtains its bytes from its socket's input stream.

This request is also aware of servlet listeners. Its `setAttribute()` method not only adds the specified attribute to the `attributes` HashMap, but also notifies any registered listeners that are instances of `ServletRequestAttributeListener`.

It also provides associations with other Catalina-specific implementations, such as the `Connector`, the `Context`, a `Wrapper`, a `Session`, and a `FilterChain`, and can also handle request dispatcher mechanics such as forwards and includes. We will discuss all these in detail in future chapters.

Response classes

The `Response` classes are actually much simpler, and work in a fairly similar fashion.

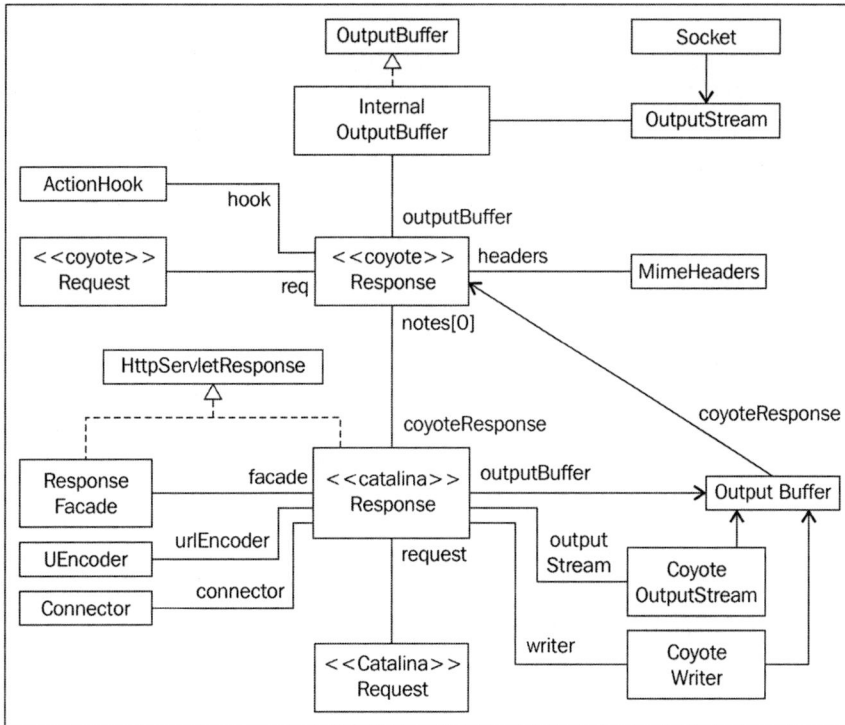

A Coyote `Response` models the internal representation of a response, and is available for use by Tomcat's internal classes.

It has an `org.apache.coyote.http11.InternalOutputBuffer` instance that lets it write the response directly out to the client socket's output stream.

A `MimeHeaders` instance represents the response headers that are being returned to the client. Cookies are added to the response by adding a `Set-Cookie` response header. Note that the `Content-Type` and `Content-Length` headers are handled by setting internal members rather than by adding a separate `MimeHeaderField` instance.

A Catalina `Response` implements the `HttpServletResponse` interface, and is handed off to user code in the form of a `ResponseFacade` that delegates the actual work to this Catalina `Response`.

A Catalina `Response` lets you write out to the socket's output stream through the output buffer of the Coyote `Response`. It also defines convenience methods to send an error response with an appropriate status code and message, to send a redirect response, as well as to rewrite the URL to append a session identifier.

HTTP classes

This set of classes represents various HTTP elements such as cookies, MIME headers, and request parameters.

MimeHeaders

This class holds the standard Internet message headers used for SMTP and HTTP as well as for MIME applications.

The nested `MimeHeaderField` class represents a single header. It holds a `name` and a `value` both as `MessageBytes` instances, and has a linked list implementation to support multi-valued headers. Its `NamesEnumerator` and `ValuesEnumerator` nested classes let you step through the names and values of the contained `headers`.

It defines methods that are used to retrieve a `MimeHeaderField` using either a subscript or a name, to create a new header, as well as to get and set header values.

Parameters and ParameterMap

A request parameter is a key-value pair that is sent either in the query string for a GET request or in the request body for a POST request. Both the name and value are strings.

An `org.apache.tomcat.util.http.Parameters` instance represents a collection of parameters for a given request. It maintains its parameters using a `Hashtable<String, String[]>` where each entry represents a mapping of a name to zero or more values.

Parameters within a query string may either be associated with values, as `name1=value1&name2=value2`, or they may be expressed without values as `name1&name2`.

An `org.apache.tomcat.util.buf.UDecoder` helper class instance performs decoding of parameters by converting `x-www-form-url-encoded` strings by replacing '+' signs with spaces and by converting '%' escapes to the corresponding character values. If no encoding is supplied, then the default case uses ISO-8859-1, where each byte is directly converted to a character.

An `org.apache.catalina.util.ParameterMap` is really a `HashMap` with a boolean member that lets you prohibit updates to the `HashMap`. This class allows you to expose parameters to user classes without running the risk of those user classes modifying them.

In general, the Coyote `Request` works with the `Parameters` class, whereas the Catalina `Request` works with the `ParameterMap`.

Invoking `getParameterMap()` on the Catalina `Request` will retrieve parameters from its Coyote `Request`, add each to the `ParameterMap` instance, set its `locked` member to `true`, and return that map to the caller.

Note that attempting to read a parameter from a Catalina `Request` kicks off the parsing of the query string. If this is a POST request with a content type of `application/x-www-form-urlencoded` (in its `content-type` header), the request's body is read in and any parameters contained within it are extracted by the `Parameters` instance.

Cookies and ServerCookie

A `ServerCookie` is an internal representation of a cookie. It has `MessageByte` instances for a name, a value, a path, a domain, and a comment. It can also indicate whether the cookie is secure, its maximum age, and version.

A `Cookies` instance holds a `ServerCookie` array. Its constructor takes a `MimeHeaders` instance, enabling it to be lazy evaluated, where information is extracted lazily from the provided headers. Each header in its `MimeHeaders` member with the name `Cookie` is processed according to the rules specified in RFC 2965, the HTTP State Management Mechanism, and is stored as a `ServerCookie` instance.

Stream classes

This set of classes deal with reading from and writing to the socket's input and output streams. They support a layer of decorators and buffers over the socket streams.

When a Catalina `Request` needs to read the body of a request, it must go through the Coyote `Request` to access the underlying input stream. The Coyote `Request` in turn delegates to its `InternalInputBuffer` to access the socket's input stream. As if that weren't enough, the `InternalInputBuffer` optionally delegates to a stack of filters that decorate the actual input stream.

A similar sequence occurs when writing data out to the socket's output stream.

InternalInputBuffer

This is the entity that is closest to the socket's input stream. It contains methods to parse the request line and request headers, which read from the socket input stream and initialize data structures within the Coyote `Request` that is associated with this buffer.

It also holds a library of filters that may be placed around the socket's input stream to modify the process by which bytes are extracted from the stream. The default input filter is an `InputStreamInputBuffer` instance that simply adds a basic `byte` array as a buffer around the input stream.

InternalOutputBuffer

This class is intimately connected to the socket's output stream. You can layer `OutputFilter` instances around the socket's output stream to influence how the bytes are written. Possible filters include the GZIP filter that adds a layer of compression to the output bytes, the Void filter that is used when there is no response body that needs to be written, and the chunked filter that is used for the chunked `Transfer-Encoding`.

The default output filter is an `OutputStreamOutputBuffer`, which simply writes out the bytes to the socket's output stream.

An optional `ByteChunk` can be set as a socket buffer around the output stream that accumulates bytes before they are actually written out over the network.

Convenience methods that help with response processing are also included. For example, `sendHeader()` writes out a `MimeHeader` as a name followed by a colon and a space followed by the value and a CR/LF. Similarly, a `sendStatus()` method writes out the response line with a protocol, status code, and a reason phrase, followed by a CR/LF. And, a `sendAck()` is provided to write out a continue response.

InputBuffer

The key method on an `org.apache.catalina.connector.InputBuffer` is `realReadBytes()` which delegates to the `doRead()` method of its associated Coyote `Request`, which simply delegates back down to its `InternalInputBuffer` instance.

An `InputBuffer` instance can be used to provide a backing stream for a `ByteChunk` or a `CharChunk` instance.

An `InputBuffer` also provides access to a `B2CConverter` instance which allows you to wrap an `InputStreamReader` around a `byte[]`. This lets you read the bytes and translate them into characters using a specified encoding.

OutputBuffer

Its `realWriteBytes()` method forces a write out to the `doWrite()` method of its associated Coyote `Response`.

Requests to flush an `OutputBuffer` will write its bytes out to the socket's output stream. The first request for a flush will cause any response headers to be sent down the wire.

A `C2BConverter` can be installed to convert characters into bytes for an appropriate encoding.

ServletInputStream and CoyoteInputStream

These classes let you read from the body of an HTTP request.

A `javax.servlet.ServletInputStream` is an abstract class that serves as an input stream for reading binary data from a client request.

An `org.apache.catalina.connector.CoyoteInputStream` is a concrete implementation of `ServletInputStream` that provides a concrete `read()` method that delegates to its wrapped `InputBuffer` instance.

A Catalina `Request` constructs a `CoyoteInputStream` and sets its associated `InputBuffer`. This `InputBuffer` instance is associated with the corresponding Coyote `Request`, giving it access to the socket's input stream.

ServletOutputStream and CoyoteOutputStream

These classes let you write to the body of an HTTP response.

A `javax.servlet.ServletOutputStream` provides numerous overloads of `print()` and `println()`.

The `org.apache.catalina.connector.CoyoteOutputStream` provides a concrete implementation of a `ServletOutputStream` that provides implementations of `write()` that actually underlie all those various overloads.

Its implementation of `write(int)` ends up writing to its associated `OutputBuffer`, which in turn causes a physical write out to its associated Coyote `Response`, which in turn writes out to its `InternalOutputBuffer`, which finally writes out the bytes to the socket's output stream.

Helper classes

Tomcat goes to great lengths to avoid garbage collection overhead for its internal classes. For instance, it uses byte[] and char[] instead of String instances to avoid the garbage collection overhead caused by the immutability of a String.

In addition, recycling objects instead of discarding them, reduces fodder for the Garbage Collector. For example, recycling a ByteChunk, which wraps a byte[], simply resets its start and end attributes to 0, but doesn't cause any memory to be collected.

As a side benefit, working with a byte[] rather than converting to chars or a String, frees us from having to worry about the character encoding. This lets us function even in cases where the encoding is not known beforehand, or when the encoding may change during the execution of the protocol (a multipart message may have parts with different encoding). In other words, we can have encoding be lazy-bound, and we can work with the byte[] until we absolutely need to convert it to a String.

These helper classes help us achieve these goals.

ByteChunk and CharChunk

The ByteChunk class functions like the Java 1.4 NIO's ByteBuffer class. It is a byte[] with index markers for a start position, end position, and a limit, and with methods for writing to and reading from this buffer.

The end marker moves as bytes are read into the buffer, to indicate the last valid byte in the array. The end position is constrained by the limit for a bounded array.

If the initial allocated space is filled, the byte[] can grow dynamically until the limit is reached (or forever for an unbounded buffer, that is, a buffer with a negative limit.)

Reads from the byte[] are indicated by moving the start marker to the right to indicate the consumption of the bytes at previous index positions.

The length of data at any given point is obtained by subtracting the end position from the start position.

This buffer may be tied to an underlying input or output stream. As a read buffer is emptied, it may replenish its bytes from the underlying input stream, and a write buffer may write out its bytes to the underlying output stream when it is full. Read and write operations invoke realReadBytes() or realWriteBytes() respectively on the associated streams.

This class has search and equality methods that are similar to `String` and `StringBuffer`, but which work on bytes instead.

The `CharChunk` class performs identically, but deals with a `char[]` instead of a `byte[]`.

MessageBytes

The Tomcat Coyote implementation relies exclusively on `MessageByte` instances instead of on instances of `String`. This class lets us work on HTTP headers using `byte` arrays without converting to either chars or `String` instances until needed.

A `MessageBytes` can hold either a string value, a `byte[]`, or a `char[]`. The `type` field indicates the type of the object used to create this instance. It is possible to change from one representation to another, for example, to generate a string value from a byte or a char array. It has setter methods that set the underlying value and the appropriate `type`.

Socket programming

Before we continue our exploration, let's make camp, and take a short detour into the grand world of Java concepts and socket programming.

> This book is concerned primarily with TCP sockets, which support the Transmission Control Protocol, a connection-oriented, reliable, protocol that provides significant value by freeing an application programmer to focus on high level issues, rather than on low level aspects such as error detection and control.

A socket is designed to provide a convenient abstraction to the discrete packet-oriented nature of network data transmission. It allows programs to pretend that all network communication is actually stream based. This has the benefit of allowing programs that use the network to use the same paradigms and idioms that are available for the processing of normal I/O streams.

Sockets make this abstraction seamless by providing the `getInputStream()` and `getOutputStream()` methods that let you read from or write to a socket as if it were a standard stream. In addition, you can decorate these bare streams using other filter streams to add additional functionality (such as buffering or the capability to read and write complex data rather than just bytes).

```
dataIn = new DataInputStream(socket.getInputStream());
dataOut = new DataOutputStream(socket.getOutputStream());
```

You could also wrap a reader or a writer around the input/output stream for character based access to the socket's underlying streams.

```
BufferedReader socketReader = new BufferedReader(
    new InputStreamReader(socket.getInputStream()));
```

A socket represents the end point of a stream based network connection. The end point on each communicating host can be represented in terms of an IP address and port number, so a TCP connection represents two pairs of such data.

A given server application may listen on a given IP address and port, and can support connections from multiple client applications running on one or more client hosts. Each end point is described by an IP address and port pair, and each distinct connection is composed of two such end points. A connection can therefore be uniquely described by identifying its end points.

All sockets are not created equal. When working with sockets, you will encounter two types of sockets — client sockets (also known as "normal" sockets) and server sockets.

A server socket is an instance of `java.net.ServerSocket`, which binds to one or more IP addresses and a port, and waits patiently for incoming connections. When a connection request is detected, it is responsible for the handshakes that are necessary to establish the connection. The net result of a successful connection request is a standard client socket, as an instance of `java.net.Socket`.

Each end point of a connection is represented by a client socket, which is an instance of `java.net.Socket`. These instances act as a pair of telephone handsets that enable the two hosts to communicate over the network, reading from and writing to the other as necessary.

When the communication is done, the two hosts close their client sockets and the connection is terminated.

The server socket on the other hand is a very long lived entity and continues to live for as long as the server is running.

The server socket spends most of its life in a loop, blocking on a call to `accept()`, which returns only when a new `java.net.Socket` can be constructed for the server side of the connection.

In a high performance environment such as with web servers, it is desirable to have our `ServerSocket` instance return to its sentry duty as soon as possible after handing off the newly accepted connection request for processing.

We achieve this by having the server socket thread hand off the new client socket to a processor thread, leaving the server thread free to return to blocking on the `accept()` call.

Socket options

You can configure how sockets work by setting socket options. These socket options have names that will seem strange to Java programmers because they carry forward their original C language names as used in Berkeley Unix where sockets were invented.

The three socket options that matter the most to us are the `SO_TIMEOUT`, `SO_LINGER`, and `TCP_NODELAY`.

SO_TIMEOUT

Normally a `read()` call will block indefinitely, waiting to read data from the socket's `InputStream`. If this takes too long, then the application will begin to seem sluggish and unusable as the processing thread is tied up for an inordinately long time.

When you specify a timeout, any read request starts up a timer. If the timeout expires before the data arrives, a `java.io.InterruptedIOException` is thrown, which can be caught and used to detect a timeout. The application can then take corrective action such as retrying or aborting the read/write attempt.

Timeouts also apply to `write()` calls, as well as to the `accept()` call on a `ServerSocket`.

TCP_NODELAY

TCP data is sent over the network using IP datagrams, where the actual data content of the transmission is wrapped with a significant amount of control overhead such as the TCP and IP header information.

The ratio of data payload to the total packet size therefore is an important measure. The smaller this ratio, the more of your bandwidth is being wasted. In other words, if each packet only carries a few bytes at a time, then the size of the headers far outweighs that of the data.

Nagle's algorithm states that TCP may send only one datagram at a time. When an ACK returns for a previous IP datagram, a new packet is sent containing any new data that has been queued up since the last transmission. This allows TCP to delay tiny packets in the hope that more data will accumulate before the packet is actually sent.

While this helps limit the consumption of bandwidth by limiting the overhead bytes that are transmitted over the network, it comes at the cost of network latency, as packets are queued and are no longer sent immediately. This can be particularly noticeable in online games where packets with positional updates may need to be sent as quickly as possible.

SO_LINGER

When a TCP socket is closed, by invoking its `close()` method, it is possible that there may yet be datagrams that have been queued for transmission, but which have not yet been sent. This includes packets that have been sent previously, but have not yet been acknowledged by the remote host.

This option controls the time, in seconds, during which we will try to resend any pending data. After this time has expired, any pending data is simply discarded. If you set this to 0, the `close()` method will immediately close the socket, discarding any unsent or unacknowledged packets.

A non zero value causes the `close()` call to block while any unsent or unacknowledged packets are transmitted. Once this timeout has passed, the socket is closed and any pending packets are discarded.

The connector subsystem—a dynamic perspective

We are now ready to explore the dynamic behavior of this subsystem.

During application startup, a `Connector` is instantiated for each `<Connector>` element that is found in `server.xml`. The `ConnectorCreateRule` invokes this constructor, passing it the protocol specified for this element. The specific protocol handler that will be installed for this `Connector` will depend not only on the protocol specified, but also on whether or not the Apache Portable Runtime library has been installed.

Initializing the Apache Portable Runtime (APR)

For Windows, everything needed for the APR connector is conveniently packaged in a dynamic library, `tcnative-1.dll`. This file was retrieved by the Ant `download` target into the `tomcat-native-x.x.xx` folder, where `x.x.xx` is the version number. The Win32 version is labeled `tcnative-1.dll.x86`, and should be renamed to `tcnative-1.dll`.

To allow the JVM to locate it, you could either add this folder to your `PATH` environment variable, copy `tcnative-1.dll` to your `CATALINA_HOME/bin` folder, or set the `JAVA_OPTS` environment variable to point to where this library resides using the `-Djava.library.path` system property.

The APR is an optional component in Tomcat, so if Tomcat is unable to locate the dynamic library, it simply uses the default pure-Java IO Connector implementation. The following console entry indicates the failure to locate the APR library:

```
INFO: The Apache Tomcat Native library which allows optimal performance
in production environments was not found on the java.library.path: ....
```

However, if the library is found, the Tomcat connectors will automatically use the APR. The console then displays a happier message as shown:

```
Feb 12, 2009 8:01:37 PM org.apache.catalina.core.AprLifecycleListener
init

INFO: Loaded APR based Apache Tomcat Native library 1.1.15.

Feb 12, 2009 8:01:37 PM org.apache.catalina.core.AprLifecycleListener
init

INFO: APR capabilities: IPv6 [false], sendfile [true], accept filters
[false], random [true].
```

> In the interests of exercising the standard Java IO `Connector`, ensure that the APR library is not found by Tomcat.

Instantiating a Connector

The following diagram describes the process of bootstrapping this subsystem.

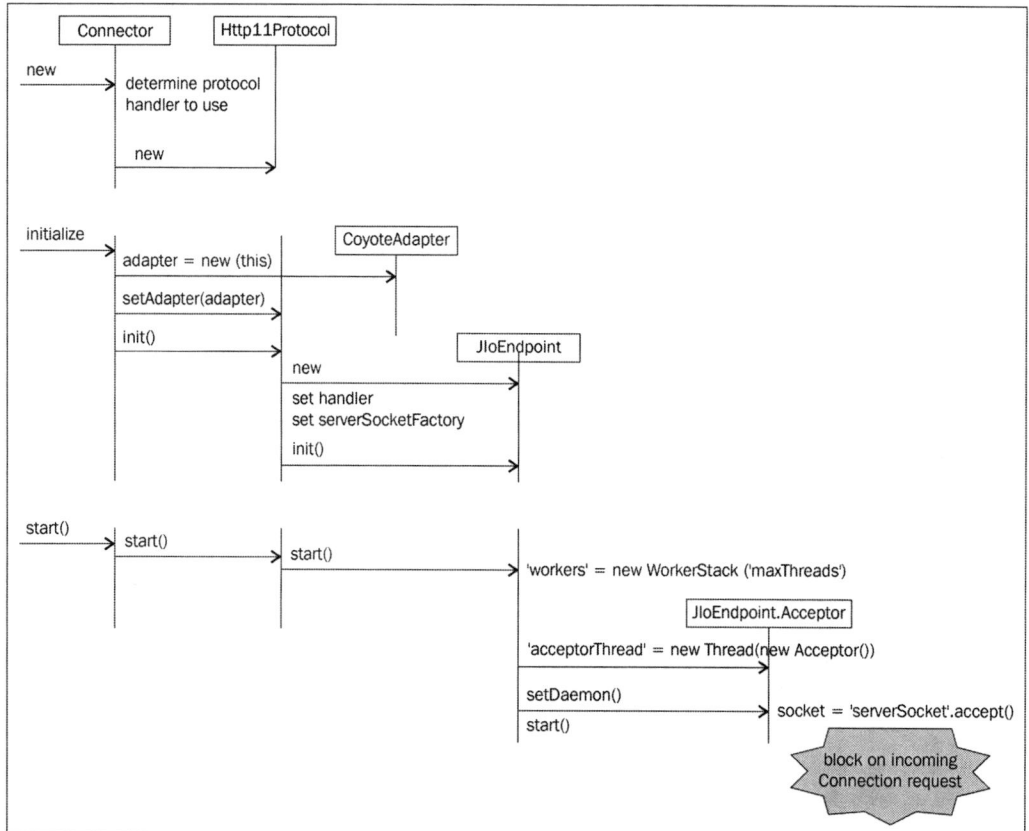

The topmost section depicts the instantiation of a new `Connector`, which drives the creation of the protocol handler appropriate for the default protocol, HTTP/1.1. If the APR library is not found, `org.apache.coyote.http11.Http11Protocol` is the standard HTTP/1.1 protocol handler.

The middle section is invoked during the initialization of the `Service`. A `CoyoteAdapter` is instantiated and provided to the protocol handler to let it hook into the request processing mechanism. The protocol handler instantiates the appropriate end point and provides it with a client socket handler, an `Http11Protocol.Http11ConnectionHandler`, and a server socket factory, `org.apache.tomcat.util.net.DefaultServerSocketFactory`.

Don't let this imposing name concern you. This factory is a thin wrapper for the creation and use of a `java.net.ServerSocket`. The end point's initialization uses the factory to obtain a new instance of a `ServerSocket`, and binds it to the specified address and port. It also configures the server socket's backlog.

The bottom section in the diagram shows what happens when a `Connector` instance is eventually started by its `Service`. The `Connector` delegates to its protocol handler, which in turn delegates to its end point implementation, which initializes an instance of `JIoEndpoint.WorkerStack` to be its pool of `JIoEndpoint.Worker` processor instances.

It also instantiates a new `JIoEndpoint.Acceptor` instance, which runs in its own thread. This thread blocks on the server socket's `accept()` call, waiting for an incoming client connection request.

With this, the initialization is largely completed. We now have a server thread that monitors port 8080 (by default) for incoming requests.

Initializing the Mapper

The second major task during the bootstrapping of the `Connector` is to initialize the mapping data structures that enable us to locate the request processing components that will need to be invoked for a given incoming request URI.

This task falls to the `org.apache.catalina.connector.MapperListener` class, which is initialized during `Connector` startup, and is then registered as a JMX notification listener. Whenever a JMX registration or un-registration notification is broadcast, it will update the `org.apache.tomcat.util.http.mapper.Mapper` instance that it shares with its `Connector`.

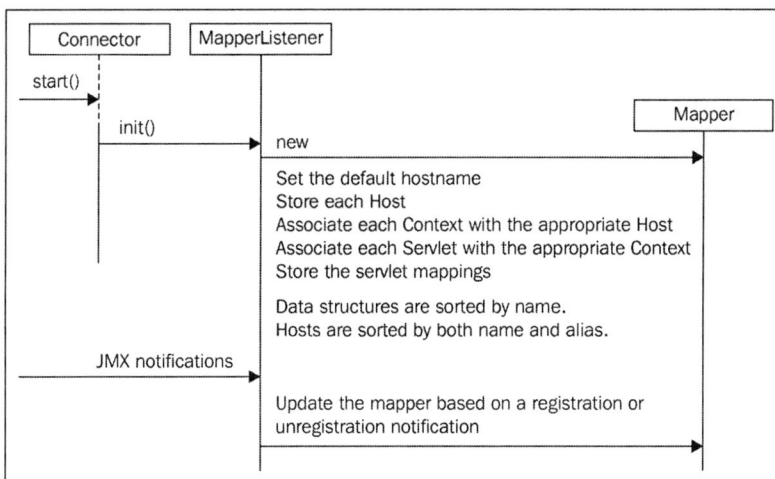

The `Mapper` instance holds references to the default host name within a given `Engine`, as well as ordered arrays of host names (including aliases) for this engine, contexts for a given host, and servlets for a given context. Servlet mappings are also maintained to enable quick determination of the servlet that will process a given request, based on the request URI and the servlet's defined mappings.

The `Connector` exposes its `Mapper` using an accessor method, `getMapper()`. As we will soon see, the adapter uses this method to access the mapper used to determine the appropriate request processing components for a given request.

A `Mapper` is queried by invoking its `map()` method, which takes a request URI, a host name, and an `org.apache.tomcat.util.http.mapper.MappingData` instance which is mutated to hold the results of the mapping operation. The `MappingData` is a very simple object that has host, context, and wrapper members that are populated, as appropriate.

The `Mapper` encodes the servlet specification's rules on how servlet mapping is to be implemented. We will see a lot more of this in Chapter 9, *The Context component*. For now, this is as far as we go.

Receiving a request

In this section, we'll trace the path of a single request. For now, we'll constrain our exploration to the `Connector` subsystem. In future chapters, we'll peel away additional curtains and peer at the puppeteers behind them.

A key aspect of a performant and scalable system is the ability to use multithreaded programming techniques to avoid blocking the main `Acceptor` thread. As a result, before we go any further, it is time once again for another digression into core Java concepts. This time it is the mechanism of thread notification.

Thread notification

The wait/notify mechanism is the preferred pattern for communication between concurrent threads. The methods that implement this mechanism, `wait()`, `notify()`, and `notifyAll()` are defined in the `Object` class, and so are available to all classes.

This pattern applies when one or more threads of execution cannot proceed until a given condition has occurred, while another thread may cause that condition to occur.

Any thread that should block while waiting for a condition to occur, must first obtain a lock on some shared lock object, before doing the testing. If the test indicates that the condition has not yet occurred, the thread must invoke `wait()` to enter the wait state.

Entering a wait state atomically does two things:

- It releases the lock.
- It causes the thread to enter a suspended wait state.

This atomicity ensures that no notification will be lost because it occurred after the lock had been released, but before the thread had entered its wait state. In other words, it ensures that no other thread could have snuck in and triggered the condition after the first thread tested the condition. Without this guarantee of atomicity, our thread might wait forever for a condition that had already occurred.

This release of the lock also has the beneficial effect of allowing more than one thread to wait on the same condition.

Now, when a trigger thread causes the condition to occur, it must also notify all the threads that have entered wait states, waiting on that condition. It does so using either the `notify()` or `notifyAll()` methods. The latter being the recommended option.

When the threads are awoken, they all attempt to gain a lock on the shared lock object. Of all the threads that are woken, only one will eventually gain the lock, detect that the condition is now favorable to continue execution, and will continue its processing. The disappointed rest will relinquish their locks and return to the wait state.

This indicates why it is important that the testing of the wait condition should occur in a loop. If a newly awoken thread detects that some other thread has beaten it to the punch in obtaining the lock and has reset the condition, it should be ready to go back to its wait state. This is easy to do when the testing occurs in a loop.

`JIoEndpoint.Worker` provides a real life example of this pattern. Its `boolean` member `available` is used for inter-thread signaling. If true, it indicates that a new socket has been placed in its `socket` member, by the acceptor, for it to process. If false, it indicates that this worker is free, and ready to accept a socket.

A `Worker` thread waits in a call to `await()` until a socket is available for processing. The `Acceptor` thread invokes `assign()` when it has a socket to assign to this worker, and blocks in there waiting for the worker to be ready to accept the new socket.

The `await()` thread waits until `available` is true, that is, until a socket is available for processing. At which point it picks up the socket, informs any waiting `Acceptor` threads that it is ready to accept another socket, and returns the newly assigned socket for processing.

```
private synchronized Socket await() {
  // Wait for the Connector to provide a new Socket
  while (!available) {
    try {
      wait();
    } catch (InterruptedException e) {
    }
  }
  // Notify Connector that we have received this Socket
  Socket socket = this.socket;
  available = false;
  notifyAll();
  return (socket);
}
```

The `Acceptor` thread that wishes to assign a socket to this worker waits in the `assign()` method until `available` is `false`—indicating that the `Worker` has begun processing its socket and is ready to accept another. At which point, it notifies the worker of the socket that is now available for processing.

```
synchronized void assign(Socket socket) {
  // Wait for the Processor to get the previous Socket
  while (available) {
    try {
      wait();
    } catch (InterruptedException e) {
    }
  }
  //Store the newly available Socket & notify our thread
  this.socket = socket;
  available = true;
  notifyAll();
}
```

End point

When we last saw the `Acceptor`, it was blocking on the `accept()` call of a `ServerSocket`, waiting for an incoming client connection. In this section, we'll look at what happens when a client attempts to connect to the listening `ServerSocket`.

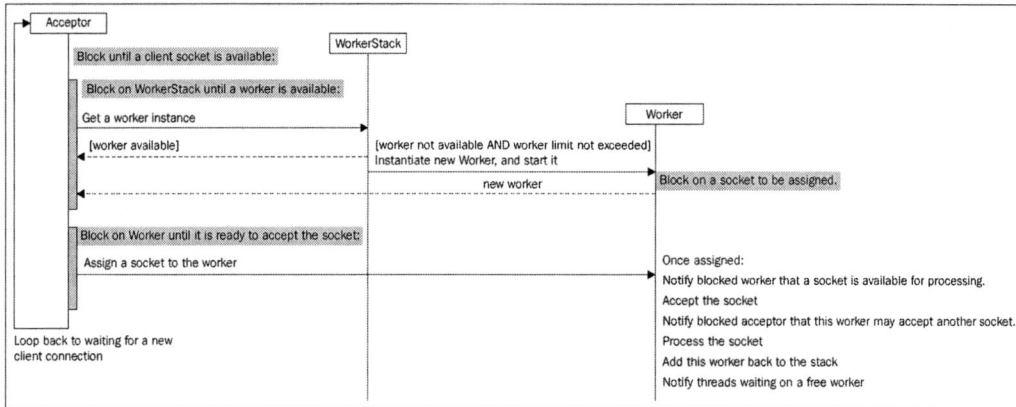

When a client connection attempt is received, the `accept()` call returns with a client `java.net.Socket` instance. In order for the `Acceptor` thread to return to waiting for the next incoming connection as quickly as possible, it must do no more than delegate request processing to a separate server thread as implemented by the active object, `JIoEndpoint.Worker`.

`Worker` instances are held in a stack that is implemented by `JIoEndpoint.WorkerStack`. This stack is bounded by the `maxThreads` attribute as configured for this `Connector`.

The stack is susceptible to multithreaded access as it may also be accessed by `Worker` threads that are returning after completing their missions that push themselves onto the stack. As a result, access to this stack is synchronized, and the `Acceptor` must first obtain a lock on it.

If there is a free `Worker`, then that worker is returned. If there are no free workers, but we either do not have a limit (that is, if `maxThreads` is negative), or have not hit our limit, a new `Worker` instance is instantiated and returned.

Else, the `Acceptor` thread has no recourse, but to wait on the `WorkerStack` instance to be notified when a `Worker` is returned to the stack and is available for assignment.

Instantiating a new `Worker` starts up a new daemon thread that blocks in the `await()` method, waiting for a client socket to be assigned to it for processing.

Whenever a client socket has been accepted, and the `Acceptor` thread invokes `assign()` on an available `Worker` instance with that socket, the `available` flag is used to indicate to that `Worker` that it can now go ahead and do its job.

The `Worker` wakes up, picks up the socket, resets the `available` flag to indicate that it is now ready for another socket to be assigned to it, notifies any `Acceptor` waiting on this condition, and proceeds to process its assigned socket.

It sets the `SO_LINGER`, `SO_TIMEOUT`, and `TCP_NODELAY` socket options as configured for the `Connector`. Then, it asks its end point's `Http11Protocol`. `Http11ConnectionHandler` to process this client socket.

Once the connection handler has processed the socket, the `Worker` recycles itself by obtaining a lock on the `WorkerStack` instance and pushing itself back onto that stack. It notifies any waiting `Acceptor` threads that the stack now has a free worker that is ready, willing, and available to process a pending client socket.

This cycle repeats for as long as the `Connector` is active and accepting connections.

Connection handler

Well, so far so good. Our `Acceptor` has accepted a connection, and has handed the client socket over to an available `Worker` thread, which has invoked the connection handler to process this new connection.

Let's pick up the story from here.

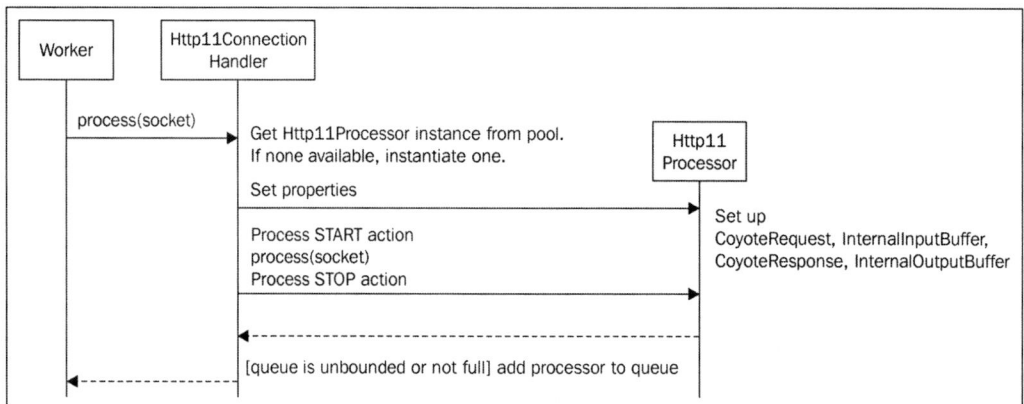

The connection handler maintains a queue of org.apache.coyote.http11. Http11Processor instances.

By now your spider senses should be tingling about yet another Java concepts diversion, and you would be right.

ConcurrentLinkedQueue

A java.util.concurrent.ConcurrentLinkedQueue is a thread safe queue that is based on linked nodes. This queue functions in a **First-In-First-Out (FIFO)** manner, where the head of the queue is the processor that has been on the queue for the longest time. New elements are inserted at the tail of the queue, and the queue retrieval operations remove processors from the head of the queue.

A ConcurrentLinkedQueue is particularly appropriate when many threads will share access to a common queue data structure, as it employs an efficient algorithm that allows one enqueue and one dequeue operation to proceed concurrently.

The typical methods on a blocking queue are:

- offer(): This method is used to add an element to the queue
- poll(): This method is used to remove and return the head element
- peek(): This method returns the head element without removing it from the queue

Http11ConnectionHandler uses an anonymous class to extend ConcurrentLinkedQueue as an unbounded queue of Http11Processor instances.

When an Http11Processor instance is needed, it is now either dequeued from this queue, or a new instance is instantiated for use. When the processor has completed its work, it will be enqueued and made available to the next request.

Http11Processor

This processor needs access to the plethora of `Connector` parameters that are either specified in the `server.xml` file, or their default values. This information is made available to the processor by passing it a reference to the endpoint instance, and by invoking various setters on it to copy over the properties that are set on the protocol handler. Its constructor also instantiates a new Coyote `Request` and `Response`.

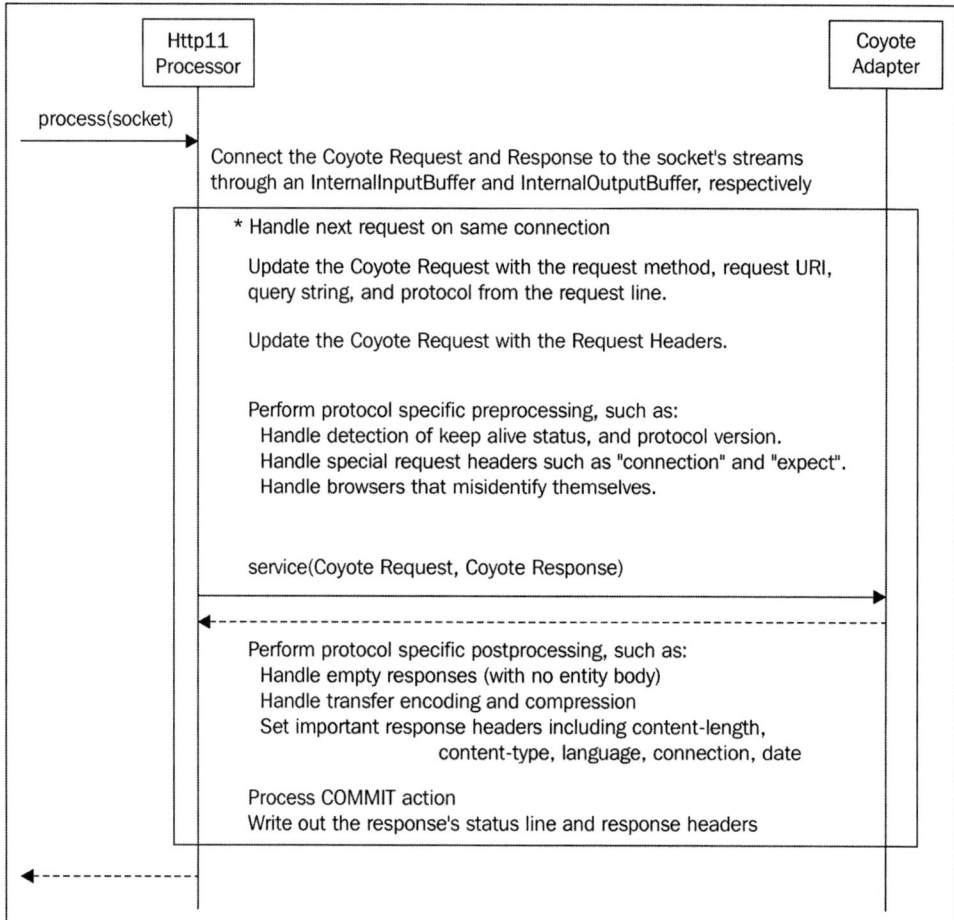

```
                 ┌───────────┐                                         ┌─────────┐
                 │  Http11   │                                         │ Coyote  │
                 │ Processor │                                         │ Adapter │
                 └───────────┘                                         └─────────┘
process(socket)
───────────────▶

         Connect the Coyote Request and Response to the socket's streams
         through an InternalInputBuffer and InternalOutputBuffer, respectively

              * Handle next request on same connection

              Update the Coyote Request with the request method, request URI,
              query string, and protocol from the request line.

              Update the Coyote Request with the Request Headers.

              Perform protocol specific preprocessing, such as:
                 Handle detection of keep alive status, and protocol version.
                 Handle special request headers such as "connection" and "expect".
                 Handle browsers that misidentify themselves.

              service(Coyote Request, Coyote Response)
              ────────────────────────────────────────────────────────────────▶
              ◀ - - - - - - - - - - - - - - - - - - - - - - - - - - - - - - - - -

              Perform protocol specific postprocessing, such as:
                 Handle empty responses (with no entity body)
                 Handle transfer encoding and compression
                 Set important response headers including content-length,
                                    content-type, language, connection, date

              Process COMMIT action
              Write out the response's status line and response headers

◀ - - - - - - -
```

The `Http11Processor` instance's `process()` method is invoked with the client socket. This process begins by connecting the `InternalInputBuffer` and `InternalOutputBuffer` to the input and output streams of the socket, respectively. It also connects these buffers to the Coyote `Request` and `Response`, respectively.

The processor handles the `keep-alive` feature of HTTP connections, and holds the connection open for as long as required.

A typical request looks as shown:

```
GET /devguide/index.html HTTP/1.1  Request Line
Host: localhost:8080
User-Agent: Mozilla/5.0 (Windows; U; Windows NT 6.0; en-US; rv:1.9.0.7)
Gecko/2009021910 Firefox/3.0.7
Accept: text/html,application/xhtml+xml,application/xml;q=0.9,*/*;q=0.8
Accept-Language: en-us,en;q=0.5
Accept-Encoding: gzip,deflate
Accept-Charset: ISO-8859-1,utf-8;q=0.7,*;q=0.7
Keep-Alive: 300
Connection: keep-alive
```

It begins by reading the request line from the socket's input stream. This request line is parsed to extract the request method, the unparsed request URI (which is the combination of the request URI and the query string separated by a question mark), the parsed request URI, the query string, and the protocol. All of these are set on the Coyote `Request`.

Next, the request headers are read from the input stream. These are added to the Coyote `Request`'s `MimeHeaders` member as new `MimeHeaderField` instances.

If the request protocol is unknown, a 505 Unsupported HTTP Version response is returned to the client.

The request headers are then queried to determine if any special processing is required. For example, the `keep-alive` flag is usually set to true for the HTTP/1.1 protocol. However, if the `connection` request header is set to `close`, then `keep-alive` must be set to false instead.

HTTP header: Connection

This header specifies options for a given connection. To indicate that a connection between the communicating hosts must be closed after sending the next message, you would send the following request header:

```
Connection: close
```

The process of establishing a connection with a remote host can be fairly time consuming. A client must determine the IP address and port of the remote host from the URI—using the Domain Name Service, followed by the handshaking required by the protocol.

In addition, TCP is a self-tuning protocol. In other words, it uses a mechanism known as **slow-start** to prevent sudden overloading of the Internet. If a host has a lot of data to send, it cannot just dump all those packets out on the Internet. Instead, it has to send one packet and wait for an acknowledgement. The receipt of the acknowledgement indicates that it now has permission to send two more packets. As each of those is acknowledged, the sender may then send four packets. This means that new connections are slower than connections that have already participated in some data exchange.

The delays that arise from both of these characteristics of socket connections can quickly add up, especially when a host needs to retrieve multiple resources from a remote host.

In such cases, rather than initiate and tear down a new TCP connection for each resource request, one optimization is to keep the TCP connection open, and to reuse it for future HTTP requests—known as a **persistent connection**.

This is the default mode of operation for HTTP/1.1. As a result, a host that wishes to terminate a connection must now explicitly send a `Connection: close` header.

Similarly, if the `expect` request header is set to `100-continue`, we flag the need to respond with a `100 Continue` response.

> **HTTP header: Expect**
>
> When a client has some large data entity that it needs to send to the server, it may wish to first check with the server that it is ready to accept that entity. The first step of this handshake is for the client to send an `Expect` request header as shown:
>
> `Expect: 100-continue`
>
> The client then waits for the server to send a `100 Continue` response before it actually sends the entity.
>
> In practice, clients should not wait forever for the server to respond, and should simply send the entity after a timeout period.

Some user agents misidentify themselves as capable of supporting HTTP/1.1 features such as `keep-alive` connections. The `Connector` can be informed of these using the `restrictedUserAgents` attribute. The processor ensures that the user agent can support these features by checking the value of the `user-agent` header against the user agents in this attribute and if a match is found, it turns off `keep-alive` connections and flags this agent's non-compliance with HTTP/1.1.

If the `transfer-encoding` header is set, we parse it for the transfer encoding names separated by commas, and set the appropriate filter on the `InternalInputBuffer`. Filters are set up as a decoration hierarchy around the input buffer, where the underlying input stream is wrapped by a filter, which in turn is wrapped by another, and so on. For instance, we might add a `ChunkedInputFilter` to support a `chunked` encoding.

HTTP header: TE and Transfer-Encoding

A transfer encoding is a reversible transformation applied to an HTTP message. It is independent of the content's format, and relates solely to how the message data will be transmitted over the network.

The `TE` request header indicates to the server which transfer encodings are supported by the client.

`TE: chunked`

The `Transfer-Encoding` header tells the receiver about the encoding that has been applied to the message.

`Transfer-Encoding: chunked`

In some cases, the server does not know the final size of the entity body being generated, and so it starts sending the data before the `content-length` is known. In such a case, the `content-length` cannot be used to delimit the data. Therefore, a different mechanism is required to indicate where the data ends. This mechanism is known as **chunked encoding.**

When using chunked encoding, the message is broken into chunks of known size. The first chunk contains the `Transfer-Encoding` header that indicates that chunked encoding is being used. Subsequent chunks are preceded by a chunk size followed by a CR/LF pair, and a portion of the entity body. The last chunk is sent with a size of 0, with only a CR/LF pair.

Another validation is to see whether a `Host` header is present in the request. This is a required header for the HTTP/1.1 protocol and its absence causes a 400 Bad Request error to be returned to the client.

If it is present, we parse the `Host` header to set the `request's serverName` and `serverPort`.

If there is no content coming through on the request, that is, the request didn't contain a `content-length` header, then we assume that this was intentional and simply set the `VoidInputFilter` as the active filter. The `VoidInputFilter` has the effect of simply returning an *End of Stream* marker for any read executed on it.

At this point the Coyote `Request` has been primed appropriately. We are now ready to begin with the actual processing of the request. The processor therefore invokes the `CoyoteAdapter` instance's `service()` method, passing it the Coyote `Request` and `Response` objects.

The processor implements the `org.apache.coyote.ActionHook` interface, which defines a single `action()` method that takes an enumeration and an `Object`. This pattern allows components, such as the Coyote `Request` and `Response`, to call back into the processor using a simplified interface.

CoyoteAdapter

The `Adapter`'s primary tasks are to construct the Catalina `Request` and `Response` objects, and to delegate request processing to its `Connector`'s engine.

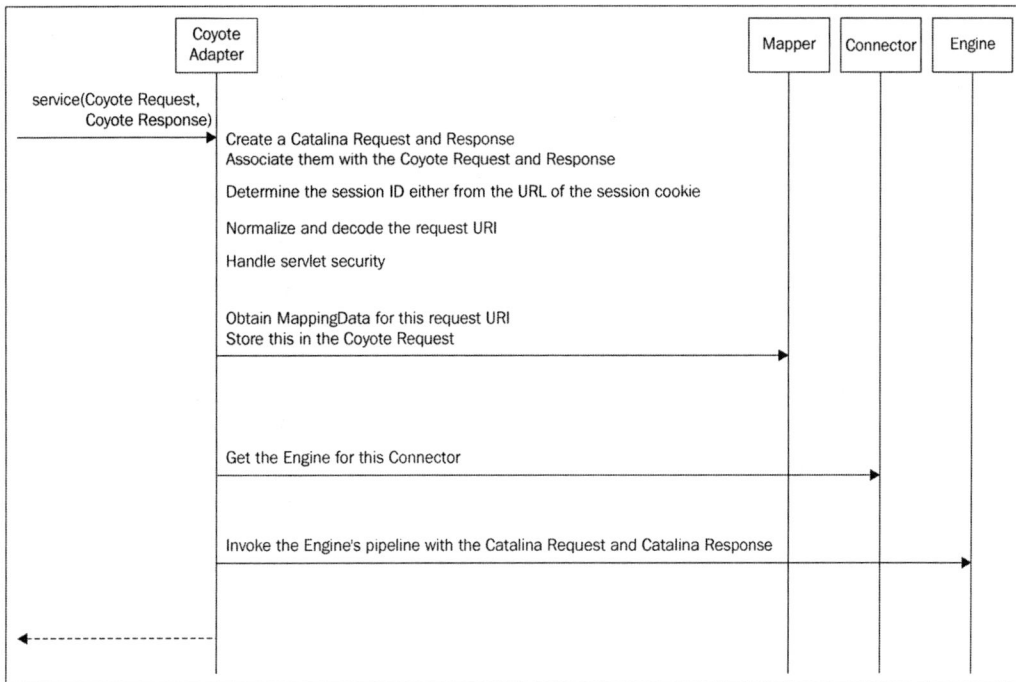

It also extracts the session identifier and sets it on the request. This identifier may be found either as a path parameter on the request URI, or in a request cookie. The adapter also sets flags on the request to indicate where it found the session identifier.

Before it delegates to the `Engine`, it consults the `Mapper` that belongs to its `Connector` to determine the host, context, and wrapper objects that should handle this request, and stores these in the `MappingData` instance associated with the Catalina `Request` instance.

This is the effective boundary of the connector subsystem.

Completing the request

Once the request processing components have generated the response, this response must be carefully shepherded back to the requesting client.

Any leftover bytes from the current request still in the input buffer are consumed, and the response is prepared for being committed. Response headers are set up and the output buffer is committed—which writes its contents to the socket's underlying output stream.

If there is no body that will be sent back, we set the active filter for the output buffer to the void filter, and we set the content length to -1. This happens for a number of status codes (204, 205, or 304) that have no associated body, or for the HEAD request method.

We now handle any compression that may be required. This is skipped if the `user-agent` request header's value matches an entry in the `noCompressionUserAgents` attribute of the `Connector`. If compression is to be used, we set the content length to -1, to force chunking.

The `content-type`, `content-language` and `content-length` response headers are set based on the response. The `Date` header indicates the current date, and a `Server` header describes the request processor.

Filters are then added to the output buffer to transform the response before it is written to the output stream. For instance, if compression is to be used, a GZIP filter is installed, while, if the `content-length` is not known, the chunked filter is used.

If this is a response that will force the connection to be dropped, for example, an internal server error, the `keepAlive` flag is reset to false. Depending on the `keepAlive` flag, the `Connection` response header is set to either `close` or `keep-alive`.

The response line is then written—the protocol followed by a space, the status code, a space, and a response message (for example, OK for 200, or Moved Temporarily for 302), as specified in `org.apache.tomcat.util.http.res.LocalStrings.properties`. This is followed with a blank line (CR/LF).

The response headers and the buffer are now written out to the socket's output stream. This completes the request processing cycle.

We turn off `keepAlive` if we already have supported up to a maximum number of `keep-alive` requests. If the connection is to be kept alive, the processor gets back to handling the next request on this same connection. Else, the processor is returned to its queue.

Summary

In this chapter, we explored the connector subsystem. We looked at the various flavors of connectors available, and we picked the standard Java IO HTTP/1.1 connector for a close review.

We discovered how the protocol handler, end point, connection handler, and processor work together to abstract away the protocol-specific mechanics of the request processing lifecycle. We also saw how the adapter is used to connect the protocol-specific processing with the remainder of the request processing engine within the servlet container.

In the next chapter we'll visit the engine component, the first component in our review of the core request processing components within Tomcat.

7
The Engine Component

So far in our journey, we have encountered the `Server`, `Service`, and `Connector` components. The `Server` and `Service` are categorized as **Top Level Components**, and represent structural aspects of a Tomcat instance. The `Server` represents the running instance of Tomcat, while a `Service` represents a grouping of `Connectors` that feed a single `Engine`. A `Connector` component, in turn, represents a connection endpoint for a given `Service`.

In this chapter, you will be introduced to additional types of components within Tomcat—**Containers** and **Nested Components**.

A `Container` is a request processing component within Tomcat, and includes the `Engine`, `Host`, `Context`, and `Wrapper` components. Containers live in a parent-child style compositional hierarchy, where a parent container contains one or more child containers, each of which may contain other child containers. Tomcat's container components implement the `org.apache.catalina.Container` interface.

A **Nested Component** is a child of a container that provides supporting functionality such as class loading, session management, or authentication and authorization.

In this chapter, we take a closer look at a key nested component, the `Pipeline`, which adds custom pre-processing of a request before it is handled by the next container, and custom post-processing of the response on its outward journey to the client.

Future chapters will consider the other container components, as well as other nested components, such as the session manager and web application class loader.

Containers

This figure provides a closer look at the compositional hierarchy of the container components, their nested components, and their request processing pipelines and valves.

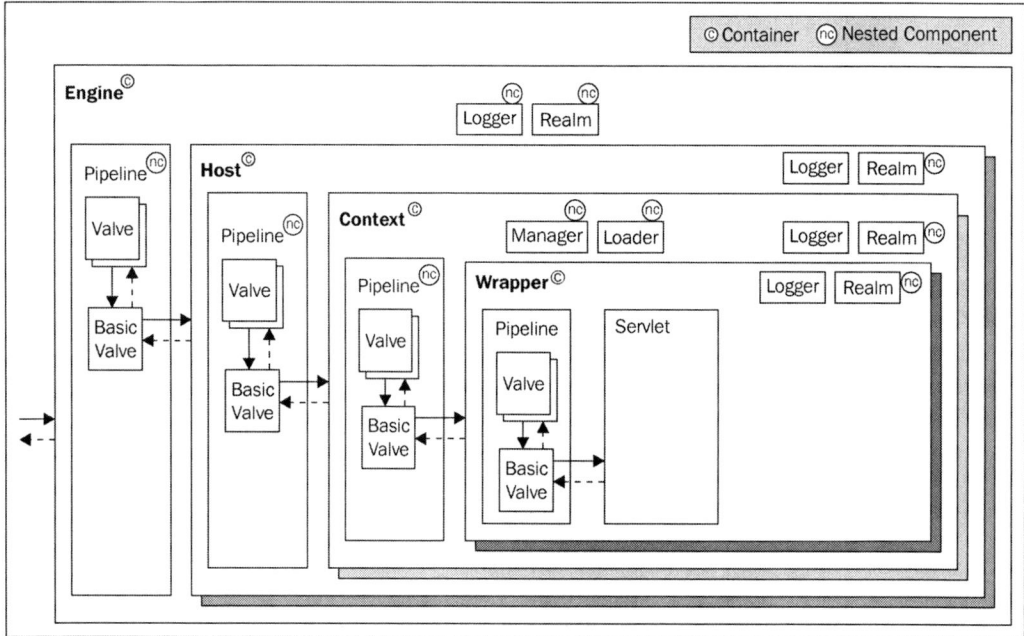

The outermost container represents the Catalina servlet engine and is the subject of this chapter.

> An **engine** cannot be contained by any component other than its service. Adding an **engine** as a child of any other container will cause an `IllegalArgumentException` to be thrown.
>
> Note that while the `Service` component does contain other components, it is not considered a container, and is instead classified as a Top Level Component.

An `Engine` contains one or more children that are of type `Host`, each of which is a virtual host. In turn, a `Host` contains a number of `Contexts`, each of which represents a single web application. A context may optionally contain `Wrapper` components, where each wrapper represents an individual servlet.

Some child containers, such as the `Host`, `Context`, and `Wrapper` can have more than one instance, as indicated by the shaded background in the image above.

The solid arrows describe the path of a request, whereas the dashed lines describe the path taken by the response. As we saw in the last chapter, the request coming into the image originates within a `CoyoteAdapter` instance.

> It is conceivable that a Tomcat deployment running as an embedded application within a network device, such as a router, might not have an `Engine` and a `Host`, but only a single `Context` and a few `Wrappers`. In other words, it is possible for certain containers within the containment hierarchy to be skipped.
>
> However, the default implementations of these containers are more restrictive in their expectations. For instance, the `addChild()` method of a `StandardEngine` will throw an `IllegalArgumentException` if a child that is not a `Host` is passed to it. Similarly, the `StandardHost` implementation only accepts children of type `Context`.
>
> Of course, this does not stop you from writing your own custom implementations of these containers that relax or remove such restrictions.

Nested components

A nested component supports the main purpose of its container. Some key nested components for a container include the following:

- A `Loader` that manages a class loader that is used to load the classes needed by its container

- A `Manager` that manages the sessions that are associated with its container

- A `Realm` that provides access to a security domain for authenticating and authorizing users

- A `Resources` component that enables the lookup of static resources associated with its container

- A `Valve` component that is used to process the request and response for its container

> Not all of these components are applicable to all containers. For instance, a Loader is actually only used by the Context.

Engine

As we saw in the last chapter, the connector subsystem was responsible for receiving the incoming request, converting it into an internal protocol-agnostic representation, and then passing it on to the engine for further processing.

All the complexity specific to a given protocol is abstracted away by the connector subsystem, allowing the engine to focus purely on the processing of the request. This has the beneficial effect of allowing a single engine to support multiple protocols such as HTTP or AJP.

An engine processes the request, by delegating to a child container, and returns the resulting protocol-agnostic response to the connector subsystem, which makes the response conform to the protocol understood by its client.

The key decision made by an engine (or as we will see later, by its basic valve) is the selection of the virtual host to which it should delegate the processing of a given request.

Configuring an Engine

The conf/server.xml file contains a default <Engine> element.

```
<Engine name="Catalina" defaultHost="localhost"> ... </Engine>
```

The important attributes supported by the Engine include the following:

- name: This is the name used to identify this engine. The default servlet engine is called Catalina.

- defaultHost: An engine directs requests to the virtual host whose name matches the name contained in the request's Host: header. If the incoming request does not contain a Host: header, or if its value does not match the name of any of the virtual Host names configured for this Engine, then the request is directed to the default host as identified by this attribute. This name is required to match the name of at least one of the <Host> elements for an engine.

- `className`: This attribute takes the fully qualified class name of an implementation of `org.apache.catalina.Engine` that should be used. The default implementation is `org.apache.catalina.core.StandardEngine`.

- `backgroundProcessorDelay`: This attribute specifies the delay in seconds (the default is 10 seconds), between periodic invocations of a container's `backgroundProcess()` method. This mechanism allows containers and their components to perform background processing on a periodic basis.

Implementation details

In this section, we'll look at how Tomcat implements the `Engine` component. This image describes the key elements of an engine's relationships.

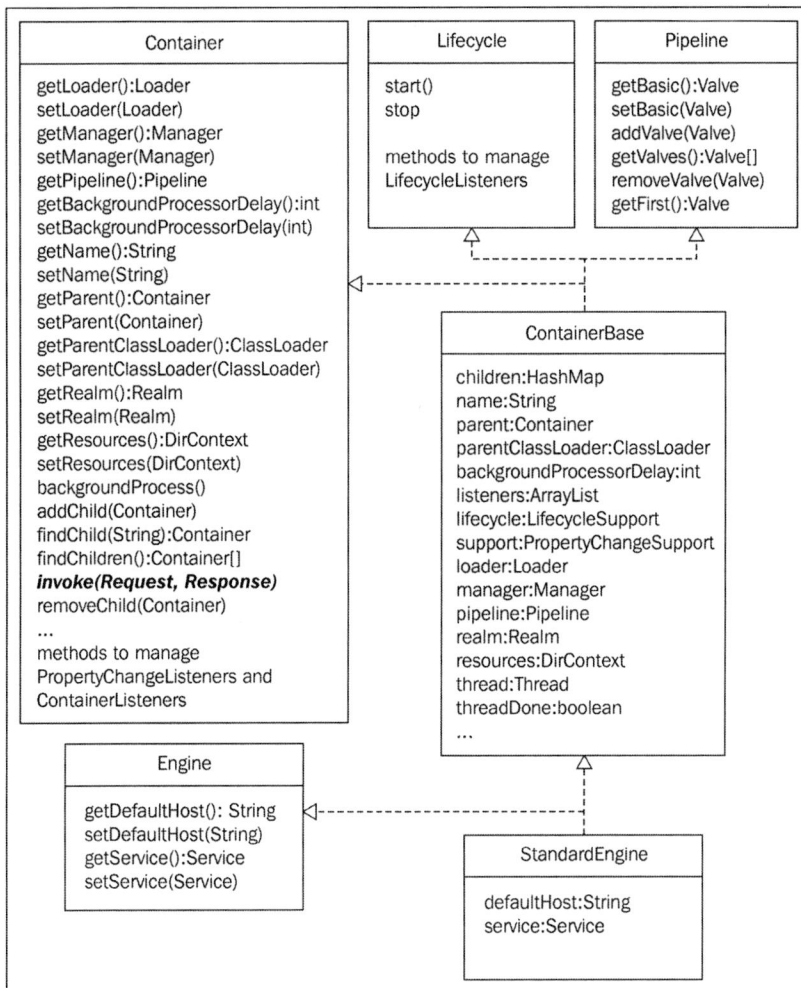

Every Tomcat container implements the `org.apache.catalina.Container` interface. The `org.apache.catalina.core.ContainerBase` class is provided as a convenience to container implementers. It not only provides default implementations for the methods in the `Container` interface, but also implements other interfaces, such as the `org.apache.catalina.Lifecycle` and the `org.apache.catalina.Pipeline` interfaces that are critical for the functioning and administration of a container.

StandardEngine

The `org.apache.catalina.core.StandardEngine` class is the default implementation of the `org.apache.catalina.Engine` interface. This class extends the abstract base class `ContainerBase`, and so conveniently inherits a lot of the common functionality of a container.

An `Engine` may only contain children that are `Host` instances. Its `addChild(Container)` override throws an `IllegalArgumentException` if an attempt is made to add a child that is not a `Host`.

A `StandardEngine` is a very lightweight object, and most of its methods, including the lifecycle methods, simply delegate to its superclass for the default implementation. As a result, our investigation of this class will continue by looking at the `Container` interface, and the `ContainerBase` superclass.

Container interface

The `org.apache.catalina.Container` interface defines the basic essence of a container, and is required to be implemented by all Tomcat containers.

It defines methods that allow you to define and manage the nested components associated with a `Container` such as a `Loader`, a `Manager`, a `Pipeline`, and `Realm`.

A `Container` may contain children, and may have a parent. The `StandardEngine`, as the outermost `Container`, cannot have a parent, and so its `setParent(Container)` method just throws an `IllegalArgumentException`.

`Containers` may also fire property change events and container events, for which listeners may register to get notifications.

Every container also has a `backgroundProcess()` method that is called periodically, based on a container's configured delay, called the `backgroundProcessorDelay`.

Every `Container` should provide an `invoke(Request, Response)` method that serves as its primary request processing method. This is the method that is called whenever a `Container` must be tasked with playing its part within the request processing lifecycle.

ContainerBase abstract class

Rather than having you implement all the methods of the `Container` interface, a convenience abstract base class, `org.apache.catalina.core.ContainerBase` is provided. Interestingly, none of the methods in this class are actually declared as abstract. Marking the class abstract just ensures that no one may directly instantiate a `ContainerBase`.

This class has members that hold references to the nested components that are most often used by containers such as the session manager, pipeline, and loader.

The responsibilities of this base class can be divided into the following categories:

- Managing parent-child relationships between containers
- Managing nested component relationships for a container
- Managing the valves for a container
- Managing listeners and notifying them of important events
- Managing the periodic processing of background tasks

We'll explore these in more detail in the following sections.

Parent and child relationships

The three main associations for a container are with its child containers, its parent container, and its nested components. In this subsection, we'll deal with the first two and leave the third for the next subsection.

The parent association is maintained using a member that points to the parent `Container`. As we have seen before, the `StandardEngine` does not have a parent container, and any attempt to set it will be met with an `IllegalArgumentException`.

A container may optionally have `children`, which are maintained in a `HashMap` that maps the child's name to the actual child object (a `Container` instance). The names for a container's children are required to be unique.

Adding a child to a container will set that container as the child's parent, and will fire an `ADD_CHILD_EVENT` container event for its `ContainerListeners`.

Other methods let you remove a child or find a given child by name. An additional finder retrieves all the children associated with a given `Container`.

Nested components

Every container can have a given set of helper components, and this set is maintained as instance members within the `ContainerBase` class.

While some components, such as the `Pipeline`, are general purpose and exist at all levels within the container hierarchy, others, such as the session manager, are only applicable within a specific container.

However, by making these generally available within the `ContainerBase`, it is conceivably possible to define these helper components at any level in the hierarchy. Various pairs of setter and getter methods let you handle each type of helper component.

Setting a new nested component on a container involves the following sequence of actions

- First, the previously set component is stopped, if it is currently active
- Next, the component is set on the container, and is started up if necessary
- Finally, a `PropertyChangeEvent` is fired that indicates the type of the component being set, as well as the old and new values for that component

Retrieving a nested component is a two step process. If the component has not been set on this `Container`, the component that was set on the parent of this `Container` is returned instead. A null is returned only if the component has not been set on any of the ancestors for this `Container`.

Valve management

A valve is a helper component that is important enough to merit its very own section later in this chapter.

A pipeline is composed of a number of valves, each of which encapsulates some element of request processing functionality. The container's own processing is encapsulated in a special valve, termed the **basic valve**, which is added to the end of this pipeline.

The base container class supports a pipeline, by providing a member that is initialized with an instance of an `org.apache.catalina.core.StandardPipeline`, right when the container itself is instantiated.

The `invoke()` method encapsulates the request processing performed by a given container. By default, `ContainerBase` implements this method by delegating processing to the first valve in its contained pipeline.

Valve management methods let you manage a container's pipeline, set the basic valve for a container, and to retrieve the first valve of a pipeline.

Life cycle methods

The `ContainerBase` class implements the `Lifecycle` interface. As a result, every container supports the `start()` and `stop()` methods, as well as life cycle listener management methods, just as with the top level components and connectors that we have already encountered.

The `start()` life cycle method invokes the `start()` method on each of this container's nested components, including the pipeline. It also invokes the `start()` method on each of its children. Finally, it starts the background processor thread. It also fires events of type `LifecycleEvent` at various points in the startup process.

The `stop()` lifecycle method does the exact reverse. It first stops the background processor thread, then it stops the pipeline, all the children, and then the nested components, by invoking the `stop()` method on each. As before, life cycle events are fired at appropriate points in this process.

A couple of things to note are that some of the nested components are optional for a component. As a result, both the `start()` and `stop()` methods do a null test for the presence of that component before trying to invoke these methods. In addition, the life cycle methods are only invoked on components that implement the `Lifecycle` interface themselves.

> A pipeline is a required nested component for a container, as a container without a pipeline is little more than a dead end.

Listener management

The `ContainerBase` also implements methods that support the management of listeners that are interested in the life cycle of containers. Its implementations of the registration and notification methods simply delegate to a `LifecycleSupport` instance, simplifying the work required to support life cycle management.

Notifications, such as `START_EVENT` and `STOP_EVENT`, are fired at the appropriate points in the corresponding life cycle methods. Similarly, the `PERIODIC_EVENT` event is fired by the `backgroundProcess()` method.

The `ContainerBase` also supports the notification mechanism for changes in standard Java Bean properties by delegating to its contained `PropertyChangeSupport` instance to relay the appropriate `PropertyChangeEvent`. Such events are fired when setting the various nested components, such as the `Loader`, `Manager`, `Realm`, and `Cluster`, as well as when setting standard bean properties such as the `name`, `startChildren`, and `parent`.

Finally, it supports notifying any listeners that are registered for container events, such as adding or removing a valve, or adding or removing a child, from this `Container`. These `org.apache.catalina.ContainerListener` instances are held in an `ArrayList` called `listeners`.

Background processing

A container may be associated with a thread that periodically invokes its `backgroundProcess()` method.

The container's `backgroundProcessorDelay` not only determines the periodicity of these calls but also determines whether the container gets its own dedicated daemon thread that periodically calls this method. If this delay is positive, then the container is given its own thread, whereas if it is negative, then this method is invoked by its parent's background processor thread.

The `ContainerBackgroundProcessor` inner class is the key to the background processing mechanism that is built into all `Container` implementations. The container's `start()` life cycle method instantiates this class and starts up this background thread.

The `ContainerBackgroundProcessor` instance's `run()` method simply sleeps for the required `backgroundProcessorDelay` specified. When it awakens, it invokes the `backgroundProcess()` method on its container, followed by that on each of its children that do not have their own background processor threads.

The default implementation of the `backgroundProcess()` method as provided by `ContainerBase` is sufficient for most containers. It calls `backgroundProcess()` on each of the container's nested components, such as the `Manager`, `Loader`, `Realm`, and `Cluster` components, as well as on each `Valve` in the container's `Pipeline`. Finally, it fires a `PERIODIC_EVENT` `LifecycleEvent` to its life cycle listeners.

The `stop()` life cycle method invokes `threadStop()` to indicate to the thread that it should terminate its processing. Next, it interrupts the thread to wake it up if it is currently sleeping and waits until the thread is done, before clearing out the background thread.

Pipeline

Now it is time to take a closer look at the container's core request processing element.

As we have seen already, an `org.apache.catalina.Pipeline` represents a series of filters, each of which is represented by an `org.apache.catalina.Valve` instance, that a request must pass through on its way into a `Container`, and that a response must pass through on its way out of that `Container`.

Pipeline execution scope

A pipeline's scope is determined by the container within which it is nested. The pipeline associated with an engine is invoked by the `CoyoteAdapter`, at the boundary between the connector subsystem and the Catalina engine. As a result, it will process every request that is received by any connector associated with that engine. In other words, an engine's pipeline can be said to have a global scope.

A pipeline associated with a host is invoked by the engine when it hands off processing to the appropriate host for which the request was targeted. As a result, a host's pipeline will process any request or response that is targeted at a given virtual host. Correspondingly, its scope is only a subset of all the requests received by an engine.

Likewise, a pipeline associated with a given context has a narrower scope, as it is invoked when the virtual host hands off the request to the web application with which it is associated.

Finally, a pipeline associated with a wrapper has the narrowest scope, as it is invoked by the context only for requests meant for the specific servlet nestled within that wrapper.

The larger the scope impact of a `Pipeline`, the more care you should take about the specific `Valves` you add into it, as there can be non-trivial performance impacts due to the composition of your `Pipeline`.

Valve execution order

When a pipeline's `invoke()` method is called, its valves are invoked in the order that they are defined, either in the `server.xml` configuration file or in the context fragment. Every pipeline has a final `Valve`, known as the **basic valve** that is invoked at the end of this invocation sequence.

A basic valve encapsulates a container's normal request processing functionality. For example, the `org.apache.catalina.core.StandardEngineValve` encapsulates the core processing associated with an engine.

StandardPipeline

A `Pipeline` is implemented by the `org.apache.catalina.core.StandardPipeline` class, which maintains its valves in a singly linked list, where each valve maintains a pointer to the next valve in the pipeline. The head and tail of this list are held in members called `first` and `basic`, respectively.

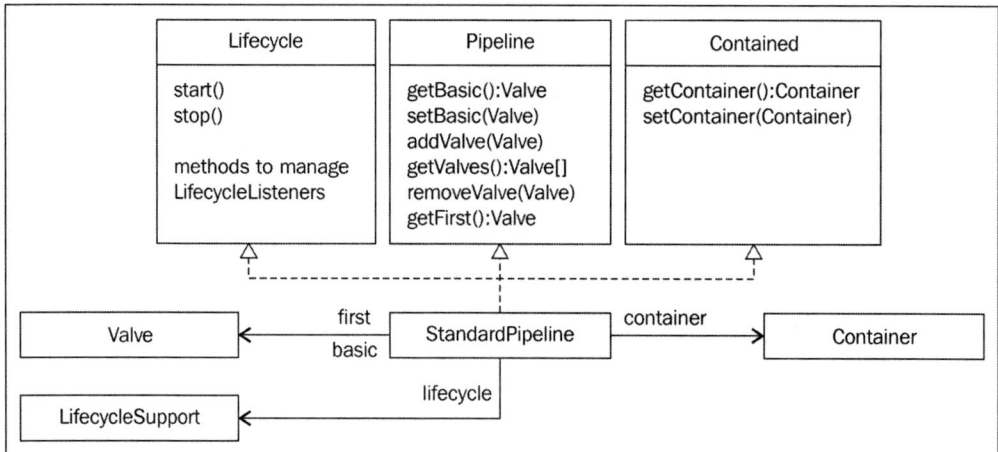

As shown, the `StandardPipeline` implements the `Lifecycle`, `Contained`, and `Pipeline` interfaces.

The Contained interface indicates that a Pipeline is associated with a single Container instance, and contributes methods to associate the pipeline with its container.

The Lifecycle interface contributes the start() and stop() methods, as well as methods to register LifecycleListener instances with this pipeline.

The Pipeline interface contributes methods to manage the valves associated with a pipeline.

Valve manipulation

The StandardPipeline's setBasic(Valve) implementation first calls stop() on the valve being replaced if the old valve is a Lifecycle instance, and then resets its associated Container. It then associates the new valve with the Container of this Pipeline, and invokes its start() method if it is a Lifecycle instance. It then sets the last valve in the pipeline to point to this new basic valve. The basic member is also updated to reference this new valve.

Its addValve(Valve) method sets the Container of the new valve to that of this pipeline. If the new valve implements Lifecycle, it then invokes its start() method. It adds the new Valve to the end of its linked list of valves. Finally, the next member of this new valve is adjusted to point to the pipeline's basic valve.

The removeValve(Valve) method removes the valve from the linked list, adjusting the list's pointers as appropriate. For instance, it adjusts the first pointer if the valve being removed is at the head. Similarly, if the valve being removed has a previous valve in the pipeline, its previous valve's next pointer is adjusted to account for its removal. The Container relationship of the removed valve is nullified, and its stop() is called if the valve being removed implements Lifecycle.

The getFirst() method returns the valve at the head of the linked list, and if that list is empty, it returns the basic valve instead.

Lifecycle methods

The start() method for a pipeline traverses its list of valves, starting at the head element pointed to by the first member, and using the next member of each Valve to continue to the next, all the way through to the basic valve. On each valve that implements Lifecycle, it calls the start() method. It fires the BEFORE_START_EVENT, START_EVENT, and AFTER_START_EVENT as it goes.

The stop() method is similar, except that it invokes the equivalent stop() method, and fires the BEFORE_STOP_EVENT, STOP_EVENT, and AFTER_STOP_EVENT events.

Valve

A `Valve` is an atomic request processing component that is assembled into the `Pipeline` of a `Container`. The name `Valve` is a metaphor for a processing unit in a real world pipeline, where a valve controls and/or modifies what flows through it.

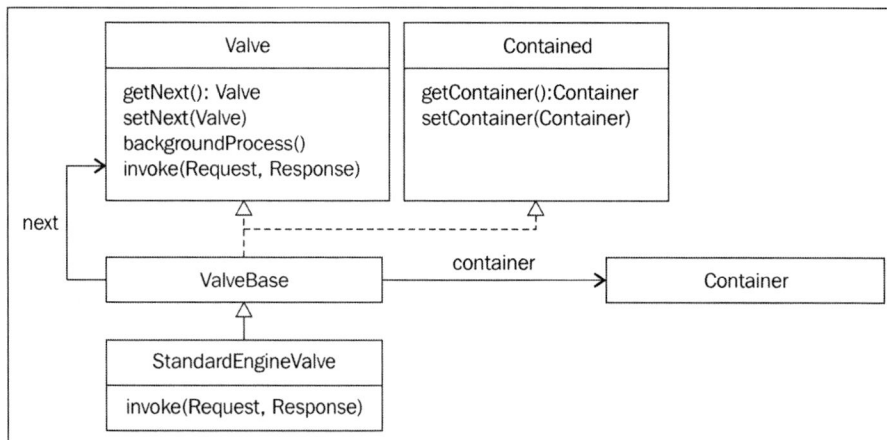

The `org.apache.catalina.Valve` interface defines methods for obtaining the next `Valve` in the pipeline; a `backgroundProcess()` method to execute a periodic task; and an `invoke(Request, Response)` method, which performs the actual processing associated with this valve.

A `Valve` may act on the request and response in a number of different ways, including:

- Examining and/or modifying the properties of the incoming request or outgoing response.

- Wrapping the request and/or response objects to supplement their functionality before passing them on.

- Completing its task and invoking the next `Valve` in the sequence, if any, by calling `getNext().invoke()` with the incoming Catalina `Request` and `Response`.

- Terminating request processing by generating and returning a complete response to the caller. A `Valve` can also terminate processing by refusing to call `invoke()` on the next valve in the sequence.

- Performing pre-processing of the request on its way in, and post-processing of the response on its way out. Any work done prior to the call to `getNext().invoke()` can be considered pre-processing, while work done after this call is the post-processing done by this valve.

However, a `Valve` should never subvert the normal request processing cycle due to its actions. In other words, it should never:

- Modify HTTP headers that are included with the `Response` on the return path of the `Response`
- Act on the output stream that is associated with the `Response` on the return path of the `Response`
- Consume bytes from the request's input stream, unless it is completely generating the response or wrapping the request before passing it on
- Change request properties that have already been used to direct the flow of processing control for this request (for example, changing the virtual host to which a `Request` should be sent from a pipeline)

Note that valves that come later in the processing pipeline may depend on work done by previous valves.

> **Comparison to servlet filters**
>
> A `Valve` is very similar in function to a servlet `Filter`.
>
> However, while the servlet `Filter` is defined in the servlet specification and so is a general construct available on a variety of servlet containers, the `Valve` is a non-portable Tomcat-specific construct.
>
> Furthermore, a `Filter` is configured declaratively using standard mechanisms in the web application's deployment descriptor. A `Valve`, on the other hand, is specified in Tomcat configuration files, and supports configuration options that are specific to the functionality exposed by that `Valve`.
>
> A `Filter` is always associated with a specific context, whereas a `Valve` can be associated with any Tomcat container.

ValveBase

The `org.apache.catalina.valves.ValveBase` class is an abstract convenience class that implements the `Valve` interface, leaving just the core `invoke()` method for your custom subclasses to define.

It defines the `next` member which points to the next `Valve` in the processing sequence. It also has a `container` member that references the `Container` associated with this `Valve`.

It provides an empty `backgroundProcess()` method, which a subclass can override to implement background processing that will be executed on behalf of its container.

StandardEngineValve

The `org.apache.catalina.core.StandardEngineValve` class encapsulates the core request processing functionality for a `StandardEngine` container.

As we saw in the last chapter, the `CoyoteAdapter.service()` method invokes:

```
connector.getContainer().getPipeline().getFirst().invoke(request,
response);
```

The container associated with a connector is an engine, and an engine by default only has a basic valve in its pipeline. As a result, this call ends up calling `invoke()` on a `StandardEngineValve`.

This basic valve's `invoke()` method simply determines the virtual host to which request processing should be delegated. It obtains the host name by calling `request.getHost()`. If you will recall from the last chapter, this is set by the `CoyoteAdapter`, by consulting the `Mapper` instance for its `Connector`.

A returned host that is null, indicates an error, which is handled by invoking `response.sendError()` to send an `SC_BAD_REQUEST` error code — 400, indicating that the host could not be determined.

If a host is found, then we delegate to its pipeline as shown:

```
host.getPipeline().getFirst().invoke(request, response);
```

Request Dumper Valve

This valve belongs to the category of general purpose valves. That is, a valve that defines generic request processing functionality that is not tied to a single container. There are over two dozen such generic valves provided by Tomcat.

The request dumper valve lets you dump the HTTP request and response headers to the logger associated with its `Container`. This valve is so simple that it takes no configuration parameters. However, its overly detailed logging can adversely affect performance when used in a production environment.

Like most valves, it extends `ValveBase`. Its `invoke()` method begins by obtaining the logger that is associated with its `Container`. It uses this logger to log various aspects of the request and response at the `INFO` level.

During the pre-processing of the request, it logs information such as the request URI, the authentication type, the content length, the protocol, scheme, server name and port. It also writes out the request's headers, including cookies, and parameters.

Then, it delegates to the next valve in the pipeline by invoking the following:

```
getNext().invoke(request, response);          // Perform the request
```

This causes the request processing mechanism to kick in, and this `Valve` waits patiently for the response to be generated before kicking into high gear again.

It then rummages through the outgoing response, logging information such as the response's content length, type, and any headers.

Obviously, all this digging around within the request and response headers is expensive, but this valve can be quite useful for troubleshooting purposes.

To use this valve, add the following `<Valve>` element to the `<Engine>` element in `server.xml`:

```
<Valve className="org.apache.catalina.valves.RequestDumperValve"/>
```

The default `server.xml` comes with this element commented out.

Start up your Tomcat container and request the default page from our previous project — `http://localhost:8080/devguide`.

The output from this valve should be logged directly to your IDE's console.

Request Filter Valve

This is a general purpose valve that allows you to allow or block client requests based on the pattern matching of various request elements . For example, an address based filter can be used to block all requests coming in from a particular range of IP addresses.

This valve demonstrates how a request can be terminated by a valve that returns a response itself, rather than delegating to the request processing mechanism.

As before, this valve is configured using the `<Valve>` element. Its `allow` and `deny` attributes take a comma delimited list of regular expression based patterns that some attribute of the request is compared against.

If the request attribute finds a match in the `deny` list, the request is terminated using a call to `response.sendError()` with a status code of `SC_FORBIDDEN (403)`. If the request attribute did not match an entry in the `deny` list, but matched one in the `allow` list, the request is allowed to proceed along to the next valve in the pipeline. If the attribute didn't find a match in either the `allow` or `deny` lists, but only a `deny` list was provided, (the `allow` list was empty), then allow the request to continue. In all other cases, the request is denied with an `SC_FORBIDDEN` error.

The specific request attribute that will be used to make this comparison is determined by the valve's `className` parameter. To filter based on the IP address of the client that submitted this request, set this to `org.apache.catalina.valves.RemoteAddrValve`. Alternatively, use `org.apache.catalina.valves.RemoteHostValve` to filter based on the hostname of the client.

The actual comparison functionality is abstracted out of these classes into an abstract base class, `org.apache.catalina.valves.RequestFilterValve`. For ease of comparison, this class converts the string based `allow` and `deny` lists into the `java.util.regex.Pattern` arrays named `allows` and `denies`, respectively.

In addition, this class provides subclasses with the `process()` method that uses the comparison algorithm described earlier to determine whether to invoke the next valve in the pipeline, or to return an `SC_FORBIDDEN` response.

Subclasses of `RequestFilterValve` implement their `invoke()` method to invoke the `process()` method with the specific request attribute that will be used for the comparison.

For instance, `RemoteAddrValve` sends in the value returned by `request.getRequest().getRemoteAddr()`, while `RemoteHostValve` sends in the value returned by `request.getRequest().getRemoteHost()`.

An example configuration to only ever allow connections from the local host, is to setup this valve in the `Context` element of either a context fragment or `server.xml`:

```
<Valve className="org.apache.catalina.valves.RemoteAddrValve"
       allow="127\.0\.0\.1,0:0:0:0:0:0:0:1" />
```

The `allow` pattern above matches the IPv6 loopback address. If this does not work for your configuration, enable the Request Dumper Valve to determine what is being sent in as the request's `remoteAddr` and `remoteHost` values.

A couple of important points to note are that the `allow` and `deny` patterns allow regular expressions, so you can go crazy in terms of the control you wish to exert.

> `RemoteAddrValve` is a lot cheaper and reliable than using `RemoteHostValve`, which requires a reverse DNS lookup to resolve the IP address from the host name.

AccessLogValve

The `org.apache.catalina.valves.AccessLogValve` is a general purpose valve that lets you create log files that contain relevant information from each incoming request. It can be configured to specify the location and name of the log file, the rolling behavior of the log file, the specific elements to be logged, as well as conditional logging of a request based on the presence of a request attribute.

The attributes supported by this `Valve` include the following:

Location and file naming attributes:

- `directory`: The directory where the log files will be placed. If this is not an absolute path, it is assumed to be relative to `CATALINA_BASE`. It defaults to `CATALINA_BASE/logs`.
- `prefix`: This phrase, which defaults to `access_log`, is prefixed to each log file's name.
- `suffix`: This phrase, which defaults to an empty string, is suffixed to the log file's name.

Advanced file attributes:

- `rotatable`: If true, then a new log file is created for each period of time as specified by `fileDateFormat`.
- `fileDateFormat`: Controls when a log file is rotated. The default, `yyyy-MM-dd` causes the log file to rotate at midnight.
- `buffered`: Controls whether an output buffer is used when writing to the log file.

Logged information attributes:

- `pattern`: The layout used for formatting log information.
- `condition`: Indicates the name of a request attribute. A request will be logged only if a request attribute with this name is found on the request.
- `resolveHosts`: Whether reverse DNS lookups should be used to convert a remote IP address to a host name.
- `timestamp`: If true, then all log messages will carry a timestamp.

The pattern supplied can include literal text interspersed with replacement parameters that are based on the syntax used by the Apache `mod_log_config` module. The complete list of parameters can be found at `http://tomcat.apache.org/tomcat-6.0-doc/config/valve.html`.

Some of the supported parameters include:

- `%a` for the remote IP address
- `%b` for the number of bytes sent, excluding HTTP headers
- `%D` for the time taken to process the request in milliseconds
- `%h` for the remote host name
- `%l` always returns '-'
- `%r` for the first line of the request
- `%s` for the HTTP status code of the response
- `%S` for the user's session ID
- `%t` for the date and time of the request
- `%u` is the remote user
- `%U` for the requested URL path

> The pattern `common` can be used as an alias for the commonly used pattern `%h %l %u %t "%r" %s %b`.

In addition, you can log additional information using the `%{xxx}y` construct, where xxx is replaced with a token name, and y is either `i` for incoming headers, `o` for outgoing response headers, `c` for a cookie, `r` for a request attribute, or `s` for a session attribute.

> This valve has been tuned to reduce the performance impact that it imposes in a live environment. However, logging has some associated cost, and that should be considered before you insert this valve into a production environment.
>
> To reduce the scope of the logging activity, insert this valve into the appropriate container. Placing it in a `<Context>` element rather than within an `<Engine>` will typically result in a significant reduction in overhead.

This valve is attached to the default host in `server.xml`, but is commented out:

```
<Valve className="org.apache.catalina.valves.AccessLogValve"
    directory="logs"
    prefix="localhost_access_log." suffix=".txt"
    pattern="common" resolveHosts="false"/>
```

Enable this on the devguide context, by adding it to our webapps\devguide\META-INF\context.xml file. Then access a standard resource within the devguide context such as http://localhost:8080/devguide. This log will generate a log file named localhost_access_log.2009-09-20.txt within output\build\logs in your Tomcat installation's base folder.

This file will contain the following entry:

```
0:0:0:0:0:0:0:1 - - [20/Sep/2009:10:23:15 -0500] "GET /devguide/
HTTP/1.1" 200 371
```

Now, let's take a look at how this valve is implemented.

Valve instantiation

A valve is instantiated by the Digester during the startup of the container. The digester instantiates the class specified in the <Valve> element's className attribute, invokes the appropriate setters corresponding to the specified attributes, and invokes addValve() on its container to register the new valve with that container.

Data members and setters are therefore provided for each of this valve's configurable attributes such as directory, prefix, suffix, pattern, and rotatable.

AccessLogElement

The setter method for the logging pattern attribute is aware of the appropriate substitutions for the common and combined patterns, and is able to replace them with the corresponding pattern sequences. Each element within a pattern sequence is converted into an instance of AccessLogElement, a nested interface within this valve.

The AccessLogElement interface defines a single method:

addElement(StringBuffer buf, Date date, Request req, Response resp, long time).

This interface is implemented by a number of nested classes within the AccessLogValve class, each of which implements the substitution of a pattern element. For instance, the ProtocolElement class supports the substitution of the %H pattern with the request protocol, whereas the HttpStatusCodeElement class supports the substitution of the %s pattern with the response's status code.

Each child class of `AccessLogValve` implements the `addElement()` method to append the appropriate substitution into the `StringBuffer` that contains the line to be logged. The other parameters allow the `AccessLogElement` subclass instance to query the environment for information required to perform the replacement for the pattern that this element represents.

For instance, a `ProtocolElement` instance overrides the `addElement()` method to invoke `getProtocol()` on its `request` argument, and to then append the result to the `StringBuffer`.

Likewise, a `RequestURIElement` represents the `%U` pattern, and its `addElement()` implementation simply appends `request.getRequestURI()` to the `StringBuffer`.

`ElapsedTimeElement` takes a constructor argument that determines whether elapsed time is to be presented in milliseconds (`%D`) or seconds (`%T`), and its `addElement()` appends the long parameter, which represents the elapsed time in milliseconds, if the `%D` pattern was used, or first converts it to seconds, if the `%T` pattern was specified.

And, when the `%S` pattern element is used, the `addElement()` method of a `SessionIdElement` uses `request.getSession(false)` to determine whether there is an associated session and then invokes `request.getSessionInternal (false).getIdInternal()` to retrieve the session ID before appending it to the `StringBuffer` instance.

Other `AccessLogElement` pattern implementations function in a similar fashion.

Literal characters are represented by the `AccessLogElement` subclass named `StringElement`, whose constructor takes the literal text as a constructor argument and stores it in its private `String` member. Its `addElement()` method then simply appends the literal text out to the `StringBuffer`, and does not need to access any of the parameters passed into it.

Named patterns

The patterns `%{xxx}i`, `%{xxx}c`, `%{xxx}o`, `%{xxx}r`, and `%{xxx}s` are inserted as instances of `HeaderElement`, `CookieElement`, `ResponseHeaderElement`, `RequestAttributeElement`, and `SessionAttributeElement`, respectively. As the class names suggest, these patterns look up the named attribute within their specified scopes. For instance, to look up a session attribute, you would use the form `%{xxx}s`.

These inner classes take the attribute name as a constructor argument. For instance, the `RequestAttributeElement` holds on to the specified attribute's name until its `addElement()` method is invoked. It then queries the `Request` for that attribute as `request.getAttribute("xxx")` and appends the returned value to the `StringBuffer`.

Valve startup

When this valve is started, it first sets up its numerous SimpleDateFormat members, and verifies that the specified directory exists, creating it if necessary. If the directory is a relative path, it is created under CATALINA_BASE, else its absolute path is used.

If the log files are rotatable, the file is named using the specified prefix, the specified fileDateFormat (or "yyyy-MM-dd" by default), and its configured suffix. For non-rotatable logs, the date portion is omitted.

A PrintWriter is then instantiated for this filename. All log file writes will be targeted at this PrintWriter.

Valve invocation

The invoke(Request, Response) method is invoked when this valve is required to write out a log entry for this request/response. This valve does not do any pre-processing of the request. Instead, it takes a timestamp, before calling invoke() on the next Valve in the pipeline. When the call returns, it takes another timestamp, and uses the two to determine the amount of time that was taken to process this particular request.

Logging is skipped if there is no logging pattern in place, or if the request does not contain an attribute that is identified using the condition valve attribute.

If the request is to be logged, a new StringBuffer and a new Date timestamp are constructed, and addElement() is invoked on each AccessLogElement element in the pattern, passing in the StringBuffer, the Date timestamp for this log request, the request and response objects, and the elapsed time for this request.

Each AccessLogElement does its thing—adding its associated information into the StringBuffer parameter.

The PrintWriter is then used to write the final StringBuffer out to the log file.

This class implements backgroundProcess(), which occasionally flushes the buffered writer to the log file. The file buffer is fairly large—128KB, and the PrintWriter is configured not to automatically flush the buffer. Therefore, this flushing ensures that data is written out at appropriate points in the process.

Summary

In this chapter, we considered our first request processing component—the Catalina engine. We looked at the containment hierarchy implemented by Tomcat and also reviewed the super class of all containers, the `ContainerBase`. Each container is associated with a pipeline that aggregates the request processing functionality for that container. We walked through the `StandardPipeline`, which is the default implementation of a pipeline. Finally, we considered the constituent parts of a pipeline, the `Valves`. We looked at the base implementation, `ValveBase`, and visited some of the key valve implementations. The valves that we explored included the `StandardEngineValve`, which is the core request component for an `Engine`, as well as some key general purpose valves such as the Request Dumper Valve, the Request Filter Valve, and the Access Log Valve. In the next chapter, we'll take a closer look at the virtual host component.

8
The Host Component

In this chapter, we're going to continue our exploration of the Tomcat containers, focusing now on the Host component.

This component is more appropriately described as a 'virtual host'. This distinction is important as it clarifies that there is often no separate physical host that is represented by this component. Instead, while a virtual host might seem very real to the users wishing to access it, in reality, it may only be one out of a number of virtual hosts that are supported by a single physical host.

Being a container, a virtual host may contain children, which in this case are web application contexts.

The standard container pattern of an implementation class with its basic valve is extended in this chapter to also include a configuration class. This configuration class, called variously as the 'configurator' or 'deployer', registers itself as a lifecycle listener of a Host, and provides support services that are central to the purpose of the container component. A host's configurator is responsible for deploying the web applications associated with that host.

> The Engine component also has a configuration class in the Tomcat source, org.apache.catalina.startup.EngineConfig. We ignored this in the last chapter, as it does not add any value to request processing.

Another key purpose of this component is to provide error handling logic for any uncaught exceptions that may be thrown during request processing. A special valve is installed in the host's pipeline to detect such an exception, and to handle it appropriately.

Virtual hosts

To users in the external world, a host is represented using a valid **Fully Qualified Host Name (FQHN)** , also known as a domain name, such as www.swengsol.com. This name is what you type into the location bar of your browser to access a particular web site.

When you request your browser to fetch a resource at a given host name, two specific steps occur.

1. Your browser tries to resolve the human-readable domain name into an IP address, which represents a unique host connected to the Internet.

> Specifying the IP address directly instead of a host name bypasses the DNS server as no resolution is necessary.

This resolution usually works by having the browser consult with a configured name server, that is, a server running the **Domain Name Service (DNS)**. The DNS database is distributed — instead of a single master database on a single server, a resolution request may be delegated to multiple servers before a match is found and returned.

> Most operating systems let you short circuit this address resolution process by configuring a mapping between the domain name and an IP address in a file such as /etc/hosts on Unix or c:\windows\system32\drivers\etc\hosts on Windows.
>
> This file is consulted before contacting the DNS server, and so this lets you run quick testing scenarios on your local workstation.

2. The browser connects to the server thread listening at a well known port for the specified protocol (by default, 80 for HTTP and 443 for HTTPS). It then relays the request for the specific resource made by the user.

In the simple case, there will be only one host name associated with a given physical host. In this scenario, every request is simply forwarded to that host.

However, the expenses involved in connecting a server directly to the Internet with a permanent IP address and with sufficient bandwidth, generally put this option out of the economic reach and technical expertise range of many small businesses. As a result it is more likely that a single physical host will house more than one logical, or virtual, host.

This is particularly popular in shared hosting scenarios, where a vendor's single physical server may house the web sites of numerous individual small businesses.

Each business has its own unique domain name, but the DNS maps each of these domain names to the IP address(es) of that single physical server. It is then up to the web server running on that physical server to demultiplex the incoming requests to the appropriate virtual host.

Tomcat virtual hosts

Before we go ahead, let's get our bearings by taking a quick look at where virtual hosts fall within the Tomcat pantheon. The following diagram will serve as a 'You are here' marker for us.

First, note that the outermost component is the `Server`, of which there is only one instance per JVM. A `Server` can have multiple `Service` instances, each of which associates one or more `Connector` instances with a single Catalina `Engine`. Each `Connector`, by default, binds to a given port on all IP addresses for that server. However, you can force it to listen to only a particular address. All requests coming into any `Connector` associated with a `Service` are channeled to the single `Engine` for that `Service`.

The `Engine` determines the virtual host that will service the request using either a request header or the IP address on which the request was received.

The `Host` is associated with one or more `Context` instances, which represent individual web applications.

A `Host` is identified by its domain name, which is what you normally type into a browser's location bar to request a resource from a remote server.

The arrows in the following diagram represent the direction of travel for a request. A response flows in the opposite direction.

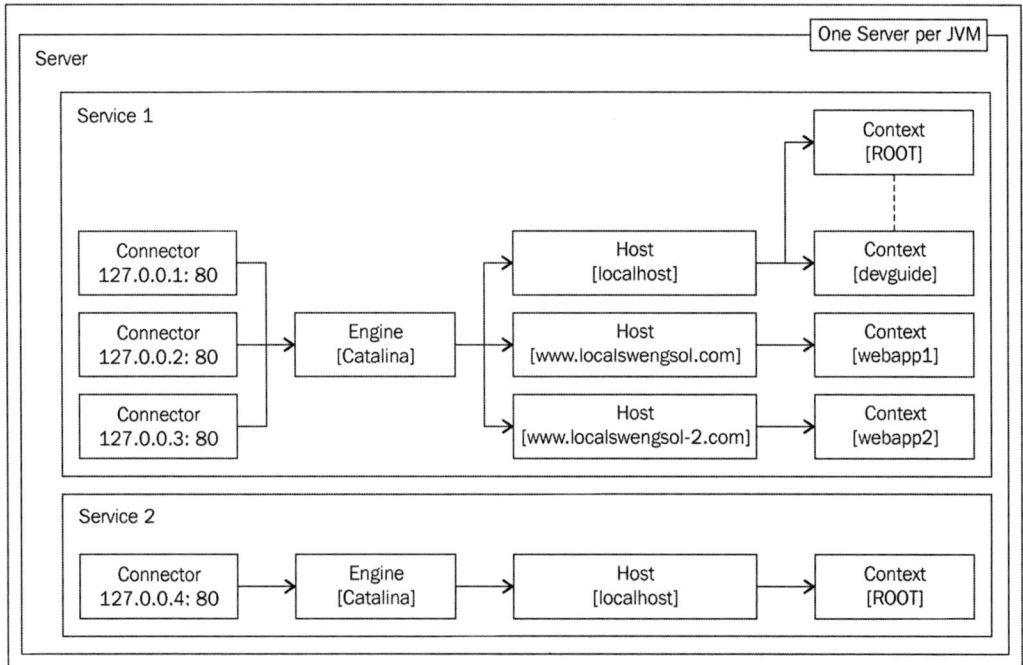

In the remainder of this chapter, we'll look at the various options available to configure and manage the virtual hosts for a Tomcat installation.

Virtual hosting scenarios

There are two main options when implementing virtual hosting—name-based and IP-based virtual hosting. The first of these has a special variant using a technique known as aliasing that we will also discuss here.

Case 1: Name-based virtual hosting

As with all types of virtual hosting, we have multiple virtual hosts that share the resources of a single physical host machine. In addition, we have a domain name per virtual host that resolves to the IP address of this physical host.

It is therefore up to the web server to determine which particular virtual host must process an incoming request.

To make this determination, the web server relies on a HTTP/1.1 request header—the `Host:` header. An HTTP/1.1 compliant browser will send this request header to indicate the specific domain that it wants to access. The server uses the value of this header to identify the virtual host that should handle the request.

```
http://www.localswengsol.com:8080/webapp1/

GET /webapp1/ HTTP/1.1
Host: www.localswengsol.com:8080
User-Agent: Mozilla/5.0 (Windows; U; Windows NT 6.0; en-US; rv:1.9.1.3) Gecko/20090824 Firefox/3.5.3
Accept: text/html,application/xhtml+xml,application/xml;q=0.9,*/*;q=0.8
Accept-Language: en-us,en;q=0.5
Accept-Encoding: gzip,deflate
Accept-Charset: ISO-8859-1,utf-8;q=0.7,*;q=0.7
Keep-Alive: 300
Connection: keep-alive
```

In this scenario, each virtual host is configured separately using an `<Host>` entry within `server.xml`, allowing each to be configured to serve up a separate set of content and applications.

Implementing name-based virtual hosting is a two-step process as follows:

- First, we create an entry in `server.xml` for each virtual host and configure each appropriately.

```
<Host name="www.myFirstDomain.com"
    appBase="webapps" … > … </Host>
<Host name="www.mySecondDomain.com"
    appBase="webapps-2" … > … </Host>
```

- Next, map all your domain names to the IP address(es) of the physical host.

For testing purposes, rather than registering a new domain name, it is easier to edit your `hosts` file.

```
127.0.0.1 www.myFirstDomain.com
127.0.0.1 www.mySecondDomain.com
```

On Windows, this file is located in the `C:\Windows\System32\drivers\etc` folder.

If you are running Windows Vista 64-bit and are unable to save edits to this file, right-click the shortcut for your file editor, and select **Run as Administrator**.

Now, when you restart Tomcat, the URL—`http://www.myFirstDomain.com` will resolve to your localhost.

> The main advantage of name-based virtual hosting is its simplicity in configuration and its ability to run multiple domain names using a single IP address, thereby conserving your available IP addresses.
>
> However, this approach has some limitations.
>
> The `Host:` header is only sent by web clients that are compliant with HTTP/1.1. Without this header, there is no way for the server to determine the host to which a given request should be directed.

There are also limitations when using HTTPS with name-based virtual hosts.

As we have seen, a web server that uses name-based virtual hosting examines the `Host:` request header to determine the target virtual host that should process the request.

However, when HTTPS is used, the browser client and the server must first negotiate SSL protocol parameters in order to establish a secure connection.

During this process, the server presents its SSL certificate to prove its identity and for use in negotiating the keys used for the session.

The problem arises at this point. The web server cannot determine which domain's certificate needs to be presented to the client browser. This is because the SSL negotiation takes place at the TCP level, which is at a lower level than the HTTP application layer protocol. To solve this problem, there must be some other way for the server to make this determination.

One solution is to use IP-based virtual hosting, which as we will see later, requires each hosted domain to have its own unique IP address. Thus, when an HTTPS request is received on one of the IP addresses bound to the web server, it simply presents the certificate associated with that IP address.

The other is to ensure that your web server and your clients support the **Server Name Indication (SNI)** extension to **Transport Layer Security (TLS)** as defined in RFC 3546. This extension causes the client to also transmit the host name during the SSL negotiation. This provides the server with enough information to return the certificate for the correct host name.

Aliasing: Multiple domains to a single set of content

This is the simplest case of name-based virtual hosting, but is more aliasing than true virtual hosting.

What is unique about this scenario is that we can support multiple domain names, each of which results in users being served identical content.

For instance, we can configure both www.swengsol.com and swengsol.com to bring users to the same set of applications and content.

This is accomplished using an <Alias> element nested within a <Host> element:

```
<Host name="www.swengsol.com" ...>
  <Alias>swengsol.com</Alias>
</Host>
```

Unlike name-based hosting, we do not have a separate virtual host element for each domain name.

Users can now specify either a host name or its alias, and both will resolve to the same content.

While to the end user it may seem that there are multiple domains involved, they are simply aliases of each other, and represent a single logical set of web applications.

Case 2: IP-based virtual hosting

With IP-based virtual hosting, each domain name on a given physical host machine is associated with a unique IP address.

How does a single physical server get associated with more than one IP address?

There are two ways to achieve this:

- You can install multiple **Network Interface Cards** (**NICs**) and bind each card to a different IP address
- You can bind a single card to multiple IP addresses by setting up virtual network interfaces—a process also known as **aliasing**

In either case, you have a single server listening on multiple IP addresses, where each IP address is associated with a given domain.

When a client browser contacts the DNS server with a given domain name, it receives the unique IP address associated with that domain.

When the server is contacted at that IP address, it simply directs the request to the single virtual host bound to that IP address.

As each server must have one IP address per domain that it will host, this solves the problem with HTTPS. The server can immediately tell which host's certificate needs to be sent to the client during protocol negotiation.

For a test setup, rather than dealing with DNS servers, we can once again edit the `hosts` file, setting a different IP address for each domain hosted on this server machine.

```
127.0.0.1 www.myFirstDomain.com
127.0.0.2 www.mySecondDomain.com
```

Unlike name-based virtual hosting, where the same IP address was mapped to every domain name hosted on the server, here a unique IP address is mapped to each domain name.

Remember to set the `useIPVHosts` attribute of the `<Connector>` element to `true` (it defaults to `false`).

```
<Connector address="127.0.0.1" port="80" … useIPVHosts="true"/>
```

Configuring a host

The default `server.xml` file defines a single engine that delegates all requests to a single 'catch-all' virtual host (named `localhost`).

```
<Engine name="Catalina" defaultHost="localhost">
    …
    <Host name="localhost" appBase="webapps"
        unpackWARs="true" autoDeploy="true"
        xmlValidation="false" xmlNamespaceAware="false">
```

This configuration is able to handle any request coming in to this `Engine`, as when a match is not found between the host name specified on a request and the host names configured for an engine, the request is simply forwarded to the default host.

The true power of this element comes from allowing you to configure additional hosts for a single engine. This allows you to support multiple fully qualified domain names on a single physical server and to partition your web application contexts by domain.

As we have seen in the last chapter, it is up to the engine to determine the virtual host that should be asked to handle the incoming request and to delegate to it.

A host's `appBase` attribute indicates that this host will monitor the CATALINA_BASE/ `webapps` folder for its contexts, the `unpackWARs` states that any WARs placed there will be unpacked before they are deployed, and the `xmlValidation` attribute controls the validation of `web.xml` files deployed in this host.

The complete set of a host's attributes can be categorized as follows:

- **Standard attributes**: These attributes define the implementation and name of the host.
    - ° `className`: It is the class name of the host implementation to be used. The default class used is `org.apache.catalina. core.StandardHost`.
    - ° `name`: This attribute is usually set to the name of this virtual host as registered with the DNS. This is also the name that is carried in the HTTP/1.1 `Host:` request header.

        An engine must specify a default virtual host that will handle an incoming request for which a destination host cannot be determined. The `defaultHost` attribute of an engine must take a name that should match the name of at least one of its configured hosts.

        The default `server.xml` uses the name `localhost` for its single host and also sets the `defaultHost` attribute of the engine to this name. This makes the single host for this engine serve as a catch-all host to which the engine sends all requests, irrespective of the host name specified in the request.

- **Deployment configuration**: These attributes determine how applications that belong to a given virtual host are deployed.
    - ° `appBase`: This parameter takes a path name that is either absolute or one that is relative to CATALINA_BASE. It identifies a folder that will contain all the host's web applications. A web application can take the form of either a WAR file or an exploded directory. A host will deploy the applications that are found in this directory.

○ deployOnStartup (default: true): If true, then any web applications found in the appBase location are automatically deployed on Tomcat startup.

○ autoDeploy (default: true): Setting this to true will cause a running Tomcat instance to monitor its appBase folder and to automatically deploy new applications without having to be restarted.

While this is a major convenience during development, this constant checking of the appBase location is done on the background processing thread and has an associated performance penalty.

○ unpackWARs: If true, then any WAR file found in the appBase directory is unpacked into its corresponding directory structure before it is deployed. If false, then a web application will be executed without first being unpacked. While this saves space in your appBase location, it increases response time because of the constant archive access that must now occur.

○ deployXML (default: true): A web application's context can be configured using a context fragment file. This file can be supplied by the web application itself (within its META-INF/context.xml) or by the Tomcat administrator as a context file in the host's configuration directory, CATALINA_HOME/conf/[engine-name]/[host-name]/[application-name.xml].

If deployXML is false, then a web application cannot supply its own configuration. Only context fragments found in the host's configuration directory will be considered.

> Note that the autoDeploy attribute controls whether applications are deployed during the host's background processing, whereas deployOnStartup controls whether applications are deployed during the host's startup processing.
>
> Setting both to true will cause an application to be deployed at startup, and then again once Tomcat is up and running. As a result, ensure that you set at least one of these to false to avoid redundant deployment of the same web application.

- Other attributes include:

    - `backgroundProcessorDelay`: This attribute specifies the seconds between the invocation of `backgroundProcess()` on this host and its child containers. A positive value causes a thread to be spawned. Otherwise, the parent's background process thread is used.

    - `errorReportValveClass`: The class name of the error reporting valve that will be used by this host. This attribute can be used to customize the look of the error pages generated by Tomcat. The default is `org.apache.catalina.valves.ErrorReportValve`.

    - `xmlValidation` (default: `false`): If `true`, then Tomcat will validate your `web.xml` files.

    - `xmlNamespaceAware` (default: `true`): Enables XML namespace awareness.

    - `workDir` (default: `CATALINA_HOME/work`): A directory used by applications running in this host to write temporary files. This location is saved as a servlet context attribute named `javax.servlet.context.tempdir`.

The `xmlNamespaceAware` and `xmlValidation` attributes are not described in the configuration section for hosts, but are still available for setting. They are used to configure the `Digester` that parses the web deployment descriptor. The former indicates whether the `Digester` should use a parser that is namespace aware, and the latter controls whether the `web.xml` file is validated against its schema prior to deployment.

When set at the `Host` level, these settings apply to all contexts within that host. However, individual contexts may override these settings.

StandardHost

The following diagram highlights key aspects of the `Host` component. A virtual host in Tomcat is represented by an instance of the `org.apache.catalina.core.StandardHost` class. This class extends `ContainerBase`, thereby inheriting all the features and abilities of a standard container. In addition, it implements `org.apache.catalina.Host` to qualify as a standard `Host` component.

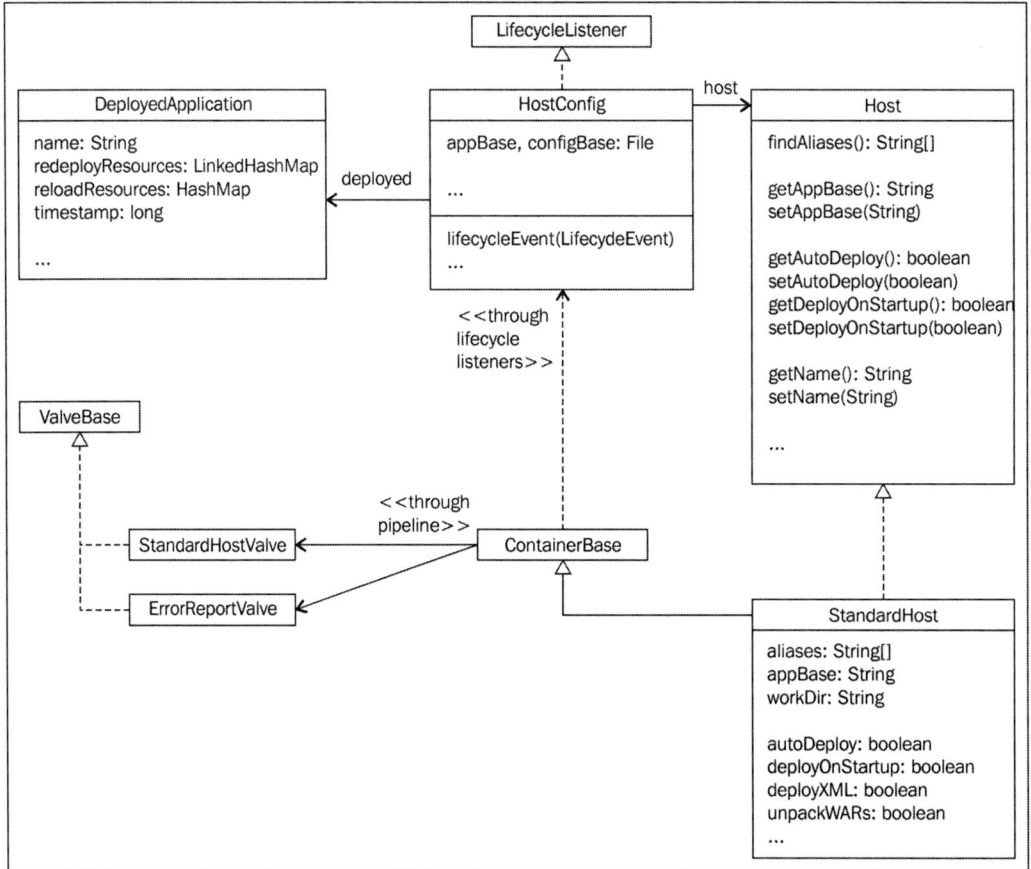

The properties exposed by the `<Host>` element are represented as data members of the `StandardHost`.

In addition, a `String` array of aliases holds the set of aliases that may be used to refer to a given host. As we saw earlier, aliases are defined for a `<Host>` element by nesting `<Alias>` elements within it.

At startup, the `StandardHost` instantiates a host configurator and registers it as a lifecycle listener. This configurator is an `org.apache.catalina.startup.HostConfig` instance and contains the functionality required to deploy and reload the host's web applications.

As a lifecycle listener, this configurator injects the appropriate functionality when it is notified of key events in its container's life. In particular, it responds to the start notification by deploying all web applications if the host's `deployOnStartup` attribute is set to `true`. It also responds to the periodic event raised by the background processing thread by checking watched resources that might signal that a particular web application must be reloaded.

By default, a host's pipeline will contain a basic valve as implemented by `org.apache.catalina.core.StandardHostValve`, as well as an error reporting valve, which by default is an `org.apache.catalina.valves.ErrorReportValve`.

A `Host` can only take children that are `Context` instances and calling `addChild()` with an instance of any other type will cause an `IllegalArgumentException` to be thrown.

All things considered, the `StandardHost` class is fairly simple. This is because most of its complexity has been moved out into its lifecycle listener, the `HostConfig`, which we will discuss next.

HostConfig

An instance of this configurator class is added as a lifecycle listener of a `Host` component during its startup phase. This listener processes the start, stop, and periodic lifecycle events for its associated `Host`.

The primary function of this configurator is to deploy the web application contexts of its `Host`. In this section, we'll take a closer look at how the deployer handles this function.

Contexts and context fragments

A `Context` is represented by an `org.apache.catalina.core.StandardContext` instance. The deployment of a web application involves the instantiation of this class and initializing it with the properties of the `<Context>` element.

The `<Context>` element can either be found as a child of the `<Host>` element within the `server.xml` file, or it can be found as a standalone XML file known as a context fragment file. The file is called a **fragment** because it contains just a lone `<Context>` element.

Irrespective of its location, the purpose of the `<Context>` element is to configure a single web application context.

A typical `<Context>` element describes the path to its document root or `docBase`, which is the path where all its static and dynamic resources live, and a context `path` which defines how the application will be referenced in a request URI. A `Context` with an empty path, "", represents the root context. This is the context that will be invoked when a request URI does not specify a named context.

> The usage of a `<Context>` element in a context fragment file is identical to its usage within `server.xml`, except that you cannot specify a context path. Instead, the base file name of the fragment file is used as the context path on the URI. To specify a path with directory separators, use a '#' character in the file name instead.
>
> A context fragment file that is contained within the `META-INF` file of a WAR file or an exploded directory has the added restriction that it can only be named `context.xml`. In this case, the context path is determined by the name of the WAR file or the exploded directory (which can also contain the '#' character).

A context fragment may be contained either within the `conf\[engineName]\ [hostName]` folder under `CATALINA_BASE`, or it may be found packaged as the `META-INF\context.xml` file within either its WAR file or its exploded directory.

The default engine is named `Catalina`, and the default host is named `localhost` — as a result, in a default Tomcat installation, you would find context fragments in the `CATALINA_BASE/conf/Catalina/localhost` folder.

Any `<Context>` element within the `server.xml` file is processed by the general `Digester` instance created during startup. This is done using an instance of the `ContextRuleSet` class, which handles the instantiation, setting of attributes, and the adding of children and nested elements, of a context.

Context fragments, on the other hand, are handled by the host's deployer, using a `Digester` that it creates to parse these fragment files, and which it holds in a static member. This digester parses context fragments, instantiates a `StandardContext` instance, and sets its properties.

> The use of context fragments is recommended for deployment, as it reduces the need to touch server.xml directly.
>
> It also facilitates hot deployment, as changes to a context fragment can be picked up without having to restart Tomcat.
>
> It is also the best option when you need to supply your web application as a self contained module.
>
> The file placement rules also allow you to better organize the context configuration files by engine and host.

DeployedApplication

Every application deployed into a Host is represented by an instance of a Context and an instance of DeployedApplication. The latter is an inner class of HostConfig that provides a convenient way to record the resources that should be watched for changes.

Watched resources are maintained in two separate maps, the redeployResources map contains the resources that would cause the application to be redeployed if a resource were to be changed or deleted, whereas the other, reloadResources, contains resources that, if modified or deleted, would cause the application to be reloaded.

For both maps, the key is the absolute path to the resource, and the value is the timestamp when that resource was last modified. This allows the container to determine if it has an out-of-date copy of that resource and allows it to determine the appropriate action to take.

> Redeploying or reloading of an entire application is controlled by the host's autoDeploy attribute. If this attribute is false, all such checks are disabled.

Note that there is a material difference between an application being redeployed and being reloaded.

Reloading a context is a much simpler process. The host invokes the stop() method on the context, followed by its start() method. The main effects here are a reloading of the web.xml deployment descriptor, and the initialization of a brand new class loader for this application.

Redeploying on the other hand, is a lot more substantial. The entire context is destroyed, and a new context initialized. The destruction of a context involves invoking its `stop()` method, and removing it from its parent host. The web application is then deployed as if it were a brand new context. This process therefore involves reloading of its context fragment file.

In general, the resources added to the `redeployResources` map include the context fragment file, the WAR file, and the context's document root.

The resources added to the `reloadResources` map include those resources that are registered as watched resources with the context. Resources are registered to be watched by adding the `<WatchedResource>` child element to the `<Context>` element. The default `context.xml` fragment file watches the `web.xml` file:

```
<Context>
    <!-- Default set of monitored resources -->
    <WatchedResource>WEB-INF/web.xml</WatchedResource>
    ...
</Context>
```

> The web application's loader component also watches for changes to its loaded classes or resources, or to its JAR files.
>
> If a change is detected, the context is reloaded, which throws away the current class loader, and initializes a new one for the context to use.
>
> This checking is enabled by setting the context's `reloadable` attribute to true.

Lifecycle events

The `HostConfig` instance responds to a start event notification by checking whether the host's `deployOnStartup` property is set to `true`, which indicates that the host's applications should be deployed on startup.

The process of deployment at startup includes deploying any context fragment files in the configuration folder for this host. Configuration folders are rooted at `CATALINA_BASE\conf` and are named for a given engine and host combination, as with `CATALINA_BASE\conf\[engineName]\[hostName]`. Any context fragments found in this folder are deployed.

The host's `appBase` points to the directory that contains the web applications for a given host, either as WAR files or exploded directories. This `appBase` can be specified either as an absolute folder location or as a folder that is relative to `CATALINA_BASE`. By default, this is the `CATALINA_BASE\webapps` folder.

> Note that this is in addition to the contexts that are created by the parsing of the `server.xml` file.

Deploying context fragments

Context fragments are found in the host's configuration directory which for the default Tomcat installation is `CATALINA_BASE\conf\Catalina\localhost`.

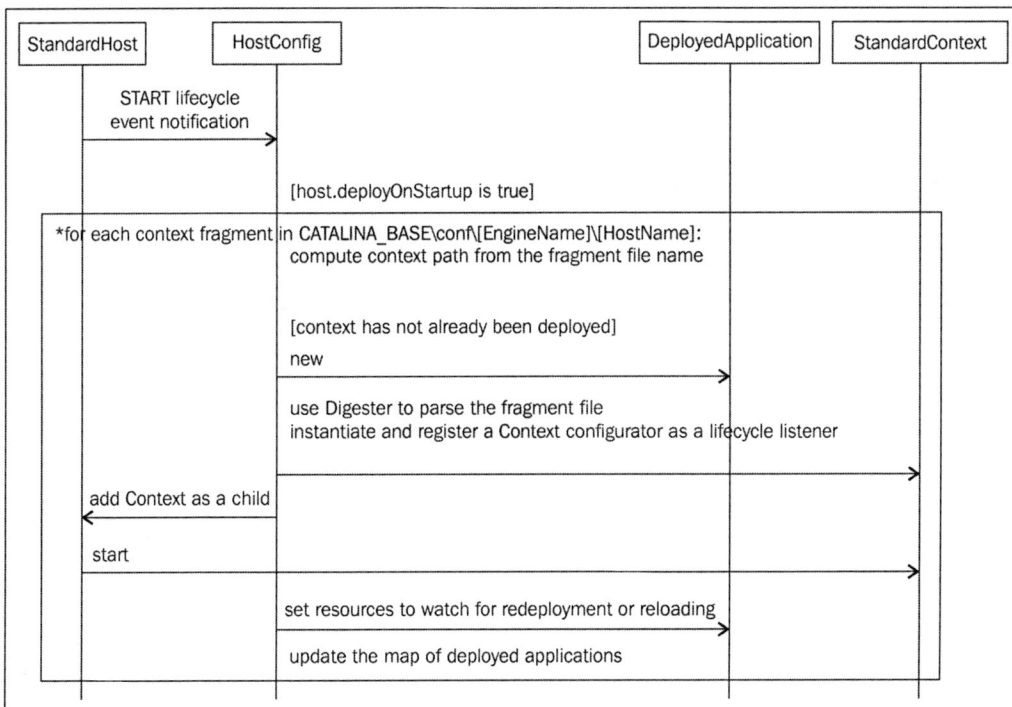

```
StandardHost      HostConfig                              DeployedApplication   StandardContext

         START lifecycle
         event notification

                   [host.deployOnStartup is true]

  *for each context fragment in CATALINA_BASE\conf\[EngineName]\[HostName]:
                   compute context path from the fragment file name

                   [context has not already been deployed]
                   new

                   use Digester to parse the fragment file
                   instantiate and register a Context configurator as a lifecycle listener

         add Context as a child

         start

                   set resources to watch for redeployment or reloading

                   update the map of deployed applications
```

The context path for the web application described by a context fragment is computed from the name of the fragment file. This context path is generated by taking the base file name of the fragment (minus the `.xml` extension), converting any '#' characters in the name to '/' characters, and prefixing it with a '/'.

As a result, a context fragment file named `myApp.xml` will result in the context path `/myApp`, whereas a file named `parent#sub.xml` is mapped to `/parent/sub`. The context fragment for the default application is named `ROOT.xml`, in which case the context path is set as the empty string, `""`.

A fragment is loaded only if it has not already been loaded, that is, it is neither in the `deployed` HashMap nor is it a child of the `Host`.

A `DeployedApplication` instance is constructed for this context.

The `Digester` is then used to parse this fragment and create and initialize a new `StandardContext` instance. A configurator for the `Context` is then instantiated and registered as a lifecycle listener. This is usually an `org.apache.catalina.startup.ContextConfig` instance. The context fragment file's path and the context path are set on our new `Context` instance.

This new `Context` instance is then added as a child of this `Host`. This kicks off the process of determining the exact `docBase` for this child context, as we will see in the next chapter.

> The `Digester` used by the configurator to parse the context fragment does not do the entire task. Its function is limited to instantiating the context and setting its properties. As we will see in the next chapter, the context's configurator will complete this processing, and will handle additional tasks such as the registering of any nested components that are associated with this context.

The context's watched resources are added to the `DeployedApplication` instance's list of resources that force a reload of the context. The resources that will cause redeployment include the context fragment file, and either the `docBase` folder or the WAR file.

Any errors found during an application's deployment through the context fragment are logged, but it does not affect the loading of other applications in this host.

Finally, the `DeployedApplication` instance is placed into its `deployed` member, which is a `Map` keyed by context path. This marks the context as having been deployed.

Deploying WAR files and exploded directories

In this phase, the WAR files located within the host's `appBase` are deployed, followed by any exploded directories found there. The process is very similar for both, and so we will treat them together.

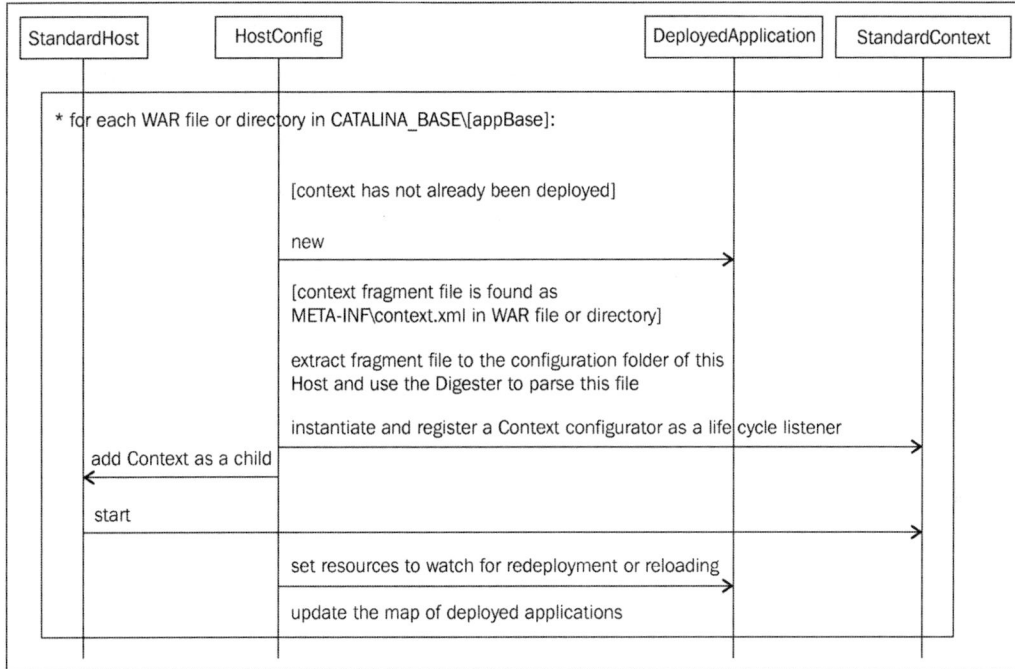

For each WAR file or exploded directory found here, a context path is generated based on the name of the WAR file or the directory, using the rules described earlier. The base file name (for a WAR file, without the `.war` extension) is extracted, all '#' characters in the name are replaced with '/' characters, and it is prefixed with a leading '/'. A name such as `ROOT.war` or `ROOT` is converted to an empty context path. Just as before, a previously loaded context is skipped.

If the security policy allows us to use the fragment provided by the context (that is, the host's `deployXML` attribute is `true`), then the application is checked to see if it provides a `META-INF/context.xml`. If such a file is found, it is copied to the host's configuration folder and named appropriately for this context.

If a fragment was found, it is parsed using the `Digester`, a `StandardContext` instance is created, and its properties are set appropriately. This context fragment is added to the `DeployedApplication` instance's `redeployResources` map.

If no fragment is available, then a default `StandardContext` instance is created to represent this web application context.

The WAR file or the exploded directory is added to the `DeployedApplication` instance's `redeployResources` map.

The process is completed as before, that is, a life cycle listener for this `Context` is added, and this `Context` is added to the host's list of children. This process ensures that the `docBase` for this `Context` is set appropriately.

If `unpackWARs` is `true` for this host, then the unpacked folder for this context must also be added to the `redeployResources` map.

Any watched resources specified using a relative path is converted to an absolute path under this context's directory. These watched resources include the default `conf/context.xml` and `conf/web.xml` files and the context fragment and `WEB-INF/web.xml` files for this web application.

Finally, the `DeployedApplication` instance is added to the `deployed` map, keyed by this application's context path.

Periodic events

The configurator also watches for periodic events that are raised by the background processing thread, based on the configured processing delay.

This method is material only if the host's `autoDeploy` attribute is `true`. It is to be noted that there is a performance penalty involved in setting this attribute to `true`. If this flag is `false`, then the method returns without any further ado.

If `autoDeploy` is `true`, we walk through each `DeployedApplication` instance in the `deployed` map, which represents the currently deployed contexts within this `Host`.

For each deployed application, it checks the application's resources for redeployment or reloading.

Each element in the `redeployResources` map is then tested. A redeploy event is indicated if either a previously existing resource has since been deleted or if an existing resource has a last modified time that does not match the time recorded in this map.

Redeployment involves removal of the child context from its parent host, invoking its `destroy()` method, deletion of any resource that is within the `appBase` or configuration folders for this host (such as the context fragment file), and the removal of its associated `DeployedApplication` instance from the map of `deployed` applications.

A reload event, on the other hand, works by detecting whether a resource in the `reloadResources` map has either been deleted or modified since it was last read. A reload involves finding the context associated with this resource, and invoking its `stop()` method, immediately followed by a `start()`.

While the above process handles changes to the key resources of a deployed web application, we also need to consider the possibility that a brand new web context may have been deployed. Therefore, the deployment of descriptors, WAR files, and directories, as described earlier, is run once again. This ensures that any new descriptors, files, or directories that have been added since the last check are deployed. In addition, any contexts that were undeployed in the previous step are now redeployed.

Examples of name-based virtual hosting

In this example, we'll set up name-based virtual hosting in our Tomcat installation.

As a first step, edit your `hosts` file to add the following lines. You may need to ensure that your user account has the appropriate privileges to edit this file.

```
127.0.0.1          www.localswengsol.com
127.0.0.1          localswengsol.com
127.0.0.1          www.localswengsol-2.com
```

This ensures that when you type in one of these domain names, your DNS resolver will return the same IP address, in this case, the loopback address for your local host.

Start up your Tomcat server, and navigate to either `http://localswengsol.com:8080/devguide` or `http://www.localswengsol.com:8080/devguide`. Both URLs should now take you to our familiar `devguide` web application's index page. Remember that you can also get here using the original URL, `http://localhost:8080/devguide`.

However, this only works on Tomcat because all the requests received by our `Engine` are simply being forwarded to the default virtual host named `localhost`. This is because no match is found with either of the host names, `localswengsol.com` or `www.localswengsol.com`.

> Resolved IP addresses may be cached locally—and throw off any modifications that you make to the `hosts` file. To clear the local DNS resolver cache, use `ipconfig /flushdns`.
>
> Note that your browser may have its own DNS cache as well.

Now, let's set up our project so that we can install additional virtual hosts and web applications into these hosts.

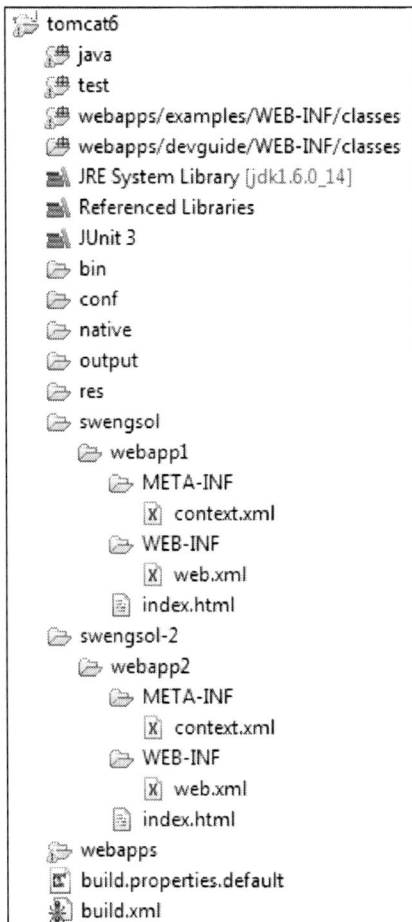

```
tomcat6
    java
    test
    webapps/examples/WEB-INF/classes
    webapps/devguide/WEB-INF/classes
    JRE System Library [jdk1.6.0_14]
    Referenced Libraries
    JUnit 3
    bin
    conf
    native
    output
    res
    swengsol
        webapp1
            META-INF
                context.xml
            WEB-INF
                web.xml
            index.html
    swengsol-2
        webapp2
            META-INF
                context.xml
            WEB-INF
                web.xml
            index.html
    webapps
    build.properties.default
    build.xml
```

This image shows our point of arrival directory structure.

Create two new sub folders named `swengsol` and `swengsol-2` as siblings of the `webapps` folder. These folders will serve as the `appBase` of the new hosts that we will add to our Tomcat deployment.

Within these folders, create the two web application contexts. These are very basic "web applications" so that we might focus on the virtual hosting aspect of this configuration.

The `web.xml` and `context.xml` files are identical across both applications and are reproduced below.

Web Application Deployment Descriptor (web.xml)

The deployment descriptor for these web applications are intentionally simplistic.

```
<?xml version="1.0" encoding="ISO-8859-1"?>
<web-app xmlns="http://java.sun.com/xml/ns/javaee"
   xmlns:xsi="http://www.w3.org/2001/XMLSchema-instance"
   xsi:schemaLocation="http://java.sun.com/xml/ns/javaee
      http://java.sun.com/xml/ns/javaee/web-app_2_5.xsd"
   version="2.5">

   <description>Tomcat Developer's Guide</description>
   <display-name>Tomcat Developer's Guide</display-name>

</web-app>
```

Context Fragment (context.xml)

The context fragments for these web applications do nothing more than add a valve.

```
<?xml version="1.0" encoding="UTF-8"?>
<Context antiResourceLocking="false" reloadable="true"
  privileged="false">
  <Valve className="org.apache.catalina.valves.AccessLogValve"
    directory="logs"
    prefix="localhost_access_log." suffix=".txt" pattern="common"
    resolveHosts="false"/>
</Context>
```

webapp1/index.html

The only difference between the two versions of this file is in the name of the web application displayed. To generate the `webapp2/index.html` file, simply replace references to `web application #1` with `web application #2` in the following listing:

```
<!DOCTYPE HTML PUBLIC "-//W3C//DTD HTML 4.0 Transitional//EN">
<HTML>
  <HEAD>
    <TITLE>Web application #1</TITLE>
    <META http-equiv=Content-Type content="text/html">
  </HEAD>
```

```
<BODY>
<P></P>
  <H3>Tomcat Developer's Guide - Web application #1</H3>
  <P></P>
  <H4>Welcome to web application #1</H4>
</BODY>
</HTML>
```

Next, let us modify `build.xml` so that these files get copied over just as the default `appBase` of `webapps` does.

build.xml

Modify the `build-prepare` target to include the lines:

```
<target name="build-prepare">
 … <lines omitted for brevity> …
  <mkdir dir="${tomcat.build}/lib"/>
  <mkdir dir="${tomcat.build}/logs"/>
  <mkdir dir="${tomcat.build}/temp"/>
  <!-- ****************** [ADDED] ****************** -->
  <mkdir dir="${tomcat.build}/swengsol"/>
  <mkdir dir="${tomcat.build}/swengsol-2"/>
  <!-- ****************** [END] ****************** -->
  <mkdir dir="${tomcat.build}/webapps"/>
 … <lines omitted for brevity> …
</target>
```

Likewise, to the `deploy` target, add these lines:

```
<target name="deploy" depends="build-only,build-docs,warn.dbcp">
 … <lines omitted for brevity> …
  <!-- ****************** [ADDED] ****************** -->
  <copy todir="${tomcat.build}/swengsol">
    <fileset dir="swengsol">
      <include name="webapp1/**"/>
    </fileset>
  </copy>
  <copy todir="${tomcat.build}/swengsol-2">
    <fileset dir="swengsol-2">
      <include name="webapp2/**"/>
    </fileset>
  </copy>
  <!-- ****************** [END] ****************** -->
 … <lines omitted for brevity> …
</target>
```

These lines will ensure that the new `appBase` locations are also copied over to the output folders.

We are now ready to test our virtual hosting scenario.

Aliasing

Let us begin with the easiest option—aliasing. Modify our `conf/server.xml`, as shown in the following snippet of code:

```
<Engine name = "Catalina" defaultHost="localhost">
    <Host name="localhost" appBase="webapps"
        unpackWARs="true" autoDeploy="false"
        deployOnStartup="true"
        xmlValidation="false" xmlNamespaceAware="false">
    </Host>
    <Host name="www.localswengsol.com" appBase="swengsol"
        unpackWARs="true" autoDeploy="false"
        deployOnStartup="true"
        xmlValidation="false" xmlNamespaceAware="false">
      <Alias>localswengsol.com</Alias>
    </Host>
</Engine>
```

In particular, note that we now have two `Host` elements defined for our `Engine`. In addition, the default `Host`, named `localhost`, is the one that is still hosting the applications in the `webapps` folder. This is also the host that will receive all requests that come in with a host name that does not match any known `Host` for this `Engine`.

Our shiny new `Host` is called `www.localswengsol.com` and has its `appBase` set as `swengsol`. We have defined an alias for this `Host` as `localswengsol.com`.

Start up your Tomcat server, and navigate to either `http://localswengsol.com:8080/webapp1` or `http://www.localswengsol.com:8080/webapp1`. Both URLs should now take you to our new web application's very spare index page.

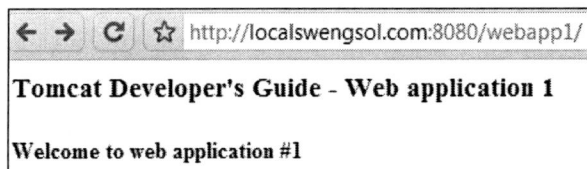

Note that trying to access the `devguide` application using `http://www.localswengsol.com:8080/devguide` will not work, as that context is not deployed to this `Host`.

As indicated earlier, aliasing allows you to present identical content through multiple request URLs. Next, we'll attempt true virtual hosting, where the different URLs result in different content.

Name-based virtual hosting

In this example, we update our `server.xml` with the following `Host` declaration:

```
<Host name="www.localswengsol-2.com" appBase="swengsol-2"
      unpackWARs="true" autoDeploy="false"
      deployOnStartup="true"
      xmlValidation="false" xmlNamespaceAware="false">
</Host>
```

Here we're bringing the second `appBase` that we had created, `swengsol-2`, into play. In addition, we use a distinct host name, `www.localswengsol-2.com`.

Remember to edit your `hosts` file to add a mapping for this host name to the loopback address.

Start up your Tomcat server, and navigate to `http://www.localswengsol-2.com:8080/webapp2`. This URL should now take you to the similarly spare index page of our second web application.

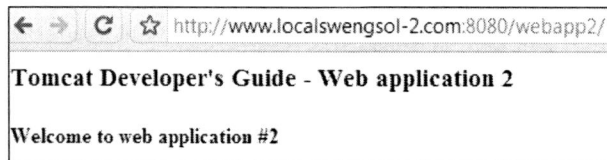

Try repeating the aliased URLs of the previous section, and you'll notice that they'll work just as before.

IP-based virtual hosting

To enable IP-based virtual hosting is just a bit more complex.

First let's ensure that each of our hosts has its own unique IP address. For our purposes, an edited `hosts` file will work just as well.

```
127.0.0.1          localhost
127.0.0.2          www.localswengsol.com
127.0.0.3          www.localswengsol-2.com
```

Then, let's update our `server.xml` to configure the connectors for each
unique IP address.

```
<Connector address="127.0.0.1" port="8080" protocol="HTTP/1.1"
           compressableMimeType="text/html,text/xml"
           connectionTimeout="20000" redirectPort="8443"
           useIPVHosts="true" />
<Connector address="127.0.0.2" port="8080" protocol="HTTP/1.1"
           compressableMimeType="text/html,text/xml"
           connectionTimeout="20000" redirectPort="8443"
           useIPVHosts="true" />
<Connector address="127.0.0.3" port="8080" protocol="HTTP/1.1"
           compressableMimeType="text/html,text/xml"
           connectionTimeout="20000" redirectPort="8443"
           useIPVHosts="true" />
```

Note the presence of the `useIPVHosts` attribute which is set to `true`. This ensures
that any mapping check for a host is done based on the IP address of the server
socket, rather than using the `Host:` request header.

Using this configuration, you should be able to access all three web applications,
`http://localhost:8080/devguide`, `http://www.localswengsol.com:8080/
webapp1`, and `http://www.localswengsol-2.com:8080/webapp2`.

StandardHostValve

This valve encapsulates the basic behavior of the `StandardHost`. It has two primary
responsibilities:

* It invokes the pipeline of the appropriate `Context` to process the request
* It handles any exceptions that occur during the processing of the request

This valve's `invoke()` method first obtains the `Context` associated with the
incoming Catalina `Request`.

It then sets the context class loader of the current `Thread` to the `ClassLoader`
associated with that `Context`. This ensures that any class loading will occur in
the context of the selected web application, and so will get a view of the world as
described by the `WEB-INF/lib` and `WEB-INF/classes` folders of that application.

It then invokes the pipeline associated with that `Context` as follows:

```
context.getPipeline().getFirst().invoke(request, response);
```

In addition to invoking the request processing pipeline, the `StandardHostValve` is responsible for detecting whether an error occurred during request processing, locating the error resource appropriate for that error, and then forwarding control to that error resource.

If this valve is unable to find a configured error resource for a given error condition, then the fallback position is to have the `ErrorReportValve` generate a default error page.

The servlet error handling mechanism

The servlet specification's error page mechanism describes how web applications may customize error pages that are displayed when an error occurs on the server.

This error page mechanism kicks in either when an uncaught exception is propagated up to the container or when the response has an error status code in the 4xx or 5xx ranges.

This mechanism is very declarative in nature and is driven by the `<error-page>` element in `web.xml`. This element maps either an exception type (using the `<exception-type>` element) or an error code (using the `<error-code>` element) to the location of the resource that will display the error page (using the `<location>` element).

The `<exception-type>` is specified as a fully qualified class name of the exception (for example, `java.lang.Throwable`), the error code is specified as an HTTP status error code (such as 404 or 500), and the location of the error handling resource is specified as a URL.

If the location URL identifies a dynamic resource (such as a JSP or a servlet), then the container will also make the request and response objects available to it. It will also store additional request attributes that will help the dynamic resource determine the specific error condition that occurred. These request attributes include the following:

- `javax.servlet.error.exception`: This attribute contains the specific exception that was thrown. You can use this exception to get its message, print its stack trace, and so on.
- `javax.servlet.error.exception_type`: This attribute contains the class of the exception that was thrown.
- `javax.servlet.error.status_code`: This attribute contains the HTTP status code.

- `javax.servlet.error.request_uri`: This attribute contains the URI of the original request that led to this error.

- `javax.servlet.error.servlet_name`: This attribute contains the logical name of the servlet in which the error occurred.

- `javax.servlet.error.message`: This attribute contains the specific error message associated with this exception condition.

Exception processing

If there is a `javax.servlet.error.exception` attribute on the request, that is, if an uncaught exception was encountered during the processing of the request, then processing continues with the next section — *Finding a custom error page by exception type.*

> As we will see in Chapter 10, The `Wrapper` Component, this request attribute is set by the `StandardWrapperValve`, when it detects that an uncaught exception was thrown in a servlet. It also sets the response's status code to 500 to indicate an internal server error.

On the other hand, if no exception attribute was detected, the processing will skip the next section, and instead will start at *Finding a custom error page by response status code.* An example of this is when you request an unknown resource from a context, which results in no uncaught exception being thrown. Instead, this results in a response being returned with its status code set to 404. The `StandardHostValve` handles this error condition by retrieving a mapping by status code, and forwarding to it. If a mapping to an error resource is not found for this status code, then it delegates to the default error page for the `ErrorReportValve`.

Finding a custom error page by exception type

Custom error pages are mapped to exception types in the web deployment descriptor, as shown here:

```
<error-page>
  <exception-type>java.lang.Throwable</exception-type>
  <location>/ErrorPage.html</location>
</error-page>
```

The search for the custom error page begins by obtaining the class of the exception stored in the request attribute and using `Context.findErrorPage()` with the name of that class. This query is repeated for each superclass of that exception, until either a mapping for that exception class is found or until the top most level of the object hierarchy — the `Object` class — is reached, which indicates that no match was found.

If no match was found, this may indicate that exception translation may have been used to translate the actual error into a generic `ServletException`. If the exception in the request attribute is an instance of `ServletException`, then the underlying root cause of this exception is extracted, and the earlier search for a mapping is repeated, walking up to the `Object` class for that root cause exception.

If an error page mapping for this exception type was not found, then the search continues, but this time, considering the response's status code instead. The response is updated to indicate an internal server error (status code 500), and then an attempt is made to locate the mapping for that error code.

Finding a custom error page by response status code

The status code set on the response is now used to locate the mapped error page. The `Context` is queried to determine the error page mapped to this status code.

At this point, if a custom error page has still not been located, then control returns out of this valve and the `ErrorReportValve` is given a chance to do its thing.

On the other hand, if a custom error page has been located, control is forwarded to it using a request dispatcher, as described in the sections that follow.

Setting request attributes

If an error page mapping was found, we then set the error related request attributes as per the servlet specification's error handling mechanism.

- `javax.servlet.error.exception`: It is set to the error associated with the `Throwable`, while `javax.servlet.error.exception_type` is set to the error's class. This is set only when a mapping by exception type was found.

- `javax.servlet.error.status_code`: It is set to the status code for an internal server error (500), if a mapping by exception type was found. Otherwise, it is set to the response error status code.

- `javax.servlet.error.request_uri`: It is set to the original request URI, as obtained from the Coyote `Request`.

- `javax.servlet.error.servlet_name`: It is set to the wrapper's name, if the result from `request.getWrapper().getName()` is not null.

- `javax.servlet.error.message`: It is set to the message contained in the `Throwable`, if a mapping by exception type was found. Otherwise, it is set to the error message associated with the Coyote `Response`.

An error page is represented by an `org.apache.catalina.deploy.ErrorPage` instance, which identifies the error code and/or exception type for which this page would be used, as well as the context relative location of this page.

Note that the `javax.servlet.error.message` attribute is set to a filtered version of the message set on the response. The filtering replaces characters that are sensitive in HTML (such as the '<', '>', '&', and double quotes) with their entity representations (that is, `&lt;`, `&gt;`, `&amp;`, and `&quot;`). This ensures that it would be impossible for an attacker to embed JavaScript code in the request URL that would then be output in an error message to an unsuspecting browser.

Forwarding to the error resource

Processing is now handed off to the custom error page resource. This is done by using a server-side forward, rather than a client-side redirect, that is accomplished using the request dispatcher mechanism that we will look at in the next chapter.

Additional attributes are added to the request. The `org.apache.catalina.core.DISPATCHER_REQUEST_PATH` attribute is set to the location of the error page. The `org.apache.catalina.core.DISPATCHER_TYPE` attribute is set to the type of the dispatcher request—in this case, an ERROR.

A request dispatcher is then obtained from the context for this error resource. It is then used to forward the request to the designated error resource. `response.flushBuffer()` is then called to commit the response.

Method termination

On the return path, the session object associated with this request is retrieved in order to set its last accessed time. Finally, the context class loader is reset to the `ClassLoader` that is used to load the `StandardHostValve` class. This will usually be the server class loader.

ErrorReportValve

This valve is used to post-process the generated response, and so will fire only after the basic valve has finished its processing. This is possible because its `invoke()` method delegates to the remainder of the pipeline before actually doing any processing for itself.

If the response has already been committed, this valve does nothing more. This would be the case when a custom error resource has been found by the StandardHostValve for a Throwable or for a response status code and has been successfully dispatched using a RequestDispatcher.

However, if the response has not yet been handled, this valve will provide the default handling behavior.

If there is a javax.servlet.error.exception attribute on the request, then it marks this as an error response, and invokes response.sendError() with an internal server error (500) status code.

It then retrieves the response's message, filters it, and generates the HTML for a default error page.

> You can have the ErrorReportValve generate an error response simply by requesting a resource that does not exist. In our case, requesting http://localhost:8080/devguide/NonExistentServlet would result in a 404 error page that was generated by this valve.

Error page mechanism example

This example modifies the devguide web application's HelloWorldServlet to throw an exception. Once you are done with this example, please undo the changes to return to the original behavior of this servlet.

We begin by editing webapps/devguide/WEB-INF/classes/HelloWorldServlet. java to force it to throw an exception:

```
public void doGet(HttpServletRequest request, HttpServletResponse
    response) throws IOException, ServletException {
    if (true) throw new IllegalArgumentException("Illegal call");
```

Now, start your server and request http://localhost:8080/devguide/ HelloWorld.

You will see the generic Tomcat error page, as shown in the following image:

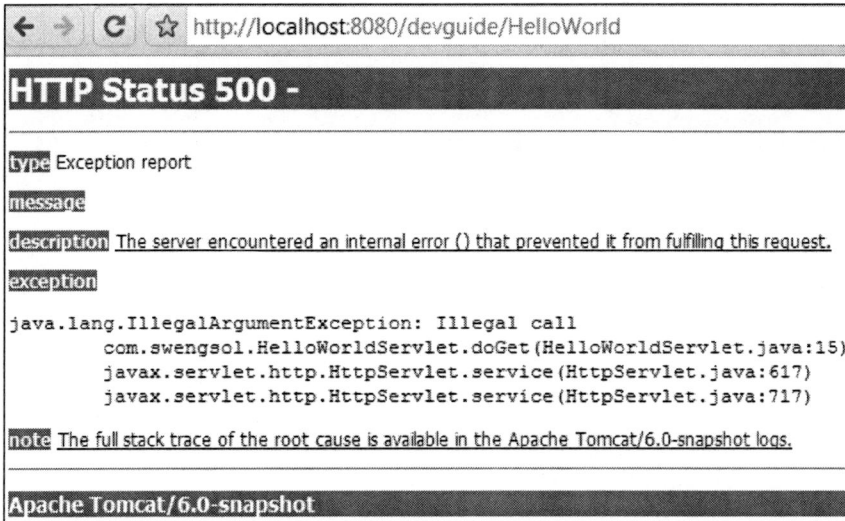

Modify webapps/devguide/WEB-INF/web.xml to add an error mapping:

```
<error-page>
  <exception-type>java.lang.Throwable</exception-type>
  <location>/ErrorPage.html</location>
</error-page>
```

> I have used an overly general exception type here. In the real world, this feature works best when you specify error resources by narrow exception types.

Finally, we add the specified error resource, webapps/devguide/ErrorPage.html:

```
<?xml version="1.0" encoding="ISO-8859-1"?>
<!DOCTYPE html PUBLIC "-//W3C//DTD XHTML 1.0 Strict//EN"
  "http://www.w3.org/TR/xhtml1/DTD/xhtml1-strict.dtd">
<html xmlns="http://www.w3.org/1999/xhtml" xml:lang="en" lang="en">
  <head><title>Error</title></head>
  <body>
  An error has occurred.
  </body>
</html>
```

Now, requesting the same page will result in your custom error page being displayed instead.

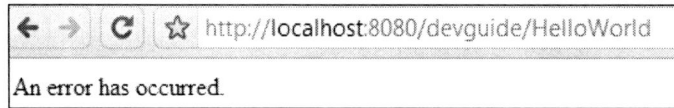

```
←  →  C  ☆  http://localhost:8080/devguide/HelloWorld

An error has occurred.
```

Summary

In this chapter, we covered the Host component within a Tomcat installation. We looked at how the Host works in concert with its configurator and valves to implement the deployment of contexts, the invoking of the context as part of request processing, and the reporting of errors that arise from this processing.

We took a close look at context fragments and the various ways in which contexts may be deployed as running web applications.

In the next chapter, we will get up close and personal with the grand daddy container of them all—the Context. Fasten your seat belts folks because things are going to get a bit rough ahead!

The Context Component

9

In this chapter, we will take a closer look at one of the most complex components of Tomcat, the context. Fortunately for us, this component makes up for its complexity by also being one of the most interesting components within the Tomcat firmament.

A lot of its complexity arises from the very central role that this component plays within Tomcat. As shown in the following image, the Context not only implements core request processing functionality, but also plays a key role in orchestrating the activities of a number of helper components.

This includes managing access to the application's resources, orchestrating the loading of an application's classes, providing a naming service, handling web application security, and registering servlets and filters.

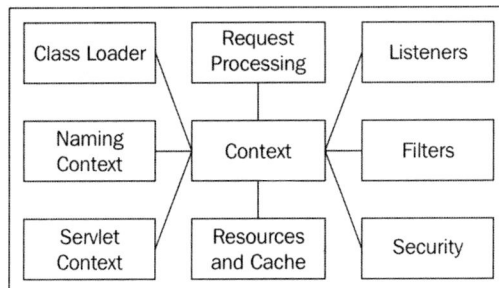

In this chapter, we will look at a number of these nested components and their implementations. We'll take a particularly close look at how Tomcat's custom class loader allows each context to have its own private view of the world, how the static and dynamic content for a context may be accessed in a storage-agnostic manner, and how key elements are engaged in processing an incoming request.

We will not cover the naming service implementation, as this is largely similar to what we have seen in the chapter on the `Server`. Security concepts are out of scope for this text and so are not discussed in detail.

There is a lot of ground to cover in this chapter, and there are a flood of new concepts waiting to be understood. In order to better organize the topics to be covered, this chapter has been organized into four main sections.

In the first section, we'll consider the general aspects of configuring this component. In the second section, we'll look at various general concepts for some key services implemented by Tomcat such as the directory interface of the JNDI API, the class loading mechanism, the implementation of custom protocols, and shared libraries. In the third section, we'll look at the process of starting up a context. Finally, we will cover an example that demonstrates a context in operation.

Let's get started!

Aspects of the Context component

The components that we have encountered up until now, such as the server, service, engine, and host, have tended to be far more interesting to administrators than to developers. It is with the context, however, that this balance begins to shift.

To serve this duality of purpose, a context actually exposes two forms of itself. To an administrator, it shows itself in its 'Context' aspect, whereas to a developer, it shows itself in its 'Web application' aspect.

Each aspect comes with its own set of configuration files; the context aspect of this component is configured using a context fragment, whereas a deployment descriptor is used to configure its web application aspect. ↘ WEB.XML

If that weren't exciting enough, each aspect can be configured at three separate levels — at the server level, at the host level, and at the individual context level. This inheritance hierarchy helps you in organizing your configuration parameters. You can move general configuration to a higher level configuration file, and then allow a more specific configuration file to override these parameters as required.

The astute reader will note that two aspects and three levels in an hierarchy allows up to six individual files being used to configure this component. This is by far the most of any component within the Tomcat family, and indicates better than anything else, the importance accorded to it by Tomcat.

The Context aspect

This aspect represents a view of this component that is purely Tomcat-specific, and is used to configure Tomcat components such as valves, loaders, resources, and session managers. This is in contrast to the web application aspect, which is compliant with the servlet specification, and so is independent of servlet container.

Configuration files

This aspect is configured using the following three files:

- **Engine scoped context fragment**: The CATALINA_BASE/conf/context.xml file contains the configuration that applies to all the contexts within a given servlet container instance.

- **Host scoped context fragment**: The context.xml.default file lives within a folder named for a specific engine and host, CATALINA_BASE/conf/ <engineName>/<hostName>/. The configuration specified in this file applies to all the contexts deployed into the specified host.

- **Web application specific context fragment**: This fragment configures a specific context, and exists either as:

    ◦ A file named <contextPath>.xml in the CATALINA_BASE/ conf/<engineName>/<hostName> folder, or

    ◦ A file named META-INF/context.xml, packaged within its web application's WAR file or exploded directory.

Using a META-INF/context.xml context fragment file limits your flexibility for two reasons. A security conscious administrator may set the host's deployXML attribute to false, forcing Tomcat to ignore any embedded context fragments. Furthermore, you will recall that the context path is determined using the name of this fragment file. An embedded context fragment file cannot be named anything other than context.xml, thereby limiting your ability to specify a custom context path.

> A context fragment may also be represented as a <Context> element within the server.xml file. However, using distinct context fragment files ensures that you do not mix server configuration with application configuration.

Document base and context path

Two critical attributes of a context are the folder in which its resources may be found—its **document base** and the path specified within a URL to access this context—its **context path**.

A context's document base references the location of either the exploded directory for the application or its WAR file. It is specified using the <Context> element's docBase attribute, either as an absolute path or as a path that is relative to the appBase directory of its host, which by default is webapps.

A context path uniquely identifies a context within a given host, and is the portion of the URL that follows the virtual host specification, but precedes the path to the resource.

A context path may be explicitly specified only when a <Context> element is used within the server.xml file. In all other cases, it is implicitly determined by the name of either the fragment file, the exploded directory, or the WAR file (minus the .war extension).

For example, a WAR file named sales.war within CATALINA_BASE/webapps is mapped to the context path /sales, while a context fragment file named reservations.xml within the CATALINA_BASE/conf/Catalina/localhost folder is mapped to the context path /reservations. These applications are then accessible at the URLs http://localhost:8080/sales and http://localhost:8080/reservations, respectively.

This convention makes it a bit unwieldy to configure a context path with '/' characters, for example, /chapter/09. In such cases, the fragment file, WAR file, or directory must be named with a '#' character wherever a '/' is desired. For example, the name chapter#09.war would result in the application being accessible at the URL http://localhost/chapter/09.

The *default web application* for a given host is a special case. It is the context to which a request is forwarded, when no context path is specified in the request URL. This web application is accessed without a context path at all, as in http://localhost:8080/path/to/resource. This context path is equivalent to an empty string and is represented in a file named as ROOT; either ROOT.xml for a fragment file, ROOT.war for a WAR file, or simply as the exploded directory ROOT.

For a complete treatment of a context's attributes, see http://tomcat.apache.org/tomcat-6.0-doc/config/context.html.

Context children

A `<Context>` element is a Tomcat container and can contain children `Wrapper` components, as well as various nested components such as loaders, realms, and managers.

[Wrapper components are defined implicitly using the web application deployment descriptor.]

WatchedResource

In the last chapter, we noted that the host watches certain resources, and if it detects that any of these resources has been modified, automatically reloads the application. The `WatchedResource` element lets you specify resources that a context's host should watch.

The default `conf/context.xml` file watches the application's deployment descriptor (`WEB-INF/web.xml`).

```
<WatchedResource>WEB-INF/web.xml</WatchedResource>
```

The path specified can either be an absolute path or a path that is relative to the context's document base folder.

Loader

This element is used to configure class loading behavior within a context. By default, this results in an `org.apache.catalina.loader.WebappClassLoader` instance being installed as the web application class loader. A `Loader` element lets you override this default class and to configure behavior such as whether or not the standard Java class loader delegation mechanism is used.

Resources

This element represents the resources associated with this web application, including classes, HTML files, and images.

Tomcat implements JNDI's Directory API to provide a view of an application's resources that is independent of the storage technology used. Out of the box, Tomcat provides resource managers that can retrieve resources either from the file system or from a WAR file. This element lets you provide your own resource manager implementation, say for loading resources from a database.

ResourceLink

This element lets you access a resource defined in the `<GlobalNamingResources>` element within `server.xml`. For example, the following element defines a global environment variable:

```
<GlobalNamingResources>
   <Environment name="country" type="java.lang.String" value="USA"/>
</GlobalNamingResources>
```

This environment entry cannot be accessed from within a servlet simply by using `java:comp/env/country`. It is only available after a `Context` adds a `ResourceLink` child element to link to this global resource.

```
<ResourceLink name="country" type="java.lang.String"
global="country"/>
```

Context parameters

A `<Parameter>` element lets you specify servlet context initialization parameters. Within a servlet, you can access this parameter by calling `ServletContext.getInitParameter()`.

```
<Parameter name="companyName" value="Software Engineering Solutions,
Inc." override="false"/>
```

`<CONTEXT-PARAM>`

By default, a `<context-param>` element in `web.xml`, with the same name, will override this parameter's value. If the `override` attribute is set to `false`, then this value may not be overridden.

Environment variables

This element lets you configure environment variables for a servlet.

```
<Environment name="maxExemptions" value="10" type="java.lang.Integer"
   override="false"/>
```

This is equivalent to using an `<env-entry>` element within a web application's `web.xml` file.

The `override` attribute works in a similar fashion as with context parameters.

The `type` attribute can take the standard wrapper types, such as a `java.lang.Boolean` or `java.lang.Integer`, as well as a `java.lang.String`.

Valves

You can nest valves to modify the request processing pipeline for a context. For instance, the following element prints out log entries for each request using the common log format:

```
<Valve className="org.apache.catalina.valves.AccessLogValve"
    prefix="localhost_access_log." suffix=".txt" pattern="common"/>
```

Manager

This child element configures the session manager for the context. A session manager is responsible for the creation, management, and persistence of server-side sessions.

This element will be explored in more detail in Chapter 11, *The Manager Component*.

Realm

```
<Realm className="org.apache.catalina.realm.UserDatabaseRealm"
    resourceName="ch09dbRealm"/>
```

A realm is a security mechanism that identifies a data source that houses authentication credentials (a user's username and password) as well as the roles to which a given user belongs. The key variability here is the type of data source used. Tomcat provides realms that support a variety of data sources, such as in-memory data sources (which are read from an XML file at startup), JDBC database sources, as well as LDAP directory sources.

Web application aspect

This is the point where the servlet specification begins to meet the Tomcat servlet container.

Whereas the context configuration is Tomcat specific, the configuration of a web application is as defined in the servlet specification. A web application's deployment descriptor is therefore portable across all Java servlet containers that support the servlet specification.

A context container's children are instances of the wrapper component, each of which encapsulates a servlet. A web application deployment descriptor defines the servlets that are configured for a given context.

Configuration files

The web application deployment descriptor contains elements that are familiar to web developers, such as servlets, filters, listeners, servlet context parameters, and error pages. This deployment descriptor can exist at the following levels:

- **Engine scoped web application deployment descriptor**: The `CATALINA_BASE/conf/web.xml` file contains deployment information that is common across all the web applications deployed into a given servlet container instance.

  This file defines a number of common servlets. This includes the `default` servlet, which serves up static resources and processes all requests that are not mapped to other servlets; the `jsp` servlet which is used to support JSP pages; as well as servlets that enable support for SSI and CGI.

  In addition, it specifies a default session timeout of 30 minutes, provides common MIME mappings, as well as popular welcome file definitions.

- **Host scoped web application deployment descriptor**: This file is named `web.xml.default` and lives in a host-specific folder named `CATALINA_BASE/conf/<engineName>/<hostName>`. It contains deployment configuration that applies across all the web applications deployed into the named host.

- **Web application-specific deployment descriptor**: This file, named `WEB-INF/web.xml`, configures the web application that contains it.

Web application resources

The resources associated with a web application are located within its document base and are comprised of static files (for example, HTML and CSS files), JAR files, property files, as well as class files.

Resources are organized using the standard WAR file format. In this organization, static content can be found directly within the document base, or in subfolders within the document base. Any JAR files for this web application are located under the `WEB-INF/lib` folder, and any class files, configuration files, and property files are found in packages within the `WEB-INF/classes` folder.

As an application's resources can exist either as compressed files within a WAR file, or as exploded files in a directory, a key design goal was to provide a storage agnostic way of accessing the resources associated with a web application.

Implementing a storage-independent mechanism for resource access makes it possible to support additional storage mechanisms, such as having resources stored as records in a database.

This independence is achieved through the use of the Java Naming and Directory Interface API. We've already seen how a naming service implementation makes it possible to look up bound resources within a container. In this section we'll see how a directory service implementation gives us true storage abstraction.

Resources

A web application resource is described by a pair of classes; a `Resource` instance that represents the resource and lets you access its content, and a `ResourceAttributes` instance that represents its attributes, such as its last modification timestamp. Both these classes are in the `org.apache.naming.resources` package.

The content associated with a `Resource` can be accessed either as a byte array or as an `InputStream`. The `streamContent()` method returns the `InputStream` that grants you access to the resource's content. If a resource has been previously cached, then its bytes can be accessed directly using the `getContent()` method, which returns a byte array containing the bytes that constitute that resource.

As we will see shortly, the specific instances of `Resource` and `ResourceAttributes` used are actually dependent on the type of storage being used. A file based store is represented by an instance of `FileDirContext`, which provides two inner classes, `FileResource` and `FileResourceAttributes`, which describe a resource that exists as a file on the file system. Each of these classes holds a `File` instance that points to its associated resource.

The inner class `FileDirContext.FileResource` overrides `streamContent()` to return a `FileInputStream` that wraps its `File` member.

The `FileDirContext.FileResourceAttributes` class overrides methods from its base class that return attributes for its contained file, such as its name, length, and the last modified timestamp. You can also query this class to determine whether this `File` instance represents a folder or a normal file.

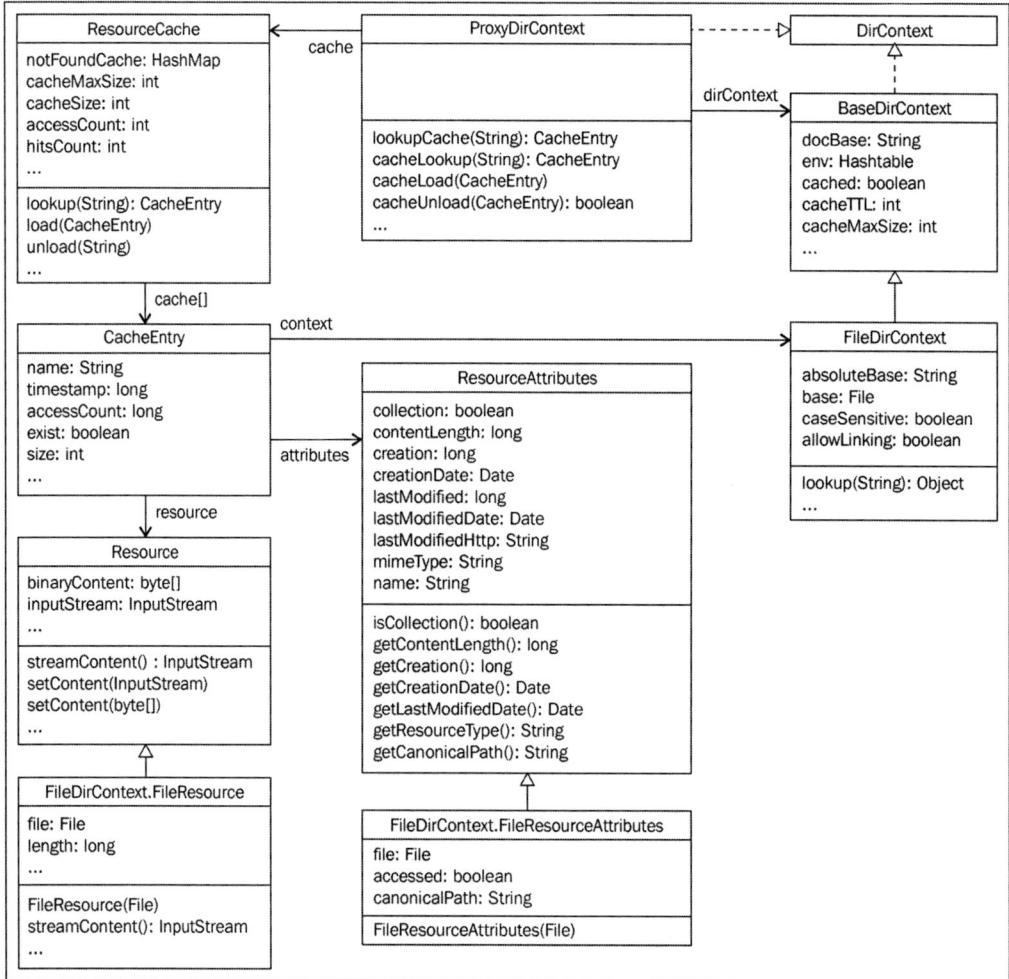

Resource cache

As a web application's resources are accessed, they are cached in order to speed up future requests for the same resource. This is orchestrated by the `ProxyDirContext`, which we will see shortly.

Caching is implemented by the `org.apache.naming.resources.ResourceCache` class, which holds cached resources as an array of `CacheEntry` instances. Each cached entry in this array is a thin wrapper around a `Resource` and its associated `ResourceAttributes`. In addition, it holds caching related information such as whether the resource exists and when it was last accessed.

The resource cache's `CacheEntry` array is sorted by the name of the resource, allowing us to use a binary search to quickly locate the appropriate entry within this array.

A secondary map, called `notFoundCache`, holds known failures. It tracks the resources that were looked up previously, but were either not found or were not readable. This saves the effort required in locating a resource that we already know does not exist.

The key methods of a `ResourceCache` include:

- `lookup()`: This method retrieves a cached resource by name and updates a cache hit counter
- `load()`: This method adds a new `CacheEntry` instance into its sorted position within its internal array and updates the cache size member

Resource retrieval

So far, we have a way to represent a resource, and we have a cache implementation. The third piece of the puzzle is a way to retrieve the resource from its storage mechanism.

BaseDirContext

A web application's resources are accessed using an instance of a concrete subclass of the abstract class, `org.apache.naming.resources.BaseDirContext`. Tomcat supplies the default implementations `FileDirContext` and `WARDirContext` that support looking up resources from either a standard file system or a packed WAR file, respectively. In this chapter, we will focus on the `FileDirContext`.

The abstract `BaseDirContext` class implements the `javax.naming.directory.DirContext` interface, which defines methods for locating objects within a directory type structure. This marks it squarely as a directory service provider for the Java Naming and Directory Interface API and ensures that a generic storage-agnostic mechanism is now available to retrieve the resources associated with a web application.

Its docBase member contains the path to the directory on the file system from where its resources will be retrieved. When used with a Context, this member is set to the docBase of its associated context.

FileDirContext

This is an actual implementation of a BaseDirContext that lets you access file system-based resources. Its File instance member, named base, points to the document base folder on the file system. The constructor verifies that the document base specified is an existing directory and is readable. It defines two key utility methods that are relied upon by the other methods in this class.

- The file() utility method takes a resource name and returns a File instance that represents that resource. It converts the name passed into it into an absolute path by prefixing it with the document base folder's location, verifies that the file does indeed exist, and that it is readable. If we are operating in case sensitive mode, it also verifies that the case of the resource name matches.

- The list() utility method takes a File instance that refers to a directory and returns that folder's contents.

The directory operations supported are as follows:

- lookup() which looks up the named resource and returns a Resource instance that references it
- unbind() which deletes the specified resource
- bind() which stores a resource with the given name
- rename() which renames an existing resource
- rebind() which overwrites an existing file with the specified resource

In addition, a getAttributes() method retrieves the attributes for a resource and returns it wrapped in an instance of FileResourceAttributes.

ProxyDirContext

As is evident from its central location in the previous diagram, an org.apache. naming.resources.ProxyDirContext plays a central role in merging resource lookup (through the BaseDirContext) with caching (through the ResourceCache). It implements DirContext and fulfills the role of being a proxy by appropriately delegating calls to its wrapped DirContext.

Clients, such as the class loader, that need access to a web application's resources will only ever use an instance of this class.

Looking up resources

The usual entry point for users of the ProxyDirContext is the public lookup() method that it inherits from the javax.naming.Context interface. This method takes the name of the resource to be retrieved and returns a Resource instance.

This method begins by delegating to the cacheLookup() method to retrieve the resource from an internal cache.

If the resource is not found or if the resource is a non cacheable dynamic resource, then a direct lookup is done by invoking the lookup() method on its wrapped FileDirContext instance.

> The ProxyDirContext does not cache any resources within the /WEB-INF/lib/ and /WEB-INF/classes/ folders. In other words, only static resources are eligible for caching.

Cache lookup

The cacheLookup() method first checks its internal cache by invoking the lookup() method on its contained ResourceCache instance. If the resource is not present in the cache, then a blank CacheEntry is instantiated for this resource, and an attempt is made to locate it using the wrapped FileDirContext instance. The located resource is either a FileResource—if it represents a regular file or a FileDirContext—if it represents a folder.

The CacheEntry instance is updated with the resource's attributes as a FileResourceAttributes instance retrieved from the wrapped FileDirContext. A resource that is a normal file has its bytes cached in the byte array for this CacheEntry.

The CacheEntry instance is then stored into the CacheEntry array of the ResourceCache. If the resource was not found on the file system, the resource name is added to the notFoundCache map instead.

A key concept with a CacheEntry instance is its time-to-live value. Whenever a new resource is cached, this timestamp is set to the current timestamp plus the cacheTTL value of the ProxyDirContext. This sets how long a particular cached resource is valid. Any access past this time will require the resource to be reloaded into the cache.

When a cache lookup actually returns a resource, the resource is checked for validity, that is, whether or not it is within its time-to-live boundary. If the resource is valid, then the cached resource is returned, and its access counter is incremented.

However, if the resource is no longer valid, then we check to see if the resource has changed on disk since it was last loaded into the cache.

If the resource has not changed on disk, then our cached version is current, and so we increment the time-to-live value for this resource, increment its access count, and return the cached resource.

However, if the resource has changed since it was last loaded, then we remove the cached entry, and this method returns null, indicating that the resource must be loaded afresh.

The context fragment file lets you specify a number of attributes that control this caching behavior. For instance:

- The `cachingAllowed` attribute (default is true) determines whether or not caching is enabled

- The `cacheMaxSize` attribute (default is 10MB) lets you configure the maximum size of the static resource cache in kilobytes

- The `cacheTTL` attribute (default is 5 seconds) lets you specify the time in milliseconds for which an entry may live before it has to be revalidated

- The `cacheObjectMaxSize` attribute (default is 512 KB) determines the maximum size of a static resource that will be placed in the cache

Miscellaneous methods

The `bind()`, `rebind()`, `unbind()`, and `rename()` directory methods delegate to the enclosed `DirContext` instance, and then unload any cached entry representing this resource, which would now be stale.

Similarly, the `getAttributes()` method takes a resource name and delegates to `cacheLookup()` the task of looking up the resource, and returns the `attributes` member of the retrieved `CacheEntry`.

Shared library mechanism

A web application's dependency on a library can be fulfilled by placing that library's JAR file in the web application's `WEB-INF/lib` folder. However, as more of your web applications deployed into a single container depend on a given library, you end up with multiple copies of the same file, littered across your contexts. This not only takes up space and feels cluttered, but also makes upgrading to a new version of this library more work than it needs to be.

A better option would be to register this JAR file as a shared library and then have each of your web applications use that shared library.

Servlet containers usually provide a shared library mechanism, where you can place libraries that must be available across all the web applications deployed into that container.

Each web application then declares, using the `META-INF/manifest.mf` file, the shared libraries that it expects to use. As per the servlet specification, a container must notify the administrator and reject the application when a dependency recorded in the manifest file is not matched by the presence of the corresponding library within its shared library mechanism.

While the servlet specification specifies the mechanism by which these dependencies are declared, the actual implementation of the shared library is specific to a container.

An implementation of this mechanism usually requires a location where these files may be placed and a single class loader per JVM that loads these files independent of web application. For this to work, this class loader must be installed as an ancestor of all the web application class loaders.

> The mechanism described in this section has been superseded by the Shared class loader that is installed using the `shared.loader` entry in the `catalina.properties` file.

Manifest file format

Declaration entries in a Manifest file usually take the form of colon delimited key-value pairs. The main entry, `Extension-List`, defines a logical name for each dependency.

```
Extension-List: javaMail javaHelp java3d
```

Additional entries then provide more detail for each such logical name. These entries take the form `<logicalName>-<Attribute-Name>`.

Each logical name entry in the manifest file indicates a dependency on some shared library.

For example, the following lines indicate that our web application requires a Java3D implementation that must be compliant with at least the 1.0 specification:

```
java3d-Extension-Name: javax.3d
java3d-Specification-Version: 1.0
java3d-Implementation-Version: 1.2.1
java3d-Implementation-Vendor-Id: com.sun
java3d-Implementation-URL:
http://java.sun.com/products/stdext/java3d.jar
```

URLs and protocol handlers

We've seen how a directory service implementation lets us abstract away the details of how a context's resources are made available. But that is only part of the story.

In this section, we'll look at how we might plug into Java's standard protocol handler mechanism to make the identification and retrieval of resources easy and intuitive. So please fasten your seatbelts as we enter the exotic world of Java protocol handlers!

Accessing resources

When a servlet container element, such as a servlet or filter, needs to access a static resource, it should avoid using hardcoded paths to that file. Hardcoding paths can hurt the portability of an application across servlet containers or result in failure when the web application is run from within a packed WAR file.

The recommended approach is to use the `getResource()` and `getResourceAsStream()` methods defined by the `javax.servlet.ServletContext` interface. These methods allow access to a packaged resource, independently of how the web application is deployed. Both methods take a path to the resource, relative to the current context root, and with a leading '/'.

The `getResource()` method lets you obtain a `java.net.URL` instance that references the specified resource, while the `getResourceAsStream()` method grants you an `InputStream` to that resource.

As we have seen, a web application's resources can exist either as files in a folder or as compressed files within a WAR file. A directory service lets us abstract away the storage mechanism using a directory context that works equally well under either scenario, or even under more esoteric storage situations, such as when resources are stored within a database.

The `getResourceAsStream()` method simply delegates to the `DirContext` instance associated with the context to look up the specified resource and returns an `InputStream` for the located `Resource` instance.

However, what should happen when `getResource()` is invoked? This method returns a `java.net.URL` that points to the named resource, which can be used to access this resource at some later time. What scheme should this URL use?

While the `file` protocol might initially look appropriate, this goes against our objective of remaining storage agnostic. After all, the resource may end up not being a file at all. The `http` protocol is a non starter, as the file is local to the context, and does not need the overhead of being requested over the wire.

Tomcat takes the ingenious approach of defining an entirely new protocol, called `jndi`, which is used to reference local resources, irrespective of the form that they take. URL strings in this protocol will take the general form `jndi://hostName/contextName/path/to/resource`.

Later, when a `jndi` URL is used to access its referenced resource, a mechanism in the Java Runtime known as the **Protocol Handler** rides to the rescue and helps retrieve a connection to that resource.

This mechanism and its implementation in Tomcat form the basis of this section.

> The `getResource()` method can also be used to obtain a URL that references a JAR file within the context's `WEB-INF/lib` folder. The URL returned in this case is of the standard `file` protocol. It is only static resources that are returned as URLs that use the `jndi` protocol.

Protocol handlers

A URL not only identifies a given resource (in its role as a Uniform Resource Identifier), but also defines its location over the network in terms of a scheme (or protocol), host, and a path to the resource.

The Java runtime natively supports URLs for common protocols such as `http`, `https`, `ftp`, `jar`, and `file`. Fortunately, Java makes it easy to add support for a custom protocol, simply by installing a handler for that protocol.

As shown in the following image, the protocol handler mechanism is composed of four cooperating classes, all within the `java.net` package. In this section, we'll walk through all these classes in more detail. Note that the image only shows the aspects of the API that are relevant to our discussion here.

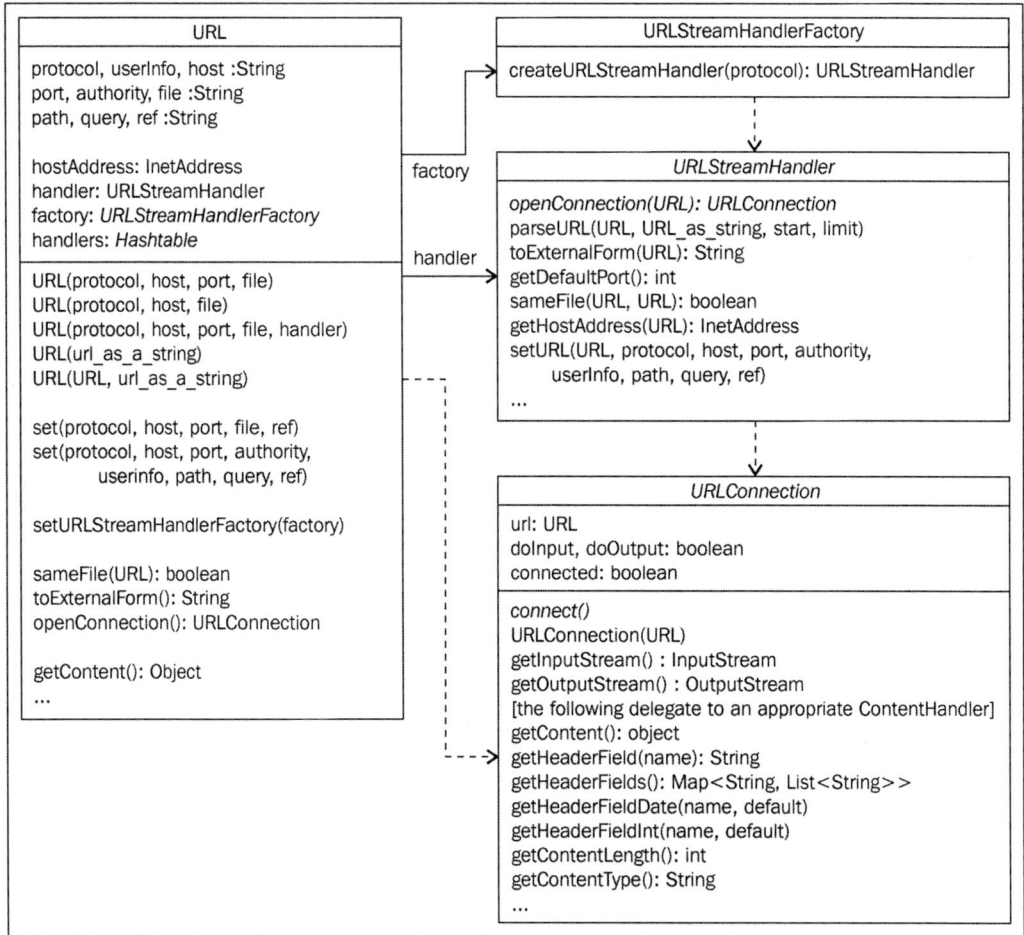

URL

protocol, userInfo, host :String
port, authority, file :String
path, query, ref :String

hostAddress: InetAddress
handler: URLStreamHandler
factory: *URLStreamHandlerFactory*
handlers: *Hashtable*

URL(protocol, host, port, file)
URL(protocol, host, file)
URL(protocol, host, port, file, handler)
URL(url_as_a_string)
URL(URL, url_as_a_string)

set(protocol, host, port, file, ref)
set(protocol, host, port, authority,
        userinfo, path, query, ref)

setURLStreamHandlerFactory(factory)

sameFile(URL): boolean
toExternalForm(): String
openConnection(): URLConnection

getContent(): Object
...

factory

handler

URLStreamHandlerFactory

createURLStreamHandler(protocol): URLStreamHandler

URLStreamHandler

openConnection(URL): URLConnection
parseURL(URL, URL_as_string, start, limit)
toExternalForm(URL): String
getDefaultPort(): int
sameFile(URL, URL): boolean
getHostAddress(URL): InetAddress
setURL(URL, protocol, host, port, authority,
        userInfo, path, query, ref)
...

URLConnection

url: URL
doInput, doOutput: boolean
connected: boolean

connect()
URLConnection(URL)
getInputStream() : InputStream
getOutputStream() : OutputStream
[the following delegate to an appropriate ContentHandler]
getContent(): object
getHeaderField(name): String
getHeaderFields(): Map<String, List<String>>
getHeaderFieldDate(name, default)
getHeaderFieldInt(name, default)
getContentLength(): int
getContentType(): String
...

java.net.URL

This class represents a location reference to a resource, and identifies the protocol that will be used to access that resource. It contains general functionality that is applicable independent of the scheme used to access the resource that it represents.

This class implements the Strategy Gang of Four design pattern to neatly encapsulate protocol-specific details into a separate stream handler instance that is appropriate for its scheme. Its methods delegate any protocol-specific work to the stream handler appropriate for the protocol, hiding the messy details from you. A URL relies on its protocol-specific strategy class to deal with a given protocol.

java.net.URLStreamHandler

When you construct a URL from a string representation, the runtime extracts the scheme and uses it to locate the appropriate URLStreamHandler subclass. Note that the URLStreamHandler itself is an abstract class.

A stream handler is tied intimately to a particular protocol and has two primary functions that are both very protocol-specific.

First, a URL's string representation is unique to a particular protocol. Therefore, its parseURL() method defines how to parse the string representation of the URL into its separate components, and to set the corresponding URL instance's members, such as protocol, host, port, file, and ref. If the URL format for a protocol is not the standard hierarchical representation, you will need to override this default implementation (as well as the toExternalForm() method) to process the URL for this protocol.

Second, it implements network operations, such as looking up the referenced host and opening a connection to the referenced resource. It implements an openConnection() method which takes the URL to which to connect, and knows about the protocol-specific URLConnection subclass that must be instantiated to enable communication with a server using the given protocol.

Once the appropriate URLStreamHandler subclass has been instantiated, all protocol-specific operations are delegated by the URL to its stream handler implementation. For instance, the URL class's openConnection() method simply delegates to its stream handler's openConnection() method.

java.net.URLConnection

This abstract class represents an active connection to the resource specified by a URL.

Its key task is to provide a way to connect to the server host. Its subclasses implement the connect() method, which establishes a protocol-specific connection to the server.

It then supports bidirectional communication with that server, allowing you to not only read from the resource using an InputStream, but also to write to it, using an OutputStream.

In addition to the raw bytes for the referenced resource, it also lets you access the protocol-specific response headers returned by the server and to set request headers for the server to process.

It can also strip away all the protocol-specific headers and deliver a resource's raw data to a content handler. A content handler is a protocol-independent entity that is responsible for converting raw bytes into a representation appropriate for their content type, for example, into an image, or a text file.

Concrete instances of URLStreamHandler and URLConnection always exist in pairs and work together to implement a given protocol.

java.net.URLStreamHandlerFactory

A URLStreamHandlerFactory implementation constructs the specific URLStreamHandler for a given URL, based on its protocol.

An instance of this factory class is set using the static URL. setURLStreamHandlerFactory() method. The factory has a single method, createURLStreamHandler() which takes a protocol and returns an instance of the appropriate URLStreamHandler subclass for that protocol.

Protocol handler implementation

As we have noted, both URLConnection and URLStreamHandler in the java.net package are abstract classes. A particular protocol is considered 'supported' only if it is accompanied by concrete implementations of this pair of classes. These implementations always occur in pairs, and a URLStreamHandler subclass always knows the specific URLConnection subclass for its protocol.

The concrete subclasses for the protocols supported by the Java Runtime are found in the sun.net package. For example, the sun.net.www.protocol.http. HttpURLConnection is the URLConnection subclass for the HTTP protocol.

In general usage, we rarely worry about the protocol handler mechanism, and most of our usage is limited to the URL class. For instance, you will normally never instantiate a URLConnection directly. You will invoke a URL.openConnection() method instead, which causes the runtime to create a URLConnection object for the URL's protocol.

When you need to implement a new protocol, however, you cannot remain blissfully oblivious of all the magic that goes on behind the scenes.

First, you must provide a concrete `URLStreamHandler` and `URLConnection` subclass pair for your new protocol. Then, you must make it possible for the Java Runtime to locate these subclasses when a protocol string is supplied.

Locating a stream handler

When a URL for a given protocol is instantiated, the `URL` constructor tries to determine the appropriate stream handler by looking in the following locations in order:

1. If the protocol has been used before, then a `URLStreamHandler` instance is retrieved from its internal cache.

2. If this is the first time that a URL for this protocol is being instantiated:

   ° It checks to see whether a `URLStreamHandlerFactory` is installed. If it is, then the protocol string is passed to the factory's `createURLStreamHandler()` method.

   ° If there is no `URLStreamHandlerFactory` installed, or if the factory failed to recognize the protocol, then the constructor looks for a `URLStreamHandler` subclass that is named, according to convention, as `<protocolName>.Handler`. For example, the `http.Handler` class is a `URLStreamHandler` implementation for the HTTP protocol.

   It looks for this class within the packages listed in the `java.protocol.handler.pkgs` system property.

   If not found there, then it looks for this class within the `sun.net.www.protocol` package. For example, the `sun.net.www.protocol.http.Handler` is the stream handler implementation for the HTTP protocol.

   ° If all of this searching fails to locate an appropriate stream handler implementation, then the constructor throws a `MalformedURLException`.

   ° If a stream handler could be instantiated, then this instance is stored in its internal cache, keyed by scheme.

Once the URL is constructed, our application code can now invoke its `openConnection()` method. This call is delegated by the `URL` instance to the `URLStreamHandler` subclass, which instantiates a `URLConnection` subclass that is paired with this stream handler. Our code can now use the `URLConnection` to interact with the remote resource.

The jndi protocol

We now know enough to revisit the `getResource()` method that returns a URL for the `jndi` custom protocol.

As we just saw, implementing a custom protocol requires you to supply concrete subclasses for the `URLStreamHandler` and `URLConnection` abstract classes, and optionally, an implementation of the `URLStreamHandlerFactory` interface.

Tomcat does this by providing the `DirContextURLStreamHandler`, `DirContextURLConnection`, and `DirContextURLStreamHandlerFactory` classes in the `org.apache.naming.handler.jndi` package.

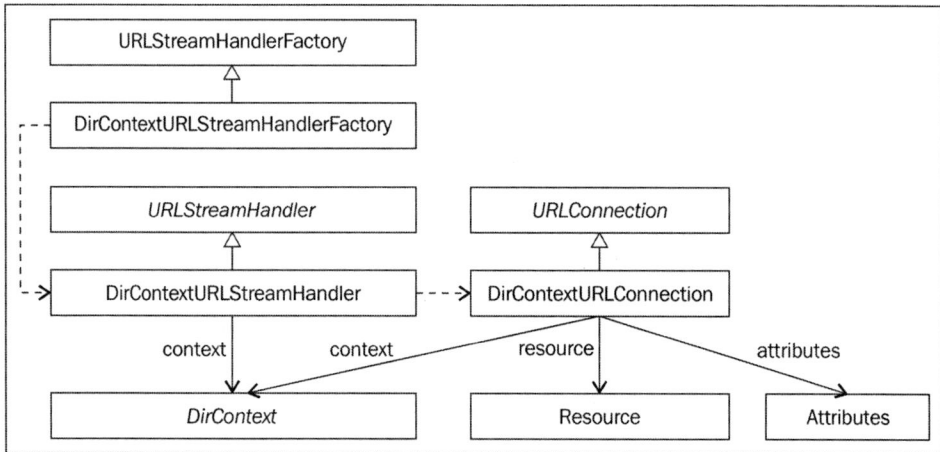

This image describes key elements of the protocol handler mechanism within Tomcat.

DirContextURLStreamHandlerFactory

Its `createURLStreamHandler()` takes a protocol name as a `String`, and if the protocol is `jndi`, it returns an instance of our `URLStreamHandler` subclass, `DirContextURLStreamHandler`.

The protocol handler mechanism is hooked to the container by the `WebappLoader.start()` method, which invokes the static `URL.setURLStreamHandlerFactory()` method with an instantiated `DirContextURLStreamHandlerFactory`.

DirContextURLStreamHandler

This class handles the parsing of URL string representations for the `jndi` protocol, as well as the instantiation of its paired `DirContextURLConnection` class.

It uses a mechanism similar to the one that we encountered when we discussed the naming service. A pair of `Hashtable` members maintain bindings by either class loader or thread, which can then be used to retrieve the appropriate `DirContext` instance (as a `ProxyDirContext` instance). This `DirContext` can be used to locate the resources for that web application.

When its `openConnection()` method is invoked, this stream handler looks up the appropriate `DirContext` and returns a new instance of a `DirContextURLConnection` that points to the specified resource within that `DirContext`.

As the URL used for this protocol is of the standard hierarchical form, the default implementation of the `parseURL()` method, as inherited from its superclass is sufficient.

DirContextURLConnection

A `URLConnection` instance represents a connection to a specific resource. It combines the appropriate `DirContext` within which this resource resides; the resource itself, as an instance of `Resource`; as well as the attributes for the referenced resource, as a `ResourceAttributes` instance.

Its stream handler provides it with the appropriate `DirContext` as well as the resource to which to connect, as referenced by its URL.

An instance of this class implements the abstract `connect()` method which will be used to retrieve the resource referenced by the URL from its wrapped `DirContext`.

If the retrieved resource is a normal file, you can then access it using the `getInputStream()` method.

This resource is identified using the `resource` member, and its attributes are stored in the `attributes` member. In the usual case of an exploded directory, these are instances of the inner classes `FileResource` and `FileResourceAttributes`, respectively.

Once this mechanism is in place, the `jndi` protocol provides a generic way of having the Java Runtime support the accessing of resources from within a context's document base, using a `ProxyDirContext` to do the actual lookup.

Java class loading

In some development environments, the developer must choose whether to use static or dynamic linking. The choice is whether a compiled executable statically contains all its library dependencies within itself, or whether it is dynamically able to locate and load its dependencies at runtime.

With Java, this choice does not exist, as all programs use dynamic linking. The loading process begins when the `java` command is invoked, and the application's main class is loaded into the JVM. All classes referenced by the `main()` method are then loaded lazily, and made available to the JVM for execution, as references to these classes are encountered.

The bytes that represent a given class usually reside on disk as a file with a `.class` extension, called a **class file**. However, the bytes associated with a class could just as easily be retrieved from across a network.

The job of locating a class's bytes and using them to instantiate a new instance of the `java.lang.Class` class falls to an instance of `java.lang.ClassLoader`. In general, a class loader takes the fully qualified name of a class and returns a `Class` object.

Fortunately, a lot of this happens invisibly to the programmer, and most Java developers rarely have to deal with the magic of how classes come into being.

The Java EE developer, however, is not quite so lucky. In the Java EE world, you often encounter multi-JVM and multi-container scenarios, replete with multiple class loader instances.

The interactions between these class loaders often show up as hard-to-diagnose bugs at runtime, and so it is critical that we spend some time looking behind the curtain to see how this magic happens.

Advantages of dynamic class loading

This approach of using a class loader to dynamically locate and load classes has some very real benefits. Understanding these will give you a better appreciation for the descriptions that follow.

- **Late binding**: As the individual classes are not statically linked into a single executable, the classes that comprise a given application need not even have existed when the application was first packaged. As long as there is a reasonable way to locate them, the application working in conjunction with a class loader will read them into the JVM for use.

  This also allows an application's functionality to be assembled by packaging the classes and resources that it needs.

- **Security**: Java was designed to allow the execution of applications downloaded across the network. Having a single choke point in which to apply security rules is a key aspect of making this work.

For instance, class loaders can be engineered to ensure that trusted system classes, such as those in the java.lang packages, may not be overwritten by identically named classes downloaded from an external source (possibly a hacked website).

- **Customizing class loading mechanics**: A dynamic mechanism provides you with a convenient hook to influence the mechanics of class loading. For instance, you could write a custom class loader that extends the basic functionality, say, by supporting encrypted class files, supporting alternative locations from which to retrieve class files (possibly, from a database), or even for supporting the dynamic generation of classes.

- **Support class variance across time and space**: A class varies 'across time' when a class has been loaded from some repository at some point in time, but has since been replaced by an updated version within that repository. A class varies 'across space' when a class with the same fully qualified name exists in two distinct physical locations.

  The dynamic class loader mechanism allows us to support both these scenarios and to treat the varying classes as distinct from each other.

  It supports variance across time by having the application decide whether the updated version should be ignored, or whether the updated version is to be loaded into the application.

  It also supports variance across space by having the application indicate which particular instance of a class is to be used. For example, the standard class loader mechanism ignores core system classes (such as those that start with java.lang) that may be found in locations other than those monitored by the Bootstrap class loader.

- **Class isolation**: An instance of a Java class is uniquely defined by its package name, its class name, and the class loader instance that loaded a given Class. This class loader instance is known as the *defining class loader* for that class.

  It is therefore possible for the same fully qualified class to be loaded in as two separate Class instances within a single JVM.

  This makes it easy to partition our loaded classes, facilitating the creation of isolated zones of operation. In a servlet container, this allows the classes in one context to be completely independent of those in other contexts deployed into the same physical host.

  This has consequences for static members, which are technically guaranteed to be unique per Class instance, and for static initializers that are run when a Class instance is first constructed. (It also has implications for the Singleton Gang of Four design pattern which usually relies on a static member to hold the sole instance of a given class.)

Class loader hierarchy

A typical Java application starts off with a hierarchy of three class loaders—known as the *delegation hierarchy*. By convention, class loading works by delegating up this hierarchy. A lower level class loader is permitted to load a class only when its entire delegation hierarchy has failed to load that class.

- **System class loader**: This is the lowest class loader in the hierarchy. It is an instance of `java.net.URLClassLoader` whose class repository consists of a list of directories and JAR file names located on the application's `CLASSPATH`. The fully qualified name of a class is used to locate the class under each repository entry. You can get a reference to this class loader using the static `ClassLoader.getSystemClassLoader()` method.

  The parent of this class loader is the Extension class loader.

- **Extension class loader**: This class loader is also an instance of `URLClassLoader`, but its repository consists of the JARs that are placed either in the `JRE_HOME/lib/ext` folder or in the path specified by the `java.ext.dirs` system property.

  It is used as a convenient way to share extension libraries that are common across a large number of applications, without having to add these to the `CLASSPATH` of each application.

  The parent of this class loader is the Bootstrap class loader.

- **Bootstrap class loader**: This class loader is at the top of the delegation hierarchy and is usually part of the JVM itself. It is implemented using native code, and is responsible for loading the core system classes, such as the `java.*` packages that are found in `rt.jar`. The classes loaded by this class loader are not associated with any defining class loader instance.

Class loader rules

Class loaders must abide by the following set of rules:

- **Consistency rule**: Once a class has been loaded, any future request for that class should always return the previously loaded instance.

  This helps avoid issues with time-based variance, where a class file on disk may have changed since the class was first loaded. This rule ensures that if an application requests a class previously obtained from its class loader, it will not be confused by a newer version being returned.

To implement this, each class loader maintains a cache of classes that it has loaded and checks in this cache before attempting to load a given class.

- **Delegation rule**: A class loader exists in a hierarchy with its parents and grandparents. The parent of every class loader that you create can be set explicitly to the class loader that you specify using a constructor argument. However, more commonly, the parent is implicitly set to the system class loader.

This parent class loader is important as it plays a key role in the loading of a class. Before a class loader may attempt to load a class, it is recommended that it first consult with its parent class loader. In other words, a class loader will attempt to load a class only if it cannot be found by any of its ancestors.

This rule is a key one for security, as it ensures that the core system classes that ship with the JVM are always loaded by a trusted class loader higher up in the hierarchy, and so cannot be overridden by a malicious class loader. This is a fairly critical rule, and an example would help to clarify the process.

When a class needs another class to be loaded, the JVM asks the defining class loader of the referring class to load it — this is usually the System class loader.

If this is the first class of the application, for example, if this is the application's main class, then a new instance of the System class loader will be used.

The System class loader begins by immediately delegating to its parent. In turn, the Extension class loader delegates up to its parent. If the request cannot be satisfied by the Bootstrap class loader, control is returned to the Extension class loader, and if it too is unable to locate the class, control is returned down to the System class loader.

If none of these class loaders could load the class, then a `ClassNotFoundException` is thrown.

On the other hand, if the class was loaded successfully by one of these class loaders, the defining class loader for that class is set to refer to that class loader, and no further action is necessary.

This scheme ensures that you cannot simply drop a class named `java.lang.String` into your application's `classpath` and have it override the true `java.lang.String`, which is included as part of `rt.jar`. Instead, the class loading request is passed all the way up to the Bootstrap class loader, which finds the `java.lang.String` class and loads it on behalf of the application.

This also allows you to place classes that are common across all web applications in a shared location, served by a distinct higher level class loader. For instance, Tomcat situates a higher level class loader, known as the Shared class loader as an ancestor of all the individual web application class loaders.

- **Visibility rule**: The entire set of classes that is visible to a given class loader is the union of the set of classes visible to each of its ancestor class loaders, and the set of classes that are on its list of repositories.

  This has very serious implications for class loaders higher up in the hierarchy. Those class loaders are unable to see classes in the repositories of lower level class loaders. For instance, a class defined by the Extension class loader cannot use a class that is served by the System class loader.

If this is the first time you've seen these rules, take the time to read this list again, as these are key to understanding how web application class loaders work.

Implicit and explicit class loading

Every class has a reference to its defining class loader. Whenever a class contains a reference to another class, its defining class loader is used to implicitly load the referenced class. This is what happens whenever code within one class uses the `new` operator to instantiate another, say when initializing a member or a local variable, as shown here:

```
// uses the class loader that defined this class - usually the System
// class loader

MyClass cls = new MyClass();
```

This implicit mechanism is used by default within Java programs. This keeps the class loading mechanism fairly unobtrusive, as all class loading happens magically, usually handled by the defining class loader for the main class of your application.

On the other hand, explicit class loading is used when you would prefer to specify the particular class loader instance that must be used to load a given class. Unlike the simplicity of implicit class loading, we now have to say:

```
// explicit classloading requires us to BYOC - Bring Your Own Class
// loader
ClassLoader loader = ClassLoader.getSystemClassLoader();
Class cls = loader.loadClass("MyClass");
MyClass myClass = (MyClass) cls.newInstance();
```

While you have to work much harder with explicit class loading, you do get a lot more flexibility in return. For example, you could have specified a custom class loader, which might customize the class loading behavior either by looking in specific repository locations, by bending class loading rules, or even by adding additional security by decrypting the bytes that represent the class obtained from some encrypted store. This is the approach taken by Tomcat's web application class loader.

Tomcat class loading

Tomcat introduces three new members into the delegation hierarchy, the Common, Shared, and Server class loaders. Tomcat also introduces a new custom class loader. Each context is given an instance of this custom class loader, which is then used to load the classes that belong to that context.

The complete class loader delegation hierarchy now looks as shown in the diagram below.

> The numbers in square brackets indicate the class loader delegation order. We'll describe them in more detail later in this section.

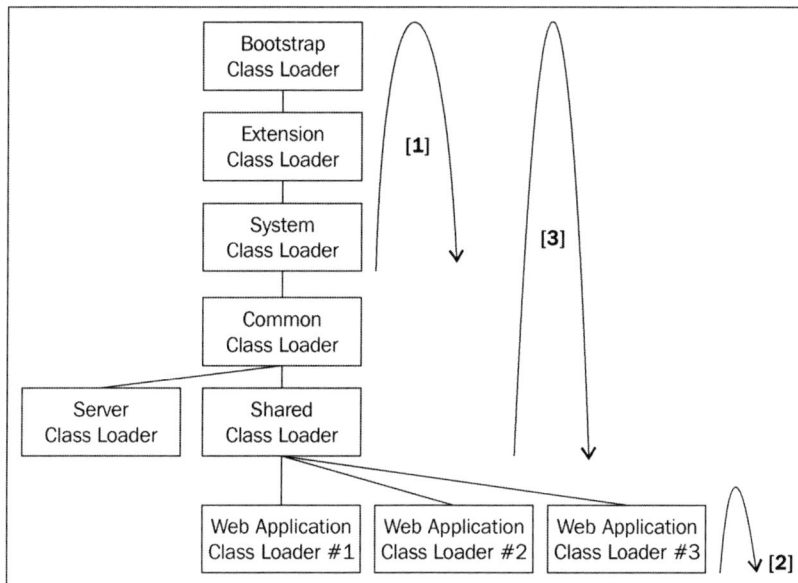

The Bootstrap loader loads the Java SE classes, that is, those contained in `rt.jar`. Likewise, the Extension loader loads classes from the JRE's extensions folder (`%JAVA_HOME%/jre/lib/ext`).

The System loader in Tomcat is merely a shadow of its former self. If you recall the discussion from Chapter 4, *Starting up Tomcat*, the startup scripts truncate the `CLASSPATH` to only include the libraries required for initializing Tomcat and for logging.

Below the System class loader comes the extensions to this hierarchy. First up is the Common class loader, which serves up the classes and resources that should be visible to both Tomcat's internal classes, as well as to all web applications. These typically include the JARs contained within the `%CATALINA_HOME%/lib` folder and include the Coyote connectors, the core Catalina components, the DBCP JARs, the Servlet API, the EL API, and so on.

Below this is the Server class loader, which can be used to load classes that are visible to the server implementation but are not available to the deployed web applications. On the other hand, a Shared class loader is introduced to load classes that are common across the web applications, but which need not be available to the server implementation.

> By default, the Server and Shared class loaders are simply set to the Common class loader. If you need these, you will need to modify the `shared.loader` and `server.loader` entries in your `conf/catalina.properties` file.

A custom class loader is created per web application context deployed within a Tomcat instance. These web application class loaders serve up the classes and resources stored within the `WEB-INF/classes` and `WEB-INF/lib` folders for a context. The classes loaded by this loader are only visible to its associated web application.

This works to isolate the individual web applications from each other. For example, static data members now become unique per web application, instead of being shared across an entire JVM. It also simplifies hot reloading where a single web application can be reloaded without restarting the JVM or affecting any of the other web applications.

This class loader is special in yet another way. It subverts the standard delegation hierarchy, and will look in its local repositories, before consulting its delegation hierarchy. However, there is one exception, it will delegate the loading of classes that are part of the Java Runtime, to ensure that these cannot be overridden.

We're now ready to discuss the numbers in square brackets in the previous image. The extended hierarchy in the previous diagram, with its modified delegation rules has the following repository search order:

- As shown by the arrow labeled [1], the web application class loader first delegates to the standard class loader delegation hierarchy.
    - ° The Bootstrap class loader serves up any core classes.
    - ° The Extension loader serves up classes held within any installed extension JARs.
    - ° The System class loader serves up Catalina startup classes as well as supporting classes.

- If the desired class is not found, the web application class loader looks within its own repositories. This is shown by the arrow labeled [2].
    - ° A web application class loader serves up classes from its `/WEB-INF/classes` folder
    - ° If not found, it serves up classes from its `/WEB-INF/lib/*.jar` files.

- If the desired class is still not found, the web application class loader now delegates to its parent class loader, as shown by the arrow labeled [3].
    - ° The Common class loader serves up classes from `%CATALINA_HOME%/lib/*.jar`. These classes are common to the web applications as well as to internal Tomcat classes.
    - ° The Shared class loader serves up classes that are common across all web applications within a given host.

This delegation hierarchy guarantees that a malicious web application context cannot subvert core runtime classes.

> The `delegate` attribute can be set on the class loader to force the search shown by the arrow [3] to occur before the arrow labeled [2]. The search order then becomes [1] → [3] → [2].

Implementing a custom class loader

Custom class loaders must extend the `java.lang.ClassLoader` abstract class and override its abstract `findClass()` method. Tomcat's `WebappClassLoader` overrides `java.lang.URLClassLoader` instead, which provides reasonable implementations for every method.

In this section, we will take a closer look at what makes a class loader tick.

Making a class available

The process of loading a class is kicked off by the invocation of the `loadClass()` method on a `ClassLoader` instance.

Loading a class involves two distinct steps, both of which must be successfully completed before a class can be used.

- **Loading the class**: In this step, the `findClass()` method of a `ClassLoader` instance is used to locate the bytecode for this class. The binary form of a class is represented using a well defined class format and typically exists as a `.class` file. However, more exotic locations may also be supported. In really mind bending scenarios, the bytecode may even be generated dynamically.

  Once the bytecode that represents the class has been found, the class is *defined* using the `defineClass()` method. In this process, the bytecode representation is converted into a `java.lang.Class` instance.

- **Linking the class**: This is an optional step that begins after a class has been successfully loaded. This process is implemented using the `resolveClass()` method of a `ClassLoader` instance, and is comprised of the following three activities:

  - First, the located bytecode is verified for structural correctness. For instance, this checks whether the bytecode is well formed, that it conforms to the language's rules, that it doesn't violate any security constraints (such as causing a stack overflow), that every instruction has a valid operation code, and that all methods have structurally correct signatures.

  - Next, the class or interface is prepared by creating its static members, and initializing them to default values. Internal data structures, such as tables that are used to efficiently look up method implementations across a type hierarchy, are also created at this time.

  - Finally, any symbolic references to other classes, interfaces, fields, methods, and constructors, encountered within the bytecode are checked for correctness, and are replaced with a more efficient direct reference.

> Class loader details are covered in the *Java Language Specification* and in the *Java Virtual Machine Specification* that can be downloaded from the Sun web site.

Before a type is ready for use, a final step known as *initialization* is used to execute its static initializer blocks, as well as the initializers for any of its static fields. This step commonly occurs when either an instance of a class is created or a static member of that class is accessed. This step is not considered a part of the class loading machinery.

The custom web application class loader

A custom class loader will usually focus on the first of the two steps involved in making a class available—loading the class. The most commonly customized aspect of class loading is that of controlling how a class is found.

The custom web application class loader provides overrides for the `loadClass()` and `findClass()` methods, which we will consider in this section. In addition, we'll see how this `ClassLoader` gains access to the classes and resources in its repositories.

Our custom class loader may be depicted as shown in the following image:

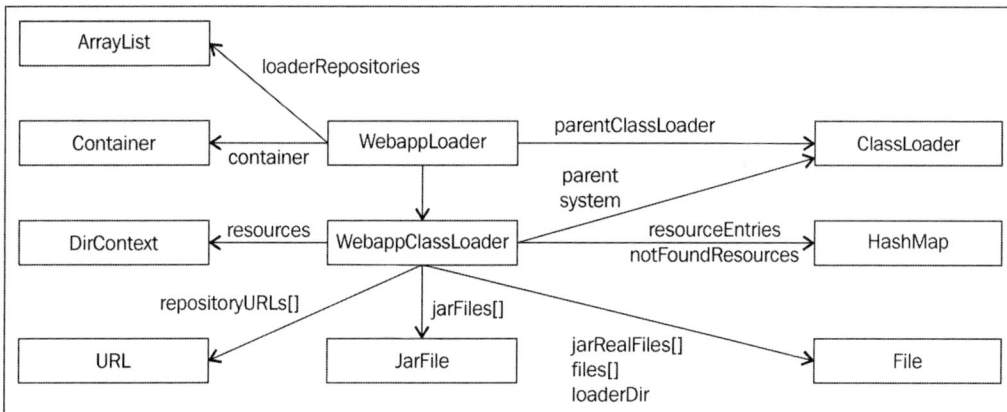

Some key points to note with a `WebappClassLoader` are:

- The repositories for this class loader can be specified as folders as well as JARs.
    - The folders that will be monitored for class files are stored in an array pair. The `repositories` array holds the names of the folders, while the `files` array holds the `File` instances that reference these folders.
    - The JAR files from which classes may be loaded are stored in three separate arrays. The file name (without the path) is stored in the `jarNames` array, its `JarFile` representation is stored in the `jarFiles` array, and its `File` representation is stored in the `jarRealFiles` array.
- Reloading of modified resources is supported by storing the names of classes, resources, or JAR files in the `paths` array, and by storing their last modified times at the corresponding index within the `lastModifiedDates` array.
- An array of class names, known as `triggers`, is used to validate whether a JAR file can be added to the set of repositories for this class loader. If a class named in this array can be loaded by the parent class loader of this class, then it should not be present in the JAR file. If the file is present, then it indicates that this JAR file should not be added as a class loader repository.

    Currently, only the `javax.servlet.Servlet` class is contained in this list, which prevents the `servlet-api.jar` file from being added to a web application class loader's repository. This JAR file is present in `CATALINA_BASE/lib` and is visible to the Common class loader.

- A `resources` member holds the `ProxyDirContext` for this class loader's associated `Context`. This member allows the class loader to access classes and resources from the web application's `WEB-INF` folder.
- To implement the Consistency rule of class loading, a `resourceEntries` map is used as a cache for loaded classes and resources. As a performance optimization, a `notFoundResources` map acts as a cache for resources that have not been found.

Class loader initialization

The `WebappLoader` class has two main responsibilities:

- It initializes a web application class loader
- It enables a background processing thread to handle the task of reloading modified class files and JARs

Its `start()` method begins by setting up the application's custom `URLStreamHandlerFactory` to the `DirContextURLStreamHandlerFactory` that we read about earlier. It then constructs an instance of `org.apache.catalina.loader.WebappClassLoader`. The web application class loader takes a specific class loader parent, usually the Common class loader, in order to hook into the Tomcat specific class loader hierarchy.

The class loader is initialized by setting its `antiJARLocking` and `delegate` properties from the context.

The `antiJARLocking` attribute (default: `false`) indicates whether or not the class loader should take extra measures to avoid JAR file locking on certain operating systems. When this attribute is set to `true`, JARs are extracted to, and accessed from, a folder named `loader` under the temporary work directory. The `delegate` property affects the class loader's delegation mechanism, as we will see shortly.

Next, it sets the `resources` `DirContext` and its work directory.

It looks up the resource named `/WEB-INF/classes` from the `ProxyDirContext`. If this is a real folder on the file system, it is added to the custom class loader's `repositories` array and a `File` reference to this folder is stored at the corresponding index in its `files` array.

However, if this folder exists within a WAR file, a folder is created in the temporary work directory, and the contents of this folder are extracted out from the WAR file. This folder is then added to the `repositories` and `files` arrays as before.

Next, it looks up the `/WEB-INF/lib` folder from the `ProxyDirContext`. It iterates over each JAR file found there, instantiating a new `JarFile` for each and adding that as a repository. If the context exists in a WAR file, then the JARs are first copied over to a `/WEB-INF/lib` folder under the work directory. The process of adding a JAR file to a class loader instance involves updating the following arrays:

- The `jarNames` array contains just the JAR file name, for example, `commons-lang-2.4.jar`.
- The `jarFiles` array holds the `JarFile` instance that represents this file.
- The `jarRealFiles` array holds the `File` instance that represents this file.

The last modified time of a JAR file is tracked by adding the name of the JAR and the timestamp to the `paths` and `lastModifiedDates` arrays respectively.

ResourceEntry

This is a simple class that represents a loaded `Class` instance. Its key members include the loaded `Class` instance, a byte array with the binary content for this class, a last modified timestamp, and a URL that points to its source.

loadClass()

A class loader receives requests to load a class through its `loadClass()` method, which takes the fully qualified name of the class and an optional `boolean` that indicates whether or not that class's references are also to be loaded.

The default implementation of the `loadClass()` method in the abstract `ClassLoader` class establishes the basic pattern. It first checks the cache of `Class` instances previously loaded by this class loader instance. If a cached instance is not found, the task is delegated up to the parent class loader, all the way up to the Bootstrap class loader. If any parent finds the class, that class is returned. However, if all its ancestors report a failure to find the class, the delegating class loader will use its own techniques to find the bytecode for this class, as encapsulated in its override of the `findClass()` method. The default `findClass()` implementation of the abstract `java.lang.ClassLoader` simply throws a `ClassNotFoundException`. A custom class loader must therefore provide a reasonable implementation for this method.

The custom web application class loader overrides `loadClass()` to first check whether this class exists in the local cache, as implemented by its `resourceEntries` map. If the class is found in the cache, it is returned from there.

If the class is not present in its local cache, it interrogates the cache maintained by the JVM for this class loader instance next. If the class is found, it is returned.

If the cache lookup turns up nothing, the class loader then delegates to the System class loader to load any Java SE classes. Remember that Tomcat abbreviates the `CLASSPATH` so that the System class loader only has access to a minimal set of Tomcat classes. However, the System class loader can still delegate up the hierarchy to load any class visible to the Extension and Bootstrap class loaders. This prevents a particular web application from overriding any of the classes that would normally be served up by these class loaders. If the class is found, we are done here. If the class is not found, then it's now up to the custom class loader to ride in and save the day.

It first checks whether the standard delegation hierarchy is to be used. This is signaled using the `delegate` attribute set on the `Loader` nested component. In addition, a `String` array named `packageTriggers` identifies the names of packages that should be loaded by the parent. If either of these conditions is `true`, it delegates loading to the parent class loader, which is normally the Common class loader. If the class is found, then we are done. If the class cannot be found by its parent class loader, then it is truly entirely up to this custom class loader.

The `findClass()` method is then invoked to search the local repositories for this class loader. We will see more about this method shortly. If the class is found, we are done.

If the class cannot be found in the local repositories, then the custom class loader has no recourse but to delegate to its parent. If it had previously delegated to the parent, then it can simply throw a `ClassNotFoundException`. If not, the parent tries its hand at loading the class. If the class cannot be found, a `ClassNotFoundException` is thrown.

findClass()

While the `loadClass()` method is the conductor who orchestrates the loading process, this method is the actual workhorse that implements the look up of the class within the class loader's repositories.

The class name is converted to a relative path name to the class file by replacing package delimiters with forward slashes and by suffixing a `.class` extension.

The `resourceEntries` map is rechecked using the fully qualified class name (not the file's relative path name), just in case it might have been added since the last check.

The relative path to the class file is converted to an absolute path by appending the relative file name to each entry within the `repositories` array. The `DirContext` instance is then used to look up the named resource and its attributes. If the resource is not found, the next entry in the `repositories` array is used, and the search is repeated.

If the resource is found, a `ResourceEntry` instance is created to represent this resource. This instance is initialized by setting its `source` and `codeBase` members to a URL, based on the full path to this file. Its last modified timestamp is set based on the attributes retrieved for this resource, and the contents of the file are read into its `binaryContent` byte array. The full path to the class file and its last modified timestamp are then added to the end of the `paths` and `lastModifiedDates` arrays, respectively.

If the resource cannot be found in any of the repository folders, the `notFoundResources` map is checked to see if this is a resource whose previous lookup ended in failure. If so, a null is returned.

Now that the class based repositories have been exhausted, it is ready to look through its JAR files. It queries each `JarFile` instance in the `jarFiles` array, attempting to locate the requested resource using its relative path.

If a resource is located, a `ResourceEntry` is instantiated, and its attributes are set appropriately. The last modified timestamp is set to the timestamp associated with its containing JAR file. Moreover, the contents of the resource within the JAR file are read into this instance's `binaryContent` byte array.

If the `antiJARLocking` attribute is `true`, then any resource files in this JAR are extracted out to the temporary work directory.

If a resource could not be located, its name is now added to the `notFoundResources` map as an optimization.

When all the dust has settled, the `ResourceEntry` instance representing this class is added to the `resourceEntries` cache using the fully qualified name of the class located. This makes it easier to locate this class when it is requested at a later point in time.

getResource()

Using this method lets you access a resource located somewhere on the class path. The name of the resource is specified using a '/' delimited path name. A resource is a file that contains data that is used to specify application properties, configuration, or some other data such as an image or sound file.

If the `delegate` attribute is `true`, it delegates first to its parent class loader to find the resource.

In the standard delegation model, it first looks within the `resourceEntries` cache for the named resource. If it is not found in the cache, then it looks in the `repositories` for this class loader, as well as in any of its JAR files, as we have seen before. The only difference is that the name for this resource does not need to be converted from a package name to a path name, as it is required to be specified using '/' file separators. The found resource is cached as appropriate.

If the resource was not found and the `delegate` attribute is `false`, it now delegates to the parent class loader.

If the resource is found, then the URL to be returned is stored within the `source` member of the `ResourceEntry` instance that was created to represent this resource.

> Repositories may be added to the underlying `URLClassLoader` that our custom class loader extends. These are termed *external repositories* and represent additional locations that are searched when a class or resource is not found within the standard locations for a context.

Context initialization and startup

So far, we've seen how a web application's resources may be retrieved, how a brand new Tomcat-specific protocol to access these resources is defined, and how Tomcat implements its own class loader. Rest assured that the hard part is over, and it's all going to be coasting downhill from here.

Our focus now shifts to starting up the context, its children, and other nested components.

As we have seen in the last chapter, a `HostConfig` instance deploys the web applications associated with its host. For instance, its `deployDescriptors()` method enumerates the context fragments that it finds in the `CATALINA_BASE/conf/Catalina/localhost` folder, deploying each in turn.

Each context fragment is deployed to a context path that is based on the name of that context fragment file. This path is computed by stripping off the extension (`.xml`), replacing any '#' characters by forward slashes and prefixing the final path by a leading forward slash. A context fragment named `ROOT.xml` is deployed to an empty path.

A bare bones `Digester` is used to parse the fragment file, which simply instantiates an `org.apache.catalina.core.StandardContext` instance and sets its properties. It does not process any of the nested children within the `Context` element.

The `Context` instance is then added as a child of its parent host, which causes the `Context` instance's `start()` method to be invoked. This is the topic that we will cover in this section.

The first step in starting a context is to initialize it.

Context initialization

The initialization process is summarized in the following image. This process starts off by creating two digesters—one to parse the context fragment file and another to parse the web application deployment descriptor.

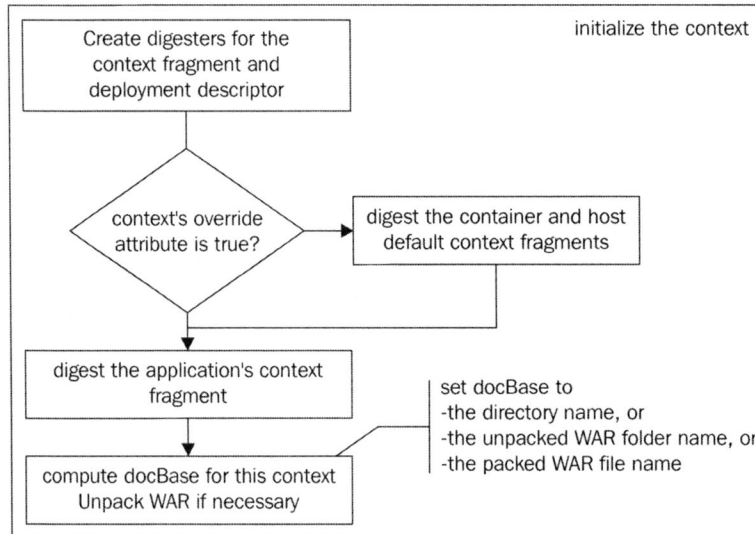

Digesting the context fragment

The deployment process initiated by the HostConfig has already instantiated the Context and has computed its path and docBase properties. As a result, the context digester created here must avoid re-instantiating the context and must not overwrite these properties.

> A ContextRuleSet parameter determines whether or not a new Context instance will be created. In the general case, the HostConfig instance has already instantiated a context, and has pushed it onto the stack maintained by the Digester.

A key task for this context digester is to parse the nested child elements such as the Listener, Loader, Manager, Parameter, Resources, Valve, and WatchedResource. The steps involved for each element typically involve instantiating the appropriate class, setting its properties from the element's attributes, and setting it on the Context instance.

For instance, when a `<Valve>` nested element is encountered, a new `Valve` is instantiated using its `className` property, its properties are set appropriately, and it is added to the `Context` by invoking its `addValve()` method. Likewise, when a `<WatchedResource>` element is encountered, it is added to the `Context` by invoking its `addWatchedResource()` method.

The naming service related elements, such as `<Resource>`, work in a similar fashion to the rules for the parsing of the `GlobalNamingResources` element. An instance appropriate for the element is constructed, such as `ContextResource` or `ContextEnvironment`, which is then added to the `Context` instance's `NamingResources` member.

The digester is now used to process the default context fragment file for the entire Tomcat installation, which is `%CATALINA_BASE%/conf/context.xml`. Next, the host's default context file is processed. If it exists, this file is named `context.xml.default` and can be found in `%CATALINA_BASE%/conf/<engineName>/<hostName>`. Finally, the context fragment file for the web application is processed. For the `devguide.xml` fragment, this file is `%CATALINA_BASE%/conf/Catalina/localhost/devguide.xml`.

Each file that is found will be parsed by the context digester, and appropriate properties will be set on the existing `Context` instance that it finds on its stack.

All the context fragment files that were found are added as watched resources for this context so that the context will be reloaded when any of these files is modified, added, or removed.

The `override` context attribute (default: `false`) affects this behavior. By default, the settings in the default server's fragment file and the default host's fragment file are digested prior to processing the context's own fragment file. However, if this property is set to `true`, these files are simply ignored, and only the settings found in the context's fragment file are used.

Setting the document base

Next, the `Context`'s `docBase` is adjusted. Remember that the document base is the location on the server where this application's resources live.

This attribute is defined when using a context fragment file but should not be specified when using a `META-INF/context.xml` file. In the latter case, the `docBase` is inferred by the application deployment process, and is set either to the name of the WAR file being deployed, or to the name of the exploded directory.

When specified, this attribute can either be an absolute path or a path that is relative to the `appBase` directory of its host.

If the docBase is not specified, it is computed by converting the context path back into a folder name. This involves replacing any forward slash characters with '#' characters and replacing the empty context path with ROOT. If the docBase is relative, it is made absolute by prefixing it with its host's appBase.

If this context's docBase represents a WAR file that is to be unpacked, then the file is unpacked into the appBase folder under the appropriate context path, and the docBase is updated to point to this exploded folder. Otherwise, if the context's docBase represents a WAR file that is not to be unpacked or if it represents an exploded directory, it is left untouched.

The unpackWAR context attribute determines whether Tomcat will automatically unpack a WAR file into the docBase directory before deploying it.

Context startup

Once the context has been initialized, the remaining startup activities follow in the sequence shown in the following image:

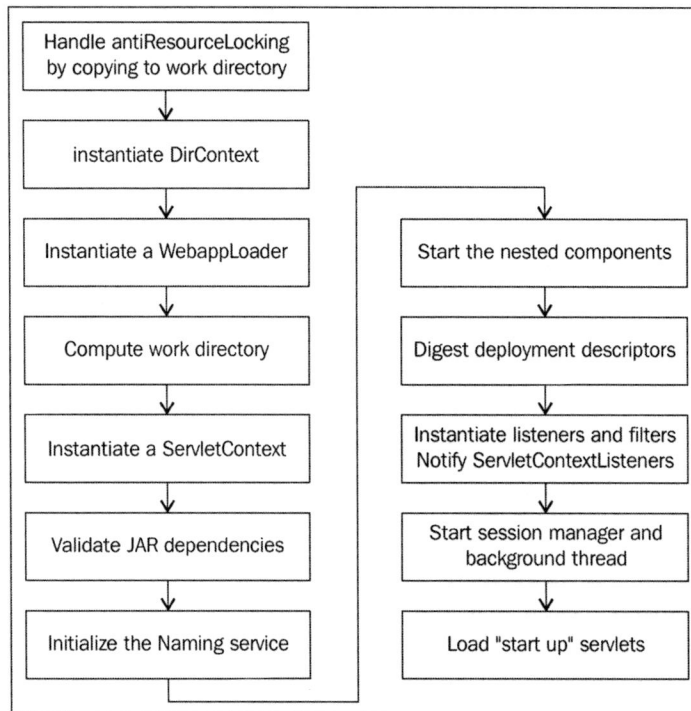

In the sections that follow, we'll address each of these in more detail.

Anti resource locking

This step is required for operating systems that might exhibit file locking issues. Setting the `antiResourceLocking` attribute to `true` forces a web application's resources to be copied to a temporary folder within the work directory.

This skirts the problem of a file lock preventing a folder from being deleted when a context needs to be undeployed. In this case, the application is always deployed into an entirely new folder within the temporary directory as identified by the `java.io.tmpdir` system property.

The folder's name is made unique by prefixing it with a sequential integer value that is a static member variable in the `ContextConfig`, called the `deploymentCount`.

The context's `docBase` is adjusted to point to this temporary directory. The original `docBase` is stored in the `originalDocBase` member of the context. This allows us to restore the `docBase` to its original value once we are done with the startup of the context.

The drawbacks with this are the extra space required to hold the entire web application each time the application is redeployed and the increased startup times.

In addition, there can be harmful side effects on some operating systems. For example, the Tomcat documentation warns that this might disable JSP reloading in a running server, or it may automatically delete a web application if it is deployed outside of the `appBase`.

Setting up the Context's resources

For a directory-based context, a `FileDirContext` is instantiated and its members are set from the corresponding context attributes. This includes `caseSensitive`, which determines whether resource names are case sensitive, as well as the `cachingAllowed`, `cacheTTL`, `cacheMaxSize`, and `cacheObjectMaxSize` attributes that we have seen before.

The document base of this `FileDirContext` is computed using `CATALINA_BASE`, the host's `appBase`, and the context's `docBase`.

A `ProxyDirContext` is instantiated to wrap this `FileDirContext`. Remember that this proxy context wraps the mechanism to locate resources on the file system, as well as the mechanism to cache these resources. A `Context` works with this proxy context, which in turn delegates to the underlying `DirContext` implementation. The proxy context is also handed off to other users, such as the web application class loader, that need to access a context's resources.

If caching is being requested, that is, if the Context attribute cachingAllowed is true, then a ResourceCache instance is instantiated for the ProxyDirContext.

The resources member of a Context holds this ProxyDirContext instance. The underlying FileDirContext is held in its webappResources member.

At this point, our Context is hooked up with a way of retrieving the resources that reside in its document base.

Setting up the Context's Loader

Next, we instantiate the class that lets us load the Context's classes, both those that reside as standalone files in the WEB-INF/classes folder, as well as those that are packaged as JAR files in the WEB-INF/lib folder.

The function of class loading is handled by the WebappLoader, which wraps a URLClassLoader subclass, WebappClassLoader.

The Context attribute that controls class loader behavior is delegate. By default, the class loader instance associated with this web application will attempt to load a class first before delegating to its parent. However, if this attribute is set to true, the class loader will follow traditional class loading mechanics of first delegating to the parent, before attempting to locate the class itself.

This is just the first part of setting up the loader. The actual class loader is not instantiated until the Loader is started. We'll get to that in just a moment.

Publish the work directory

A temporary work directory for this context is computed as CATALINA_BASE/work/<engineName>/<hostName>/<modifiedContextPath>, where the context path is modified by stripping off the leading '/' and replacing any intermediate slashes with underscores. As a result, the context path /chapter/09 becomes chapter_09.

This directory is converted to an absolute path, rooted at CATALINA_BASE, and is set as a servlet context attribute named javax.servlet.context.tempdir. Servlets within this context can then query this attribute to determine the work directory.

The workdir attribute of a <Context> can be used to configure the folder to be used as the work directory.

Setting up a servlet context

In this step, an ApplicationContext is instantiated and set on the context member of the context.

This class implements the ServletContext interface, which represents a servlet's operating environment in the servlet specification, and provides a way by which a servlet may access its container.

In Tomcat, this is implemented as an instance of the org.apache.catalina.core. ApplicationContext class. However, because an ApplicationContext holds references to internal Tomcat structures, it is not safe to allow servlets to directly access an ApplicationContext instance.

Instead, an ApplicationContext implements the standard pattern of maintaining a member of type ApplicationContextFacade that implements the ServletContext interface. This facade is handed off to the container's servlets and filters, and it simply delegates to its enclosed ApplicationContext.

A ServletContext provides a number of useful methods. For example, you can:

- Get the major and minor versions of the servlet specification that this container supports
- Query the MIME type associated with a given filename
- Obtain a RequestDispatcher instance to forward or include requests
- Determine the real path of a virtual resource
- Set and retrieve initialization parameters

The ApplicationContext instance works very closely with the Context to provide implementations of all these methods. Its important members include the Context instance, a Map for context initialization parameters, and a Map for context attributes.

Validating optional JARs

A static initializer in the ExtensionValidator class looks for shared libraries in the directories specified by the java.ext.dirs and catalina.ext.dirs system properties, as well as on the System Classpath, as specified by the java.class.path system property. This list comprises the 'available' libraries.

It then validates the web application's dependencies by first accumulating all the dependencies, identified within the manifest file for the web application, as well as within the manifest files for each JAR found in the web application's WEB-INF/lib folder. This list comprises the 'required' libraries.

A dependency is considered fulfilled when a required library is matched with an available library such that both have the same extension name, and the available library's specification and implementation versions are not older than those of the required library.

Any dependency that is not satisfied is an error condition and aborts a context's startup.

Naming context

The `Context` attribute `useNaming` determines whether or not a `NamingContextListener` is instantiated and added as a lifecycle listener on the `Context`. The principles for the naming context operation are very similar to what we had discussed in Chapter 5, *The Server and Service Components*.

Starting nested components

The `Loader` component is started by calling its `start()` method. This causes it to install the stream handler factory, which can handle the `jndi` protocol, by invoking the `URL.setURLStreamHandlerFactory()` method. It then instantiates a `WebappClassLoader` instance and sets the context attributes that affect its behavior. This includes the `delegate` attribute that indicates whether or not this class loader should first delegate to its parent and the `antiJARLocking` attribute that determines whether the contents of JAR files within this application are extracted out to a temporary folder in the work directory.

In addition, the context's `ProxyDirContext` is handed off to the class loader to allow it to access the resources contained within the `/WEB-INF/classes` and `/WEB-INF/lib` folders associated with this context.

The various array-based data structures of the class loader that we have seen earlier are also initialized.

The `start()` method is also invoked on the context's children, as well as on its pipeline.

Configuring the web application aspect

The context is now ready to receive configuration elements that are set up in the web application deployment descriptor.

The web application digester is intended to process the various elements that can live in the web.xml file. As we have seen with other digesters, the process is fairly standard—you instantiate a class to represent the named element, set its properties from the element's attributes, and then store that initialized instance on some parent object. In this case, the parent object is a Context instance.

The elements encountered are rooted at the web-app element and include definitions for error pages, filters, servlets, initialization parameters, listeners, environment entries, resources, session configuration, welcome files, and so on.

For instance, when a <servlet> element is encountered, the createWrapper() method is invoked on the Context instance to instantiate a blank Wrapper instance and to set any listeners on it. Next, this wrapper is added as a child on the Context. The name of the specific servlet class that this Wrapper will wrap is set, along with the servlet name, and its load on startup flag. Any initialization parameters are set by invoking addInitParameter() on the Wrapper instance. Additional parameters are set as necessary.

Similarly, when a <servlet-mapping> element is read, the addServletMapping() method of the Context is called with the servlet name and URL pattern.

Filters are handled by instantiating a new org.apache.catalina.deploy.FilterDef instance, setting properties such as the filter's name and the name of its implementing class, setting initialization parameters, and adding it to the Context using the addFilterDef() method.

A filter mapping is instantiated, initialized with the filter name, servlet name, URL patterns, and dispatcher setting, and is added to the Context using the addFilterMap() method.

The <session-timeout> and <welcome-file> elements are responded to by invoking the Context's setSessionTimeout() and addWelcomeFile() methods, respectively.

You can investigate the complete set of rules by checking out the org.apache.catalina.startup.WebRuleSet class.

Just as with context fragment files, a web application is configured at three levels.

First, there's the default %CATALINA_BASE%/conf/web.xml that applies to all the web applications within the entire container. Next, there's the %CATALINA_BASE%/conf/<engineName>/<hostName>/web.xml.default that applies to web applications within a given host. Finally, there's the /WEB-INF/web.xml that applies to a specific web application.

The `Context` instance is pushed on to the `Digester` stack, so it is updated with whatever we find in the file being parsed.

The found deployment descriptors are added as watched resources for this `Context`.

At this point, our `Context` instance has been completely initialized from all its constituent configuration files, whether fragment files or application deployment descriptors.

The Mapper

We first encountered the `Mapper` class in Chapter 6, *The Connector Component*, when we saw how the `Connector` component causes an instance of this class to be initialized. This class has a number of nested classes that help in the mapping process.

The `Mapper$Context` nested class holds the context path, the array of welcome file names, and the `ProxyDirContext` for this context. It also has a number of arrays of the `Mapper$Wrapper` nested class. Each instance of this class holds a reference to the actual `org.apache.catalina.core.Wrapper` instance.

Servlet mappings defined in `web.xml` are maintained in three sorted arrays—extension mappings are used for patterns such as `*.jsp`, wildcard mappings are used for patterns such as `reservations/*`, and exact match mappings are used for patterns like `/HelloWorldServlet`.

A separate default mapping for the pattern / is not held within an array—it's held in a single member named `defaultWrapper`, as there can be only one default servlet.

We'll see a lot more of this component in Chapter 10, *The Wrapper Component*.

Starting listeners

The context's listeners, as registered in the deployment descriptor, are now started. Each listener is loaded using the context's `WebappClassLoader` instance and is then instantiated.

Instances of `ServletContextAttributeListener`, `ServletRequestAttributeListener`, `ServletRequestListener`, and `HttpSessionAttributeListener` are classified as *event listeners*, while `ServletContextListener` and `HttpSessionListener` instance are termed *life cycle listeners*.

Any registered `ServletContextListener` instances are now notified of the context's startup by invoking their `contextInitialized()` methods.

Starting application filters

For each defined filter, an `org.apache.catalina.core.ApplicationFilterConfig` is instantiated.

The context's `WebappClassLoader` is used to load and instantiate the filter's implementation class, and its `init()` method is invoked. An entry is then added to the context's `filterConfigs` map, which maps the filter's name to its `ApplicationFilterConfig` instance.

Some filters are marked as restricted by adding an entry in the `RestrictedFilters.properties` file, which is found in the `org.apache.catalina.core` package. An attempt to install a restricted filter in a non-privileged context results in an exception being thrown.

A privileged context is identified using the `privileged` context attribute. Setting this attribute to `true` will cause this context's parent class loader to be the Server class loader rather than the Shared class loader. By default, both of these are set to the Common class loader.

> This is a security risk and should only be allowed for trusted contexts, such as the `Manager` application, as it allows this context to have privileged access to internal Tomcat classes and container servlets such as the `Manager` servlet.

Session manager and the background thread

Once the context has been configured, an `org.apache.catalina.session.StandardManager` instance is set as this `Context`'s session manager, and its `start()` method is invoked. We'll consider this component in more detail in Chapter 11, *The Manager Component*.

The context container's background thread is started, as long as its `backgroundProcessorDelay` attribute is non zero. This attribute sets the interval in seconds between invocations of the `backgroundProcess()` method on the `Context` and its child containers, including all wrappers.

The background thread can be used to perform session expiration and class monitoring for reloading. By default, the context will use the background processing thread of its parent host. Specifying a positive delay causes a separate thread to be spawned instead.

A parent will not invoke `backgroundProcess()` on a child container if it detects that the child has its own thread to handle background processing (that is, it has a positive delay).

Loading servlets on startup

In this step, each child wrapper for this context is queried to see if it should be loaded on startup (that is, its load on startup value is not -1). Each such wrapper is added to a sorted `TreeMap`, whose key is the `loadOnStartup` value for the wrapper, and whose value is an `ArrayList` of the child wrappers that have that `loadOnStartup` value.

Once the `TreeMap` has been populated, we iterate over the keys in the sorted order of the `loadOnStartup` values. For each key, the `ArrayList` of `Wrapper` instances is retrieved and the `load()` method is invoked on each `Wrapper` instance.

This completes the startup process, and the context is now marked as available.

Request processing

As of the last chapter, the received request ended with the `invoke()` method being called on the `StandardHostValve`. That valve extracts the context being targeted from the request and sets that context's class loader as the current thread's context class loader.

The context's pipeline is then invoked to process the request, which results in the `invoke()` method of the `StandardContextValve` being called. This method first checks whether a protected resource is being requested. Any request for a resource within the `/WEB-INF` or `/META-INF` folders results in an HTTP response status code of 404, which indicates that the requested resource is not available.

This method also implements a busy wait, if it senses that the context is in the process of being reloaded. It sleeps for a second at a time, until the context has been reloaded and is available once again. If the context was indeed reloaded, then the context class loader, as set by the `StandardHostValve`, becomes obsolete and so is replaced with the context's new class loader.

The `Wrapper` instance, as set on the Catalina `Request` by the mapping process, is then retrieved. A 404 Not Found response is returned, if this wrapper is either not set or if it is not available.

Next, any `ServletRequestListener` instances for this context are retrieved and the `requestInitialized()` method is invoked on each listener found.

The `Wrapper` instance's pipeline is then invoked, which as we will see in the next chapter, actually executes the intended servlet's logic.

This is followed by invoking the `requestDestroyed()` listener method on each `ServletRequestListener` instance that is observing this context.

Finally, we reset the context class loader before returning.

Hot deploying a context

The `reloadable` attribute of a context indicates that resources should be watched for modification and that a reload of the context should be triggered if an application's resources have been modified.

> While reloading a context is invaluable during development, it requires significant runtime overhead and so should be left turned off in a production environment.

Determining if a reload is necessary

As we saw in the last chapter, a context may be reloaded when a watched resource is modified or deleted. In addition, a key responsibility of a `WebappLoader` is to provide a `backgroundProcess()` method implementation that is called by its parent container's background processing thread. Note that this method is of use only for a context whose `reloadable` attribute is set to true.

This method delegates to its `WebappClassLoader` instance, which checks each class or resource name in the `paths` array to see whether it has been modified since it was last accessed, by comparing its corresponding `lastModifiedDates` entry with that of the resource. Next, it obtains a listing of all the JAR files available and compares them against the `jarNames` array that was built earlier to see if a new one has been added, or if an existing one has been deleted.

If a resource file has been modified, or the JAR listings do not match, then we are due for a reloading of the context. We do this by invoking `reload()` on the context.

Reloading a context

The `reload()` method of a `StandardContext` simulates a web application restart by invoking the `stop()` method followed by the `start()` method.

The `stop()` method works as an inverse to the `start()` method. It invokes the `stop()` method on each of its `Wrapper` child instances, invokes `release()` on each filter instance in its `filterConfigs` map and then clears out this map, stops the background processing thread if any, stops the session manager, invokes the `contextDestroyed()` method on all its registered `ServletContextListener` instances, and calls the `stop()` method on its pipeline.

It then clears out its children wrappers and servlet mappings, its filter definitions and mappings, error pages, welcome files, parameters and any application-specific servlet context attributes, as well as any MIME mappings. It also deletes the temporary folder created by the anti-resource-locking mechanism.

It clears out any attributes set in its associated `ServletContext`, nulls out its `ProxyDirContext` reference in the `resources` member (the underlying `DirContext` is safe in the `webappResources` member), and stops its nested components such as the loader.

Stopping the web application's class loader involves invoking `stop()` on its wrapped `WebappClassLoader` instance and setting its class loader reference to null. This deregisters any JDBC drivers loaded by this class loader and walks through each loaded class to null out any static fields to work around any garbage collection issues. It then clears out all the arrays used to manage this class loader's resources and its caches.

In effect, this reverts the context to an uninitialized state.

The `reload()` method then invokes `start()` to begin the process of redeploying this context.

Reloading is very useful as it lets you pick up changes to class files and resources. Unfortunately, this is only accomplished by restarting the entire context. This sets up a brand new class loader and causes all previously loaded `Class` instances to be discarded. Any instances of classes are also released for garbage collection.

Fortunately, JDK 1.4 introduced a better mechanism that lets you make a change to a class, but lets all existing instance members retain their previous values. No static initializers or instance initializers are run, and static variables retain their values.

This mechanism, known as **HotSwap** or **class redefinition**, lets you fix a problem in a class, recompile it, dynamically replace the old instance with the new one, and then continue debugging with the fixed code, all without losing a step. The key point here is that you can make a fix within a debugging session and have it take effect without restarting the session.

This functionality is part of the **Java Platform Debugger Architecture (JPDA)** and is only available while an application is being executed under the control of a debugger.

See `http://java.sun.com/j2se/1.4.2/docs/guide/jpda/enhancements.html` for more details on this feature.

Context example

In this section, we'll modify the `devguide` web application to install a custom class, a context parameter, a filter, a `ServletContextListener`, and a `ServletRequestListener`. When the application is run, watch the console output to see when the filters and listeners are invoked.

Deployment descriptor

Edit the `devguide` web application's `web.xml` deployment descriptor to add in the following lines:

```
<listener>
  <listener-class>
    com.swengsol.listeners.MyServletContextListener
  </listener-class>
</listener>
<listener>
  <listener-class>
    com.swengsol.listeners.MyServletRequestListener
  </listener-class>
</listener>
<context-param>
  <param-name>contextVariable</param-name>
  <param-value>Example Context Value</param-value>
</context-param>
<filter>
  <filter-name>MyAppFilter</filter-name>
  <filter-class>com.swengsol.filters.MyFilter</filter-class>
</filter>
<filter-mapping>
  <filter-name>MyAppFilter</filter-name>
  <servlet-name>HelloWorld</servlet-name>
</filter-mapping>
```

Source files

The Java class files that comprise this web application's code base include a sampling of the various components of a web application. Their intent is to provide an understanding of the plumbing connections that are made, rather than to implement any material functionality.

HelloWorldServlet.java

This is an example servlet that simply prints out a **Hello World** message when invoked using the URL, `http://localhost:8080/devguide/HelloWorld`. While this servlet won't win any awards for either form or function, it represents the use of a custom class and the retrieval of an initialization parameter. Note that the URL displayed for the `index.html` resource uses the custom `jndi` protocol.

```java
package com.swengsol;

import java.io.IOException;
import java.io.PrintWriter;
import java.net.URL;

import javax.servlet.ServletException;
import javax.servlet.http.HttpServlet;
import javax.servlet.http.HttpServletRequest;
import javax.servlet.http.HttpServletResponse;

import com.swengsol.helpers.Message;

public class HelloWorldServlet extends HttpServlet {
    private static final long serialVersionUID = 1L;

    public void doGet(HttpServletRequest request, HttpServletResponse response)
        throws IOException, ServletException {
        response.setContentType("text/html");
        PrintWriter out = response.getWriter();
        out.println("<html>");
        out.println("<head>");
        String title = "Hello World - Tomcat Developer's Guide";
        out.println("<title>" + title + "</title>");
        out.println("</head>");
        out.println("<body bgcolor=\"white\">");

        Message msg = new Message();
        msg.setMessage("Hello World - Tomcat Developer's Guide");
        out.println("<h1> "+ msg.getMessage() + "</h1>");

        URL u = getServletContext().getResource("/index.html");
        out.println("URL for the resource <i>/index.html</i> is " + u);
        out.println("<p />");
        out.println("Servlet initialization parameter: ");
        out.println(getServletContext().getInitParameter("contextVariable"));
        out.println("</body>");
        out.println("</html>");
    }
}
```

Message.java

This class provides an example of a utility class that will be accessed by our servlet.

```java
package com.swengsol.helpers;

public class Message {
  private static int num = 0;
  private String text;
  public void setMessage(String text) {
    this.text = text;
  }
  public String getMessage() {
    return text + " - " + Integer.toString(num++);
  }
}
```

Listeners

Two listeners are implemented, one that listens for context initialization and destruction events and the other that fires before and after each incoming request.

MyServletContextListener.java

This listener prints notifications of context start and destroy events to the console.

```java
package com.swengsol.listeners;

import javax.servlet.ServletContextEvent;
import javax.servlet.ServletContextListener;
public class MyServletContextListener implements
ServletContextListener {
  public void contextDestroyed(ServletContextEvent sce) {
    System.out.println("> Servlet Context Listener: " +
                       "Context Destroyed");
  }
  public void contextInitialized(ServletContextEvent sce) {
    System.out.println("> Servlet Context Listener: " +
                       "Context initialized");
  }
}
```

MyServletRequestListener.java

This listener prints notifications of request based events to the console.

```
package com.swengsol.listeners;

import javax.servlet.ServletRequestEvent;
import javax.servlet.ServletRequestListener;
public class MyServletRequestListener implements
ServletRequestListener {
  public void requestDestroyed(ServletRequestEvent sre) {
    System.out.println("> Servlet Request Listener: " +
                       "Request Destroyed");
  }
  public void requestInitialized(ServletRequestEvent sre) {
    System.out.println("> Servlet Request Listener: " +
                       "Request Initialized");
  }
}
```

MyFilter.java

Finally, we install a filter which also does nothing more than print out some log messages.

```
package com.swengsol.filters;

import java.io.IOException;
import javax.servlet.Filter;
import javax.servlet.FilterChain;
import javax.servlet.FilterConfig;
import javax.servlet.ServletException;
import javax.servlet.ServletRequest;
import javax.servlet.ServletResponse;
import javax.servlet.http.HttpServletRequest;

public class MyFilter implements Filter {
  private FilterConfig fc;
  public void init(FilterConfig config) throws ServletException {
    this.fc = config;
    System.out.println("> Filter: " + "Initializing filter");
  }
  public void destroy() {
  }
```

```
public void doFilter(ServletRequest request,
                     ServletResponse response,
   FilterChain chain) throws IOException, ServletException {
   HttpServletRequest req = (HttpServletRequest) request;
   System.out.println("> Filter: " + req.getRequestURI());
   String name = req.getRemoteUser();
   if (name != null) {
      System.out.println("> Filter: " + "User " + name);
      fc.getServletContext().log("User " + name +
         " is doing something.");
   }
   chain.doFilter(request, response);
  }
}
```

Summary

Congratulations! You have successfully completed one of the most complex chapters in this book. We had a lot of ground to cover in this chapter, with general concepts and Tomcat implementation specifics flying fast and furious.

In the first part of this chapter, we considered the configuration of both the context aspect, as well as the web application aspect of this component. We also looked at the multitude of configuration files that may be brought to bear on these two aspects.

Next, we looked at a number of general concepts. We considered a JNDI-based Directory service implementation that was used to access a web application's resources in a storage-independent manner. We took an in-depth look at class loading principles in general and at the Tomcat web application class loader in particular. We then toured the arena of Java protocol handlers and considered an implementation of the jndi custom protocol that is used to access context resources in a generic manner. Finally, we looked at the shared library mechanism used to provide a common repository for libraries that are shared across multiple web applications.

We then proceeded to look at the context startup process in a sequential manner. We observed how the context was updated by the digester's parsing of the context fragments and deployment descriptors. We also noted how filters, listeners, and servlets are installed into the context, and how servlets are loaded on startup if needed.

We ended by looking at the request processing flow with the context's basic valve.

In the next chapter, we will look at the process by which an invoked servlet handles the incoming request.

10
The Wrapper Component

We are finally at the workhorse of the Tomcat component hierarchy — the **Wrapper**. This unassuming component is what breathes life into your servlets, and consequently is a very critical component to a web developer.

In the default case, where Tomcat is not running in a clustered configuration, the container is expected to use only one servlet instance per `<servlet>` element in the web deployment descriptor. It is this single instance that is wrapped by a `Wrapper` component.

The servlet specification requires each servlet to implement the `javax.servlet.Servlet` interface, which defines the `init()`, `service()`, and `destroy()` life cycle methods. The primary role of a `Wrapper` component is to invoke these methods at appropriate times in the lifetime of a servlet instance.

When a servlet implements the `SingleThreadModel` interface, the `Wrapper` might actually manage a pool of servlet instances, while ensuring that only one thread is executing within a servlet instance's `service()` method at any given point in time. This interface is dangerous, as it gives developers a false sense of confidence in a multi-threaded environment, and as a result has been deprecated. In this chapter, we will not discuss this mode of operation any further.

StandardWrapper

This image depicts some key aspects of the `org.apache.catalina.core.` `StandardWrapper` component. As shown, this component extends `ContainerBase`, marking it as a container. However, a wrapper exists at the lowest level of the container hierarchy, and any attempt to add a child to it will be met with scorn, and an `IllegalStateException`.

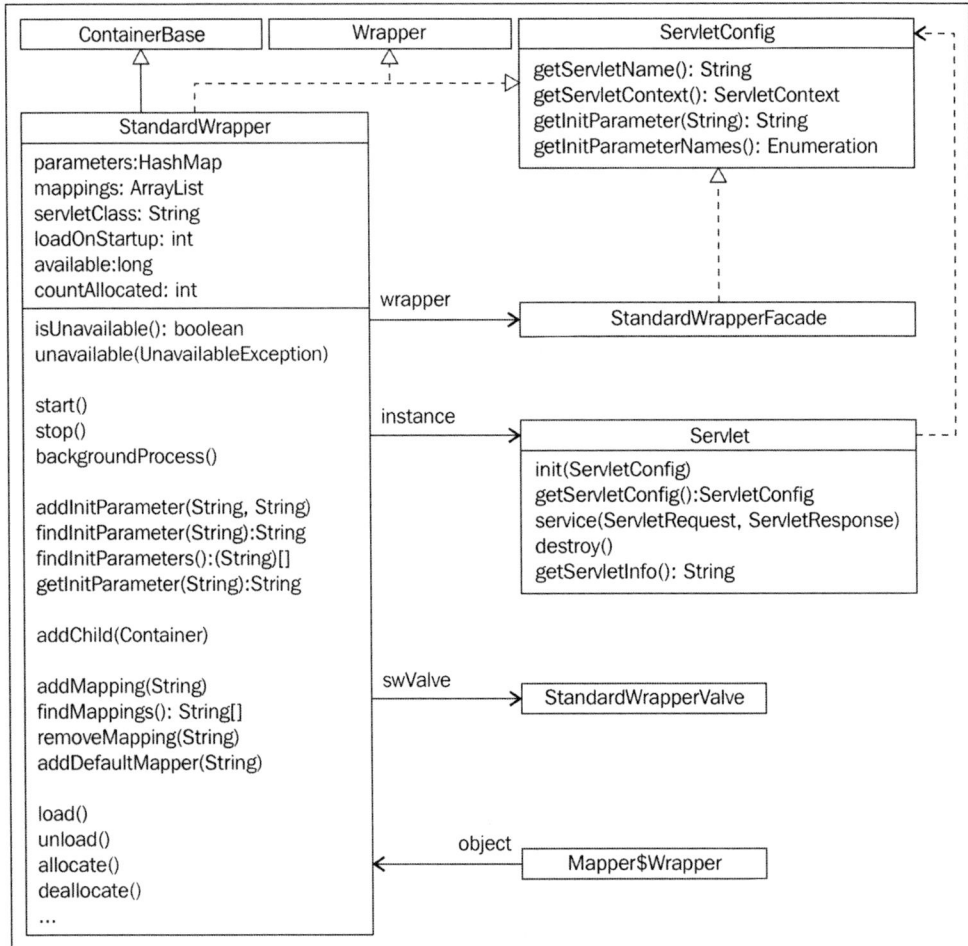

As the `web.xml` deployment descriptor is parsed, any `<servlet>` elements within it are converted into `StandardWrapper` instances and are added as children of the context.

Key members of the `StandardWrapper` instance include the following:

- a `mappings ArrayList` which represents the collection of `<servlet-mappings>` elements in the `web.xml` file that are associated with this servlet

- a `parameters HashMap` which holds the servlet's initialization parameters

- a `servletClass` member that holds the implementation class for the servlet

- a `loadOnStartup` integer which indicates whether this servlet should be loaded and initialized at context startup.

The `StandardWrapperValve` is a wrapper's key request processing component, and is set as its basic valve.

The actual servlet being managed is represented by the wrapper's `instance` member. The wrapper gives the wrapped servlet a chance to initialize itself, by calling its `init()` method. It passes a `ServletConfig` instance to the `init()` method to provide the servlet with a way to access its external environment. Both the `StandardWrapper` and `StandardWrapperFacade` classes implement `ServletConfig`, allowing an instance of this facade to be passed into the servlet's `init()` method.

The `StandardWrapperFacade` narrows the public API of the `StandardWrapper` to the methods in the `ServletConfig` interface while ensuring that a servlet may not access the internals of the Tomcat container.

A `countAllocated` member tracks the number of requests that are currently 'in flight' for a given servlet instance. It is incremented when the wrapper's `allocate()` method is called to retrieve the servlet instance in order to have it process a request, and is decremented when the wrapper's `deallocate()` method is called once the request has been processed.

A Tomcat-specific extension to the servlet specification is provided through the `backgroundProcess()` method. If a servlet implements the `org.apache.PeriodicEventListener` interface, its `periodicEvent()` method will be invoked periodically on the background thread.

> Members that support the dreaded `SingleThreadModel` (such as the `instancePool` stack) won't be discussed in this chapter.

Servlet lifecycle

The process of adding a wrapper to its context causes the wrapper's `start()` method to be invoked. A key task of this method is to set its `available` member to zero.

This member indicates the time (in milliseconds) when a servlet is expected to be ready to serve requests. If this is zero, the servlet is ready and able to serve. If it is a positive value, then the servlet is expected to be available at the specified future time, and requests for it are handled by returning an `SC_SERVICE_UNAVAILABLE` response. On the other hand, a servlet whose `available` member is set to `Long.MAX_VALUE` is considered to be permanently unavailable, and requests are responded to with an `SC_NOT_FOUND` error.

As we saw in the last chapter, servlets can also be marked as needing to be loaded during the context's startup process using the `<load-on-startup>` element in the web deployment descriptor.

Loading a servlet

A context loads a wrapper by invoking its `load()` method.

A non-null `instance` member for a wrapper indicates that this wrapper's servlet has been previously loaded, instantiated, and initialized. In such a case, the `load()` method simply returns that instance. This is in compliance with the servlet specification that states that only one instance should exist per JVM for each servlet declaration found in the web deployment descriptor.

However, if the servlet has not been initialized previously, the wrapper's `instance` member will now be initialized.

The fully qualified class name of the servlet is specified by the `servletClass` member, which is initialized with the value of the `<servlet-class>` element in the `web.xml` descriptor.

Servlets may be divided into two broad categories. First there are the normal servlets that conform to the servlet specification and which web developers know and love. Second, there are the *container servlets* that have special privileges when running in the Tomcat container.

A container servlet implements the `org.apache.catalina.ContainerServlet` interface, which confers upon it the ability to receive a reference to its enclosing wrapper, through which the container servlet may gain access to the rest of Tomcat's internals.

In addition, while normal servlets are loaded using the web application class loader, container servlets are loaded using either the Common or Server class loader. Examples of container servlets include the Manager servlet and the now deprecated Invoker servlet.

Only a privileged context may load a container servlet. A privileged context is indicated by setting the `privileged` attribute of its `<Context>` element to true.

The servlet class is loaded using the appropriate class loader and the loaded class is instantiated. Its `init()` method is then invoked to give it a chance to initialize any expensive resources, such as database connections, before it is eligible to handle incoming requests.

The `init()` method is passed a `ServletConfig` parameter that allows it to obtain the servlet name, the servlet context, as well as any initialization parameters as specified in the web deployment descriptor. The `StandardWrapper` passes itself to the `init()` method, wrapped as a `StandardWrapperFacade` instance.

The loaded and initialized servlet instance is then stored in the wrapper's `instance` member, and is ready to service incoming requests.

> A failure at any stage of this loading process results in the wrapper's `available` member being set to `Long.MAX_VALUE`, indicating that the servlet is permanently unavailable, and in an exception being thrown.

Mappers

A container uses the mapping rules defined by the servlet specification to map an incoming request URI to the appropriate context and servlet that will process the request.

In this section, we will explore these rules and then discover how this mapping is implemented within Tomcat.

Mapping rules

The target context is determined based on the longest context path on the URL that matches one of the contexts for the specified virtual host.

Once a successful context match has been found, the remainder of the URL, up to the query string, is considered for a match with the wrappers associated with that context. Each of the rules below is tried, in a case sensitive manner, until the first match is found, at which point the matched wrapper is returned.

- **Exact path matching**: The servlet path on the request is checked *for an exact match* with the servlet path in the `<servlet-mapping>` element. An exact match pattern must start with a / and must not end with a /*. An example of an exact match would be the servlet path `/customers/invoices`.

- **Wildcard path matching**: Next, the container attempts to find *the longest matching path* between the servlet path on the request and one of the servlet paths in the `<servlet-mapping>` elements.

  If a match is not found, the last part of the path is repeatedly dropped and the remainder is compared until a match is found. The longest match found is used to identify the target servlet.

  This is typically used to find paths that start with a / , but which end in the /* wildcard pattern. An example of such a servlet path is `/customers/*`.

- **Extension matching**: If the servlet path ends with an extension, then that extension is compared against any `<servlet-mapping>` element that have a pattern that starts with *. and ends with that extension. An example of such a servlet path is `/customers/invoices/editInvoice.jsp`.

- **Default servlet matching**: There can be only one default servlet for an application. This default servlet is mapped to a servlet path of /. If none of the above rules are able to locate a match, the container will delegate to this default servlet.

> The default servlet is declared in the `web.xml` file within `CATALINA_BASE/conf`, and is implemented by the `org.apache.catalina.servlets.DefaultServlet` class.

Partial URLs

In addition to the above mapping rules, the container also considers a special type of request known as a *valid partial request*, which is a request that references a directory rather than a specific resource.

Such a request takes the form `http://www.swengsol.com/context/` or `http://www.swengsol.com/context/folder/`, where `context` is the context path for this application and `folder` is a directory for this context that is not mapped to a servlet or JSP page.

When a *valid partial request* is detected, the container will complete the request URL by appending a *partial URL* to it.

Where does this partial URL come from? Well, the web deployment descriptor has a `<welcome-file-list>` element that lets you specify welcome files in the application. These are termed *partial URLs*, as they are not complete paths to a resource, but instead are simply resource names, such as `index.html`, `welcome.htm`, or `index.jsp`, that are identified without any leading or trailing `/`.

When a valid partial request is received, a container walks through the welcome file list defined for the specified context. The container appends the name of each welcome file defined, to the valid partial request and checks whether a static resource or servlet is mapped to that request URI. The first resource that matches gets to handle the request.

If no match is found, the request is handled by the default servlet defined for this context.

> A request URI that represents a folder, such as `http://www.swengsol.com/context/folder` is first redirected to `http://www.swengsol.com/context/folder/`, which in turn is handled by appending the appropriate welcome file partial URLs to locate the appropriate resource.

Now that we are familiar with the matching algorithm, let's look at how Tomcat implements these rules.

Tomcat mappers

The `org.apache.tomcat.util.http.mapper.Mapper` class implements the matching rules defined by the servlet specification.

> This is the same `Mapper` that we encountered in Chapter 6, *The Connector Component*.

As always, let's begin by observing the structural relationships that govern a mapper.

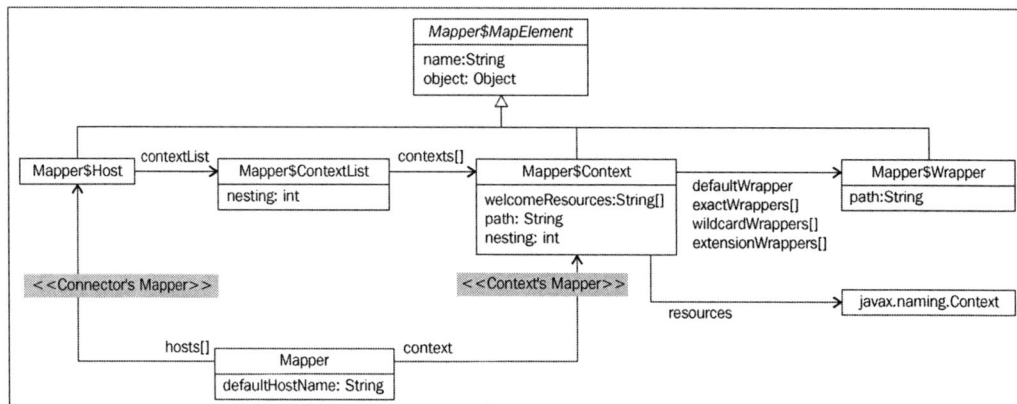

```
                                    Mapper$MapElement
                                    name:String
                                    object: Object

              contextList                    contexts[]
Mapper$Host              Mapper$ContextList           Mapper$Context                         Mapper$Wrapper
                        nesting: int                  welcomeResources:String[]   defaultWrapper    path:String
                                                      path: String                exactWrappers[]
                                                      nesting: int                wildcardWrappers[]
                                                                                  extensionWrappers[]
  <<Connector's Mapper>>              <<Context's Mapper>>
                                                                                          javax.naming.Context
                                                                              resources
            hosts[]                       context
                        Mapper
                        defaultHostName: String
```

Most of the classes in this diagram are static nested classes within the `Mapper` class.

Pay particular attention to the `Mapper$MapElement` class. This base class provides a simple name to object mapping, where the actual object stored depends on the subclass. For example, instances of `Mapper$Context` and `Mapper$Wrapper` pair a logical name with their associated `StandardContext` and `StandardWrapper`, respectively.

This lets the `Mapper` function as a kind of naming service for lookups, where the context and wrappers are bound by name to their associated 'real' Tomcat component.

Each `Mapper$Host` instance in the `hosts[]` array represents a virtual host within the engine, and is associated with a `Mapper$ContextList` instance that contains the `Mapper$Context` instances for that host.

In turn, each `Mapper$Context` instance has `Mapper$Wrapper` instances that represent its child wrappers. It also holds a reference to the resources of its associated `StandardContext`.

The wrappers for a context are categorized into distinct arrays based on the mapping rules that we saw earlier. The arrays are sorted to allow for efficient lookup.

For each servlet mapping added to a `Mapper$Context`, its `url-pattern` is examined to determine the category into which it falls:

- **URL pattern is an exact servlet path (exact path matching)**: A `Mapper$Wrapper` is instantiated with its `name` set to this exact path and its `object` member set to the associated `StandardWrapper`. This instance is inserted into the sorted `exactWrappers` array.

- **URL pattern ends in a /* wildcard (wildcard path matching)**: A `Mapper$Wrapper` is instantiated with its `name` set to the path up to, but not including, the /*, and its `object` member is set to the associated `StandardWrapper`. This instance is inserted into the sorted `wildcardWrappers` array.

- **URL pattern starts with *. and ends with an extension (extension matching)**: A `Mapper$Wrapper` is instantiated with its `name` set to the extension and its `object` member set to the associated `StandardWrapper`. This instance is inserted into the sorted `extensionWrappers` array.

- **URL pattern is just a / (default servlet matching)**: A `Mapper$Wrapper` is instantiated with its `name` set to an empty string and its `object` member set to the associated `StandardWrapper`. This instance is directly set on the `defaultWrapper` member, as there can only be one default mapping.

This process is repeated until the `Mapper$Context` instance has been updated with all the mapping rules that have been defined for it in the deployment descriptors.

As we will soon see, a `Mapper` actually exists in two forms.

First, there's the mapper associated with a given connector, whose scope includes all the hosts within an engine, all the contexts within that host, and all the mapping rules within that context. This mapper is consulted for each incoming request to determine the appropriate request processing components. In this form, the `context` member is not used and all lookups proceed from the `hosts[]` array.

Second, there's the mapper associated with a single context, whose scope only includes the mapping rules for the wrappers associated with that context. This mapper is used by the request dispatcher mechanism. In this form, the `hosts[]` array is not required and all lookups start at the `context` member.

In the next few sections, we'll take a closer look at both these forms. We'll look at how the structural relationships shown in the previous image are established, and how they are used to map requests to their appropriate handlers.

The connector's mapper

As we saw in Chapter 6, *The Connector Component*, a MapperListener instance is responsible for actually initializing the connector's mapper and setting up its structural relationships. It relies on JMX notifications to be apprised of the various components that are registered for a Tomcat instance, and updates the mapper accordingly.

When an incoming request is received, the CoyoteAdapter kicks off the process of determining the request processing components that should handle that request. It does so by invoking the Mapper instance's map() method with the virtual host name, the URI, and a MappingData instance.

The map() method sets its results on this MappingData instance, which can then be queried by the caller to obtain these values.

> The org.apache.tomcat.util.http.mapper.MappingData class helps with carrying the inputs into, and the results out of, the mapping process. The primary results of a mapping operation include a StandardContext instance, an optional StandardWrapper instance, as well as various URI components.

The resulting context and wrapper instances are also set directly on the Catalina request to make them readily accessible to other components that process this request.

Locating the host and context

The map() method first locates the host named on the request from the internal hosts array. It updates the MappingData.host member with the found host.

It then uses the context path from the request URI to match one of the contexts in the selected host's ContextList array.

The MappingData instance's context and contextPath members are set to the StandardContext instance and the name member for the located Mapper$Context, respectively.

At this point the MappingData instance has been updated with the StandardHost and StandardContext instances.

The final step is to locate the wrapper.

Locating the wrapper

It begins by looking for an exact match by scanning for the servlet path within the `exactWrappers` array. If an exact match could not be found, the array of `wildcardWrappers` is scanned next. Then, an extension based match is considered by looking through the `extensionWrappers` array.

If the incoming request URI's servlet path is empty, the current request's processing is terminated by sending a client-side redirect to the root of the context path, after appending a / to the URI.

If a matching wrapper is found in any of these arrays, the `MappingData` instance is updated appropriately, and returned.

In a more general sense, a request for `http://www.swengsol.com/context/folder` processing terminates with a redirect to `http://www.swengsol.com/context/folder/`. The general effect is the same—a / is suffixed to the folder name and a client-side redirect is issued to terminate the current request.

If no match has been found, then this might be a valid partial request. In which case, we complete the request URL by appending each of the partial URLs as defined in the `welcome-file-list` element of the deployment descriptor. Each welcome file name is appended to the partial valid request, and the `exactWrappers` and the `wildcardWrappers` matching algorithms are used. This allows the supporting of the mapping of servlets as welcome files. If a static file matching this URL is found, then it checks if any extension mapping is defined by looking within the `extensionWrappers` array.

If no match is found, and if this is a static file being requested, then the `MappingData` is updated to use the default wrapper, and the `MappingData` instance's `requestPath` and `wrapperPath` variables are set to point at the resource.

The default servlet for a context acts as the fallback handler for a request, if no match is found for the requested resource. This is also where the redirection for a folder request, as we discussed earlier, occurs.

A `404 Resource Not Found` response is generated by the default servlet when no match is discovered for a resource.

Setting up the StandardContext mapper

The instantiation of a `StandardContext` also creates a mapper, which is used to track the child wrappers for that context. This is an abbreviated `Mapper` that is rooted at a single context. This mapper is used by the `RequestDispatcher` to determine the target servlet (as we will see in a later section).

> External requests have their mappings determined by the connector's mapper. However, internal requests that occur due to a server-side forward or an include operation do not pass through the connector, and as a result require this alternative mapping mechanism.

This mapper is updated with servlet mappings as the deployment descriptors are digested. For each `<servlet-mapping>` element encountered, the context retrieves its `StandardWrapper` child and adds the pattern to its `mappings` member.

The servlet mappings are then registered with the context's mapper. This process is identical to what we noted earlier. Each servlet mapping is converted to a new `Mapper$Wrapper` instance that is then associated with the single `Mapper$Context` instance for this mapper. The wrapper is added to an appropriate sorted array for this context, by matching rule type. This is repeated until the mapper has been initialized with all the information needed to convert a URL for this context to a wrapper instance.

Finally, the `context` member of this `Mapper` is initialized with the context path, an array of welcome file names, and the context's resources, as configured for its associated context.

The process of locating a resource using this mapper is identical to that for the connector's mapper. The only difference being that no resolution of the host or context is necessary, as all lookups are for the mapper's single context.

Request processing

As we saw in the last chapter, the context's basic valve first notifies any `ServletRequestListener` instances by invoking their `requestInitialized()` method, and then calls `invoke()` on the servlet wrapper's pipeline.

A wrapper's pipeline, by default, only has a single valve, the `StandardWrapperValve`. It calls its wrapper's `allocate()` method to obtain an instance of its wrapped servlet to process the incoming request.

If this is a normal servlet (that is, it does not implement the deprecated `SingleThreadModel` interface), then there will always be only one instance of a given servlet per wrapper, and it is this instance that is returned to service every incoming request for this servlet.

While servlets that are marked to be loaded on startup are instantiated and initialized by the context within its `start()` method, the rest are lazily initialized on first use.

The wrapper is requested to allocate a servlet instance to handle this request. If an instance has not yet been allocated for this wrapper, the servlet is first loaded using `load()`. This is a critical section of code and must be synchronized on the wrapper instance to prevent race conditions when attempting to load and initialize this servlet.

Once a servlet instance has been allocated, the `countAllocated` member is incremented, and we are now ready to kick off the actual processing of the servlet request.

Any filters are now added to the request processing pipeline. To indicate to the filter mechanism that this request is a standard incoming request, the `org.apache.catalina.core.DISPATCHER_TYPE` request attribute is set to `ApplicationFilterFactory.REQUEST_INTEGER`, and `org.apache.catalina.core.DISPATCHER_REQUEST_PATH_ATTR` is set to the servlet name — to assist with pattern matching for filters.

Remember that filters are used to preprocess the request before the servlet has a chance to handle it and post process the response after the servlet has done its job. More than one filter may be applied in sequence, and the entire sequence is referred to as a 'filter chain'.

The filters that make up the filter chain for a given request are determined at runtime by considering the dispatcher type, the servlet being targeted and the request's URL pattern.

We will shortly see the mechanics of this process. For now, let's just continue along with the story.

Once the filter chain has been established, it is assigned the task of processing the request. The filter chain is responsible for invoking the outermost filter. Each filter performs its processing and then asks the filter chain to continue on to the next one. Once all of the filters have run, the final step is to invoke the `service()` method of the servlet instance.

This process works in reverse on the way out, allowing the response to be post processed by the filters in the chain.

Finally, the wrapper's `deallocate()` method is invoked to decrement the `countAllocated` member.

The valve's `invoke()` method returns the completed request to the `StandardContextValve`, which in turn invokes the `requestDestroyed()` method on any interested `ServletRequestListener` instances to notify them of the completion of this request.

Filters

In this section, we'll see how a filter chain is constructed to handle an incoming request.

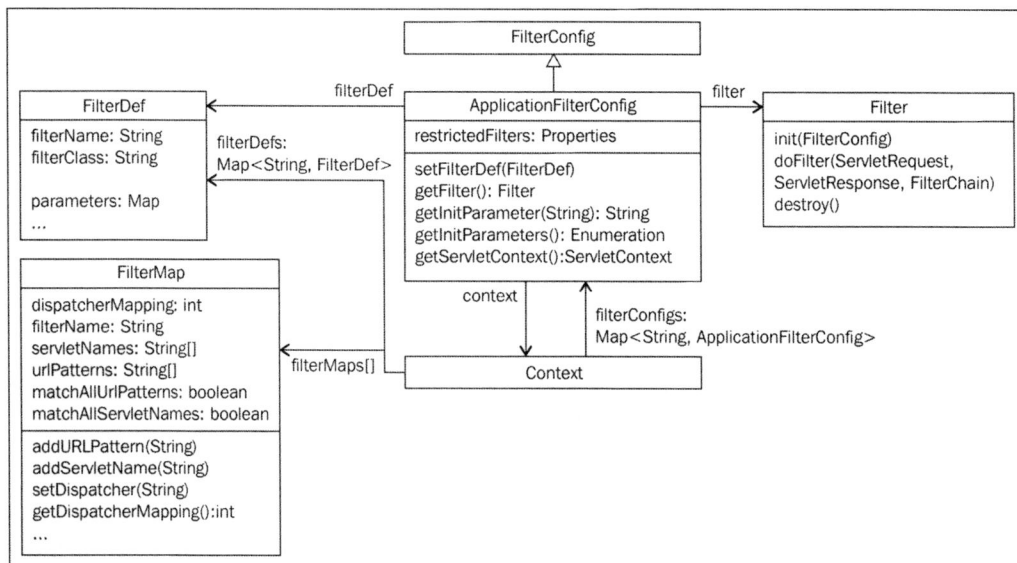

A `FilterDef` represents the `<filter>` element in the web application deployment descriptor. It describes a filter in terms of its name, its implementation class, and initialization parameters.

A `FilterMap`, on the other hand, represents the `<filter-mapping>` element. This element describes the servlet names, URL patterns, and dispatcher mappings that cause the filter to be engaged.

A `FilterMap` instance defines when a filter will be invoked. By default, a filter is invoked for incoming requests. However, you can specify that a filter should be invoked even for request dispatcher actions (forwards and includes), as well as error page mechanism actions.

The specification of when the filter will be invoked is encoded as a single integer, `dispatcherMapping`, whose bits are set to indicate the desired trigger actions. The `servletNames` and `urlPatterns` members contain the mappings for which a filter will be invoked, either as servlet names or using URL patterns. Using the * wildcard for servlet names and URL patterns indicates that a filter must be invoked for all servlets or URL patterns respectively. The `boolean` members `matchAllUrlPatterns` and `matchAllServletNames` are presented as a convenience.

A `StandardContext` instance tracks its declared filters using a `filterDefs` member, which maps filter names to `FilterDef` instances, and its filter mappings using its `filterMaps` member which references an array of `FilterMap` instances. These members are populated from the deployment descriptors during the startup process.

During startup, a `StandardContext` loops through the `filterDefs` map, constructing an `ApplicationFilterConfig` instance for each filter definition.

These `ApplicationFilterConfig` instances are stored, mapped by filter name, in the context's `filterConfigs` map. An `ApplicationFilterConfig` is a wrapper for a given `javax.servlet.Filter` instance. It is constructed with its `StandardContext` and the `FilterDef` that it will wrap.

It first checks against its list of restricted filters, in `org.apache.catalina.core.RestrictedFilters.properties`, and will only instantiate a restricted filter within a privileged `Context`. It then uses the appropriate web application's class loader to load the filter class, instantiates it, and invokes its `init()` lifecycle method as per the servlet specification. The `ApplicationFilterConfig` holds on to this instantiated `Filter` in its `filter` member.

Filter chain construction

Now that we've seen how the filters are registered with the context and how they are initialized, we'll look at how they are assembled into a request processing chain.

A request can be classified in terms of its *dispatcher type*. That is, whether it is part of regular request processing, whether it is part of `RequestDispatcher` processing of a forward or an include operation, or whether it is part of the error page mechanism.

All request processing components that affect filters are required to set the `org.apache.catalina.core.DISPATCHER_TYPE` request attribute to indicate the type of activity being performed.

In addition, each filter advertises its interest in a particular *dispatcher type* using the `<dispatcher>` child of its `<filter-mapping>` element.

A filter is added to the filter chain for a given request only if that filter is interested in processing the dispatcher type for that request, and if a match is found either on the servlet's URL pattern, or on the servlet's name.

A request processing component also sets the `org.apache.catalina.core.DISPATCHER_REQUEST_PATH` request attribute to indicate the destination URL. The filter factory uses this request attribute to determine whether a particular filter is applicable based on that filter's mappings.

The `invoke()` method of the `StandardWrapperValve` is responsible for constructing the filter chain for a given request. It entrusts this task to the singleton `ApplicationFilterFactory`, by invoking its `createFilterChain()` method, and passing it the incoming request, the `StandardWrapper` instance, and the wrapped servlet.

This method begins by instantiating a new `ApplicationFilterChain` and sets its `servlet` member to indicate the final processing element in the chain.

We then retrieve the `filterMaps` from the wrapper's parent context. If there are no filter mappings for this context, the `ApplicationFilterChain` with its single servlet member is returned.

However, if there are mappings present, we iterate over each `FilterMap` element in the returned array. If the mapping doesn't match the current dispatcher type or the request's URL pattern, we ignore it. However, if a match is found on both, we ask the `StandardContext` for the `ApplicationFilterConfig` associated with this filter, and add this instance to the `ApplicationFilterChain` instance.

We then repeat this search, iterating over each `FilterMap` element, this time looking for a match with the current dispatcher type and the servlet's name, and adding any matched `ApplicationFilterConfig` instance to the `ApplicationFilterChain`.

This matching of URL patterns is done by walking through each URL pattern in the `urlPatterns` array of `FilterMap`, and comparing each with the request URL. The first test is whether there's an exact match between the two. Next, we check whether the filter map's pattern is a wildcard map that encompasses the current request URL (either is, or ends with, `/*`). Finally, if the filter map's pattern starts with `*.`, we check for a matching extension.

> The filters in a chain are ordered by order of declaration within the deployment descriptor. In addition, filters that match on URL patterns occur before filters that match on the servlet name.

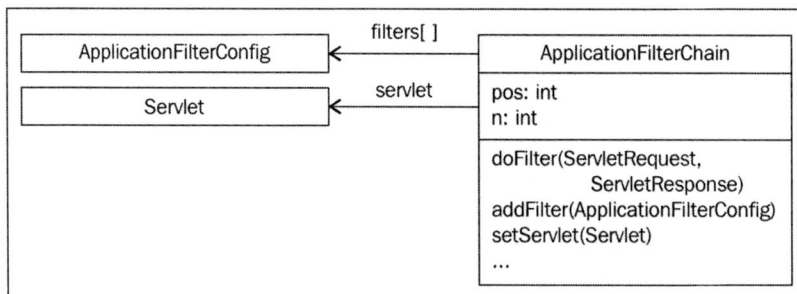

As shown, the final constructed `ApplicationFilterChain` instance contains an array of `ApplicationFilterConfig` instances (each of which represents an initialized `Filter` instance) and a servlet. It also has two integers—n, which indicates the number of filters in the chain and pos, which represents the currently executing filter.

Filter chain invocation

Once the filter chain has been constructed, the `StandardWrapperValve` delegates to it by invoking its `doFilter()` method, passing it the request and response. From then on, it's the filter chain that manages the processing of the request.

The `doFilter()` method is particularly interesting in that it must call all the filters in the chain in the sequence established by the mappings, it must allow any of the filters to abort or modify request processing, and at the end of the filter chain must call the servlet's `service()` method, before proceeding back outward in reverse order.

It does this by passing itself as a parameter to the `doFilter()` method that it invokes on each filter in the chain.

The individual filter does its preprocessing and must then invoke `doFilter()` on the next filter in the chain. It doesn't do this directly however. Instead, it invokes `doFilter()` on the `FilterChain` parameter that has been passed to it. The `FilterChain` is then responsible for tracking the next filter in sequence, and calling its `doFilter()` method. If there are no more filters in the chain, it invokes the `service()` method of the servlet.

At each stage, a particular filter may provide an alternative request or response object, if it wishes to affect the input or buffer the output either of any subsequent filters or the servlet itself.

Request dispatcher

When a request is received by a servlet, it may choose to either generate the response itself, relinquish processing to another servlet (known as **forwarding**), or request one or more other servlets to generate portions of the complete response (known as **including**).

The servlet container provides the request dispatcher mechanism in order to allow a servlet to engage other servlets in generating a response.

A few important rules apply to the process of dispatching a request:

1. A servlet forwards a request when it is either not interested or not able to generate the response. In this case, it wholly delegates request processing to the forwarded servlet. Any output written by the original servlet is flushed.

2. Attributes added to a request are available to the forwarded or included request.

3. The resource being forwarded to, or included, may either be dynamic or static. A dynamic resource, such as a servlet, is invoked to generate the output, whereas a static file is directly included.

4. This mechanism works across contexts within the same container. You can use the getContext() method of a ServletContext to obtain the context associated with a given context path. You can ask the retrieved context for a RequestDispatcher appropriate for that context.

5. Parameters associated with a RequestDispatcher are scoped only for the duration of the include or forward call. In other words, if you supply additional parameters, say using a query string, those parameters are not visible once the included servlet has finished executing.

6. One servlet may include another, which in turn may include yet another, in a chain miles deep. A similar servlet call chain can be constructed when forwarding a request.

Obtaining a request dispatcher

To begin this process, you must obtain an instance of the javax.servlet. RequestDispatcher interface, which is implemented in Tomcat by org.apache. catalina.core.ApplicationDispatcher. The following methods let you obtain a request dispatcher instance:

- The getRequestDispatcher() method of a ServletContext can be invoked with a path that begins with a / and is relative to the context's root. If the path contains a query string, it is passed on to the forwarded or included servlet.

  This method uses the context's mapper to identify the resource that should handle requests to the specified path. The URI passed to the mapper is modified to include the context path, and to remove any query string (indicated by a ?) or parameters (indicated by a ;). As we have seen before, the results of the mapping operation are returned in a MappingData instance.

  If no servlet match is found for this request URI, the static content at the specified path is returned instead.

If a servlet match is found, an `ApplicationDispatcher` is instantiated, and initialized with the mapped `StandardWrapper` instance, the context, the complete request URI, the parsed servlet path, any path information, as well as the query string from that URI.

Alternatively, you could call the `getNamedDispatcher()` method of a `ServletContext` passing it the name of a servlet within that context, as specified in the `<servlet-name>` element of the `web.xml` descriptor. This method locates the context's child wrapper with the given name and returns it wrapped up in a new `ApplicationDispatcher`.

- The `getRequestDispatcher()` method of a `ServletRequest` can be invoked with a path that is relative to the path of the current request.

  This method converts the specified servlet-relative path to a context-relative path and then invokes the `getRequestDispatcher()` method of the `ApplicationContext`.

The key aspects of an `ApplicationDispatcher` are depicted in the following image:

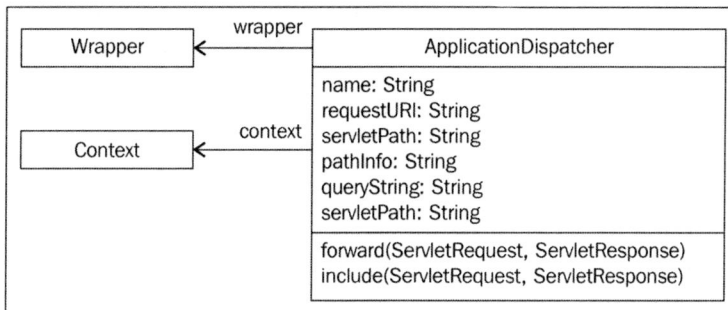

As shown, an `ApplicationDispatcher` contains a wrapper that represents the target servlet. If the dispatcher was retrieved by name, its `name` member is set, whereas its request URI and parsed components are set if a path based dispatcher was used instead.

Once a request dispatcher has been obtained, you may include or forward to it using the `include()` and `forward()` methods of the `RequestDispatcher` interface.

Using a request dispatcher

The servlet specification has strict mandates as to what path elements should be visible to the target servlet. These path elements include the request URI, the context path, the servlet path, the path information, and the query string.

The content of these path elements depends on:

- The dispatcher type, that is, whether this is a forward or an include operation.
- The type of dispatcher being used, that is, whether a path-based dispatcher or a named dispatcher is used.

> A name-based forward or include occurs when the `getNamedDispatcher()` method is used to obtain the request dispatcher.

Forwards

For name-based forwards, the request dispatcher is obtained purely using the servlet's name and no path information elements are specified. As a result, the request passed to the target servlet must have its path elements set to match those of the request coming into the servlet doing the forwarding.

For path-based forwards, the request passed to the target servlet must have its path elements set based on the URI used to obtain the request dispatcher. Furthermore, the path elements associated with the first servlet in the call chain are available to all subsequent servlets, by having the container set the following request attributes.

```
javax.servlet.forward.request_uri
javax.servlet.forward.context_path
javax.servlet.forward.servlet_path
javax.servlet.forward.path_info
javax.servlet.forward.query_string
```

This ensures that no matter how deep in the call chain a particular target servlet lives, it can still reach out and determine the path of the original request from the client.

Includes

For includes, the included servlet must receive the same request as that received by the servlet performing the include operation.

For path-based includes, the path information used to obtain the request dispatcher must be made available to the included servlet by setting the following request attributes:

```
javax.servlet.include.request_uri
javax.servlet.include.context_path
javax.servlet.include.servlet_path
javax.servlet.include.path_info
javax.servlet.include.query_string
```

This ensures that any included servlet can access the parameters used to generate the request dispatcher that resulted in its invocation.

> No special attributes are set for either name-based forwards or name-based includes.

Wrapper classes

The complete servlet call chain can get fairly involved. In addition, the request or response seen by one servlet in the chain may be different from the request or response viewed within another servlet in that chain.

In order to make this work, we need a way of modifying the request and response objects to expose different information, in a non destructive manner, depending on where they are accessed within the call chain.

This is accomplished by employing the Decorator Gang of Four pattern. We use this pattern to have a wrapper that wraps either another wrapper or the actual subject. Both the wrapper and the subject implement the same interface, and so can be used interchangeably with each other.

There's always just one subject underneath all this wrapping. A wrapper's user works with the wrapper as a complete substitute for the original subject and is not even aware of the switch.

In our case, the subjects are instances of `HttpServletRequest` or `HttpServletResponse`, while the wrappers are instances of `ApplicationHttpRequest` and `ApplicationHttpResponse`, respectively.

Each forwarding servlet adds wrappers around the request-response pair that were passed to it, and hands off this wrapped pair to the intended target servlet. The wrapper is smart enough to handle requests for the special servlet specification attributes and to mock the originating request URI appropriately.

This continues ad infinitum until a pair is handed off to the final servlet that actually does the processing. The servlet that receives the wrapped request and response is not aware of the magic that has occurred, and simply takes the request and response pair at face value.

On the way out, each servlet removes the wrappers that were introduced for it, until only the original request and response remain, at the servlet at the top of the call chain.

The two major benefits of this mechanism are:

- It ensures that the wrapper can modify the view of the attributes, parameters, and other path members that are provided to a given servlet.
- It ensures that attributes and parameters added to a previous wrapper or to the original subject are accessible to an outer wrapper. It does this by setting up a delegation mechanism for attributes and parameters, whereby one wrapper delegates to its wrapped object all the way down to the original request or response.

On the way out, as wrapper pairs are removed on the conclusion of a servlet's activity, this also ensures that the view available to an invoking servlet is consistent with its own call chain.

Wrapper class structure

The following image describes the servlet request hierarchy. A generic servlet request is represented by the `javax.servlet.ServletRequest` interface. Its methods describe a request in terms of its protocol, host, port, address, content type, attributes, and parameters. The `javax.servlet.HttpServletRequest` turns this generic request into an HTTP request by adding support for cookies, headers, query strings, and so on. Both the Catalina `Request` and its associated `RequestFacade` extend this HTTP request.

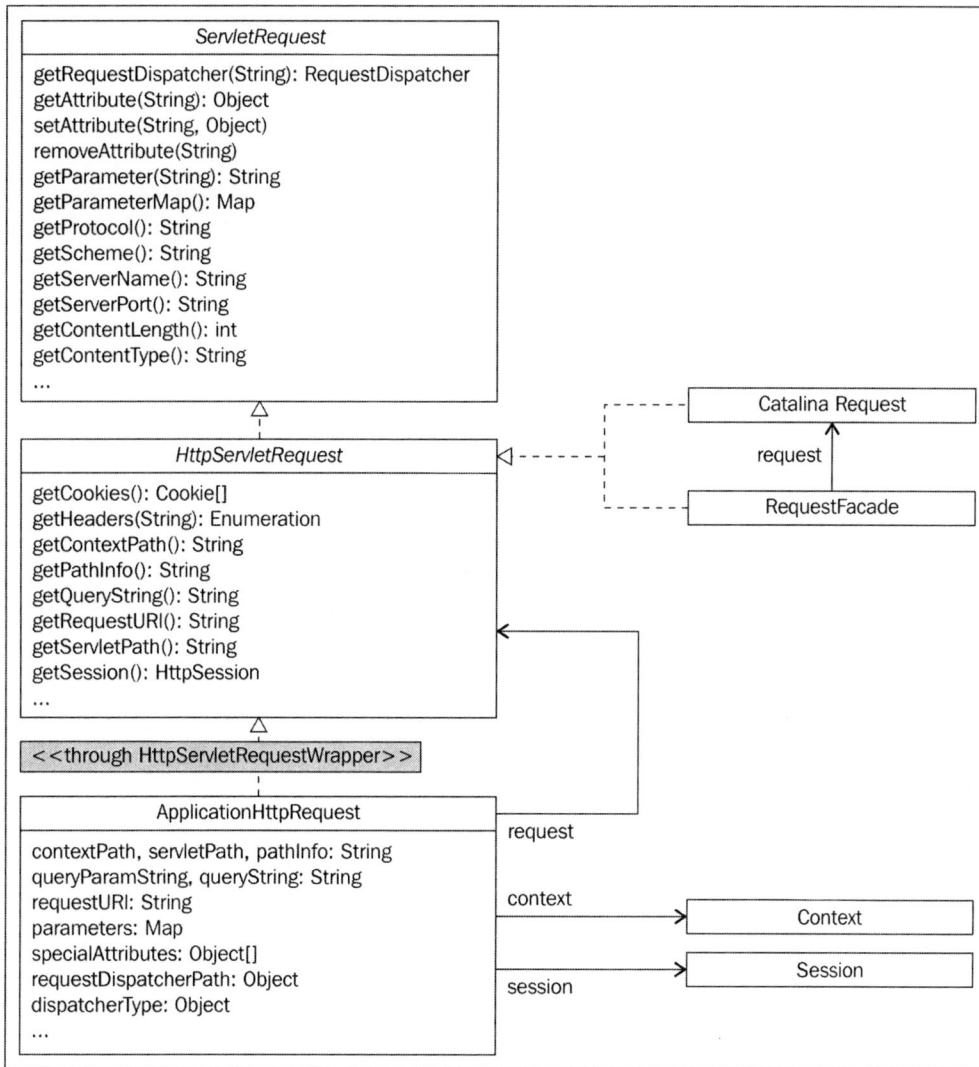

An `org.apache.catalina.core.ApplicationHttpRequest` wraps an HTTP request (by virtue of being a `javax.servlet.http.HttpServletRequestWrapper`) and extends its functionality to support the request dispatcher mechanism.

Each time a request is forwarded or included, it is wrapped in one such wrapper. This wrapper can be used wherever a standard request can, because it ultimately extends a `ServletRequest`.

For the most part, this wrapper acts as a simple pass-through object and responds to commands by delegating to its wrapped request.

However, a key area where it takes control is in managing the attributes and parameters during a forward or include operation.

For example, its getAttribute() and setAttribute() overrides can handle requests for the special attributes that are mandated by the servlet specification such as javax.servlet.forward.request_uri. Its overrides let these special attributes masquerade as standard request attributes.

It also overrides the parameter retrieval methods by ensuring that any query string parameters passed to an included or forwarded servlet are merged with the parameters on the original request. If a query string parameter matches a parameter on the request being wrapped, the value(s) for this parameter on the query string will precede any previous values for that parameter.

The response hierarchy works in a similar manner, where an ApplicationHttpResponse wrapper either wraps another wrapper or the underlying javax.servlet.HttpServletResponse subject.

Processing a forward

The servlet that is the target of a forward operation is responsible for generating the entire response. Therefore, any uncommitted partial response generated by the forwarding servlet must be cleared by invoking resetBuffer() on the response.

> If output has already been committed to the client, that is, isCommitted() on the response returns true, then an IllegalStateException is thrown which terminates the forward operation.

A request wrapper, an ApplicationHttpRequest instance, is instantiated to provide the altered reality for the target servlet that will be invoked. As the response is completely overridden by the servlet to which we will forward, the original response can be passed along without needing to be wrapped.

The request wrapper's attributes are first initialized by copying them over from the request being forwarded. These elements include the request URI, the context path, the servlet path, the path information, and the query string.

For a path-based forward, the special attributes as specified by the servlet specification must now be set. These special attributes are set only on the very first wrapper around the original request. Once these have been set, subsequent wrappers will not overwrite these. These special attributes are based on the original incoming request, and include various elements of the incoming request URI. In addition, the request wrapper's path elements and the query string are updated from the equivalent members of the `ApplicationDispatcher`. This ensures that the request now is mocked up to look as if it originally was intended for the URL that was specified when the request dispatcher instance was created.

On the other hand, for a name based forward, the special attributes need not be set. Additionally, the request dispatcher is not provided with a request URI, and so the wrapper's request components are set up based on the request that came into the servlet doing the forwarding.

The `org.apache.catalina.core.DISPATCHER_TYPE` request attribute is set on the wrapper to indicate that this is a FORWARD operation and `org.apache.catalina.core.DISPATCHER_REQUEST_PATH` is set to the forwarded servlet.

The rest is very similar to the `invoke()` method on the `StandardWrapperValve` that we saw earlier. This method is invoked with the wrapped request, our new `ApplicationHttpRequest` instance, as well as with the original incoming response. It sets the context class loader to the web application class loader, verifies that the servlet is available, invokes `allocate()` on its wrapper to obtain the servlet instance, sets up the filter chain, and invokes `doFilter()` on the filter chain to process the request.

The output generated by the target servlet is written out to the original request. Note that we didn't need to wrap this, as the target servlet of a forward operation is solely responsible for generating the output.

Once the target servlet is done, the filter chain is released, the servlet is deallocated, and the context class loader is reset.

Including a resource

The include process works in a very similar fashion as the above.

The wrapping of a response is a bit more involved than before, as unlike the forward case, we cannot simply overwrite the original response. Instead, we always instantiate a new `ApplicationHttpResponse` instance that wraps the outermost response object.

For a path-based dispatcher include, the special request attributes are set from the equivalent data members of the `ApplicationDispatcher`.

For a named dispatcher include, we indicate that a named dispatcher is being used by setting a request attribute, and we set the request wrapper's servlet path from the `ApplicationDispatcher`. As per the servlet specification, no special attributes are set.

For both types of includes, the `org.apache.catalina.core.DISPATCHER_TYPE` request attribute is set to indicate an `INCLUDE` operation and the `org.apache.catalina.core.DISPATCHER_REQUEST_PATH` attribute is set to a concatenation of the servlet path and extra path information.

Examples

The following servlets demonstrate the servlet and wrapper mechanisms.

Servlets

These servlets build on the example created for the last chapter. As a result, you should simply include the following classes, static files, and declarations in the example from the preceding chapter.

> Do check out the 'Request Info' servlet from the `examples` web application at `http://localhost:8080/examples/servlets/servlet/RequestInfoExample`. This is an example of wildcard-based matching, and you can experiment with it by providing additional information at the end of the request URI. For example, `http://localhost:8080/examples/servlets/servlet/RequestInfoExample/path/info`.

Declaration

The following servlet elements are added to the web deployment descriptor to enable our new servlets:

```
<servlet>
  <servlet-name>GreetingForwarder</servlet-name>
  <servlet-class>
    com.swengsol.ForwardingServlet
  </servlet-class>
</servlet>
<servlet-mapping>
  <servlet-name>GreetingForwarder</servlet-name>
  <url-pattern>/GreetingForwarder</url-pattern>
</servlet-mapping>
<servlet>
```

```
    <servlet-name>GreetingIncluder</servlet-name>
    <servlet-class>
      com.swengsol.IncludingServlet
    </servlet-class>
  </servlet>
  <servlet-mapping>
    <servlet-name>GreetingIncluder</servlet-name>
    <url-pattern>/GreetingIncluder</url-pattern>
  </servlet-mapping>
  <servlet>
    <servlet-name>TemplateServlet</servlet-name>
    <servlet-class>com.swengsol.TemplateServlet</servlet-class>
  </servlet>
  <servlet-mapping>
    <servlet-name>TemplateServlet</servlet-name>
    <url-pattern>/TemplateGenerator</url-pattern>
  </servlet-mapping>
```

ForwardingServlet.java

This servlet demonstrates how a forward to the GreetingIncluder servlet can be accomplished using a path based dispatcher. This servlet can be accessed using the URL: http://localhost:8080/devguide/GreetingForwarder.

```java
package com.swengsol;

import java.io.IOException;
import java.io.PrintWriter;

import javax.servlet.ServletConfig;
import javax.servlet.ServletException;
import javax.servlet.http.HttpServlet;
import javax.servlet.http.HttpServletRequest;
import javax.servlet.http.HttpServletResponse;

public class ForwardingServlet extends HttpServlet {
  private static final long serialVersionUID = 1L;
  public void init(ServletConfig config)
    throws ServletException {
    System.out.println("In init..."+
        this.getClass().getName());
  }
  public void doGet(HttpServletRequest request,
  HttpServletResponse response)
  throws IOException, ServletException {
    request.getRequestDispatcher("GreetingIncluder").
      forward(request, response);
  }
}
```

Static resources

The following HTML snippets will be included by our `IncludingServlet`.

The contents of the `webapps/devguide/main.html` file are as shown:

```
<p>
This is some important text that matters to someone or the
    <i>other</i>.
</p>
```

The `webapps/devguide/secondary.html` file's contents are:

```
<p>
This is secondary text included by parameterization.
</p>
```

These files are incomplete fragments that are included by the *including* and *template generator* servlets.

We also update the index page to add a link to our new servlet. The contents of the `webapps/devguide/index.html` file are as shown:

```
<!DOCTYPE HTML PUBLIC "-//W3C//DTD HTML 4.0 Transitional//EN">
<HTML><HEAD><TITLE>Hello World</TITLE>
<META http-equiv=Content-Type content="text/html">
</HEAD>
<BODY>
<P />
<H3>Tomcat Developer's Guide</H3>
<P />
<ul>
    <li>
      <a href="HelloWorld">
        Hello World Example Servlet
      </a>
    </li>
    <li>
      <a href="ContactList">
        Contact List Servlet
      </a>
    </li>
    <li>
      <a href="GreetingForwarder">
        Forwarding and Including Servlet
      </a>
    </li>
</ul>
</BODY>
</HTML>
```

IncludingServlet.java

This servlet demonstrates multi-level inclusion. It is accessed using the
`GreetingForwarder` servlet that we saw earlier.

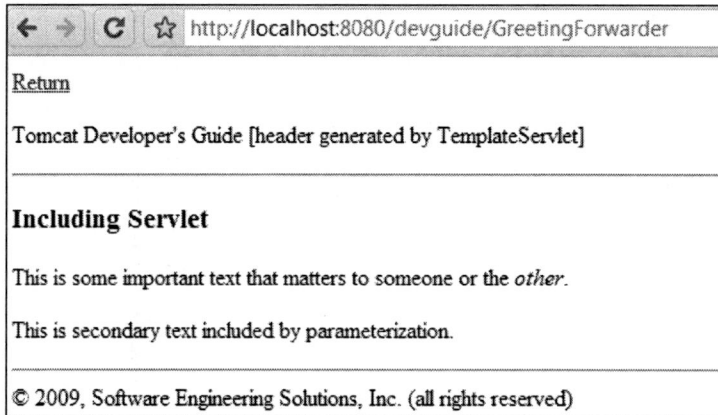

When you invoke this servlet, it includes output from the `TemplateGenerator`
servlet, as well as from a static resource, `main.html`. In addition, the
`TemplateGenerator` is also used to retrieve static resources.

```java
package com.swengsol;

import java.io.IOException;
import java.io.PrintWriter;

import javax.servlet.ServletException;
import javax.servlet.http.HttpServlet;
import javax.servlet.http.HttpServletRequest;
import javax.servlet.http.HttpServletResponse;

public class IncludingServlet extends HttpServlet {
  private static final long serialVersionUID = 1L;

  public void doGet(HttpServletRequest request,
  HttpServletResponse response)
    throws IOException, ServletException {
    response.setContentType("text/html");
    PrintWriter out = response.getWriter();

    String servletName = "TemplateGenerator";
    out.println("<html>");
    out.println("<head>");
    out.println("<title>" +
      "Including Servlet" + "</title>");
```

```
    out.println("</head>");
    out.println("<body bgcolor=\"white\">");
    request.setAttribute("bannerType", "header");
    request.getRequestDispatcher(servletName)
       .include(request, response);
    out.println("<h3> Including Servlet </h3>");
    out.println("<p>");
    request.getRequestDispatcher("main.html")
       .include(request, response);
    request.removeAttribute("bannerType");
    String resource =
       "?bannerType=file&resource=secondary.html";
    request.getRequestDispatcher(servletName + resource)
       .include(request, response);
    resource = "?bannerType=footer";
    request.getRequestDispatcher(servletName + resource)
       .include(request,response);
    out.println("</body>");
    out.println("</html>");
  }
}
```

TemplateServlet.java

This servlet has no independent identity, and its sole purpose is to provide common template generation functionality. Its client servlets will include it, passing in a request parameter indicating the type of template output desired.

For example, specifying the `bannerType=footer` parameter will cause this template servlet to write out footer HTML to the response.

This servlet can also include static resources, when a `bannerType` of `file` is specified, with a resource parameter that provides a relative path to the static resource.

```
package com.swengsol;

import java.io.IOException;
import java.io.PrintWriter;

import javax.servlet.ServletException;
import javax.servlet.http.HttpServlet;
import javax.servlet.http.HttpServletRequest;
```

```java
import javax.servlet.http.HttpServletResponse;
public class TemplateServlet extends HttpServlet {
  private static final long serialVersionUID = 1L;

  public void doGet(HttpServletRequest request,
  HttpServletResponse response)
    throws IOException, ServletException {
    PrintWriter out = response.getWriter();
    String copyright =
      "&copy; 2009, Software Engineering Solutions, Inc.";
    String bannerType =
      (String)request.getParameter("bannerType");

    if (null == bannerType)
      bannerType =
        (String)request.getAttribute("bannerType");
    if(bannerType != null) {
      if (bannerType.equalsIgnoreCase("header")) {
        out.println("<a href=\"index.html\">");
        out.println("Return</a><p />");
        out.print(
          getServletContext().getServletContextName());
        out.print(" [header generated by "
          + getServletName() + "]");
        out.print("<hr />");
      } else if (bannerType.equalsIgnoreCase("footer")) {
        out.print("<hr />");
        out.print(copyright);
        out.print(" (all rights reserved) <br />");
      } else if (bannerType.equalsIgnoreCase("file")) {
        String resourceName =
          (String)request.getParameter("resource");
        if (null != resourceName)
          request.getRequestDispatcher(resourceName)
            .include(request, response);
      } else {
        out.print("Default template? <br />");
      }
    } else {
      out.print("!!!no banner type specified!!! <br />");
    }
  }
}
```

Summary

With this chapter, we've covered the key request processing containers within Tomcat. The wrapper is at the final end of this processing chain, and as we have seen represents an actual servlet.

We also looked at how filters can be used to modify request processing. The connector's mapper was reviewed in greater detail, and we looked at an alternative mapper used by the request dispatcher.

The request dispatcher mechanism was also discussed, and we considered the process of forwarding and including requests.

We ended the chapter by considering a real world example of servlet and filter usage, combined with the request dispatcher mechanism.

11

The Manager Component

HTTP is intrinsically a stateless protocol. Each incoming request is a separate independent event, and once the server has responded to a given request, it does not hold any information about the requesting client.

This statelessness was well suited for the original intent of the Internet as a global file sharing mechanism, where a client may connect to a server and request a particular file. The client would then wait on that connection for the server to respond with the contents of the specified file. Once the file had been transferred, the connection would be closed and the server would retain no active memory of the client that it had just serviced.

This resulted in an architecture that was highly performant and scalable, as a server incurred minimal overhead while performing its core task of accessing and transmitting a file.

The challenge, however, is that any non-trivial web application does much more than just retrieve a file or resource. In applications such as a shopping cart, it is important to remember details of an interaction that may span multiple request-response pairs.

This information can include the contents of the shopper's cart, payment details, shipping options, and so on. This information represents the conversational state of the application and can be discarded once the application has persisted the user transaction to a data store.

In order to support conversational memory across multiple requests from the same client, a server must allocate a data structure that represents this state, associate an identifier token with this data structure, and ensure that some mechanism is used for a returning client to return this token to the server.

When a request carrying a token is received by the server, it is immediately able to look up the state associated with that token, and so recovers its conversational state for the requesting client.

This combination of the conversational memory data structure and its associated identifier is termed a web **session**.

A *manager* component assists its associated context in working with sessions. It is responsible for creating session instances for its context, managing these session instances, looking up existing sessions by identifier, and helping active sessions survive application reloads or server restarts.

The manager component and its managed sessions form the topics covered in this chapter.

Session propagation mechanisms

Before we dive into the implementations of the session and its manager, let's address the issue of how the identifier is returned by the client to the server.

As was stated above, the server generates a unique identifier for the conversational state holder for a client and communicates this identifier to the client.

Statefulness will only work if the client returns that identifier back to the server, for each request that is part of that conversation.

When each new request is received, a server attempts to locate this identifier, and use it to look up the conversational state associated with this client.

If a request comes without this identifier, the server has no way of recognizing that client, and so it treats the request as having come from a brand new client.

There are two common mechanisms that are used to ensure that the session identifier is communicated across each interaction between the client and the server—cookies and URL rewriting.

Cookies

When using cookies, the server sets a cookie named `jsessionid` on the response. The value of this cookie is set to the session identifier. Once this cookie has been received by the client, it is returned on every request made by that client to the server that set the cookie. This enables the server to retrieve the session associated with that client.

However, cookies have received a lot of bad press due to their potential for abuse, especially in tracking a client's browsing behavior. As a result, some users may turn off cookies in their browser. In such cases, a fall back mechanism, known as URL rewriting, is used.

URL rewriting

The servlet specification calls this 'the lowest common denominator of session tracking', as this mechanism relies on nothing more than the standard HTTP protocol. With this technique, the URL of every link is modified by appending the session identifier as a special parameter, named `jsessionid`, as shown:

```
http://host/contextPath/resource.jsp;jsessionid=a302eV9i_3mCvQ
```

Obviously, there is a potential for a lost session if even a single URL does not have the session identifier appended. Clicking on a non-rewritten link will generate a request that will not have the information required by the server to locate the associated session.

> The session identifier is passed using a HTTP construct known as a 'path parameter'.
>
> According to `RFC 3986 Uniform Resource Identifier: Generic Syntax`, reserved characters, such as a semicolon, comma, or equals sign, can be used by URI producing applications to convey additional parameters to the URI dereferencing algorithm.

While Tomcat uses the semicolon reserved character and a parameter named `jsessionid`, another vendor might use the comma reserved character and might directly append the session identifier itself, without the parameter name.

```
/path/servletname,a302eV9i_3mCvQ
```

Yet another container might simply pass the session identifier as a modified path information parameter as shown:

```
<a href="/path/servletname/jsessionid=a302eV9i_3mCvQ">Linky</a>
```

In each case, the dereferencing algorithm built into the specific container knows how the session identifier is encoded, and is able to extract the relevant session identifier from the rewritten URL.

Now, let's get back to the main topic of this chapter.

Session

A session is represented using an instance of the `javax.servlet.http.HttpSession` interface. A Tomcat session also implements the `org.apache.catalina.Session` interface.

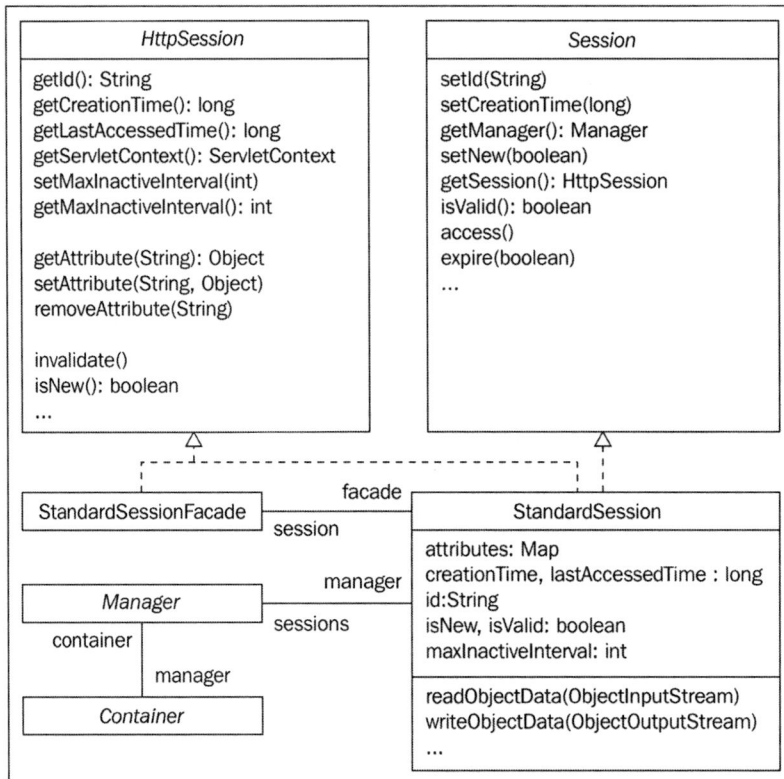

The `org.apache.catalina.session.StandardSession` class is the standard implementation of the `HttpSession` interface within the Tomcat container.

Note the presence of the `StandardSessionFacade` which implements the same pattern that we have seen countless times before, of narrowing its subject's API to prevent a servlet programmer from accessing Tomcat's internals. It wraps a `StandardSession` instance and exposes the API defined by the `HttpSession` interface. All calls to it are delegated to the wrapped `StandardSession` instance.

As we noted in the last section, a session object is associated with a unique identifier and an attribute store that manages a binding of objects by name.

We will see more about the `org.apache.catalina.Manager` class later in the chapter. For now, note that it has a map of the `Session` instances that it manages, which are keyed by session identifier.

Session identifiers

In addition to a `getId()` method which returns the session's identifer, a `setId()` method can be called to set the session's identifier. The latter method is normally called when a new session is created by the manager. It involves adding the session to its manager's `sessions` map, which is keyed by session identifier, and notifying all the listeners associated with that session.

A session event is first fired to notify any registered listeners, which are `org.apache.catalina.SessionListener` instances, by invoking their `sessionEvent()` method with a notifier indicating the creation of a session. Any application event listeners of type `HttpSessionListener`, that are associated with the manager's context, are also notified by invoking their `sessionCreated()` method.

The former is considered an internal notification, and so the `StandardSession` instance is passed to the event, whereas the latter notification is part of the servlet specification, and a `StandardSessionFacade` is passed in to the application event listeners, instead.

Session attributes

An `attributes` map holds the attributes associated with a session.

The `setAttribute()` method, as defined by the servlet specification, allows an `Object` to be bound to a `String` name.

This method begins by unbinding any attribute previously bound to this name, within the `attributes` map. If the value being bound is a `HttpSessionBindingListener`, and if listeners are to be notified, then its `valueBound()` method is invoked. The value is then added to the `attributes` map, bound to the specified name.

If listeners are to be notified, then two additional events are fired. If the previous object had implemented `HttpSessionBindingListener`, its `valueUnbound()` method is invoked. It also notifies each of its context's `HttpSessionAttributeListener` instances, by calling either `attributeReplaced()` or `attributeAdded()`, as applicable.

> Calling `setAttribute()` with a null value is an alias for calling the `removeAttribute()` method.

The `getAttribute()` method simply retrieves the named object from the `attributes` map.

The `removeAttribute()` method takes an attribute name and a flag indicating whether or not listeners should be notified. It first performs a validity check on the session and throws an `IllegalStateException` if the session is invalid. It then removes the attribute from the `attributes` map. If notification is requested, and if the removed object is an `HttpSessionBindingListener`, it invokes its `valueUnbound()` method; it also invokes the `attributeRemoved()` method on each `HttpSessionAttributeListener` associated with its context.

> As with everything in life, a session doesn't come for free. It takes some memory on the server for its map of attributes.
>
> In highly loaded servers, this memory burden can be significant. As a result, sessions are designed to timeout after they have been inactive for a configurable period of time, usually 15 to 30 minutes. As we will see shortly, a session is considered inactive after a timeout period has passed without a request being received received from its associated client.
>
> In addition, a session may also be explicitly invalidated, which is typically done when a user logs out or otherwise terminates the conversation.
>
> Recommended practices when working with sessions are to avoid loading large objects into it, to prune sessions of obsolete data objects, and to release sessions when they are no longer needed.

Session lifetime

When a request processing component requests a session to be established, the server will create a `StandardSession` instance and associate it with a unique session identifier. This session identifier is then transmitted to the client, either in a cookie or a URL parameter. During this stage of its life, the session is considered to be 'new'.

A session instance is considered to be 'established' only after it has been *joined* by the client.

Joining occurs when a request from this client comes in containing the session identifier either as a cookie in a request header or as a path parameter on the request URL. This indicates that the client and the server now share a common understanding of their session.

A session's `isNew` member is initially set to `true`, and is set to false only after the client joins the session.

Until a session has been joined, the server cannot make any assumptions about the client's state.

> A session is only valid within a given web application. In other words, a session identifier maps to a session object that is unique to a given context.

Session creation and access

A session is associated with three timestamps—the time it was created (`creationTime`), the time of the current access (`thisAccessedTime`), and the time of the last access (`lastAccessedTime`).

These times are initialized when the `setCreationTime()` method is called, and are initially all set to the time of creation.

Whenever a request is received from the client associated with this session, the `access()` method is called to update these access times. This method sets `lastAccessedTime` to the previous value of `thisAccessedTime` and then sets `thisAccessedTime` to the current time.

Session validity

The `expiring` and `isValid` data members indicate the condition of a given session instance.

The `isValid()` method determines whether or not a session is valid. A session is valid if it has not timed out, and if its `isValid` member is `true`.

Remember that the `thisAccessedTime` member holds the timestamp when this session instance was most recently accessed.

A session has timed out if its `maxInactiveInterval` member is set to a positive value, and if the difference between the current time and the session's `thisAccessedTime` member is greater than its `maxInactiveInterval` value. In other words, a request has not been received for this session for at least as long as the inactive timeout specified for the session.

The `expire()` method is then invoked to invalidate the session and to notify all its listeners of this expiration.

> Checking for validity using the `isValid()` method has the side effect of expiring an invalid session.

Session expiry

The `expire()` method takes a `boolean` indicating whether listeners should be notified about the expiring session.

If its listeners must be notified, this method gets any `HttpSessionListener` instances registered for its context, and invokes the `sessionDestroyed()` method on each.

It then sets the `isValid` member to `false` to mark itself as invalid.

Next, it updates various members that track session lifetime statistics for a manager instance. These members include:

- `sessionMaxAliveTime` which tracks the longest lifetime in seconds of any session created by this manager
- `expiredSessions` which holds a count of expired sessions for this manager
- `sessionAverageAliveTime` which holds the average lifetime in seconds for sessions created by this manager

The `remove()` method of its `Manager` is then called to remove the expiring session from its map of active sessions.

If requested by the caller, any internal listeners are informed of the destruction of this session.

Finally, it unbinds the attributes associated with this session. Each attribute in the `attributes` map is removed. If listeners are being notified, event notifications are now broadcast. If the attribute's value is an instance of `HttpSessionBindingListener`, then its `valueUnbound()` method is invoked. In addition, each `HttpSessionAttributeListener` is notified by invoking its `attributeRemoved()` method.

> You can also expire a session by invoking the `invalidate()` method, which directly invokes `expire()`.

The harvesting of expired sessions is done on a background thread and is implemented by its manager's `backgroundProcess()` method. This method simply calls the `isValid()` method on each of its sessions and relies on the side effect of that method to cause the expiry.

Session cleanup

A session exists from the time that a server instantiates a session instance to the time when the session is no longer required.

The length of this timeout period is defined in the `web.xml` deployment descriptor and is set on the session's `maxInactiveInterval` member. If set to 0 or negative, a session will never expire.

An expired session is no longer available for access even if its associated client returns the appropriate session identifier in a later request.

A servlet may also explicitly invalidate a session due to a user's action. For example, the user clicking on a logout link may result in the server expiring the session.

Session lifecycle events

As shown in the following image, a number of event listeners can be associated with a session.

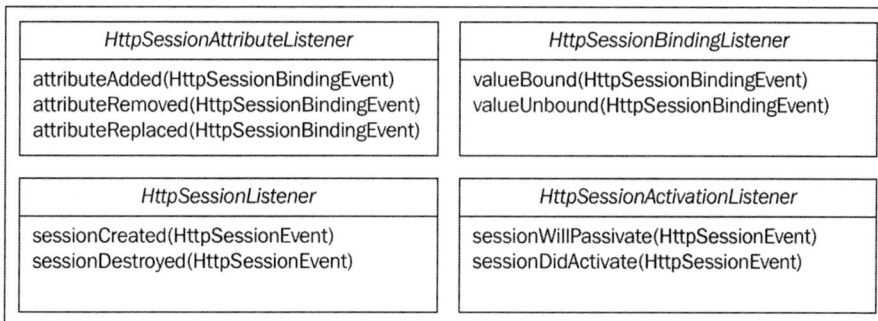

HttpSessionAttributeListener	*HttpSessionBindingListener*
attributeAdded(HttpSessionBindingEvent) attributeRemoved(HttpSessionBindingEvent) attributeReplaced(HttpSessionBindingEvent)	valueBound(HttpSessionBindingEvent) valueUnbound(HttpSessionBindingEvent)
HttpSessionListener	*HttpSessionActivationListener*
sessionCreated(HttpSessionEvent) sessionDestroyed(HttpSessionEvent)	sessionWillPassivate(HttpSessionEvent) sessionDidActivate(HttpSessionEvent)

For instance:

- Listeners that implement the `HttpSessionBindingListener` interface can be notified when they are bound to or unbound from a session
- Listeners that implement `HttpSessionListener` can be notified whenever a session is created or destroyed
- Listeners that implement `HttpSessionAttributeListener` can be notified when an attribute is added to, replaced in, or removed from, a session
- Listeners that implement `HttpSessionActivationListener` can be notified before a session is passivated or after a session is activated

Object binding events

An object can be bound to a session instance by name. If this object needed to be notified when it was placed into, or removed from, a session, then it would implement the `javax.servlet.http.HttpSessionBindingListener` interface, which defines the `valueBound()` and `valueUnbound()` methods.

The former is called before the object is made available through the `getAttribute()` method of the `HttpSession` interface, while the latter is called after the object is no longer available through the `getAttribute()` method.

Session lifecycle events

Lifecycle events are fired when an `HttpSession` is created or destroyed. An object that wants to be notified of these lifecycle events must implement the `javax.servlet.http.HttpSessionListener` interface, which defines the `sessionCreated()` and `sessionDestroyed()` methods.

The former is called when the container first creates a session. At this point, the session is still considered new and the client has not yet joined the session.

The latter is called when the session is about to be invalidated by the container, either because the session has timed out or a servlet has called the session's `invalidate()` method.

> When a web application is being shut down, session listeners must be notified of session invalidations before context listeners are notified of the application being shut down.

Attribute change events

Attribute events are fired after an attribute has been added to, removed from, or replaced in, an HttpSession. Replacement occurs when a servlet calls setAttribute() with a name that's already bound to that session.

An object that wants to be notified of these events must implement the javax.servlet.http.HttpSessionAttributeListener interface.

Session migration events

Sessions are serialized and deserialized when a context is reloaded, when the container is restarted, or when used in a clustered environment.

The javax.servlet.http.HttpSessionActivationListener interface defines methods that allow an object stored in a session to properly handle such events. An attribute that implements this interface takes control of its own serialization and deserialization.

Its sessionWillPassivate() method will be called before the container serializes the session so that the attribute has a chance to prepare itself for dehydration.

Its sessionDidActivate() method will be called after the container has deserialized the session so that the attribute has a chance to get itself ready for hydration.

For example, an external resource such as a database connection itself is not implicitly serialization friendly. Instead, on passivation, it could serialize the information needed for the connection, and then close the original connection. When the session was activated, the serialized information could be used to recreate the connection.

Session serialization

Sessions may be persisted to a secondary store to allow them to survive the reloading of a context or the restart of a server. During this process, the Manager invokes passivate() on a session to give it a chance to update its internal state to get ready for passivation.

Serialized sessions are reloaded when the Manager is restarted. The Manager invokes activate() on a session as it is being reloaded to allow it to ready itself for activation.

Before we continue, let's take a slight detour to consider Java's serialization mechanism.

Serialization

Java serialization is the process by which an object is converted into a stream of bytes that can be persisted to a file or transmitted over the network. The original object can be regenerated from this byte stream later, either at a different place (say, in a different JVM) or at a different time.

To avail of this serialization functionality, classes are only required to implement the `java.io.Serializable` marker interface. The default mechanism works its magic using reflection to gain access to the internal state of an object.

Members declared as `transient` are ignored by the default serialization process. This is done intentionally to let you identify members that can either be determined later or which hold references to objects within the native operating system, such as file handles, threads, or sockets. The former can be reinitialized after deserialization, while the latter may have little or no meaning when this object is deserialized.

To serialize an object, you create an instance of a `java.io.ObjectOutputStream` which you wrap around the actual `OutputStream`, such as a `FileOutputStream`, to which the serialized output will be sent. You then invoke the `writeObject()` method of the `ObjectOutputStream`, passing it the object to be serialized.

In the reverse of this process, you create an instance of a `java.io.ObjectInputStream` to wrap an `InputStream`, such as a `FileInputStream`, and then invoke its `readObject()`, which returns the deserialized object instance that you can cast appropriately.

While this default behavior is often quite sufficient, a serializable class may choose to take control of this process by providing overrides for the `readObject()` and `writeObject()` methods.

These overrides can invoke the `defaultReadObject()` and `defaultWriteObject()` methods on the `ObjectInputStream` and `ObjectOutputStream` respectively if they need to access the default serialization mechanism.

Once the default processing has completed, the `readObject()` and `writeObject()` methods may add special processing, such as the handling of transient data elements or additional validation checks.

A few considerations arise when serializing objects that are worthy of mention here.

Versioning

If the class has been modified since the object was serialized, the deserialization process may encounter discrepancies between the serialized form of the original object and the current structure of the class.

This problem is addressed by assigning a version number to each class, which is written out as part of the serialized form of the class. During deserialization, the previously serialized version number is compared with the current version for the class. If a mismatch is detected, then the JVM will refuse to deserialize the object.

Class loading

The serialized form of an object contains the name of the class along with other metadata (such as a signature that identifies a particular version of the class, a set of flags that indicate whether the class implements `Serializable`, and whether it provides custom `readObject()` and `writeObject()` implementations).

The entity doing the deserialization (either a different JVM or a different part of the application within the same JVM) must be able to access the class specified by the serialized class name.

By default, the class name is resolved relative to the class that called `readObject()`. However, in a web application scenario, the class doing the deserialization is a Tomcat internal class. As a result, its defining class loader will not be able to see a class located under the `WEB-INF` folder of a particular web application.

Fortunately, the standard `ObjectInputStream` implementation lets you take control of the class resolution mechanism by overriding the `resolveClass()` method. This method takes an `ObjectStreamClass` instance that describes the class being deserialized and returns its associated `Class` instance.

Tomcat provides a custom `ObjectInputStream`, which is appropriately called `CustomObjectInputStream` in the `org.apache.catalina.util` package. This class takes a web application class loader as its constructor argument. It overrides the `resolveClass()` method to load the class with its provided class loader. This ensures that the class being deserialized can be loaded appropriately.

Serialization in a StandardSession

As we will see shortly, in the section *Session Persistence Mechanism*, a session's manager is responsible for ensuring that a session's state is persisted to secondary storage as appropriate for that manager.

During this process, the manager first invokes `passivate()` on the session. This causes the session to call `sessionWillPassivate()` for each bound attribute that is also an `HttpSessionActivationListener`. This gives the attribute a chance to get itself ready for dehydration. For instance, a database connection object might respond to this by ensuring that it closes itself gracefully to release resources, and to ensure that the connection string is available for later activation.

The manager sets up the appropriate `ObjectOutputStream` to point to the file that will contain the serialized sessions and ends up calling `writeObject()` on each session to have them serialize themselves out to the appropriate `ObjectOutputStream`.

The `StandardSession` class implements `Serializable` to identify itself as being capable of being serialized. Furthermore, it defines the `readObject()` and `writeObject()` methods to indicate that it wants to take control of the serialization mechanism. These methods take total ownership of the serialization and deserialization mechanism. That is, they do not invoke either `defaultReadObject()` or `defaultWriteObject()`.

The `writeObject()` method writes out the `creationTime`, `lastAccessedTime`, `thisAccessedTime`, `maxInactiveInterval`, `isNew`, `isValid`, and `id` members to the specified `ObjectOutputStream`. It then walks through its `attributes` map. Any non serializable attributes are simply discarded by calling `removeAttributeInternal()` with the appropriate notifications fired. It then writes out an `Integer` indicating the number of serializable attributes and invokes `writeObject()` on the stream with each serializable attribute.

The key activity for the `activate()` call of the `StandardSession` is to invoke `sessionDidActivate()` on each session attribute that is also an `HttpSessionActivationListener`. This gives the attribute a chance to restore itself to its former glory. For a connection object, this might involve reconnecting to the database resource.

The `readObject()` method takes an `ObjectInputStream` that identifies a byte stream that contains the serialized version of a `StandardSession`, and performs the reverse of this operation.

Session multi threading

The servlet specification recommends that a developer should assume that the same session identifier will be returned from all windows or tabs of a given client browser.

In other words, a user who opens multiple browser tabs or windows to access a particular server, could result in multiple request threads, each of which accesses the same session instance in a multithreaded manner.

THREAD
SAFETY

The container will ensure that the internal data structures within the session instance are accessed in a thread-safe manner. However, it is up to the developer to ensure that thread-safety is considered when accessing any application specific objects stored in the session.

The recommended practice is for each request to synchronize on the session instance before attempting to work with the session instance.

Manager

An instance of the `org.apache.catalina.Manager` interface is responsible for managing the sessions for a given context.

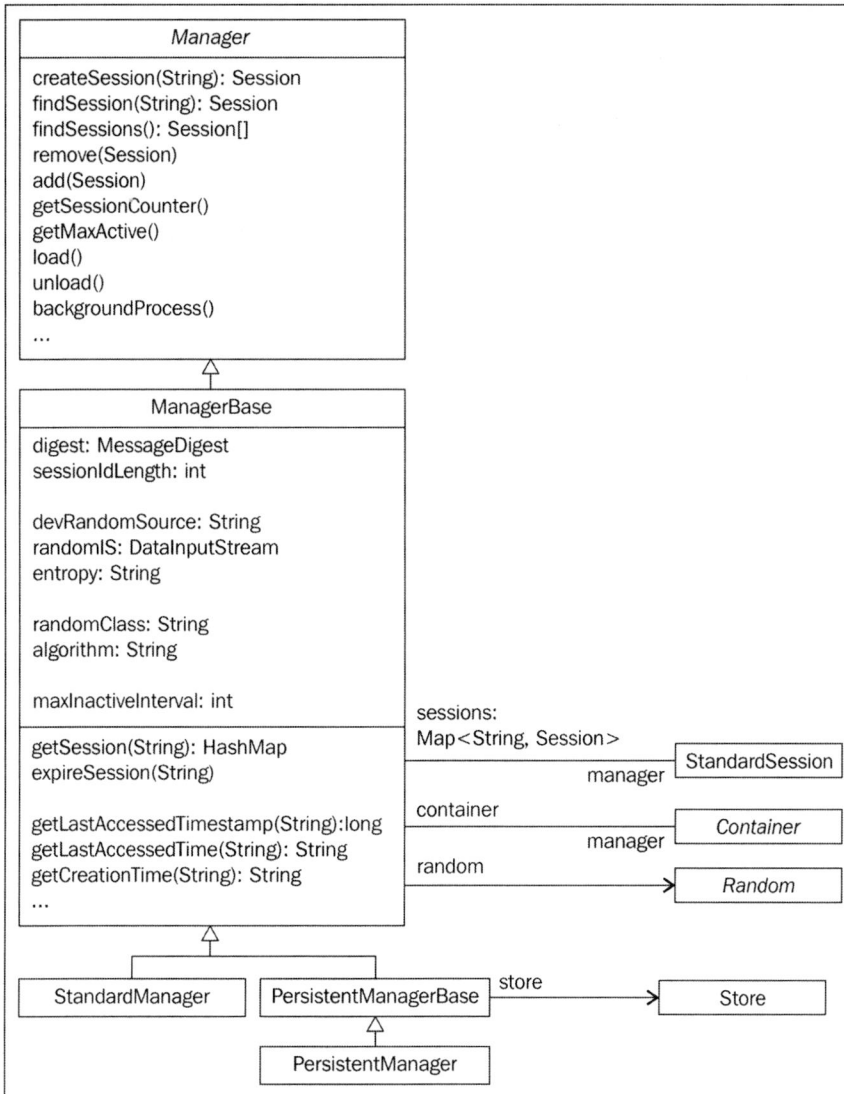

As shown in the previous image, the main responsibilities of a `Manager` include creating and managing the session instances for its context.

It is specified using the `<Manager>` element in `server.xml`, which has attributes such as the maximum inactive interval, also known as the session's timeout, and the session identifier length. These attributes are used as defaults for the sessions created by this manager.

Its `load()` and `unload()` methods support the persistence of sessions to secondary storage. These methods do nothing when persistence is not supported by a given `Manager` implementation.

Its `backgroundProcess()` method is called on a periodic basis by its context to allow it to do housekeeping chores such as harvesting expired sessions.

Implementations of this interface, such as the `StandardManager` and `PersistentManager` classes in the `org.apache.catalina.session` package, add support for additional features such as session persistence or session swapping.

A `StandardManager` supports session persistence across restarts of a manager, such as when the entire server is shut down and restarted or when a particular web application is reloaded.

A `PersistentManager` uses a `Store` to swap active sessions to disk. It can be configured to:

- Persist sessions across restarts of the container
- Support fault tolerance by backing up sessions on disk to allow recovery in the event of crashes
- Limit the number of active sessions kept in memory by swapping less active sessions out to disk

Before we look at these actual implementations, however, let's first look at a convenience base class that implements the `Manager` interface and provides functionality that is commonly required by actual `Manager` implementations, the `ManagerBase`.

ManagerBase

`org.apache.catalina.session.ManagerBase` is a convenience base class that provides the data structures and session management logic that is common across most session manager implementations.

At the heart of any `Manager` is the collection of sessions for which it is responsible. This is implemented as a `ConcurrentHashMap` member named `sessions`. The key to this map is the session identifier and the value is an instance of a session.

In addition, each `Manager` is also associated with a web application context, as represented by its `container` reference.

A key function of a `Manager` is to create unique session identifiers. This function is critical to security, so before we proceed onwards, let's take a short detour into the world of session identifier generation.

Session security

As we have seen, a session is kept alive by having the client browser return the appropriate session identifier on each request it sends to the server.

Unfortunately, this introduces significant security risk to web applications.

If a malicious user were to present the session identifier for another user's existing session, the malicious user would be largely indistinguishable, to the server, from the valid user who initiated the session.

It is therefore critical for a container to ensure that a malicious user is not able to guess a currently active session identifier in a reasonable time frame, even with a brute force attack.

In order to approach this ideal, the container must:

- Employ a cryptographic **Pseudo Random Number Generator (PRNG)** to generate the session identifier.
- Generate a session identifier that is at least 16 characters – or 128-bits in length.
- Expire sessions after a given period of inactivity or lifetime.

Employing a cryptographic Random Number Generator

The first step in preventing a malicious user from guessing an active session identifier is to ensure that the identifier that is generated is as random as we can possibly make it.

Java supports random number generation using two separate classes, `java.util.Random`, and `java.security.SecureRandom`. The former belongs to the class of random number generators known as *statistical pseudo random number generators* (PRNG), whereas the latter belongs to the class of *cryptographic pseudo random number generators*.

Statistical PRNGs are not suitable for secure use since they produce values that are fairly easy to predict. For instance, a Random is seeded with the current time, and it is possible for an attacker to predict the future random values that will be generated by it.

Cryptographic PRNGs, such as SecureRandom, are able to produce values that are sufficiently random, at least within the constraints of a deterministic system. However, this is only true if it is seeded with an array of truly random bits. An adequately seeded cryptographic PRNG will generate numbers that are random enough for most purposes.

> For effective security, this seed (known as **entropy**) must be truly random and it must be sufficiently large.
>
> A seed that is either not truly random (such as the system time, which can be guessed rather easily), or with too few bits, will not provide adequate security and can turn out to be the weak link in your security chain.

What makes it a challenge to generate true entropy is that computers are deterministic machines, and given the same set of inputs will always generate the same outputs. By themselves, they cannot generate truly random bits. As a result, we must rely on external devices connected to a computer to generate the entropy that we need. Some common sources of entropy are the durations between key presses or mouse clicks, mouse cursor positions, process or task statistics, or external device characteristics.

In a Java runtime environment, the configuration of the entropy gathering device is set using the securerandom.source property in the java.security file. A snippet from this file is shown in the following screenshot:

```
#
# Select the source of seed data for SecureRandom. By default an
# attempt is made to use the entropy gathering device specified by
# the securerandom.source property. If an exception occurs when
# accessing the URL then the traditional system/thread activity
# algorithm is used.
#
# On Solaris and Linux systems, if file:/dev/urandom is specified and it
# exists, a special SecureRandom implementation is activated by default.
# This "NativePRNG" reads random bytes directly from /dev/urandom.
#
# On Windows systems, the URLs file:/dev/random and file:/dev/urandom
# enables use of the Microsoft CryptoAPI seed functionality.
#
securerandom.source=file:/dev/urandom
#
# The entropy gathering device is described as a URL and can also
# be specified with the system property "java.security.egd". For example,
#   -Djava.security.egd=file:/dev/urandom
# Specifying this system property will override the securerandom.source
# setting.
```

By default, the source of the seed is set to the URL, `file:/dev/urandom`. This is a special device available on Linux or Unix systems that serves as a true source of entropy by permitting access to environmental noise collected from device drivers and other sources. On Windows, the Microsoft CryptoAPI is used to generate entropy instead.

If an exception occurs when accessing this URL, an algorithm based on system/thread activity is used as the source of entropy.

Generating a session identifier of adequate length

In addition to being generated by a cryptographic PRNG seeded with adequate entropy, the session identifier must be at least 16 characters (128-bits) long.

If it is any shorter than this, you leave yourself open to brute force attempts by users trying to generate a session identifier that matches that of an active session on the server.

This length can be specified as an attribute to the `Manager` element in the `server.xml` file. This length defaults to the recommended 16 characters.

Using an inactive timeout to expire sessions

One tactic that can be used to thwart a patient attacker is to reduce the size of the target. This can be done using two session timeout related techniques.

First, sessions that have been left inactive for more than a specified timeout period can be eliminated. This ensures that users who have gone on to do other things are not indefinitely at risk because of an open session that they left behind.

Second, we can limit the maximum time for which a session may be kept alive. This ensures that even if an attacker has hijacked a session, the session cannot keep it alive forever. This is unfortunately not mandated by the servlet specification.

With this out of the way, let us return to the issue of generating a session identifier.

Generating a session identifier

By default, a Tomcat session identifier consists of 16 bytes, where each byte is represented using two hexadecimal characters.

The mechanism for generating the random bytes to be used as the identifier for a new session depends on the following:

- **A source for random bytes**: This is the special device identified by the devRandomSource member, which defaults to /dev/urandom. To facilitate reading random bytes from this source, an InputStream is instantiated to wrap it. This input stream is stored in the randomIS member.

- **A cryptographic PRNG**: If the source were not able to generate a sufficient number of random bytes, then the fallback option is to use a cryptographic PRNG to generate these bytes. The fully qualified class name of the PRNG to be used is specified in the randomClass member, which defaults to java.security.SecureRandom. This class must be instantiated and seeded with a sufficiently random entropy.

  This entropy can be provided as an attribute of the <Manager> element in server.xml. If this attribute is not set, then it must be generated.

  If the **Apache Portable Runtime (APR)** libraries are installed, then sufficiently strong entropy is obtained by invoking the random() method on the org.apache.tomcat.jni.OS class.

  If the APR libraries are not available, an alternative method is used to generate the entropy needed. First, the toString() method is invoked on the Manager instance, which returns the class name, suffixed by @ followed by the object's hashcode (a String of 8 hexadecimal characters).

  The entropy thus obtained is divided into groups of 8 bytes. The final entropy is then generated by exclusive-ORing each group, starting with the current time in milliseconds.

  Unfortunately, while the algorithm is not simplistic, the entropy may not be as strong as might be preferred. The random parts for the weakest source of entropy are the system time (whose value can be inferred) and an object's hashcode.

- **A message digest algorithm**: The algorithm to be used is represented by the algorithm member and defaults to MD5. A message digest instance that implements this algorithm is obtained and is stored in the digest member. This message digest is used to digest the generated random bytes for the session identifier, in order to further obfuscate the generated random sequence from observers.

> If an exception is thrown when trying to instantiate the class specified by the randomClass member, the java.util.Random PRNG is used instead. Given how insecure this PRNG is, it is important that you look for logged error messages that indicate that this is happening.

Now we're ready to walk through the details of the process by which a `Manager` generates a session identifier.

The `generateSessionId()` method of a `ManagerBase` is implemented as two loops. The inner loop generates unique session identifiers, while the outer loop verifies that the generated session identifier is not already in use by an active session in the manager's `sessions` map. If it is, then the generated session identifier is discarded and the inner loop is retried.

The inner loop repeatedly invokes `getRandomBytes()` with a byte array until it has retrieved the requisite number of random bytes as determined by its `sessionIdLength` member. The `getRandomBytes()` method obtains random bytes by reading from the `randomIS` member, lazily initializing this member if necessary.

If sufficient bytes could be read from this device to fill the byte array argument, those bytes are returned. Otherwise, it falls back to using the cryptographic PRNG to generate these random bytes instead, by invoking the `getRandom()` method to obtain the PRNG.

The `getRandom()` method lazily initializes the `random` member, seeding it appropriately, with entropy obtained by invoking the `getEntropy()` method. Entropy is either retrieved from the `<Manager>` element's `entropy` attribute, from an installed APR library, or by processing the `Manager` instance's string representation.

The `generateSessionId()` method further mangles these obtained random bytes using an MD5 message digest function to obscure the generated sequence of random numbers.

Each digested byte is converted to 2 characters, the first representing the hexadecimal value for the high order 4 bits, and the second representing the hexadecimal value for the lower order 4 bits.

This process is repeated until the digest is exhausted, or it has accumulated the required number of bytes (as set by `sessionIdLength`). This will result in a 32 character string (with characters whose values fall between '0' and '9' or 'A' through 'F').

If the digest was exhausted before the session identifier's length limit was reached, the inner loop is repeated to collect additional bytes.

Session construction

Now that we've generated a session identifier, let's step back to look at the creation of the session as a whole.

The createSession() method is invoked to create a new session. This method results in a new org.apache.catalina.session.StandardSession instance being instantiated, passing it a reference to its Manager instance.

This instance is marked as 'new' by invoking its setNew() method. Remember that a session is considered new until it is joined by the client.

The session is also marked as valid by invoking its setValid() method. The session's creation time is set to the current time using setCreationTime(), and its setMaxInactiveInterval() is invoked with the value of the Manager instance's maxInactiveInterval member.

If this method was passed a session identifier, then that is now passed to the session's setId(). If no session identifier was passed, then generateSessionId() is invoked to generate a new session identifier.

The sessionCounter member of this session's Manager is incremented to record the creation of this new session, and the initialized session instance is returned.

Background processing

The Manager provides a backgroundProcess() method that is invoked at regular intervals by its parent and is used to process expired sessions. The isValid() method is invoked on each session in the sessions map to give it an opportunity to expire itself.

Other methods

The init() method performs some JMX registration and invokes getRandomBytes() to initialize the random number generation process.

The findSession() method takes a session identifier and returns the corresponding session from the sessions map for that identifier.

The findSessions() method returns an array with the sessions in the sessions map.

StandardManager

The `org.apache.catalina.session.StandardManager` is the most common implementation of `Manager` used with Tomcat.

A `<Manager>` is an optional child for the `<Context>` element in the `server.xml` file.

When it is not explicitly specified, a `StandardManager` instance will be instantiated for the context.

Manager element attributes

You would supply a `<Manager>` element if you wanted to either provide an alternative `Manager` implementation, or if you wanted to override the default properties that are set on the `StandardManager`. Some important attributes that can be specified for this element are described in this section.

Session identifier generation attributes

These `<Manager>` element attributes affect how the session identifier is generated. We have already seen their usage in an earlier section.

The `algorithm` attribute takes the name of the message digest algorithm that is used in the `generateSessionID()` method to transform the generated random bytes into a session identifier. By default, this is set to MD5.

The `entropy` attribute lets you specify the seed for the PRNG instantiated by Tomcat. If this attribute is not set, the seed is computed based either on an APR method call or by manipulating the `toString()` form of the `Manager` instance. In highly security conscious environments, it is recommended that this be set to an adequately long `String` value.

The `randomClass` attribute lets you specify the fully qualified class name of the random number generator used in generating session identifiers. This is set by default to `java.security.SecureRandom`.

The `sessionIdLength` attribute, defaults to 16, and sets the length of session identifiers that should be created by this `Manager`.

Session attributes

These <Manager> element attributes affect the Session instances that are created by this manager.

The maxInactiveInterval attribute determines the period of client inactivity in seconds, after which a session is timed out or invalidated. By default this value is set to 60 seconds.

The maxActiveSessions attribute configures the maximum number of sessions that may be active at any given time for this Manager instance. By default, this is set to -1, which indicates no limit. If this is a positive integer, then createSession() requests will result in an IllegalStateException being thrown once the specified limit has been reached.

The processExpiresFrequency attribute determines how often housekeeping tasks (such as the expiring of sessions) will occur. When set to 1, these tasks are executed on each invocation of backgroundProcess(). The default value is 6, so housekeeping is done once every sixth invocation of this method.

The pathname attribute sets the file in which session state is preserved across application restarts. This path is either absolute or it is relative to the context's work directory. It defaults to the relative path, SESSIONS.ser. To disable persistence across server restarts, set this attribute to an empty string.

Session persistence mechanism

A key function of a StandardManager is to keep sessions alive across a web application reload or a server restart.

In this section, we'll take a look at how this is achieved.

When the stop() method of a StandardManager is called, all currently active sessions are saved to the file identified by its pathname member. The stop() method sets up a stream decoration that wraps this file using a FileOutputStream, a BufferedOutputStream, and an ObjectOutputStream. Once this structure is ready, it writes out an Integer representing the total number of active sessions in the sessions map. It then invokes passivate() on each session in this map, asking each session to serialize itself out to the ObjectOutputStream. Once a session has been persisted, expire(false) is invoked on it to cause it to expire without notifying its listeners.

On the reverse side, when the `StandardManager` instance's `start()` method is called, it reads in any previously persisted sessions. After the session persistence file is located, the number of persisted sessions is first read. It then reads that number of sessions from the file. For each session read, a new `StandardSession` is instantiated. This instance is initialized with the object data read from the persistence file, its manager is set, and it is added to the `sessions` map of its `Manager`. Finally, its `activate()` method is invoked to ask it to initialize itself.

Once all the sessions have been reloaded, the persistence file is deleted.

> If no file for persistence is found, the persistence mechanism is disabled, and both the load and unload mechanisms are short circuited.
>
> Setting the `pathname` attribute to an empty string will have this effect and is a simple way to remove this processing from your server startup and shutdown.

Persistent manager

A persistent manager adds the ability to swap out active sessions to a persistent storage mechanism (such as a file or a database table), once they have been inactive for a configured duration. Sessions may also be persisted across a normal restart of Tomcat.

> This `Manager` implementation is marked as experimental in the Tomcat documentation. It even comes with a warning that states that this class has not been thoroughly tested. However, as this is a fairly interesting departure from the default manager implementation, we will discuss it in this chapter.

A persistent manager is configured in `server.xml` using the `<Manager>` element. It takes a `<Store>` child element that defines the specific persistent storage mechanism that this manager will use.

The attributes of a persistent `Manager` include many of the same attributes that we have already encountered, such as the `algorithm`, `className` (which in this case defaults to `org.apache.catalina.session.PersistentManager`), `entropy`, `randomClass`, `maxActiveSessions`, `maxInactiveInterval`, and `sessionIdLength`.

In addition to these, it takes the following attributes:

- `maxIdleBackup`: This is the interval, in seconds, since the last access to a session before it is eligible to be backed up to the session store. By default, this is set to `-1` to disable it.

- `minIdleSwap`: This is the interval, in seconds, since the last access to a session before it is eligible to be persisted to the session store and passivated out of the server's memory.

- `maxIdleSwap`: This is the time interval, in seconds, since the last access of a session before it should be persisted to the session store and passivated out of the server's memory. By default, this is disabled by setting it to `-1`, so sessions are not forcibly swapped out, no matter how long they are idle. If enabled, then this value should be equal to or longer than the value specified for `maxIdleBackup`.

- `saveOnRestart`: If true (the default), sessions are persisted to the store when the manager is shut down properly, and are reloaded when it is started up again.

> *Backing up* a session involves writing the session out to a persistent store, but not actually removing the session from memory and passivating it.
>
> *Swapping out* a session involves not only backing up the session, but also removing the session from memory and passivating it.

The `PersistentManagerBase` is a convenience abstract class that extends `ManagerBase` by adding a persistence mechanism. The only implementation supplied by Tomcat is `org.apache.catalina.session.PersistentManager`. Its `store` member references a `Store` implementation that provides the persistence support for a persistent manager.

Persisting sessions

The key action in a persistent manager occurs during the start and stop lifecycle events.

The `start()` method initializes the random number generator and checks whether the `store` member is null. If it is null, an error is logged, and persistence is disabled. Otherwise, it invokes the `start()` method on its `store`.

The `stop()` method invokes `unload()` if this manager has a configured `Store`, and if it is expected to save sessions on restarts (`saveOnRestart` is `true`.) Otherwise, it simply walks through its current sessions, calling `expire()` on any session that is still valid, and ends by invoking `stop()` on its `store`.

The unload() method saves any currently active sessions in the persistence store. This method does nothing if persistence is not enabled—that is, if store is null. For every valid session, the swapOut() method first invokes passivate() on the session, and then invokes writeSession() to persist it using store.save(). The session is then removed from the map of sessions maintained by its Manager.

The load() method works in reverse. If persistence is enabled, it retrieves all the session identifiers from the store by invoking its keys() method. For each session identifier, it invokes swapIn() with that identifier.

The swapIn() method returns null if persistence is disabled. Otherwise, it invokes store.load() with the specified identifier to look up the session in the store. If it is not found, then a null value is returned. If a session is found, but it is invalid, it is not added to the map of active sessions. Instead, expire() is called on it, and it is removed from the Manager, by invoking the removeSession() method. If the session is valid, it is brought back to life by connecting the session to the persistent manager by invoking it's setManager(), and its new-ness is broadcast by calling its tellNew() method. The session is then added to the sessions map, and its activate() and endAccess() methods are invoked.

Finding a session

The default behavior of findSession() in ManagerBase is to return the Session got using sessions.get(id), where id is the identifier of the session we are trying to find. A persistent manager must take into account that a session may have been swapped out to the store. Therefore, it first delegates to the ManagerBase implementation, and if a session is not found, it invokes swapIn() with the identifier.

Background processing

A persistent manager overrides processExpires() to define its own custom processing. It walks through each Session in the sessions map calling isValid() on each, which has the side effect of expiring any invalid sessions. Then, it begins the process of handling swapping and backing up of sessions.

- **Swapping out sessions that are idle:** If maxIdleSwap is negative, no swapping out of idle sessions occurs. Valid sessions, last accessed more than both maxIdleSwap and minIdleSwap seconds ago, are swapped out to persistent storage by invoking their swapOut() method.

- **Swapping out sessions if too many are active:** If maxActiveSessions is negative or if it is greater than the number of current sessions, nothing is done. Else, each session that was last accessed more than minIdleSwap seconds ago is swapped out to persistent storage by invoking swapOut() with that session. Sessions are swapped out until the number of active sessions is brought below the maxActiveSessions limit.

- **Backing up sessions that are idle**: If `maxIdleBackup` is negative, backing up of idle sessions is disabled, and no backing up is necessary. Valid sessions that have not been accessed for at least `maxIdleBackup` seconds are backed up by invoking `writeSession()` to write them out to persistent storage.

Store

A persistent `<Manager>` element must have a nested `<Store>` child element. Out of the box, Tomcat comes with two `org.apache.catalina.Store` implementations:

- A file based store, `org.apache.catalina.session.FileStore`, which we will cover in this chapter
- A JDBC based store that we will not cover here

The `org.apache.catalina.session.StoreBase` abstract class is provided as a convenience implementation of the `Store` interface. This base class mostly just holds a reference to its `Manager`. It implements `Lifecycle`, and provides default `start()` and `stop()` methods that do not do much.

Its `processExpires()` method is invoked by the background reaper thread to clear out any expired sessions. Its default implementation retrieves the persisted session identifiers, invokes the abstract `load()` method for each identifier, and expires any invalid sessions.

FileStore

The `org.apache.catalina.session.FileStore` class is a concrete `Store` implementation that supports a file based persistence mechanism.

It takes a `directory` attribute which defines the directory into which the individual session files will be written. By default, these persisted session files are written to the application's temporary work directory. The specified directory can either be absolute or relative to the work directory.

It also takes a `checkInterval` attribute that indicates the seconds between checks for expired sessions (the default is 60 seconds), among those that are currently swapped out.

The `directory()` method returns a `File` that represents the directory in which the persisted session files will be stored.

The `file()` method takes a session identifier and returns a `File` within the specified `directory` that has the session identifier as its name and with a `.session` extension.

The `keys()` method returns an array of session identifiers currently in the store. It iterates over the contents of the `directory`, extracting just the base file name for each file found, and adding it to this array.

The `save()` method takes a `Session` instance and invokes `file()` to create a `File` instance with this session's identifier as its name. It opens an `ObjectOutputStream` on this file, and serializes the `Session` instance to that stream.

The `load()` method takes a session identifier and uses `file()` to locate the appropriate file. This is where it gets interesting. By default, an `ObjectInputStream` uses a class loader to resolve the class named in the serialized byte stream. This class loader may not be able to see the class that we need. For example, when the class lives within a `Context` and is visible to its web application class loader. To handle this, `load()` uses a `CustomObjectInputStream`, which uses the `WebappClassLoader` instance of its `Context` to load this class. Otherwise, a standard `ObjectInputStream` is used to do the deserialization.

In either case, we invoke `createEmptySession()` on the `Manager`, which returns a blank `StandardSession` instance that references its creating `Manager`. We then invoke `readObjectData()` on the session instance to read from the byte stream. This method simply delegates to `readObject()`. This session instance is then returned.

Summary

Congratulations! This is the point at which you reach around and pat yourself on the back. With this component you have finally completed your tour of a large swath of the Tomcat request processing machinery.

In this chapter, we looked at the reason for the existence of sessions. We also considered the importance of unique session identifiers to security. We reviewed the mechanism of Java serialization and considered how Tomcat leverages it to persist sessions.

The manager component is responsible for the creation and management of sessions, and so we reviewed Tomcat's implementations of this component. We also looked at options to persist sessions across manager restarts.

We ended the chapter by looking at a file store based persistent manager implementation, which supports the persistence of sessions to a configured directory.

Index

[PACKT]
PUBLISHING

Thank you for buying
Tomcat 6 Developer's Guide

Packt Open Source Project Royalties

When we sell a book written on an Open Source project, we pay a royalty directly to that project. Therefore by purchasing Tomcat 6 Developer's Guide, Packt will have given some of the money received to the Apache Tomcat project.

In the long term, we see ourselves and you—customers and readers of our books—as part of the Open Source ecosystem, providing sustainable revenue for the projects we publish on. Our aim at Packt is to establish publishing royalties as an essential part of the service and support a business model that sustains Open Source.

If you're working with an Open Source project that you would like us to publish on, and subsequently pay royalties to, please get in touch with us.

Writing for Packt

We welcome all inquiries from people who are interested in authoring. Book proposals should be sent to author@packtpub.com. If your book idea is still at an early stage and you would like to discuss it first before writing a formal book proposal, contact us; one of our commissioning editors will get in touch with you.

We're not just looking for published authors; if you have strong technical skills but no writing experience, our experienced editors can help you develop a writing career, or simply get some additional reward for your expertise.

About Packt Publishing

Packt, pronounced 'packed', published its first book "Mastering phpMyAdmin for Effective MySQL Management" in April 2004 and subsequently continued to specialize in publishing highly focused books on specific technologies and solutions.

Our books and publications share the experiences of your fellow IT professionals in adapting and customizing today's systems, applications, and frameworks. Our solution-based books give you the knowledge and power to customize the software and technologies you're using to get the job done. Packt books are more specific and less general than the IT books you have seen in the past. Our unique business model allows us to bring you more focused information, giving you more of what you need to know, and less of what you don't.

Packt is a modern, yet unique publishing company, which focuses on producing quality, cutting-edge books for communities of developers, administrators, and newbies alike. For more information, please visit our website: www.PacktPub.com.

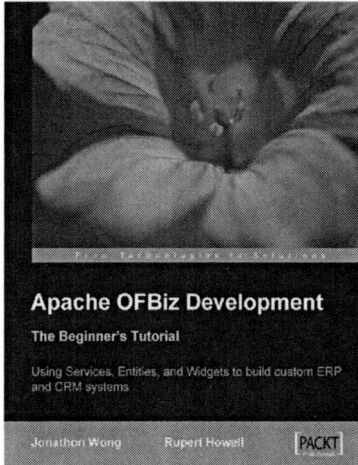

Apache OFBiz Development:
The Beginner's Tutorial

ISBN: 978-1-847194-00-8   Paperback: 472 pages

Using Services, Entities, and Widgets to build custom
ERP and CRM systems

1. Understand how OFBiz is put together

2. Learn to create and customize business
   applications with OFBiz

3. Gain valuable development and
   performance hints

4. A fully illustrated tutorial with functional
   step-by-step examples

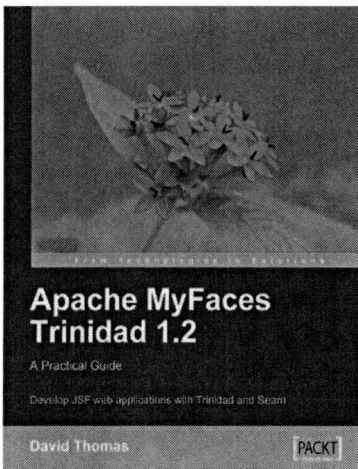

Apache MyFaces Trinidad 1.2:
A Practical Guide

ISBN: 978-1-847196-08-8   Paperback: 300 pages

Develop JSF web applications with Trinidad
and Seam

1. Develop rich client web applications using
   the most powerful integration of modern web
   technologies

2. Covers working with Seam security,
   internationalization using Seam, and more

3. Get well-versed in developing key areas of
   web applications

4. A step-by-step approach that will help you
   strengthen your understanding of all the
   major concepts

Please check **www.PacktPub.com** for information on our titles

LaVergne, TN USA
12 July 2010
189257LV00003B/18/P

9 781847 197283